TO SERVE AND COLLECT

TO SERVE
AND COLLECT

CHICAGO POLITICS
AND POLICE CORRUPTION
FROM THE LAGER BEER RIOT TO
THE SUMMERDALE SCANDAL

RICHARD C. LINDBERG

New York
Westport, Connecticut
London

Library of Congress Cataloging-in-Publication Data

Lindberg, Richard, 1953–
   To serve and collect : Chicago politics and police corruption from
the Lager Beer Riot to the Summerdale Scandal / Richard C. Lindberg.
      p.   cm.
   Includes bibliographical references and index.
   ISBN 0–275–93415–2
   1. Police—Illinois—Chicago—History.   2. Police corruption—
Illinois—Chicago—History.   3. Chicago (Ill.)—Politics and
government.   I. Title.
HV8148.C4L55   1991
364.1'323'0977311—dc20   90–38713

British Library Cataloguing in Publication Data is available.

Library of Congress Catalog Card Number: 90–38713
ISBN: 0–275–93415–2

First published in 1991

Praeger Publishers, One Madison Avenue, New York, NY 10010
An imprint of Greenwood Publishing Group, Inc.

Printed in the United States of America

∞

The paper used in this book complies with the
Permanent Paper Standard issued by the National
Information Standards Organization (Z39.48–1984).

10 9 8 7 6 5 4 3 2 1

To the memory of Margaret Stone:
''Distant echoes from a melancholy life.''

Contents

     Crime Syndicate, 1921–31   147

     Close Up on the Chicago Police:
     Tommy O'Connor Breaks Out   219

10   Pawns of the Machine: The Cermak-Kelly-Nash Years,
     1933–47   227

     Close Up on the Chicago Police:
     Confessions of a Vice Cop   259

11   A System at Fault, 1947–60   263

     Appendix I: Statistical Data, 1866–1960   327

     Appendix II: Law Enforcement in Cook County,
     1855–1960   331

     Notes on Sources   337

     Bibliography   341

     Index   347

     About the Author   367

Photographs follow page 218.

Preface

The history of any city is often mirrored in its police force. Just as Chicago was a city on the make, so too was its principal law enforcement agency. Scandal, disgrace, and rampant political corruption characterized the administration of the Chicago Police Department for 100 years until the conditions became such that the very people who channeled the graft were forced to admit that the system was no longer salvageable.

In most European countries a state police was maintained under the control of the central government. Policing agencies on the continent were generally modeled after the French *gendarmes*, but in the United States it was up to the local municipality to provide for the protection of its citizens. The ethnic coalition that guided Chicago's political destiny in the late nineteenth and early twentieth centuries was composed of liquor men, gamblers, and resort keepers who viewed politics as a means to an end. The police of this period strengthened the numerous "mini-machines" that flourished in the sprawling corridors of the inner-city wards. In return for protecting the saloon, the gambling den, the sporting house, and chasing down anarchist undesirables who might overturn that order, the policeman could expect a degree of job longevity, financial recompense, and the gratitude of the politician. That often counted more than attending to lost children, solving burglaries, or keeping the peace.

A policemen's lot was never a happy one. Disease, despair, and the prospects of an early death awaited the police officer assigned to the mean streets. He had to keep his wits about him and be resourceful because his own livelihood depended not on how well he did his job but how he pleased his masters.

Too often his choices were not guided any sense of moral obligation to the community but a desire to survive the environment. Those fortunate enough to be singled out for appointment by the ward boss, who "had it in right" with the civil service commissioner, paid their fealty in a variety of underhanded ways. To continue his employment on the force the policeman was often called on to perform political work for the alderman or peddle tickets to prep football games or fund-raising events that lined the coffers of the ward organization. The policeman quickly realized there were perils involved in arresting gamblers and brothel keepers who had "clout."

The hours were long and the wage was miserly for what was expected of them. In the early years of this century, payless paydays were all too common. Was it any wonder then that the policeman compromised his standards, especially in regard to gambling laws, liquor prohibition, prostitution, and other offenses in which the moral seriousness of the crime was a matter of interpretation? Certain unscrupulous members of the department profited from their acquaintances with the gambler politicians because there was a bounty of graft awaiting the "smart boys" who knew how to play ball.

Police inspectors and district captains became autonomous in their respective neighborhoods as a result of the decentralized nature of Chicago politics. They permitted vice to flourish, impervious to the intentions of the superintendent or city reform agencies. In some quarters the police were expected to close down the gambling dens and chase streetwalkers out of the district. But in the tenderloin areas vice was allowed to thrive in an environment that fostered police graft. The policy of vice segregation, however noble in theory, kept in motion the wheel of graft with the police as the axle. Lacking a definitive statement of policy from the municipal administration, corruptive arrangements between the rival vice syndicates and politicians were inevitable. These occurred in cycles.

What inevitably followed the detection of scandal was a clamor for reform. Then after the conscience of the city had been awakened and the hierarchy reshuffled, the department returned to pre-scandal levels. Police reform usually meant civilian control of some kind. But in the long run the unwelcome intrusions of a well-meaning citizens' group into what was essentially a militaristic agency could not succeed, and neither would the police sanction any plan to recruit "spies" from within the ranks to report on wrongdoing. Before 1960, internal regulation of any kind was sarcastically referred to as "piperizing," named for Alexander Piper, the turn-of-the-century police administrator who handed in a scathing report to the City Club in 1904.

Assailed by the reformers for his apparent unwillingness to execute sworn duties, and in greater jeopardy of being transferred to the "woods" if he did, the policeman sought his identity through fraternal societies like the Benevolent Association. And in the early years, the various ethnic brotherhoods served as an important link to a distant nostalgic culture that was a stark contrast to grim urban Chicago. Members in the Policemen's Benevolent Association were entitled to share common job-related experienced as well as work toward mutually advantageous goals. By its very nature the business of policing was secretive and mistrustful of external stimuli perceived to be a threat to its own self-interests. The fraternal orders formed by the police after 1868 contributed to the general feeling that this was not so much an occupation but a highly insulated, oath-bound brotherhood.

The pace of reform between 1855 and 1960 moved at a glacial speed. The police reflected the old axiom that "Chicago ain't ready for reform." For 100 years the evils of the system prevailed: graft, spoils, and political treachery at the highest levels. Promotions and appointments were brokered to friends of the administration, or those with the ability to pay. Captains became wealthy and entrenched in their districts. There was a ring of truth to the old adage of the "millionaire cop," especially if the individual could perpetuate his powerbase in a highly concentrated vice district. In the days of the "gaslight era" the action was centered in the 22nd Street "badlands." By the 1940s vice had shifted northward to the East Chicago Avenue District. Separated by a generation, the thrust of technology, and a presumably greater degree of professionalism, the police demonstrated the same familiar patterns of behavior. When O. W. Wilson arrived in Chicago in 1960 he found a police department mired in a nineteenth-century mindset. When all was said and done, nothing had changed very much.

This is a book about the history of the Chicago police, but is is also about the impact of city politics, gambling, vice, and organized crime in the department. It is a tragic, improbable story.

Acknowledgments

A book of this nature could not have reached its successful conclusion without the help of some very special people. I wish to cite the valuable assistance rendered to me by Dr. Steven Riess, Professor of Urban History at Northeastern Illinois University (UNI). I cannot overlook the added help and inspiration given me by Dr. Joseph Morton and the late Dr. C. David Tompkins, also of the distinguished UNI faculty. I received valuable insights from the collective wisdom of several notable Chicago historians and crime writers, including Bill Reilly, local mob expert; Nathan Kaplan, a man of rare insight; Barbara O'Shaughnessy; Former Mayoral Press Secretary Frank Sullivan; Bill Helmer; and Bill Young.

I am also indebted to Ron Chambers, Neal Trickle, Tom Murphy, Tim O'Connell, Kenan Heise, and Wayne Klatt. Special thanks to Bob Deckert, my artist; the late Art Manger, retired vice detective; Dennis Bingham, editor of Chicago's *Police Star* magazine; attorney Russell Stewart; Pat Egan; retired detectives Burt Neilson and James Janda; Al "Wallpaper" Wolff, last of the Untouchables; Chuck Lindberg; my wife Denise for her enduring fortitude; and finally Robert Mathias Krupp who first suggested the idea to me in 1985.

TO SERVE AND COLLECT

1

The Police and the Emerging City

The pioneers who ventured out of Fort Dearborn to build the town that was to become the city of Chicago did so at great peril to themselves and their property. Bands of hostile Potawatamie and Illinois Indians roamed the marshlands and sailed the rivers. The 1812 Fort Dearborn massacre was a distant memory by 1835, as the last of the Native Americans abandoned their homeland for the spacious western plains. Secure behind the walls of the old fort, U.S. Army regulars sat idly by while the townsmen dispensed frontier justice as best they could. South of the fort stood a camp ground for the wagon trains, filled with optimistic pilgrims winding their way west.

The town crier walked through the campgrounds carrying a lamp and bell in search of lost children and the miscreants who may have carried them away. Chicago was growing. And to its port came the speculators. gamblers, and whiskey men who recognized opportunity when they saw it. Policing was haphazard. At best, the townsmen could "tell the criminals to get out of town or suffer the consequences."[1] Most of them decided to remain, and soon the first gambling dens and saloons in the guise of "drug stores" appeared in the commericial district.

The demands for better municipal services led to Chicago's incorporation in 1831. Four years later the state legislature increased the executive powers of the village trustees by granting them the right to appoint constables. O. Morrison, who had formerly served as the town collector, was elected Chicago's first high constable. In this capacity he served as a paid officer of the municipal court.[2] The position was markedly similar to what already existed in Boston, except that the officer was not the appointee of wealthy selectmen. He was accountable only to the court, and was charged with the maintenance of public health, the removal of obstructions, the reporting of fires to the trustees, and the "removal of all idle and suspicious persons not actually or usefully employed in aiding to extinguish such fires, or in the preservation of property thereof."[3] The constable did not wear a uniform or special insignia. but instead carried a "staff of office" that was painted white.[4]

The village trustees enacted several important ordinances during this time. Firearms were outlawed and the first of the controversial Sunday closing laws was passed on September 1, 1834. The temperance question in a town as raw and untamed as Chicago was an issue certain to fester among the Irish and German immigrants who were just beginning to arrive. To control public gambling, an 1835 ordinance levied a $25 penalty each time a person was brought before the trustees for keeping a gaming house of faro bank, and $25 each day thereafter.[5]

The City Charter was granted in 1837. The office of high constable became an elective one and John Shrigley became the city's first law enforcement official to take office as a result of a public election. Shrigley was the law in frontier Chicago—the only law. Like most police officials in the United States at this time, Shrigley was not well versed in law enforcement, for this was not yet a profession but a gritty job reserved for the strongest, most fearsome members of the community. Shrigley was a barrel-chested brute who owned a saloon.[6] According to Alexander Beaubien, one of Chicago's original settlers, it was a common sight to see Constable Shrigley subdue an offender with his fists, and then drag him off to Cook County's first "calaboose": a log cabin stockade on the corner of Madison and Michigan Avenues (which was a swampy marsh on the edge of lake Michigan in 1837.) John Shrigley was said to be a "very clever" man with his fists.

Shrigley was reelected in 1838. He continued in office until 1839, when Samuel J. Lowe, whose title was changed to "chief to the city watch," took over. The constabulary, composed of just four men in 1837, soon proved incapable of protecting the city's population which was growing by the day. Despite persistent complaints from the *Chicago American* that "it is a great evil that the number of police is so contemptively small," the size of the city force never exceeded ten, even in the 1840s.[7] Samuel Lowe's successor, Orson Smith, convinced the mayor and the common council to appoint three assistants: Henry Rhines, Hugh Henry, and William Wesencrest. So it was that in 1840 the first policing *agency* came into being. But real power still rested with the mayor, who served as the city's chief officer. The situation remained chaotic because the night watchmen who roamed the city during the evening hours remained independent of the constable, who was the only one with actual arresting power at this time. The night watchman reported fires and "observed" movements of suspicious characters who were seen prowling the city at night. When a burglary was committed, the only reasonable way to apprehend the robber was to engage a private "thief catcher." People who could afford to pay a reward usually printed a notice in the gazette. The thief catcher would then use whatever means—legal or illegal—

to recover stolen goods. Frequently these individuals worked in tandem with the robbers who preyed on the community at large.

In 1845 Orson Smith was replaced by Philip Dean, who added six "assistants" during his tenure. The number of city wards was increased to nine in 1847, with one constable assigned to each district under the direction of Ambrose Burnham. During Marshal James Howe's four-year reign in the 1850s, the fledgling department numbered 13. Howe, a pioneer baker, was a frequent target of the newspaper editors of the day who derided him for his naivete. Yet the administration of the "pie man" was marked by a perceptible decrease in crime. Howe earned $800 a year, and his 13 constables were paid $37.50 per month. Chicago continued on a two-tier police system.

The unification of the Night Watch and the Day Constabulary occurred in Chicago as it had in Boston after the Broad Street Riots of 1837 and the London Gordon Riots of 1780—as a result of a major civil disturbance.

The Lager Beer Riot of 1855

Between the years of 1850 and 1871 the city population swelled from 30,000 to nearly 300,000 inhabitants. Although they were second in sheer numbers to the Germans, Chicago's foreign-born Irish totalled 40,000 by the time of the great fire.[8] These Irish settlers who crossed the Atlantic were the victims of the great agricultural famine of the 1840s. The poorest of them congregated in the teeming enclaves of Boston, New York, and other Atlantic seaboard cities.

Here the Anglo-American effectively excluded them from the mainstream with the familiar warning: "No Irish Wanted." The fortunate ones who escaped disease, poverty, and oppression negotiated their way west into the Ohio Valley and Chicago, which had lately became a center of commerce and transportation. The Irish backlash was not as extreme there as it had been in Boston, but Chicago did have its own Anglo coalition, which had influenced the city's political and social life from the time of the earliest settlements.

Excluded from direct participation in the city's cultural life, the Irish maintained a fierce group identity, which often evolved around the local parish or with neighbors who had emigrated from the same county. Relief from the drudgery of urban life could be found in a bottle of corn whiskey, a game of chance, and trust and kinship of other Irishmen in the community. They organized their own benevolent associations, such as Ancient Order of Hibernians and the Sons of Erin, to preserve a way of life recently threatened by the Illinois Maine Law Alliance.[9] This coalition of abolitionists and anti-Douglas, anti-Catholic Democrats was commonly referred to as the Know-Nothings. For nearly a decade they battled the Democrats for control of the City Council. Municipal elections became free-for-alls, in which gangs of rowdies intimidated voters with sticks, rocks, and offensive ethnic slurs.

Irish voters succeeded in placing Isaac Millikin in the mayor's chair in 1854, but only after considerable bloodshed. A policeman was knocked down and beaten in the Seventh Ward, the traditional stronghold of Democratic partisans. "We don't care a damn for Millikin, but hurrah for lager beer!" exclaimed one Irish voter—obviously not interested in the outcome of the election.[10] But his victory over Amos Throop, the candidate endorsed by the *Chicago Tribune*, delayed the inevitable clash between temperance and libertinism.

Events reached a crisis level a year later when Dr. Levi D. Boone, and ultra-conservative physician who was the grand-nephew of frontiersman Daniel Boone, was elected mayor. Boone was a Know-Nothing who had just completed his term in the City Council. He endorsed the *Tribune*'s position that the social problems of the day were directly tied to the "rowdy Irish elements who live in constant violation of the law."[11] Candidate Boone promised his supporters that he would rid Chicago of its Irish and "low Dutch" (Germans). Once in office his supporters in the Council passed a series of restrictive laws requiring all applicants for positions in the police and fire departments to provide proof of birth in the United States.

Boone's choice to head up the Police Department was Cyrus Parker Bradley, who traced his lineage back to Haver Hill, Massachusetts, where his great-grand-father was killed during an Indian raid.[12] Captain Bradley, the Puritan blueblood, was a dynamic figure who influenced policy making in the department for almost a decade. He wrested control of police affairs from his immediate superior, Marshal James Donnelley, because Mayor Boone counted on him to uphold the Sunday closing laws—something the marshal did not endorse wholeheartedly.

Cyrus Bradley entered public life after running the affairs of the Horace Norton Company, Chicago's leading forwarding merchant in the years before the Civil War. The Norton Company owned the only warehouse south of the Chicago River. In 1850 he was appointed fire marshal, and helped organize the Benevolent Association years before the police got around to forming one of their own. With the support of the business community Bradley was elected city collector, and then appointed deputy sheriff of Cook County. It was later written that Bradley was "one of the most energetic and able men ever connected with the fire and police service in Chicago, . . . doing so much to bring order and efficient municipal government out of the changes and struggles for excellence in these early times."[13] Bradley put the department on a firm footing, but his own attitudes reflected the sentiments of Chicago's ruling class: the tide of European immi-gration into the city posed a serious moral threat to the God-fearing Yankees who happened to arrive there first.

When liquor licenses for drug stores and tipping houses were raised to $300 a year, there was an immediate outcry from the German communities north of the river. A restive crowd of brewers, tradesmen, and patrons of the sample rooms gathered in Ogden Park the morning of April 21, 1855, to protest the actions of the mayor and Judge Henry Rucker, who had postponed a decision to free several men imprisoned in the Bridewell for violations of the Sunday closing law. Inflamed by the incendiary comments of Alderman L. D. LaRue, whose 8th Ward supporters included many Germans, the mob pushed forward to free the prisoners. At the front of the curious procession was a fife and drum band, and several men who wielded meat cleavers and crude fowling pieces. As the crowd approached the Clark Street Bridge, the Market Square was in plain sight, but they were halted by Captain Luther Nichols, who commanded several volunteer companies enlisted for emergency duty by the mayor.

Nichols, who headed up the Police Department day patrol, was one of Chicago's "Old Settlers." He arrived in Chicago in 1832 during the Blackhawk War. For a short time in the early 1840s, he served as fire chief of the volunteer brigade. Nichols met the mob holding the traditional "staff of office"—a white baton signifying that he was acting in a official capacity. [14] This did not discourage the mob, which taunted the police with catcalls and a shower of rocks. What followed was a short, bloody siege which remarkably did not claim any lives. Officer George Hunt was shot in the leg by a young German agitator named Peter Martens. The assailant was later tracked down and killed by Sheriff James Andrews. Hunt was awarded the bronze star for gallantry and given a City Hall job, which he held down for the next 32 years. [15]

There were a score of minor injuries, but Bradley and the mayor prevented further incidents of violence by declaring martial law once the bridges and public square had been cleared of rioters. Judge Rucker prepared the necessary writ, freeing the incarcerated men. Two months later another prohibition referendum was placed before the voters, but it was overwhelmingly defeated by Chicagoans fed up with Boone's policies.

The police showed a degree of restraint that would all but disappear in the coming decades, as they attempted to preserve order in the chaotic struggles between labor and capital, Bradley's men were outnumbered and unprepared to deal with the angry throngs that threatened the established order. If not for the presence of the militia, events might have gotten out of hand.

Recognizing these inadequacies, Boone reorganized the force. Under the old system 28 night watchmen had been separate and apart from the day constabulary. The night-time force patrolled the city for 12 straight hours each night, with no substitutes provided for by City Council. Overworked and fatigued from such long vigils, the night force was naturally contemptuous of the day police. Boone added a mid-day shift and reduced the hours of the night-time squad. For the first time the police were required to wear uniforms. Until this time Chicago policemen had worn ordinary street clothing with a small star affixed to their coat collars. If an officer did not wish to involve himself in a street quarrel, or a dispute, he only had to remove the star, or conceal it with the lapel of his coat. The notion of a uniformed police department was repugnant to many Americans, who still equated military red with the colonial occupation. For these reasons, the New York City Police Department was outfitted in navy blue uniforms by James Gerard in 1855. [16]

The Democratic newspaper ridiculed this latest maneuver by Boone as an "attempt to show off the police as his prized cattle."[17] The deeper significance lay in the fact that for the first time, the police department had attained a degree of professionalism, as it shed its essentially civilian orientation.

The Nativist movement in Chicago declined following the Lager Beer Riot. Accounting for nearly one-fifth of the city population, the Irish helped elect Democrat Thomas Dyer as the next mayor in 1856. The Dyer campaign touched off a series of election skirmishes between Irish Democrats and Protestant Republicans in the bloody 7th Ward, an urban ethnic melting pot that typified the problems the nineteenth-century police faced in trying to maintain order in a hotly contested mayoral contest. "Head knockers" made the rounds of the polling places while the police stood idly by, or chose not to risk their own personal safety over a political quarrel.

Mayor Boone was easily defeated by Dyer, a flamboyant Irish businessman less inclined to enforce strict temperance measures. Rowdy celebrants attended his inaugural parade. A scandalous assembly of gaudy demimondes and their men followed the procession through the clogged, dusty streets of the business district.[18]

Once in office the new mayor further antagonized his opponents by retiring the popular captain, Cyrus Bradley, and abolishing the title of chief of police. James Donnelley, who was elected city marshal on the Dyer ticket, assumed command. Departing with Bradley were some of the most capable officers on the force, who resigned as an act of protest. New applicants soon lined the courthouse square to fill the vacated positions.[19] The *Chicago Tribune*, stung by the election results, described the new men as "the worst of the border ruffian type—many of whom were well known to the Bridewell keeper." Such pointed accusations were an expression of the "No Irish" philosophy of the *Tribune's* editors.[20] But even the normally supportive *Chicago Democrat* wondered what forms of lawless tyranny would seize the city: "Villains of all kinds will now act boldly with little fear. Citizens must look out for themselves at least until the new administration completes it restoration."[21]

Unfortunately for Dyer, a financial panic gripped the city for most of 1856. Incidents of burglary and hold-up increased as idle unemployed men drifted into Chicago, filling the railroad terminals and alms houses. The police, now composed of young Irish recruits, seemed incapable of solving a string of robberies within the residential community. Public confidence in the police waned, even as Dyer expanded the force to meet the threats. At the time the department consisted of 112 men, a dozen more than the ordinance allowed. Expenditures were $99,972—a stiff price to pay for a police force so few people had confidence in. The *Tribune* meanwhile praised the thief-catching abilities of Cyrus Bradley, now engaged in private practice. Following his dismissal from the mayor's police, Bradley organized one of the city's first private forces—the Chicago Detecting and Collecting Police Agency.

The notion of a paid private force to recover stolen property was certainly not a new one. As U.S. cities gradually shifted from the constabulary and night watch to a single unified force, retired constables frequently worked outside the law and for a fee.

In terms of efficiency, the private agencies of Bradley and Allan Pinkerton exceeded the meager abilities of the city police. Methods of crime detection were still very primitive. (The detective department within the police was not organized until 1861.) The private eye had a much greater incentive to venture into unsafe areas than his underpaid counterpart on the city force. And when Bradley's men returned thousands of dollars in stolen merchandise to five Lake Street merchants, the *Chicago Tribune* commended "his energy and skills in saving these gentlemen a large amount of property and he is entitled to every credit for his promptness."[22]

Soon there were scores of ambitious competitors making the rounds of the business district. G. T. Moore of the Merchant Police boasted that "though there have been upwards of twenty burglaries within a block of my district, during that time there has been but two among my customers and in those the attending circumstances was such that blame was not attached to my men."[23] The Merchant Police patrolled each alley along the beat four to five times an hour, vigilant and on guard for suspicious characters and the outbreak of fire. For these services, Moore charged each of his customers 50 cents per night.

The city police were officially charged with these responsibilities, of course. But during the turbulent years before the outbreak of the Civil War the city administration's larger concern was the threat of mob violence, a feature of urban life throughout the nation at this time. Volunteer military companies were actively engaged during the Lager Beer Riot and held on a permanent retainer by Mayor Dyer, who promised them a greater role during his term of office:

While I trust that we may never see the day the law will require the aid of a bayonet to enforce the large organization of citizen soldiers ready at any moment to support the constituted authorities, [sic] must act as a preventative of violence on the one hand, and as a sure guarantee that all the laws must be executed. I shall be in favor of dealing liberally to this branch of our protective interests.[24]

John Wentworth, the charismatic editor of the *Chicago Democrat*, questioned the thinking of the mayor in allowing a band of citizen soldiers to be armed and ready in a city that was in no immediate danger of an Indian attack. Wentworth reserved his sharpest criticisms for the private agencies and Cyrus Bradley in particular, who was a bitter political enemy. Wentworth suggested that Bradley and Pinkerton were having a field day rounding up all the criminals they had personally invited to Chicago to discredit the municipal authority. "Long John," as he was known to his friends and supporters, renounced his former ties with the Democratic Party to run as the Republican candidate for mayor in the spring election of 1857. Wentworth appeared on the dais along with Abraham Lincoln. There is no record of the future President's thoughts, as Wentworth spoke long and passionately about the Irish question, and the need to restore only men of native birth to the city police department. He vowed to rid the city of the "Hibernians and their ignoble neglect of duty."[25]

On election day the mayor allowed the saloons to remain open. The convivial atmosphere and the election rhetoric enflamed the South-Side Irish coalition into acts of confrontation with the Germans from the North Side, who were casting their votes for Wentworth. Shortly before noon over 150 Irishmen advanced on the polling places armed with clubs, knives and rocks. A young German voter named Charles Seifert was seized and beaten to death as he exited the polling place. The Republican *Tribune* and Democratic *Times* were, as usual, divided in their opinions as to the real cause of the murder. One claimed that it was a Wentworth device to discredit the mayor, while the other blamed the rowdy Irish.

Wentworth won the election against a political unknown named Carver. A number of officers retired by Dyer were restored to their former positions, and the duty of collecting city licenses was taken away from the police and rightfully given over to the tax collectors.[26] These were purely organizational moves on Wentworth's part.

Because the mayor was not a man to tolerate the motives and ambitions of a political foe like Bradley, he set out to restore a measure of lost credibility to the city force. To achieve these aims, Wentworth ordered a vice crackdown against the dive-keepers who maintained the brothels and saloons in the notorious red-light district known as the "Sands." This district north of the Chicago River was populated by a transient crowd of longshoremen, prostitutes, gamblers, and real estate speculators anxious to turn a dollar in Chicago.[27] Typical of most nineteenth-century tenderloin districts, this one thrived on the city's periphery, where police interference was minimal.

Wentworth stood at the front of the police column that advanced on the Sands houses the morning of April 20, 1857. This move was made following the court's refusal to legislate the disreputable houses out of existence. A scheme to purchase the property of the former dive-keepers, and clear it for redevelopment, had gone for naught. Former Mayor William B. Ogden conceived the idea, but organized vice historically demonstrates a firm resistance to all kinds of pressure, legal and otherwise. Thus "Long John" took matters into his own hands. Together with the deputy sheriff and 30 policemen, Wentworth supervised the dismantling of the district. The inmates had been lured away from the Sands under false pretenses: a horse race and cock fight had been advertised in another part of the city, as a ruse on the part of the mayor.

The remaining tenants were allowed to vacate before five buildings and several shanties were torn down. Several thousand Chicagoans turned out to cheer Wentworth, who, despite his capricious ways, was seen as a folk-hero to many. Later the same day, the remaining buildings were set on fire by the vice-keepers, probably as a gesture of contempt toward landlord Ogden. Wentworth's actions were largely symbolic, and did little to eradicate deteriorating vice conditions in Chicago. Through the Civil War years, the Sands continued to serve the tastes of men seeking a game of chance or intimate soiree with one of the residents of the district.

The existence of gambling "hells" in Chicago is noted as early as 1835, when an ordinance levied a $25 penalty each time a person was brought before the trustees for running a faro bank.[28] By 1849 it was estimated that Chicago had more faro banks than Philadelphia: a total of three.[29] Faro was the most popular card game of its day, because it provided the illusion of easy victory for the unwary participant. The game was supervised by a sharp-talking dealer assisted by two men who handled the exchange of money and kept a watchful eye for cheaters. Wagers were placed on cards drawn from a dealing box, which was controlled by a mechanical device. The presence of the box provided a false sense of security to the players, who assumed that the game was honest.

The faro bank often required a prominent backer, who might lead a better class of people to the game and ensure that police interference in the game was minimal. Chicago offered an inexhaustible supply, which led to a degree of permanency in the community previously unknown in the days of the steamboat trade. The existence of gambling and the presence of ladies of easy virtue in a self-contained district naturally provided a boon to more legitimate enterprises such as saloons, hotels, restaurants, and the livery trade which conveyed patrons to and from the area. As the reputation of the Sands spread, thrill-seekers, the curious, and the underaged youth of the city flocked to the levee to partake of the excitement.

From the pulpits of the churches and in the columns of the daily newspapers was frequently heard the cry of the reformer to "do something." Wentworth was mindful of the public's dim perceptions of his police. As a former editor of the city's leading news journal, he had pushed for strong reforms. His raid on the infamous Sands earned a partial reprieve, so he continued this tactic against the gambling "hells" and dance halls of Chicago. Sometimes, though, his marauding tactics backfired.

On July 17, 1857, police under the direction of Captain Bartholomew Yates broke up one of the city's largest faro banks, located on the third floor of Spear Bazaar, which was a bowling alley and saloon. After weeks of rooftop surveillance, Bartholomew's men broke through the windows from ropes that were tied to drain pipes on the top of the building. Fifteen of Chicago's top gamblers were arrested and taken to the Bridewell. When attorney C. S. Cameron attempted to bail the men out, he was accosted by Wentworth, who pummeled the man with a series of blows to his face and chest. The lawyer was then ordered imprisoned. The next day a warrant for Wentworth's arrest was sworn by Cameron. A lawsuit followed which was later settled to the satisfaction of both parties. But the mayor's vice raids, however noteworthy, did not cure the lingering ills of gambling and prostitution.

The gambling parlors and houses of ill fame that had previously existed on the edge of the city merely shifted their base of operation to Randolph Street, near the center of the Chicago commercial district. Formerly this area between

State and Dearborn had been the domain of some of the great brewing companies, but the subsequent years witnessed the intrusion of an altogether different clientele.

Three powerful gamblers who enjoyed limited police protection marshalled control of the fragmented vice coalition by the time of the Civil War: Jack Haverly, "Cap" Hyman, and Roger Plant. Plant, a diminutive Englishman, was married to a street-smart procuress who learned her trade on the Liverpool docks. She used these talents to attract customers to their "Under the Willow" resort, which stood just a few blocks from the courthouse and in plain view of the city hall. During the war Plant and his wife expanded their operation by purchasing flats adjacent to the saloon. In effect, Roger's place became a "barracks of vice." The police were smart to leave Roger alone. He paid the toll regularly, and to close down his place would have been harder than "pulling an elephant by the tail."[30] This kind of criminal activity peacefully coexisted alongside the more legitimate businesses because shopkeepers soon realized extra income by renting out the second floors of their buildings to transients.

Jack Haverly was a gambler who was representative of the new generation of Irishmen climbing the socioeconomic ladder through more legitimate means. During the Civil War he ran a popular dime museum and minstrel show that was frequently advertised in the pages of the *Chicago Tribune*. Before the Great Fire of 1871 gutted his real estate holdings, Haverly was the lessee of the Post Office. On the side, he also ran a faro bank and funneled race track odds to the newspapers, who routinely printed this information despite their stern views concerning wagering. During the 1880s Haverly divested himself of his gambling enterprise to devote himself to running Hooley's downtown theater.

Cap Hyman, a contemporary of Haverly, was known as the boss of "Gambler's Row" along Randolph. His habit of reaching for his pistol at the slightest provocation earned Gambler's Row another dubious nickname—the "Hairtrigger Block." Like so many of the other Civil War gamblers who did not share Haverly's desires to attain social position, Hyman's life was fast and loose. He squandered his money within 15 years, and died destitute in the insane asylum.

To ensure a continued profit for all concerned, it was first necessary to keep the district free of police interference. Cordial relationships with the local captain were essential. When Cap Hyman took a bride, the guest of honor at the high-toned Lakeview resort where the reception was held was none other than Jack Nelson—captain of the Armory Station in the heart of the Gambler's Row district. Jack Nelson was appointed by Wentworth during the mayor's second term of office in 1861.

While his police openly consorted with underworld characters, Wentworth steadfastly maintained that "the only legitmate or proper detectives are those sustained by the law."[31] However, the city police seemed incapable of executing the law in a courageous and honest manner. The problem was Wentworth, who time and again involved himself in trivial matters—sometimes with disastrous consequences. In October 1857, Wentworth targeted a group of residents in the

German quarter of the north division for harassment. His reasons are unclear, but the *Tribune* accused him of spitefulness against a voting consituency that opposed his views. Complaints about a rabid dog had crossed the mayor's desk, so five officers and a lieutenant were sent to the north division to shoot down the feral animal. Between midnight and 2:00 A.M. the police killed four leashed and pedigreed dogs. The burning ember from a missed shot was thought to have settled into a pile of hay in a nearby stable and a fire began which destroyed 17 buildings between States and Clark Streets.[32]

The perpetrator of the foul deed was not easily recognized, because shortly after taking office Wentworth discarded the traditional blue uniforms in favor of a simple leather badge affixed to the policeman's headband. In ordinary street clothes, a police officer was not easily distinguished; to conceal himself, all he had to do was hide the star, a common practice in those days. In defense of his actions, Wentworth argued that "there is nothing like leather to remind a policeman of his station."[33]

John Haines won the next municipal election. He was a part-owner of a Michigan copper mine, and was derisively known to his opponents as "copper stock." His men were thus "coppers."[34] A Chicago colloquialism became a standard part of U.S. slang. Haines, whose two terms of office bridged the first and second Wentworth eras, restored the military blue uniforms, and did the best he could under trying circumstances. But he inherited certain objectionable officers who were holdovers from the previous administration. One of them was George "the Beast" Brown, who was hired by a Wentworth partisan, Lieutenant Deacon Ambrose. Brown was assigned to the red-light territories to procure evidence that might be used by the prosecuting attorney in Recorder's Court.

Beast Brown did his job too well. He patrolled the low dives each night, playing "Brigham Young" among the fallen angels. Soon there were complaints that Brown was overzealous in the discharge of his duties. Then it was revealed that he had collected monetary advances from the city comptroller just before setting out on his mission. This money was never accounted for, and a grand jury was summoned to investigate the matter. Haines, who had no direct knowledge of Brown's activities, was questioned at length by the grand jury. However, the real responsibility rested with Wentworth, who went into self-imposed exile in New York for several years.

Mayor Haines completed two terms of office, but stepped aside in 1860 when John Wentworth returned to Chicago to seek the mayoral nomination for the second time. The Democratic candidate was former Mayor Walter Gurnee. He had reluctantly accepted the party's nomination solely to check the ambitions of Wentworth, known to his opponents as "Johannus Elongatus." During this critical period, as the country teetered on the brink of the Civil War, Wentworth looked past the city election toward the national nominating convention scheduled for Chicago. It was an event he considered to be the centerpiece of his career in public service.

Once again, Long John fanned the flames of anti-Irish hysteria. His pro-

nouncements were endorsed by Joseph Medill, who warned of the dire consequences that awaited on election day, when "the Irish, if not aided, at least
permitted by the Police were accustomed to take possession of the polls regularly
at three o'clock in the afternoon; drive ordinary citizens away from the vicinity
and continue voting until after they had secured the majority marked down on
the Democratic side."[35]

The pre-election rhetoric appealed to the emotion and prejudices of the elec-
torate on both sides. The streets overflowed with processions of torch-carrying
Irishmen who formed a line a half-mile long at the balloting window. "It was
a demonstration that fully revived the memory of the Dyer Dynasty and the Dyer
parade," the *Tribune* observed. A handbill circulated a week before the election
reminded 7th Ward Republicans of their obligations to alderman candidate Gurdon Hubbard: "Go to the polls early and vote for G. S. Hubbard and the whole
Republican ticket. One more victory in the noble seventh and the Celts will
never peep again."[36]

Mayor Haines, whose ruptured friendship with Wentworth might have been
reason enough to give the police the day off, nevertheless urged restraint on
election day. The saloons were ordered closed at 7:00 A.M. and the police were
stationed at key voting places to guard against outbreaks of violence. This no
doubt worked to the advantage of Wentworth, who won the election by 2,000
votes.

Examining the roster of police in 1860, Wentworth discovered that 49 of the
107 members were Irish. It was alarming to the mayor, who already considered
some budgetary cutbacks to finance construction of the Wigwam, a convention
hall that would host the Republican Convention. Some of the holdovers, particularly the policemen who had served on the force since Dyer's administration,
would be discharged. But the facts were inescapable: the Irish were a rising
political power whose time had at last come.

Notes

1. *Chicago Democrat*, November 2, 1835.
2. Joseph Kirkland, and John Moses, *History of Chicago*, vol. 1. (Chicago and New
York: The Munsel Company, 1859), p. 112.
3. *Chicago Democrat*, November 11, 1835.
4. Ibid.
5. Ibid., September 2, 1835.
6. Peter Pruyne to Edmund Kimbark, April 2, 1834 (Chicago Historical Society
Collection).
7. *Chicago American*, July 12, 1839.
8. Michael F. Funchion, *Chicago's Irish Nationalists: 1881–1890* (New York: Arno
Press, 1976), p. 9.
9. Ibid., p. 17.
10. *Chicago Tribune*, March 8, 1854. Millikin defeated Throop by 1,089 votes.
11. Ibid., June 26, 1854.

12. Cyrus Parker Bradley Memorial, March 1865 (Chicago Historical Society Collection).

13. Bonnie S. Forkosh, *History of the Chicago Police Department 1820–1886* (unpublished, Chicago Police Department Public Information Division, 1968), p. 30. Under Bradley's skilled direction the first detective bureau was organized in 1861. Before this time the city marshals would designate members of the department as needed to investigate criminal activity.

14. *Chicago Tribune*, April 21, 1872, for a retrospective look at the Lager Beer Riot of 1855. The temperance issue was again at the forefront of Chicago politics and this published account of the riot was no doubt intended to shape public opinion on behalf of Mayor Medill. See also Richard W. Fenner, "In a Perfect Ferment," *Chicago History* 5 (Fall 1976): 167; and Rudolf A. Hofmeister, *The Germans of Chicago* (Chicago: The University of Illinois, 1976), pp. 55–57, 136–37.

15. John J. Flinn and John E. Wilkie, *History of Chicago Police Department from the Settlement of the Community to the Present Time* (Chicago: Policemen's Benevolent Association, 1887), p. 78.

16. James Richardson, *The New York Police: Colonial Times to 1901* (New York: Oxford University Press, 1970), p. 89. *Chicago Tribune*, July 25, 1861.

17. *Chicago Times*, March 19, 1855.

18. *Chicago Tribune*, March 3, 1856: "All day the city swarmed with riff-raff and refuse that they turned out. They filled the Dyer carriages. They carried Dyer flags. They strained their throats in hurrahs for Dyer. The groceries ran whiskey for Dyer's honor."

19. Ibid., April 8, 1856.

20. Ibid., April 12, 1856.

21. *Chicago Democrat*, April 18, 1856.

22. *Chicago Tribune*, September 16, 1856.

23. Ibid., October 6, 1858.

24. Ibid., March 12, 1856, for a transcription of Dyer's inaugural address.

25. Ibid., March 2, 1857.

26. Ibid., March 18, 1857.

27. Walter Cade Reckless, *The Natural History of the Vice Areas in Chicago* (Ph.D dissertation, University of Chicago, 1925), p. 14. Also, Herbert Asbury, *Gem of the Prairie: An Informal History of the Chicago Underworld* (New York: Alfred Knopf, 1940); and Emmett Dedmon, *Fabulous Chicago: A Great City's History and Its People* (New York: Atheneum, 1981), pp. 28–30.

28. *Chicago Democrat*, September 2, 1835.

29. David Johnson, "A Sinful Business: Origins of Gambling, 1840–1887," in David Bayley, ed., *Police and Society* (Beverly Hills: Sage Publications, 1977), p. 22.

30. Dedmon, *Fabulous Chicago*, p. 79.

31. *Chicago Tribune*, July 9, 1857. Wentworth accused the opposition press of attempting to undermine his administration in a number of devious ways. To sustain this charge the mayor ordered his lieutenants to submit reports of burglaries in their respective districts. In the third district, for example, only three cases of robbery were reported in the month of June—but the report made no allusions to the many unsuccessful attempts.

32. Ibid., October 12, 1857. Until the Great Fire of 1871 this conflagration was the worst in city history. The *Tribune* traced Wentworth's motives to a selfish desire to foment hostility toward the Republican Party among the German voters residing in the north division.

33. Frederick Francis Cook, *Bygone Days in Chicago* (Chicago: A. C. McClurg, 1910), p. 172.

34. Ibid., p. 172.

35. *Chicago Tribune*, February 9, 1860.

36. Ibid., March 5, 1860. Gurdon S. Hubbard easily won the alderman race in the 7th Ward. Arriving in Chicago in 1818, Hubbard was the city's first insurance salesman, lumber dealer, and meat packer.

2

Ethnicity, Fraternal Orders, and the Police

"Isn't there something in the police ordinance requiring that policemen shall be citizens of the state?" the *Tribune* asked shortly after the infamous Dyer procession. The empty complaints of the nativist rang out across the city for years—even as the City Council, the Department of Public Works, and the Police and Fire Departments fell under control of the Irish ward bosses, who ran their districts like medieval fiefdoms.

A close look at the Police Department in 1866 reveals that the Irish were still second in numbers to the native-born Americans. However, all eight of the men assigned to detective duty were Irish, as were three captains and two sergeants (See Table 1).

Twenty years later the Irish so thoroughly dominated police affairs that Mayor Carter Harrison appointed Frederick Ebersold, a German, to serve as superintendent lest he alienate this strong voting constituency. "Men of Irish descent now fill a large share of the offices at my command," he explained. "It seems to me that 160,000 Germans should be recognized."[1] In 1890, 25 percent of the entire force were born in Ireland, and this study does not take into account the great number of first- and second-generation Irish who served in the department.[2] Native-born Protestants often found the notion of public service self-degrading—not a respectable career path for a young man of refinement, despite its earnings potential. During the 1860s a typical U.S. police officer could expect to earn $600 to $700 a year. This compared favorably with the wages of mechanics and other unskilled laborers. But the loss of prestige and inherent job dangers discouraged many from considering this line of work.

Table 1
Nationality of Policemen: 1866

Nationality	Number of Men	Percentage
Americans	51	31
Irish	45	27
Germans	44	26
English	9	5
Norwegians	8	4
Nova Scotians	6	3
Danes, French, Scots, Welsh, Swedes	1 ea.	.6

Source: *Chicago Tribune*, January 1, 1866. Reprint of Superintendent's Report to the City Council for 1865. The detective department was composed of eight men, six of whom were of Irish descent.

As the well-to-do fled the decaying inner city after the Civil War, immigrant Irish, who were recent victims of the potato famine, settled into the crowded tenements near the central business district. Chicago's Irish understood the English language and were more politically adept at the game of politics than their counterparts from Eastern Europe. The ambitious members of their community utilized these advantages to build a base of support within their wards. In exchange for jobs, good municipal service, and occasional intervention on behalf of a constituent in trouble with the law, an Irish alderman could expect a degree of job longevity.

As the nineteenth century drew to a close, the City Council increasingly was populated by a collection of ward bosses who ran their neighborhoods from the corner saloon or pool hall. They were colorful and utterly corrupt, and they earned for themselves the sobriquet "gray wolves." Charlie Martin, "Bathhouse" John Coughlin, Ed Cullerton, the gambler Mike McDonald, and John Powers were the everyday reality for the people in the ghetto—not the high-minded ideals of a "Committee of Fifteen" or a visiting Sunday church group. In return for a Christmas turkey, a street-cleaning job for the young man in need of work, or an even break in court, the slumdweller was expected to do his duty on election day.

Alderman Powers served his West Side 19th Ward faithfully for nearly 40 years. His district was an ethnic melting pot of 26 different nationalities.[3] His political base perpetuated itself from 1888 until 1922, long after the Irish had ceased to be the dominant immigrant group within the ward. The local bosses influenced assignments and promotions in and out of the Democratic districts they represented. The police soon realized that their livelihood was inextricably tied to the fortunes of the ward organization.

Satisfying the dominant political party was just one unfortunate aspect of the job. Of greater concern was the irregular hours and high occupational death rate.

In 1898 the death rate among patrolmen was ten per 1000, as compared with 14.63 for the general city population. Violence, consumption, and pneumonia were listed as the three most common causes of death among patrolmen.[4] In 1904, two-thirds of the force worked eight hours a day, seven days a week. Most of these men were rank-and-file officers who walked a beat in all kinds of weather. Some of them were stationed at the numerous city crossings—one of the most dangerous assignments on the force before the introduction of traffic signals. The Chicago Loop was a veritable maze of delivery wagons, streetcars, and pedestrian traffic, all eager to make up for lost time. Fourteen of the 498 men who died between 1872 and 1906 were victims of accidents at the crossings.

Working conditions for the men assigned to the station houses were substandard. Following the Great Fire of 1871, in which $53,500 in real estate property was destroyed, the city appropriated emergency funding to construct new station houses. In some cases the police were installed in temporary locations that became permanent as the City Council attempted to deal with budget shortfalls and the effects of various economic recessions. When Mayor Edward Dunne personally inspected some of the antiquated buildings in the fall of 1906, he was shocked to discover that there was no hot water at the two Chicago Avenue stations and 100 prisoners shared one working toilet with police officers. Shower baths were installed in every precinct and the matrons who administered to the prisoners were supplied with clothing disinfectants.[5]

Frequent pay furloughs further impaired the policeman's overall morale. Mayor Carter Harrison II made it a point to "dock" the men three days pay or held back their pay checks to compel them to make significant contributions to the Democratic party, especially around election time.

Few, if any, of these men received formal education past grammar school. New officers were given on-the-job training. Recruits learned to identify a criminal or confidence man from older officers who through the years had observed "devious behavior" by cultivating a good memory, or by noting a crook's demeanor in a crowd.[6] An offender could be arrested and brought in simply because his past exploits and associations with other criminals were well known to the police. Formalized classroom instruction in police technique and the Chicago municipal codes were not introduced until the reform superintendency of LeRoy T. Steward in 1910.

Petty thieves, homeless children, and destitute women were considered part of a "bad lot" or a "degenerate class." As one officer observed in 1898, "there are plenty like him. The Ninth District is full of these types."[7] The policeman often assumed the role of accuser and sole witness to an offense. They failed many times to distinguish between average citizens "out for a good time" and streetcorner loungers creating a public nuisance.

To sustain an accusation of vagrancy or public drunkenness, proof had to first be established that the conduct was an annoyance to others. In a typical case in 1890, Superintendent Frederick Marsh suspended two officers who clubbed a suspect inside a saloon. "That makes the offense all the more serious," he explained. "Policemen ought not to go into saloons while on duty unless they go in the performance of their duties."[8]

The police had little regard for existing social conditions or the ways in which deviant behavior might be reformed. Once he received an appointment to the force from the alderman or saloon keeper, the policeman often found himself the authority figure in a teeming city slum—very often the same neighborhood in which he had grown up. Public attitudes toward the officer reinforced his own perceptions of his external environment. The Maxwell Street Station served the congested, crime-ridden 19th Ward. Poorly lit streets, tough saloons, crowded alleys, and tenement buildings that housed eight to ten people per flat made this district a natural breeding ground for crime. Residents were resentful and suspicious of the bluecoats.

The blare of the calliope whistle signalling the approach of the paddy wagon served warning to the residents that one of their own was in trouble. The offenders were often hidden from sight and their wounds dressed in the maze of rambling slum buildings while the police were helpless to make an arrest.

The public perception of the police officer as a fat, bumbling loafer was fed by the newspaper cartoonists of the day (see Figures 1–3). Criticized by the press for his shortcomings and manipulated by the politicians, the rank-and-file sought identity through political, social, and ethnic outlets at which they could share common job frustrations and work toward mutually acceptable goals. The fraternal societies that were formed after 1868 were not unlike the ones organized by European immigrants to preserve their language and culture in a new hostile world. The police used their fraternal orders to lobby against the ills of civil service reform. They fought for passage of pension laws, and collected money for the aged and infirmed. The issues were important to the entire department, and they crossed political and social lines.

Although well paid by contemporary standards, Chicago policemen of the mid-nineteenth century faced the inherent dangers of crippling disablement or early death. Officers assigned to a city beat often fell victim to roving gangs of young thugs who populated the streets after dark. The policeman was alone in the commission of his duties since the City Council was usually slow in appropriating the necessary funds to hire new recruits for particularly sensitive areas. Bringing an offender to headquarters for booking required courage—and an occasional show of force. Lurking in the shadows were garroters ready to intercede on behalf of their comrade. Outnumbered and restricted by law in the use of his revolver, the policeman became the victim and not the arbitrator of a dispute.

For months past it has been patent among the gangs of rowdies who infest our city, that to assault a police officer was a manly and judicious act; that he was compelled by law to confine his defensive operations to the use of a club and that a policeman who would draw a revolver and shoot an assailant would be immediately dismissed from the force.[9]

Figure 1

Attending to unlicensed dogs while the city is in the clutches of the gangsters, burglars, and pickpockets is the implied message of this 1921 cartoon. (Deckert/Briggs)

Figure 2

THE POLICEMAN WAS WILLING TO DO HIS DUTY, BUT—

1. The inspector—"Look here, you'll have to do your duty. No favors to anybody hereafter. I'll go with you and see that you do your full duty."

2. "Say! Inspector, here's a salon open after hours. Shall we pull the proprietor?"
"No, he's a particular friend of the alderman."

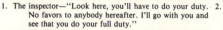

3. "Now, here's a quiet little game up here. Shall we pinch the bunch?"
"No, the place is run by a friend of the alderman."

4. "Here's a wholesale house obstructing the sidewalk. Shall we arrest the proprietor?"
"No! Great Scott! He's one of the biggest contributors to the campaign fund."

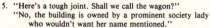

5. "Here's a tough joint. Shall we call the wagon?"
"No, the building is owned by a prominent society lady who wouldn't want her name mentioned."

6. "Here's a man spitting on the sidewalk. Shall we pinch him?"
"You bet! We'll teach him to respect the law."

Reprinted from the *Chicago Tribune*, March 24, 1904. Again, we see the familiar McCutcheon policeman attempting to do his job but impeded by the Division Inspector who wants to see the anti-spitting ordinance enforced. (Deckert/McCutcheon)

Figure 3

Following the publication of the 1904 Piper Report, which accused the police of habitual loafing in saloons, John McCutcheon took the department to task in this biting satire. Note the time on the clock, the presence of a "loose" woman in the saloon, and the holdup outside. (Deckert/McCutcheon)

Chicago was the first city in North America to introduce the patrol signal service in 1881. It changed the usual ways of policing a city neighborhood, and significantly reduced the incidents of violence against patrolmen. There is some debate, however, about who actually conceived the idea. The Simon O'Donnell version of the matter is that the idea came to him while investigating a murder in the West Twelfth District one night in 1880. A streetcar driver who saw the

Figure 4

William McGarigle, chief of police, 1880–82. (Illustration by Bob Deckert)

killing reported the crime to O'Donnell, who was sitting in a buggy in front of the station. The captain sped to the scene and quickly located a clue that led to the swift apprehension of the murderer. He was so pleased with the speed with which the case was cleared up that he spoke with Professor John P. Barrett, superintendent of the fire alarm telegraph, about the advisability of installing police call boxes similar to the ones the Fire Department already had in place.

According to Austin Doyle, departmental secretary and future superintendent, he first discussed the need with Mayor Carter Harrison at a German Society picnic in the summer of 1880. While returning to City Hall, Doyle suggested to the mayor that it would "be a great thing for the Police Department if there could be some means devised whereby the men on beat could communicate with the station at any time they desired to do so." Doyle, or so the story goes, made arrangements with Barrett to construct an experimental patrol box at Twelfth and Halsted Streets. A telephone wire was strung from the box to the Twelfth Street Station on Johnson Street. A telephone—a new-fangled invention in 1880—was installed in the box, permitting the policeman to communicate directly with the station. The prototype model was an instant success. That winter, 375 hexagonal pine boxes, measuring seven feet high by three feet in diameter, were installed in Chicago to the dismay of many of the patrolmen, who feared an inevitable reduction in manpower. With the patrol system in place there would be no chance to shirk duty if hourly reports had to be made from a box to the station. In other words, a man couldn't "hole it" for a smoke or a drink if the dial had to be "pulled" at a certain time. Inside the box was an alarm dial with a pointer that could be placed on 11 different categories by the user; included were such crimes as thievery, riot, and forgery.

The boxes were fastened to telegraph poles with a direct line to the station. Citizens of good standing who were known to the police were provided with two keys to gain access to the lock boxes in their wards. Each key was lettered and numbered at the station. When the alarm sounded, a wagon and driver with two policemen on board were dispatched to the site, arriving within three minutes. Keys belonging to the person who sounded the alarm remained locked in the box until the police arrived. This discouraged prank calls.

Chief William McGarigle expanded the patrol system and brought it to the attention of police agencies outside Chicago. At his suggestion, Professor Barrett placed a glass pyramid on top of the box, crowned by a street light to illuminate the neighborhood. The wooden boxes remained in service in Chicago for many years until they were replaced by the smaller iron boxes in the 1930s and 1940s.

The impact of the call box system was immediate. Austin Doyle reported that 11,530 arrests made in 1883 were directly tied to calls placed through the patrol service.[10] Discipline was strengthened since the patrolmen on duty were required to report into the station house once an hour using the lock box. Men could be transferred out of low-crime areas as the police trusted the neighborhood watch to the businessmen and residents who were given keys. Said one lieutenant: "I would rather have fifty men in a district well patrolled with watch boxes than seventy-five men unprovided with them.''[11] The attitude of the men was reflected in a popular limerick of the day:

> Says Clancy: "I'm glad that I'm not on the force now—
> I couldn't in honor keep friends with them things.
> The counthry has surely gone clane to the divil.
> Since lightnin' id doin such work for the rings."
>
> "With these sir, the boys can't get up half a shindy
> Before the alarm brings the wagon around;
> And bedad sir, they'll gobble the whole av the part
> Before the first man's fairly laid on the ground."
>
> "Ah! once I was proud of my star and billy!
> I walked like a turkey cock happy and free;
> But now sir I wouldn't be happy as a peeler,
> No, no sir! I thank ye—not anny for me."

As the news of the patrol system spread across the country, other cities sent delegations to Chicago to consider ways of adopting it to their own locales.

By the late 1880s the trend in U.S. policing had gradually shifted toward professionalism. There was an increasing awareness that this was career work and not merely a job. New innovations in crime detection required that a policeman should at least be able to read, write, and understand basic concepts. The Bertillon Method of prisoner classification was based on measurements and subdivisions of the human body that do not change after an individual attains full physical growth. By measuring body parts of a suspect, such as the length of the middle and little fingers and the circumference of the head, police were able to identify and exchange information about criminals regardless of the disguises they employed.

In 1888 Chicago became the first U.S. city to put the Bertillon system into limited use. Former Detective George Porteous became its earliest advocate and due in part to his recommendations the Harrison Street Station became the first precinct to purchase a set of the measuring instruments.

After a prisoner was bound over to the grand jury on a criminal charge, he was transported to Harrison Street for classification. Measurements of the head, outstretched arm, foot, knee, and ears were taken. Two photographs from the front and sides were taken, and attached to index cards maintained by a special office of the department.[12] By 1895 six cities (Chicago, Cincinnati, Detroit, Philadelphia, Milwaukee, and Washington, DC) had adopted the system for general use. The Bertillon method remained the accepted system of classifying prisoners until the 1910s, when fingerprinting gained widespread acceptance.

Chicago led the way in advancing the sophistication of police work. But, unfortunately, the city remained mired in partisan politics and self-interested causes. The Policemen's Protective Association was founded February 20, 1868, with membership open to all men serving in active duty. Since the city made no direct provisions for the families of officers who died or were injured in the line of duty, the Protective Association served as a relief agency, providing food, clothing, and burial money.

In 1872 its name was changed to the Policeman's Benevolent Association, and it was granted a state charter in January. In its early years the leadership sponsored a number of worthwhile events, including charity balls and an annual picnic that was open to the public. The 1885 event attracted 18,000 spectators to the suburban Driving Park, where the policemen competed in a variety of athletic events and sharpshooting contests.[13] Money raised from the annual picnic went into a relief fund administered by the treasurer. By the 1920s, the Association continued to sponsor special fund-raising events, but the leadership attached greater significance to the public participation. Their annual "field meet" was a two-day event in which the entire department participated, either through ticket sales or in the athletic arena. In addition to the added revenues, the police maintained that the field days engendered good will in the community while providing excellent entertainment in return. But events of this nature invariably distracted the policeman from his real duty to the city. Rank-and-file members were pressured to sell a quota of tickets in their precinct or face the risk of reprimand by the captain: "I have a list for my district and anyone who buys fewer tickets than the year before is personally interviewed by me. I want to know the reason why."[14]

The day-to-day control of the Association passed from the Republicans to the Irish Democrats, reflecting the demographic shift of the city and the changing nature of Chicago politics in the 1870s and 1880s. Increasingly, the Association involved itself in partisan political struggles, as it went far beyond its stated intentions, published in an 1877 handbook: "The particular business and objects for which such association is formed, areas to wit: to create a fund and provide means for the relief of the distressed, injured, sick, or disabled members of the Association and their immediate families."[15]

The Fire Department also had a fraternal society with similar bylaws. There was, however, one notable amendment that the police charter did not have: "And all property and money acquired by the said association shall be held and used solely for that purpose."[16] Slush funds, political lobbies, and misappropriation of funds characterized the management of the Policeman's Benevolent Association. However, they were virtually unknown in the Fire Department, which remained true to the charter's original intent.

Guided by opportunistic officers like Chief Michael Brennan, the Association sanctioned a variety of illegal money-making schemes while attempting to "muscle" downstate legislators for a favorable vote on pension issues. In 1887 a separate pension bill was passed by the General Assembly with a little help from a police lobby headed by Brennan and Inspector John Bonfield, who collected $1,000 from the men to be used to sway votes in Springfield. The measure passed, and a board of trustees was appointed to administer to all Illinois cities with a population of 50,000 or more.[17]

Following the World's Fair of 1893 the city was in the grip of a financial panic that left thousands homeless and out of work. With the city treasury depleted and the department facing across-the-board salary reductions, Brennan gave his approval to a bribery scheme in which certain alderman were to be "braced up" with Association contributions in exchange for a favorable vote.[18] Brennan supervised the distribution of $400 that had been left over from a special "agitation fund" raised in 1892 to coax Springfield legislators to pass a bill increasing the tax rate to 2.5 percent. At the time, Brennan was retired from the force following a change to a Republican administration. However, he continued to serve the Association while in the employ of banker Edward S. Dreyer. Brennan then raised over $2,000 from the members, which he handed over to a Committee of Three to use as bribery money for legislators who were inclined to vote against the tax increase. This increase, if passed, would mean a pay raise.

This method of buying an alderman's or state senator's vote was known in police circles as "corrupt treating." Public officials who were shy about accepting cash honorariums might be bought off in other ways. Sometimes an alderman might be seen in a well-known restaurant with an Association member, or have choice tickets to the theater or a sporting event. Of course, Brennan denied that any money withdrawn from the Association was used for these purposes. The General Assembly did not pass the tax increase and the crisis was finally resolved by requiring the men to take a furlough without pay.

Financial mismanagement on the part of the Association trustees was a disturbing but certainly not uncommon way of doing business. Because of Brennan's close dealings with Edward Dreyer, the Association was nearly bankrupt in 1898. For years Dreyer was a fixture in Democratic Party affairs. Through the influence of his employee and close personal friend, Michael Brennan, the Association was persuaded to deposit its membership dues and other income into a special account with Dreyer's bank—the National Bank of Illinois. As treasurer for the West Park Board, Dreyer had access to significant amounts of county tax money. In 1897 he deposited $300 of embezzled park funds into his own personal account at the bank. This money was reinvested in a bogus land scheme. When news of the swindle leaked out, Dreyer was handed a penitentiary sentence. The National Bank failed shortly thereafter, and the Association was out $12,000.[19]

To recoup these losses the new superintendent, Joseph Kipley, approved another crooked money-making scheme involving the publication of a departmental history to be sold by subscription to the city's leading merchants and philanthropists. A prize fight was first considered, but contests of this sort were in violation of local city ordinances. The idea to publish a book was certainly not a new one. In 1887 John Flinn completed a manuscript that was circulated in the city. The revenue from book sales was pumped back into the treasury, which encouraged Kipley to publish a sequel. Patrolman Walter Magnus of the East Chicago Avenue Station was appointed receiver of the funds in the name of the Association. This was arranged without so much as a voice vote from the delegates. Only four people were privy to this scheme: Kipley, Mayor Carter Harrison, City Oil Inspector Bobby Burke, and Amos D. Atwell, a solicitor of the business interests. Atwell was a well-known confidence man who was run out of Detroit for obtaining money under false pretenses. But Kipley seemed oblivious to his shortcomings when he handed over a document bearing the mayor's signature asking for support from the business community. In return for making the right contacts, Atwell was to receive 25 percent of the gross and Magnus 5 percent. The Benevolent Association refused to cooperate in the scheme, leaving Kipley with several thousand dollars of subscription money and no book. The project was cancelled and the two confederates were seen fleeing to the train station without so much as leaving a forwarding address. When questioned by a special subcommittee of the state senate, Kipley had this to say: "I heard about Atwell but I never heard that he was guilty of the charge you make, or has been arrested in every city. I sent him out to do what he did. I think he is a successful individual."[20]

An honest police superintendent less inclined than Kipley to use the resources of City Hall to further Association aims might have gone a long way in separating the department from political interference. Francis O'Neill replaced Kipley in 1901. He made it known that membership in the newly formed Protective Association would be cause for immediate dismissal. The Protective Association was a splinter group organized to support the aims of John Hopkins, a political enemy of Mayor Harrison. Members pressured aldermen for a favorable vote on the issue of a two-platoon system. The Fire Department already had such a system in place and the men's work hours were shortened as a direct consequence.

The Protective Association was forced to disband but it retained the services of Alderman Powers as treasurer and Lieutenant Thomas Kane of the Sheffield Station as president. Kane was a political appointee who owed his position to his uncle, former Mayor Hopkins.[21] Kane and a political crony, State Senator Tom Dawson, reorganized the Protective Association into the "Mexican Plantation Company." Four thousand acres of farm land in the interior of Mexico had been quietly bought up by agents acting on behalf of Kane. Shares of stock in the bogus land company were sold to unwitting Association members for exactly the same amount as the dues that had been charged before O'Neill forced it to disband.[22]

Reform groups paid little attention to the goings on within the fraternal associations because for the most part, their activities were disguised to the public and did not affect the well-being of the city. Proper direction therefore had to come from the superintendent's office to ensure that the rank-and-file members did not cross the boundaries of acceptable behavior. During the term of Leroy T. Steward (1909–10), politically active members were disciplined and in some cases removed from the force.[23] As a result the Benevolent Association was forced to maintain a lower profile during this period.

However, Steward vacated the office when Carter Harrison returned to the mayor's office in 1911. Harrison rewarded John T. McWeeney, an old-line officer who did not share Steward's liberal views, with the top job in the department. Years earlier, when Civil Service was about to become compulsory, McWeeney admonished the commission that there were men in his station "who if the mayor should fire them could go and force him to reinstate them."[24] Chief McWeeney was one of a group of old-time political officers who saw no impropriety in maintaining cordial relations with the leaders of the county party like Bobby Burke and his successor, James "Hot Stove" Quinn. Quinn was the owner of the Village Inn, a vicious resort located at 63 W. Erie Street. Policemen at the East Chicago Avenue Station maintained a strict "hands off" policy, lest they offend this politically connected brothel master. But even Jimmy Quinn lacked the necessary clout to block passage of the 1911 Reorganization Act, which created the office of Civilian Deputy (see Table 3 in Chapter 5). McWeeney scoffed at reformers who would have a group of civilians telling policemen what to do, so he approved a plan to have the United Police organization "brace" up the aldermen.

The United Police was a variation of an old theme—merely the same gang of corrupt police officials who tried to sell worthless Mexican land holdings to the rank-and-file in 1905. The leaders of the organization were some of the most avaricious officers in the department, including Inspector John Wheeler, who was later fired for accepting bribes from the 1st ward resort keepers, his protégé Captain Patrick Harding, and Inspector Nicholas Hunt, friend and protector of stockyards gambler Jim O'Leary.

At the forefront of the United Police stood its president, Sergeant William F. Stine of the Irving Park Station. His shady dealings filled an entire roster book. He supplemented a $100 monthly salary by removing corpses from the Dunning Mental Institution and selling them to local medical colleges.[25] Just before the issue of a police salary increase came up for a vote in the city council, Stine engineered a $66,000 slush fund to be distributed "where it could do the most good." Before the November city elections, Stine circulated a handbill in the station houses listing the candidates who had make token pledges of support to the United Police.

Just before the money was to be distributed to the alderman, Stine requested a three-month furlough to investigate a job possibility with his cousin in Texas. He took with him a locked strong box containing $42,000 in United Police assets, but did not leave a forwarding address. Detectives traced Stine to Baraga, Michigan, in June 1911, but through a lack of conclusive evidence and a general unwillingness on the part of the United Police to prosecute, the matter was quietly dropped.

Membership was open to everyone in the department, but only the highest-placed officers reaped any benefit. In 1909, 72 percent of the cash held in reserve was used to pay legal fees for various officials accused of malfeasance. Inspector Edward McCann was sentenced to a term in the state penitentiary for accepting bribes from resort owners, but used $2,000 of agency funds for his appeals. Former Chief John Collins received $360 in his own battle to avoid prison, while

Inspector Patrick Lavin was given $565 to fight an earlier indictment for complicity in a jewelry story robbery.[26]

The distribution of money was never seriously considered by anyone outside the department until the strong-arm techniques against opposition aldermen finally got the best of them. Charles Reading of the 33rd Ward told of coercive tactics by certain members in the precinct. "I told the fellow to do his worst," the alderman explained. "I guess he did, and other policemen did too. I can name no less than a dozen who spent their time campaigning against me for reelection. They rode up and down the line on the street talking against me because I voted against a salary increase which was impossible, for there was no money."[27]

Alderman Ellis Geiger, chairman of the Council committee on police, proposed an investigation into lobbying efforts of the United Police. Geiger was opposed by a number of aldermen who counted on the support of the police to help them carry their wards at election time. "As white men and Americans they have the right to oppose an ordinance affecting their welfare," blustered Alderman "Bathhouse" John Coughlin in defense of the United Police and their efforts to kill the reorganization bill.[28]

As usual, the United Police thumbed their noses at Civil Service by retaining Michael Ryan, Jr. as their legal counsel. Ryan was the son of Michael "White Alley" Ryan, who commanded the Levee tenderloin, and a nephew of Patrick Dwyer, who headed up the United Police. The effort to break the power of the organization was planned months earlier by reform-minded aldermen. Because of the veiled secrecy surrounding Stine's slush fund and the usual reluctance on the part of the police to testify against one of their own, indictments were slow in coming. Cooperative witnesses were finally produced, but only after the state's attorney threatened them with a wave of perjury indictments.

During the hearings the grand jury learned that division inspectors collected five to ten dollars per man, which would then be placed into the agitation fund. Wheeler, Hunt, and Harding personally travelled to Springfield with $5,000 to be used in the fight to prevent police matrons from inclusion in the revised pension laws. Thirty men were eventually indicted for their role in the United Police scandals. But with a view toward obtaining leniency, President Dwyer announced the formal dissolution of the United Police on January 16, 1913. "I am glad to hear of it," commented Mayor Harrison. "They long ago have outlived their usefulness, if in fact they were of any use."[29] The Police Reorganization Bill passed the Council and the United Police faded into memory. The reformers had scored a temporary victory. But in time the department would return to former levels of scandal as concerned citizens again wondered what steps might be taken to separate politics from policing.

Notes

1. Richard Lindberg, *Chicago Ragtime: Another Look at Chicago, 1880–1920* (South Bend: Icarus Press, 1985), p. 18.

2. *Register of the Chicago Police*, vol. 1, *1890–1897*, Chicago Historical Society Manuscript Collection. See pp. 1–303 for an alphabetical listing of all police officers active during this period. The *Register* includes place of birth, date of appointment, and sundry comments by supervisors.

3. *Chicago Tribune*, February 13, 1898, for an account of conditions in Powers' ward. The division of nationalities in the 19th ward is a good example of the inner-city ethnic coalition that fueled Chicago's decentralized machine. In the west end of the ward resided 18,065 middle-class Irish. Between Taylor and 12th Streets, 5,784 Italians, 4,980 Russian Jews, and 2,944 Bohemians comprised the impoverished classes of the neighborhood. Alderman Powers, known as the "Prince of the Boodlers," once boasted that he provided 2,600 people of various nationalities with jobs on the public payroll. In addition to jobs, Powers provided bail bonds on demand, exemptions from city ordinances for local businessmen, turkeys at Christmas, and a shoulder to cry on when a loved one died. Powers was the official "mourner" of the 19th ward. Humbert S. Nelli, *The Italians in Chicago: 1880–1930* (New York: Oxford University Press, 1970), pp. 92–100.

4. *Chicago Inter-Ocean*, April 15, 1907.

5. *Chicago Tribune*, September 7, 1906. This report, filed one year after the Piper investigation, shows that little was done to correct the unsanitary conditions in the substations to which the committee had first drawn attention.

6. David R. Johnson, *The Search for an Urban Discipline: Police Reform as a Response to Crime in American Cities* (Ph.D dissertation, University of Chicago, 1972), pp. 197–98.

7. *Chicago Tribune*, February 13, 1898.

8. Ibid., January 21, 1890.

9. Ibid., August 24, 1865.

10. *Report of the General Superintendent to the City Council (1883)*, p. 27. See also John Flinn and John Wilkie, *History of the Chicago Police from the Settlement of the Community to the Present Time* (Chicago: Policemen's Benevolent Association, 1887), pp. 397–407; and *New York Times*, February 27, 1881.

11. *New York Times*, February 27, 1881.

12. Matthew Wilson McLaughery, "History of the Bertillon System," *Fingerprint Magazine*, April 1922, p. 3. See also, *Chicago Times Herald*, December 15, 1895. Superintendent Robert McLaughery (1891–93) first introduced the Bertillon method of prisoner classification to the Joliet Penitentiary when he served as warden in the late 1880s. In a letter to the members of the Wardens' Association he urged uniform adaption of the anthropometric system pioneered by Alphonse Bertillon in 1879, and submitted to Louis Andrieux, the prefect of police in Paris.

13. *Chicago Daily News*, June 22, 1885.

14. *Chicago Police Problems* (Champaign: University of Illinois Press, 1931), p. 246.

15. Policemen's Benevolent Association of Chicago (Collins & Hoffman Printers, 1877), p. 2. Chicago Historical Society Collection.

16. Charter Constitution and Bylaws of the Paid Fire Department of the City of Chicago (Hazlitt & Reed Printers, 1877), p. 4. Chicago Historical Society Collection.

17. *Chicago Police Problems*, p. 234. The revenue to fund the plan came from several different sources including: (1) a 1.5 percent assessment paid by each member of the department, provided it did not exceed $300 a month; (2) revenues from the sale of unclaimed property; (3) 4 percent of all saloon licenses (which was another good excuse to ignore the one o'clock closing laws); (4) fines for carrying concealed weapons; and

(5) money collected from the special events. The pension fund provided men with 20 years of service a salary of exactly half of their base earnings. The recipient had to be at least 50 years old. But as the department grew, so too did the number of eligible beneficiaries. From just 609 members in 1908 the figure increased to 1,111 by 1914. In 1908 the police telegraph operators joined and soon after that the police matrons. The rank-and-file lobbied against their inclusion in the pension plan because the payouts to a growing list of retirees exceeded the actual income. The dilemma was finally resolved in 1921 with the passage of a law that placed Chicago and all other Illinois municipalities with over 200,000 residents on an actuarial reserve basis. See also a *Tribune* account of the recurrent financial problems plaguing the pension board, July 28, 1914.

18. *Chicago Tribune*, February 25, 1894.

19. Edward Dreyer obituary, *Chicago Tribune*, June 22, 1918.

20. Senate Report on the Chicago Police System presented by the Committee of Investigation by the 40th General Assembly, 1897–98 Session, p. 17. Kipley occupied nearly every top position in the Police Department during his checkered 20-year career. He was highly regarded by the mayor for his exceptional "thief-catching" abilities, but his pettiness and political maneuvering proved to be his own undoing. Kipley's troubles began in 1900 when he picked a fight with Bobby Burke, secretary of the Democratic County Committee who was later appointed city oil inspector. Burke and Kipley were once the best of friends, but at the urging of Mayor Harrison the chief distanced himself from Burke. In 1901 Burke retaliated by campaigning for Luke Colleran, chief of detectives, to take Kipley's place. For a time the cadre was split into two warring camps until Harrison put pressure on Kipley to resign.

21. Kane was later assigned to the state's attorney's police, considered for years to be one of the softest jobs in Chicago law enforcement.

22. *Chicago Tribune*, July 15, 1905.

23. *Chicago Herald-Examiner*, October 3, 1909; November 30, 1909.

24. McWeeney's statements can be found in the *Tribune*, March 31, 1895.

25. Ibid., April 20, 1911.

26. Ibid.

27. Ibid.

28. Ibid., December 18, 1912.

29. Ibid., January 18, 1913.

Close Up on the Chicago Police:
A Ride to Jail in the Patrol Wagon

There was no such thing as a Miranda Act back then. Anyone could be arrested in Chicago and all one had to do was look like a rough character—or arouse the policeman's suspicion. The nineteenth-century cop had a phrase for this: you were picked up "on description," and it was so noted in the arrest book after your name. The harrowing experience a man under arrest faced back then began the instant the officer or detective informed him that he was being taken into custody. When Thomas Byrnes ruled the New York police with an iron hand, his men would often say, "The inspector wants to see you in his office." The presence of the uniformed cop and the mere mention of his name sent a clear message. There was nothing so dramatic as "I'm arresting you in the name of the law!" That was a comical invention of the pulp fiction writers. If a Chicago policeman wanted to take you in, he would simply ask, "Want to walk over to the station with me?" A more compassionate officer might add, "I've got to take you over to the station now, but I guess it will come out all right."

Most of the time it was a short walk down the street if the arrestee offered no objection. If there was resistance or if a detective made the arrest, the patrol wagon would be summoned via the corner signal box. From the central barn located at Michigan and Monroe, the two officers and the driver were spurred to action. An electric buzzer would be pressed, and the team of horses would be saddled in 17 seconds. If traffic was light the team could cover a city mile in less than three minutes. The patrol wagon was equipped to handle any emergency. Each wagon carried with it the necessary equipment:

1. stretcher and hangers suspended to the sides

2. three blankets

3. one air pillow

4. two tarpaulins for the dead

5. a coil of rope for use at fires

6. six pairs of handcuffs

7. straitjacket for the violently insane

8. medicine chest containing a bottle of brandy, vinegar for snake bites, painkiller, court plaster, tourniquet, scissors, rolls of bandage, and a sponge

9. a grappling hook for dragging the river

The noise of a fast-moving patrol wagon was deafening. The clang of the bell was barely audible as the iron wheels jostled noisily over the cobblestone pavement of Chicago's downtown streets. Arriving at the scene of a street fight or shootout, the wagon officers assisted their comrades in loading the prisoner into the wagon, often amidst the jeers and angry epithets of the street throng. If the prisoner was the rebellious sort, he would be rudely shoved into the back of the wagon and held in place by one of the burly officers. The Patrol Service required that its members be the strong, physical type.

It was an established routine. During the peak years of the Patrol Service a seasoned wagon team could make 18 runs a day, covering 12,000 miles a year. During the "can-rushing season"—that time of year when the heat and humidity of summer increased beer sales—emergency calls to the patrol barn doubled. Sundays, Mondays, and Chicago election days were the quiet times.

At the Harrison Street Station, the patrol wagon descended down a long, narrow ramp that led into the basement. The persons in detention were brought before a barred office window and asked to identify themselves. The prisoners were frisked and their names entered into the arrest book, known to the desk sergeant as the "sheet." After being relieved of his possessions, the prisoner was offered the services of the police court attorney and led away to his cell, where a wooden plank and a solitary tin cup awaited. Sometimes there would be as many as five or six souls crowded into the narrow space, sharing that one glass of water.

If a suspect was to be questioned, the police began the gamesmanship of the "sweat." They would move slowly down the corridor, casting a menacing glance at the person from whom they hoped to receive information. Then, when the time was right, he would be led up to the captain's office where the real grilling took place. Prisoners would be told that their families and friends had all gone back on them, and there was little else to do but confess. This process was a painful, degrading experience, mercifully ended only when the captain agreed. Returned to his cell, the prisoner next encountered the bondsman, who determined his fee by the person's ability to pay. A grinning jackal of a man, the

professional bondsman resembled a river boat gambler in his loud, garish clothing. He had a kind word for everyone, and a memory for names and places. It
was his business to know people, and trade on the collective misery of the
system.

If the arrested man was to be bound over to the grand jury, he was led out
of the cell of the local precinct station and taken to detective headquarters to be
"shown up." Standing under a hot, glaring light, he answered the sergeant's
questions before a room of onlookers. When this process was complete, the
prisoners were herded back into the patrol wagon handcuffed to their cellmates
and returned to the station. Frequently, prisoners shared quarters with special
witnesses, whose only crime was that they happened to be present when a crime
was committed. This was the Chicago version of the "witness protection program"—a cell in the precinct jail.

The patrol wagon rumbled back to the barn to await the next call and to record
in the ledger the destination and comments. Day crews were on duty from 7:00
AM until 6:00 PM when they were relieved by the night-time drivers. The experienced wagonmasters had no use for nerves. Each trip out of the barn carried
with it inherent dangers—or some pathetic, loathsome sight, which only experience and time could chase from their memories.

3

The Failures of Reform: Chicago under the Police Commission and Civil Service

The essence of politics and the role of the politician underwent a metamorphosis before the Civil War. No longer the genteel patrician of the business and commercial classes, the politician who represented a bustling city ward was invariably Irish, foreign-born, and a service carrier who traded jobs and favors for votes at election time. The votes were delivered to the boss of the local machine—a coalition of loosely affiliated ward organizations composed of immigrants.

These local officials had an important stake in their police and fire departments as sources of patronage and good municipal service. The Republican Party, as the traditional spokesman for the nation's business and reform groups, watched with growing alarm the erosion of its urban power base to the Democrats—the party it associated with "rum, Romanism, and rebellion." As Republicans were forced to relinquish influence to the Democrats, they often sought ways to regain lost ground. One way to do this was to impose rigid state control over the urban police in the form of an appointed board responsible for policy making, transfers, promotions, budgetary considerations, and overall discipline. Their stated intentions were to "divorce politics from the police," a nineteenth-century cliché that really meant returning a degree of control to their party. Republicans succeeded in instituting state-run boards in New York (1857), Detroit (1865), New Orleans (1868), Cincinnati (1877), Boston (1885), and Omaha (1887).[1]

The motivation was clear and on the surface it had a degree of merit: rid the police of political interference by engaging businessmen of sterling reputations to oversee the affairs of the department.

However, the experience of state-controlled boards in Boston and New York tended to prove that change at the top would not always solve the deep-seated problems, despite an early flash of success. In Boston the board eliminated a great deal of budgeted bloat. A police school was opened and the first pension bill was passed during the first year.[2] The situation was a little different in New York, where bitter factional fighting existed for years between Tammany Hall and the Republican-dominated legislature in Albany. Despite the opposition of Mayor Fernando Wood—a man cut from the same cloth as Wentworth—the Republicans pushed through a metropolitan board. As in Boston, it achieved peak efficiency in its first few years, but was later plagued by scandal and political turmoil.[3]

As in New York, the actions of a wily and capricious mayor led to the formation of the Chicago Police Commission, which was sanctioned by the legislature on February 22, 1861. Shortly after beginning his second term of office, Wentworth returned the police to civilian clothing. Then, to the considerable alarm of everyone, he reduced the force to half its previous size. This was seen as a way to raise revenue for the construction of the Wigwam, which was to host the national nominating convention. But an alarming increase in crime convinced Governor Richard Yates that Wentworth was not sound in his judgments.

Hindsight should have taught Wentworth that attempting to block the police bill would be one political battle he could not hope to win. But the mayor considered the Police Commission an outrageous affront to local self-determination. Thus he decided to fire the entire force one night. There were 1,500 job seekers who had recently filed applications in the court house. Perhaps Wentworth thought that the Commission would out of necessity be compelled to hire these men, who could later serve him on election day. A recent change to the City Charter pushed back the mayoral election from March to April. With his popular support eroding each day, Wentworth's move was a desperate gamble.

He ordered the men to vacate their posts for a midnight meeting in his office. After praising them for their efforts on behalf of the city he informed the men that the new board intended to fire them all anyway, and that he would save them the trouble.[4] From midnight until 10:00 A.M. on March 27, 1861, Chicago was without benefit of police protection. Fortunately, no one knew about this, and the night passed quietly.

The next day the Police Commission convened for the first time. The politically ambitious Republican Jack Rehm was appointed deputy superintendent, with full control over appointments. On April 6, Cyrus Bradley was brought out of retirement to serve as superintendent. Bradley and the mayor had not patched up their differences, and Bradley's appointment was another slap at Wentworth's authority.

The Commission accomplished a great deal in the first month of its existence. Thirty-three new men were mustered into the force, and guidelines were passed to establish height and weight requirements. No serving policeman could be under five foot six inches in height.

The new men were supplied with smartly styled blue uniforms that distinguished them from the ordinary citizenry, and by mid-summer Bradley had improved the overall discipline and appearance of the Police Department. But these were cosmetic improvements that over time could not obscure the problems of a state-controlled commission. The police board, though well-intentioned, became as much of a political tool as any self-serving mayor. Because the term of appointment of the three commissioners were staggered, the hold-over members often exercised greater influence over the recruitment of new applicants than the incoming member. Patrolmen soon realized they would have to court the favor of the commissioner of the division to which they were assigned.

The first board was composed of men handpicked by the governor. The three members and their terms of office were: Alexander Coventry (six years), William Wayman (four years), and Frederick Tuttle (two years). Each of the men drew lots to determine the length of their appointed terms, with popular elections scheduled to begin in 1863. Succeeding commissioners would then be elected to terms of six years.[5] The Commission Bill stipulated that members were required by law to reside in their respective divisions for five years prior to election. Their duties were further broadened by the state when they were given responsibility for the annual budget of the Fire Department, and Departments of Health and Safety. This not only undermined the effectiveness of the firefighters, but also distracted them from their real duties as law enforcement officers.

Assessing the relative strengths and weaknesses of the board years later, Jake Rehm recalled that "the measure simply meant taking the police from the control of one set of politicians and putting it in the hands of another set."[6] The political bickering between board members seeking special considerations for their districts was most apparent after 1863, when the revised City Charter reduced the elective terms of the commissioners to three years. Under this arrangement, the mayor was made an ex-officio member of the board. The act also set a voting quorum of three instead of two, with the treasurer's job eliminated in favor of the newly created secretary's position. This realignment only served to create a political deadlock between the members which encouraged partisan votes over key issues when the opposing member was absent. In its first test the board was unable to agree on a compromise candidate to replace Jake Rehm, who resigned as superintendent after succeeding Cyrus Bradley. Bradley himself had quit to become the collector of South Chicago. The resources of the superintendent's office were severely restricted by the board. None of these men was content to remain a ceremonial figurehead, and they all vacated their offices as soon as this realization set in.

The issue of Rehm's successor reached a crisis level in the early summer of 1864. Each commissioner pushed for the nomination of a man from his own division. Wayman's man was Democrat William Turtle, captain of the West Division Police. Coventry pushed for Jack Nelson, the Republican who commanded Gambler's Row, and Commissioner Richard Newhouse (who succeeded Tuttle) nominated Charles Walsh, commander of Camp Douglas, the Confederate prisoner of war camp on the South Side. With the board in a hopeless deadlock, Coventry mysteriously absented himself from Chicago. Wayman, whose term of office was about to expire, entered into a secret agreement with Newhouse and Democratic Mayor Francis Sherman to install Turtle as the new superintendent. Rumors to the effect that Wayman had been paid off circulated in the city.[7] The Democratic ticket had lost badly in the recent spring election so this was clearly a "grab-game" by the two commissioners to regain control of the force, which was dominated by Republicans.

Turtle took office on September 26 after his appointment was confirmed by the City Council. With no previous experience in police work, William Turtle advanced to the highest office in three short years. Before his 1861 appointment he had served as town collector in suburban Northfield. Guile, cunning, and blind ambition translated into success for this Englishman who was also a Free Mason. After taking office he suspended the Republican officers loyal to Coventry. In retaliation, two detectives named Samuel A. Ellis and Charles Storer brought suit in circuit court, charging Turtle with unlawfully occupying an office and usurping power without benefit of a popular election.

The question of Turtle's right to occupy office was further clouded by revelations of Commissioner Newhouse's adulterous relationship with a single woman.[8] Newhouse was forced to resign, thereby returning control of the board to the Republicans by a 2–1 margin. A meeting was convened on Friday, June 10, 1864, but Mayor Sherman was unable to attend. Since the board was reduced to three, a quorum of two was sufficient to act on new business. Cyrus Bradley was appointed commissioner, and the two suspended detectives were reinstated to active duty.

In defense of what seemed to be an underhanded move, Coventry declared that no one had really forced Newhouse to resign, as the Democratic press had charged, but rather that the deposed commissioner had begged for his release. Attorneys for Turtle accused Bradley and Storer of conspiracy and illegal trespass of office. The mayor stood behind Turtle and vowed to ignore any new police business or affix his signature to official documents that contained Bradley's name. This imbroglio divided the department along party lines until Judge Williams handed down the verdict that upheld Turtle's appointment. The judge wrote to the mayor that it was not the intent of the state legislature to allow the board to change its mind after the fact. Bradley's claim was dismissed and his resignation was accepted on July 23.[9] William Turtle continued to occupy the office until 1866, amidst charges that he masterminded a scheme in which Union Army deserters were released after they had paid a $50 "fee" to the department.[10] Turtle was accused of malfeasance of office on several occasions, but when the issue of his retention or dismissal came up, one of the new commissioners from the opposition party spared him the humiliation of censure. The board member who spoke on Turtle's behalf was John Wentworth, who had been appointed to fill out Richard Newhouse's unexpired term.[11]

External supervision of an essentially militaristic organization by business people unfamiliar with policing technique could never be as effective in the long run as good internal self-regulation. The Turtle-Bradley affair illustrated this point, but there were some more painful lessons to be learned before the city finally came to grips with the issue. A City Council probe spearheaded by Alderman John Comiskey in 1868 traced the blame for the existing corruption directly to the board, which he accused of "delinquency, omission, and failure to perform the duties of them by law, and their oath of office in permitting confidence men and other thieves to be prowling around the railroad depots of the city, encouraging by their example, all other officers and members of the force to do likewise."[12]

One of the reasons corruption escalated during the commission years was the difficulty in removing objectionable men from the force. The existing rules allowed a suspended officer to appeal his case. While awaiting his day in court he would have enough time to line up witnesses and produce evidence to compel the judges to overturn the commission's prior ruling. A shrewd officer might reverse his suspension by petitioning the mayor for relief if he knew that the board and the executive branch of city government were in disharmony.[13]

The rivalries between the mayor and the board reached a crisis level during the administration of Joseph Medill (1872–73). An otherwise prudent man in the ways of running a big city newspaper, Medill endorsed the position of the radical temperance movement, which revived the Sunday closing furor. After a drunken police officer slammed his fist into a reporter from the *Chicago Morning News* during a saloon row, the Committee demanded the removal of Superintendent William W. Kennedy, an Irish-Catholic who took a more liberal stance concerning the Sunday liquor laws. Medill fired Kennedy and replaced him with Elmer Washburn, former warden at the Joliet Penitentiary, on August 13, 1872. Skeptics in the City Council questioned the legality of Medill's move, and the need to go all the way to Joliet when there were capable men in Chicago—like Mike Hickey.

Medill justified his actions as being consistent with the additional powers granted him under the ordinance of the new state constitution, approved by the legislature on April 7, 1872. Known as the "Mayor's Bill," its consequences were far-reaching. It gave the mayor the power to remove at will the men in city government he considered incompetent or objectionable. It was a powerful tool, and in the hands of Medill it was devastating.

Politics, the Saloon, and the Police Board

Elmer Washburn was a man of ripe experience in public affairs but sadly lacking in his perceptions. He pledged to uphold the Sunday closings, and to ensure that each and every man in the department maintained the laws. Not since the time of Mayor Boone had the distillers and brewers faced such formidable opposition. The Germans and Irish were naturally concerned, because this decision affected their livelihoods. Chicago's foreign-born Irish constituted 12.5 percent of the work force by the 1870s, yet held down 14.7 percent of all liquor jobs.[14] The numbers are even more telling within the German community: immigrant Germans accounted for 21.3 percent of the city population, with 42.8 percent engaged as saloon keepers.[15]

The liquor business, like the gambling fraternity, prospered during the post-Civil War period. Liquor licenses were cheap and were often paid for by the breweries and malting companies. A person who was interested in opening a saloon was obliged to pay the city collector $52 a year and file a bond under the ordinance of the state laws for a "grocery"—another word for a grog shop. Each of the bonds required two notarized signatures, thereby ensuring that the applicant would return with his dollar at renewal time.

In 1839 the legislature transferred licensing to the individual locales, which effectively discouraged any statewide prohibition movement.[16] The saloon owner merely had to pay the fee and supply the necessary bond to operate in the neighborhood. Until the time of Medill, Chicago mayors rarely interfered in this process. Thus by 1874, there were an estimated 4,000 saloons operating in Chicago.[17] Once licensed, the saloon became the gathering place of the working class. A reputable establishment might attract local businessmen for lunch; more importantly, however, this was where ward politics were openly conducted. A barkeep might entertain certain political aspirations, or may have begun his business to supplement a career in public life. By 1874, 15 percent of the City Council were actively engaged in the liquor trade, either as barkeeps or suppliers.[18] For the policeman walking the beat in a blizzard or rain storm, the saloon was a safe haven and a place to escape the drudgery of a 12-hour shift. Elmer Washburn introduced the 12-hour shift after he discovered that the men on three staggered shifts worked varying hours. Complained one officer: "He sits there in his office and thinks it's all easy enough, but he'd find it a damned sight different if he had to go out there and travel with us."[19]

Police regulations prohibited men from lounging in saloons while on duty, but this rule was rarely enforced. The chance to share in local gossip and mingle with the ward characters who might be able to "do something" for them down at the hall were important reasons that policemen on duty were less than enthusiastic for Washburn and the Committee of Seventy. A number of highly placed officers like Jake Rehm and William McGarigle had separate careers in the liquor trade. Following his 1882 defeat for the position of sheriff, former Superintendent William McGarigle (1880–82) purchased the "Turf Exchange" at 128 Clark Street from a former detective named Thomas Currier. Currier had been dismissed from the force because he circulated handbills in support of McGarigle's candidacy. After McGarigle received an appointment to serve as warden of the County Hospital, he then sold the Turf Exchange to another officer who had fallen into recent disfavor—Patrick Ryan. Ryan then entered into a partnership with the gambler "Blind" John Condon, and the two of them operated a faro bank and crap game in the backroom for years.[20]

Within the department, three-time Superintendent of Police Jake Rehm was the brewer's closest ally. For years he ran a 12th Street brewery before he entered into a partnership in the malting business. Closely allied with publisher Anton

Hesing and other political leaders of the German community, Rehm's influence was far-reaching, even after he was officially "retired" to run his malting concerns. In 1869 he slated his close friend Michael Hickey to run for commissioner.[21] Hickey was a venal and dangerous police captain who had been cited in the Comiskey probe of 1868 for running a bail-bonding racket out of the Armory Station. Hickey was the eyes and ears for Rehm, but this time he lost the election to Mark Sheridan, a former Irish nationalist who lined up against Washburn and Medill in their efforts to please the Committee of Seventy.

First organized on September 12, 1872, the Committee's attitude was that previous mayors had for too long been "afraid of the liquor interests, and had lacked the moral courage to do right. They would rather violate their oaths of office than to offend the voting public of their saloons to which they owe their elections."[22] Medill argued with the Committee of Seventy, but in the end acceded to pressure when 2,000 Chicagoans turned out at the Board of Trade to express their support of Sunday closings.

The board, which was divided on the matter, was composed of two Republicans and a Democrat in the fall of 1872 when this issue came to a head. The members included Mancel Talcott, who was one of the founders of the First National Bank and a strong temperance advocate; Ernest F. C. Klokke, a manufacturer of campaign uniforms and the commander of the "Minuteman," a precision drill team composed of Republicans; and the volatile Democrat Mark Sheridan.

Sheridan was a former Irish nationalist who fought the British on his home shores before emigrating to the United States as a boy. He was an uncompromising foe of temperance, which he probably equated with the oppression he had faced in Ireland. Sheridan was hot-headed, foul-tempered, and if the *Chicago Tribune* is to be believed, an inebriate: "The recent conduct of Police Commissioner Sheridan, who presented himself at the meeting of the Board on Thursday in an incapable state of intoxication, has caused his friends considerable anxiety. Were this the first time he had been guilty of a similar proceeding, something might be said but it is well known that he has had several opportunities to reform but has not done so."[23]

The battle of the board was on, pitting Medill and Washburn against Sheridan and Klokke, with Talcott trying to preserve the peace. This proved to be an impossible task and Talcott resigned in November. In accordance with the provisions of the Mayor's Bill it was necessary to appoint a successor that Medill believed would be accepted by the council—Charles A. Reno of the West Division. Reno aligned himself with the side of Sheridan, which created a greater resolve on the part of the mayor to undermine the duties of the board.

Klokke complained that Washburn would bury them in trivialities. His real concern seemed to be the proper length of the policeman's frock coat, and what the proper width of a billyclub should be. Regarding a more serious matter, such as an amendment to the statutes requiring a prisoner to seek written permission from the justice of the peace to secure bail, he simply ignored their counsel.[24]

Concerning public gambling and the Sunday closing laws, Washburn stopped consulting the board members when he considered sending out a raiding party. Sheridan maintained that a police raid could not be conducted without the assent of the commission. But too often the gambling house had been "tipped" minutes before the police arrived. Mike McDonald, the successor to Cap Hyman and Jack Haverly, was rumored to have influence over the board members and certain highly placed officers, including Mike Hickey. In the 1870s he ruthlessly closed down his competitors, forcing them to sell interests in their "bank" or risk the consequences of future raids. When brothers Jeff and Al Hankins refused to bend a knee to "King" Mike, their establishment at Clark and Madison was closed down by a squad of Hickey's men.[25] Elmer Washburn refused to be party to any gambler's attempt to win influence, and he showed no biases in his indiscriminate raids against the rival factions. Washburn's unapproved raids quickly became a nuisance not only to McDonald, but also to his wealthy business clients who suffered the public ridicule of being taken to the station and having their names printed in the morning papers.

McDonald offered Washburn two bribes—for $11,000 and for $25,000—but the chief refused.[26] The superintendent was incorruptible, but the Sunday closing laws were nonetheless unjust, unpopular, and the ultimate downfall of the administration. Medill might have saved his reputation and gone down in history as one of the city's outstanding mayors for his efforts to rebuild the city after the Chicago Fire, if not for the saloon issue. Medill refused to retreat from his promise to uphold the law. When the board surreptitiously "fired" Washburn for carrying out raids without the proper authorization, Medill retaliated by dismissing Klokke and Reno on January 29, 1873. Sheridan was the most outspoken of the commissioners, but the mayor was powerless to remove him because under the terms of the Mayor's Bill, a public official could not be dismissed if his election occurred prior to the adoption of the new state constitution. A few troublesome police captains, including Mike Hickey, were also "retired" for the good of the service.

Hickey's long tenure in office is a fable of Chicago politics. Consider that on July 11, 1873, the captain was suspended pending investigation when it was revealed that he had received $430 from Lizzie Moore, the proprietor of a notorious Chicago bagnio who had reported the theft of some diamonds and watches. Hickey mysteriously "found" the merchandise in a Pittsburgh pawn shop. After the money had been paid to him, the goods were returned. The women reported the incident to the courts only after she became suspicious when Hickey said he would retrieve the jewels himself. A trial board cleared him of all wrongdoing, and he was returned to active duty shortly before the mayor's axe fell. Regarding the cases of Hickey and the commissioners, the city attorney and the corporation counsel agreed that the mayor's actions were legal and binding.[27] In 1876 the City Council launched another investigation into Hickey's private dealings following published reports in the Chicago *Post* that the commissioner collected bribes from sneak thieves and fences. The newspaper dug up evidence of a very shady real estate transaction between Hickey and one Dan

Webster, owner of a house of ill repute. After weighing the evidence—conclusive as it seemed—Mayor Monroe Heath sent word to the aldermen on November 27, 1876 that he would take no actions against Hickey. "There is no doubt in my mind but this attack on the chief of police was originated and came from some leading gamblers or bunko men and was aimed at the entire department with the hope of crippling them," Heath stated. His reluctance to remove an objectionable police chief, even one who was a great detriment of the administration, was typical of many Chicago mayors.

Klokke argued that by virtue of his election to a county office, the mayor's power was not binding. The deposed commissioners filed an application *quo warranto* against the two appointees, Carlisle Mason and Levi P. Wright. Medill had enough trouble finding someone to accept the vacant offices, and this latest outburst from Klokke and Reno made him all the more furious. He leveled a new round of accusations against the men, blaming them for the Chicago Fire: "The responsibility was with the men that controlled these departments [the Police and Fire Board]. I have thought that since the fire that if our police force and fire department had been efficient, the fire would have never crossed from the West Side to the South."[28]

Judge Joseph Gary, who would later figure prominently in the Haymarket case, ruled that the mayor's authority to remove members extended to all boards organized under the new state charter. But a legal loophole permitted Captains Hickey and Frederick Gund to be reinstated because Medill had neglected to advise the City Council of their removal.[29]

For a few months at least, calm settled over the department. But when Washburn reinstated an officer that Mark Sheridan had recently suspended, the old charges and verbal taunts between the mayor and the board resumed.[30] Again Sheridan demanded Washburn's immediate resignation. During one stormy board meeting the commissioner and the chief had to be separated before they exchanged blows. Sheridan menacingly brandished an inkwell that he intended to plant in Washburn's skull.[31] Sheridan was wrong, Medill explained, to assume that he had any power to suspend an officer without the formality of a written charge.[32] He considered the confrontation a simple case of two men laboring under a degree of emotional insanity.

Commissioner Mason tried to arbitrate the matter, but took ill and resigned his post on July 19, 1873. From his sickbed he blamed the other commissioners for his illness. Weary of the incessant bickering and the collapse of his popular support, Medill resigned office to embark on an extended tour of the continent. Lester LeGrand Bond served as the interim mayor until the autumn elections.

A coalition of liquor men and Irish Democrats, known as the People's Party, elected Harvey Doolittle Colvin, Chicago's next mayor. He won by 10,000 votes, thanks to the efforts of Anton Hesing and Mike McDonald, whose growing influence in political matters delivered the deciding votes to Colvin. But in return, Colvin offered little to the Irish community in terms of jobs and clout. Mark Sheridan urged the mayor to appoint Mike Hickey to the superintendent's position, but the stain on his character was reason enough to look elsewhere. The Tribune, still smarting over the Medill fiasco, charged that Sheridan and McDonald visited the prostitute Lizzie Moore in an attempt to persuade her to recant her damaging testimony against Hickey so that he could be cleared of all charges in the Pittsburgh fencing case.[33]

Colvin bypassed Hickey and chose Jack Rehm, who embarked on his third term of office. Washburn, who was not considered for any position, resigned to become the president of the Stockyards National Bank. In 1891 he made an unsuccessful bid for mayor on the Citizen's ticket before retiring to private life for good.

Chicagoans greeted Colvin warmly following two dry and lean years of economic hardship and nativist backlash. In his inaugural address to the city the new mayor signalled a new tolerance by expressing his beliefs that the police should concentrate on prevention rather than punishment. Three months later the Sunday closing laws, so offensive to the German community, were repealed. In an affront to Medill, Klokke and Reno were restored to the Police Commission while the hard-working Levi Wright was notified of his dismissal.

From the beginning the Colvin administration was beset by scandal. His election represented the successful integration of the gambling syndicate, the liquor trade, and downtown nightlife into city government. During these depression-ridden times business was conducted from Gambler's Row and Jake Rehm's office. Confidence in the mayor and the police chief to uphold the laws was severely tested when it was revealed that Rehm was the ringleader of one of the most notorious graft rings in the city.

The Downfall of the Police Commission

The liquor men who figured so prominently in Colvin's election campaign found themselves under indictment or in jail by the close of his term. A scheme to defraud the government of its tax revenues by falsifying production records was hatched in Chicago by Rehm, and involved men in all branches of the whiskey business in Chicago, St. Louis, and New Orleans. Reputable distillers were blackmailed in excess of $400,000. Government prosecutors were able to trace the crime directly to Rehm and his confederates, who had used police resources to disguise the deed.[34]

The first arrests were made in May 1875. Facing a possible prison term, Rehm agreed to testify against the other members of the Whiskey Ring if four conditions were met: (1) his counsel was to be allowed to plead for full immunity; (2) Rehm should not be sent to the state penitentiary; (3) any jail sentence handed down should not exceed six months; and (4) Jake was to be allowed to testify "fully and freely" as to all he knew.[35] Alderman James Hildreth and City Assessor George Von Hollen avoided the ignominy of a jail sentence by fleeing to Canada, where weak extradition laws made arrest all but impossible. Another man was acquitted, and two cases were thrown out for lack of confidence in the ability to select another jury that might believe Rehm's story. Jake's plea-bargaining tactics earned him some enemies, but he received a six-month sentence in the county jail and a reduced $20,000 fine—which is what he hoped for all along. Other Colvin backers were not as fortunate. Anton Hesing, the respected German publisher, received a stiff two year sentence, and even the *Chicago Tribune*, normally a bitter opponent, expressed sympathy over his plight. The sentences closed a particularly odious chapter in Chicago politics and effectively discredited Mayor Colvin, who had attempted to marshal control of the various municipal boards into one source of patronage that might deliver 3,000 votes of city workers into his column on election day.

At stake was the control of the Boards of Health, Fire, Police, and Public Works. It was a case of addition by subtraction, and to carry out this plan Colvin enlisted the support of Jake Rehm.

Colvin and Rehm sought to eliminate the board altogether and replace it with a figurehead officeholder, to be known as the city marshal. In the case of the other city and county boards, Hesing and some of the other administration "turncoats" who revolted against the mayor would be frozen out or removed.[36]

Like Medill three years earlier, Colvin sought the legal means to take such a drastic action. He solicited the opinions of some of the finest legal minds in the city, including Charles B. Morse of the Chicago Bar Association, who maintained that the City Council had no such powers. He was supported by the corporation counsel, but a dissenting vote was cast by City Attorney James P. Root, who argued that the Mayor's Bill gave the Council the power to establish the necessary machinery "as will suit the particular locality."[37] Root was referring to Section 73 of the bill, which stated that "the City Council may by ordinance or resolution discontinue any office so created and devolve the duties thereof on any other city office."

A Committee on Police carefully considered Mayor Colvin's resolution before deciding to recommend passage on June 25, 1875. The office of city marshal came into being, but it was poorly defined. According to the Council provisions, the marshal "shall be charged with the duty of preserving the peace of the city preventing crimes, and arresting offenders."[38] There was little distinction between this office and that of a lowly crossing guard.

Recognizing the farcical nature of the job, several prospective nominees turned it down, including former Mayor Francis Sherman, now engaged in running his hotel business. George Dunlap, a member of the Board of Trade and a former executive with the Northwestern Railroad, accepted the position at $4,000 per annum. He had a staff of three clerks, a secretary, and nothing to do since budgetary matters and personnel issues were handled out of the Superintendent's office. He attempted to perform his meager duties in a capable, honest matter, but quickly realized that real power was returned to the Rehm-Hickey clique. The superintendent vetoed a proposal to clean out the detective department, and he blocked a proposal to pull some of Mike McDonald's gambling houses along Randolph Street. Summing up his plight, the *Tribune* noted "that the Marshal wields an empty baton, and that while he may issue orders till the day of doom, he can do little more than saw the air with a sword of lath. They see just as clearly that Rehm has power to dismiss them if they fail to obey his wink.''[39]

Dunlap resigned in disgust just four months after taking office. Shortly thereafter, the marshal's position was eliminated forever. What Dunlap didn't realize was that Jake Rehm also planned to resign; this was before the Whiskey Ring became public knowledge. The money Rehm had gathered from his liquor frauds was placed in a secret campaign war chest to be used to promote his candidacy for city collector in the North Division. After Jake resigned to pursue his ambitions, Colvin appointed his confederate, Mike Hickey, to fill out the term. After 14 years of civilian control, the department was worse off than it had been the night that Wentworth fired the entire force for political reasons.

For the next 20 years the Police Department remained decentralized to a degree unheard of in New York and other eastern cities. The control of appointments rested with the ward bosses and gamblers who comprised the neighborhood links to the machine. At the head of the department stood the superintendent, who owed his allegiance to the mayor and the gang of rapacious ward characters like McDonald and the Hankins brothers. After the city elections, the spoils were given out to deserving party hacks while the officers loyal to the defeated party were dismissed.

Even that rare animal—the honest superintendent—was limited in his options. Jake Rehm was really the last of the strong police chiefs, but his integrity was always in question. From 1879 until 1905, not one police chief was reappointed following a mayoral change. Austin Doyle, who ran for clerk of the criminal court on the Colvin ticket in 1873, lasted three and one-half years as head of the department. His term was a record for longevity until Joseph Kipley was appointed by the younger Harrison in 1897. Both Doyle and Kipley were Democrats, and their unflagging support of the two Harrisons translated into extended terms of office.

The Whiskey Scandal, the corruption of the various county boards, and Colvin's own failure to unify the fragmented ethnic coalition that first elected him led to the break-up of the People's Party in 1876. Former members drifted back into Democratic circles to push for the election of Carter Harrison I, who was inclined to continue the liberal saloon policies of the People's Party. But while Colvin was a businessman elevated to public life by Anton Hesing, Mike McDonald, and Jake Rehm, Harrison was not. He was a skilled politician who recognized the urgency of bringing the diverse ward elements into a unified body that he might control. And while he would rely on the warm support offered by gamblers and the liquor factions, Harrison's actions would not be guided *solely* by their directions.

The Failure of Civil Service Reform

After Mayor Harrison was elected in 1879, it was not long before the Republicans once again decried the moral decay of the city and the corrupt acts of the gamblers and politicians who controlled appointments and jobs. Writing for *McClure's Magazine* years later, Lincoln Steffens summed up the prevailing attitudes toward bossism by declaring that "political corruption . . . is a process. It is not a passing symptom of the youth of a people. It is the natural process by which a democracy is made gradually over to a plutocracy."[40] While the corruption of the bosses was hardly unique to Chicago, events always seemed to get out of control. On the one hand, the poor and the needy were provided with food and shelter during the long winter months. And in the summer free ice was distributed through the intervention of the aldermen or a refrigeration company that might have had an exclusive city contract. But the example set by the "gray wolves" of the Council, who sold valuable city real estate to the traction magnates, indicated a casual disregard for the principles of open debate and self-determination. Fifty-year franchises were parceled out to the gas trust and street railways while the pockets of the boodling aldermen were lined by Charles Yerkes, boss Roger Sullivan, and others.

Even a promising young up-and-comer like William McGarigle found the lure of graft money an easy temptation. He was just 29 years old when Carter Harrison touted him for police superintendent. McGarigle brought a college education and ten years of experience to the job. He rose to prominence in the Detective Department under Jake Rehm, and for a time served as Elmer Washburn's private secretary. During his 18 months in office, beginning in 1880, he introduced some interesting new innovations and much-needed reforms.

First, he systematized the reporting procedures of arresting officers by creating a workable bookkeeping system at the station houses.[41] Then, a traffic division was organized for the first time, with 65 men assigned on a permanent basis to street crossings, bridges, and tunnels to regulate the flow of traffic through the downtown streets. McGarigle placed Chicago at the forefront of the suffrage movement by offering career work for women in the station houses. At the urging of the Women's Christian Temperance Union, McGarigle appointed the first police matrons to the force in 1882, detailing them to three notorious precincts on the crime-ridden West Side. Although not involved in actual police work, the matrons attended to runaway girls, the sick, wounded, and lost children. This freed the patrolmen to attend to their city beats.[42]

McGarigle realized that increased cooperation among the police chiefs of major cities was necessary if the departments were to become agents of social control, and not merely extensions of a political machine. Previous attempts to organize the big city police into a cohesive network had met with little success. In 1881, McGarigle called for a conference of police chiefs to be held in Chicago. This national conference was the first of its kind, and it occurred 11 years before the Police Chief's Union was first organized.[43]

The chiefs from 25 U.S. cities arrived in Chicago in December to discuss a number of topics, including the cooperative exchange of photographs of known fugitives from city to city and a proposal to adopt a national insurance plan among the various agencies. A constitution was drafted, and the organization became known as the National Police Association. Before the conference adjourned, the visiting chiefs previewed the patrol-call box system that was being implemented across the city. Within a few years most of the cities along the east coast adopted a similar system.

Reforms, however noteworthy, are almost meaningless if the leadership is corrupt and self-serving. McGarigle's brilliant career quickly unraveled after his term of office. After a brief and unsuccessful stab at politics, McGarigle accepted an appointment as warden of the County Hospital on September 1, 1883. It was a position with enormous political clout and graft potential. As a member of the county board he became the go-between for contractors seeking to do business with the various local offices. Building contracts were given out based on the amount of money paid to the "gang." Meanwhile, conditions at the hospital remained appalling, prompting a major newspaper investigation in 1887. A dozen prominent figures, including Mike McDonald's brother Edward and former Chief McGarigle, were indicted and jailed for their involvement. But McGarigle's cozy dealings with Sheriff Canute Matson served him well. Matson drove McGarigle to his Lakeview home from his cold cell in the city jail. While the sheriff waited in the front parlor, McGarigle kissed his wife and children goodbye, hopped out the bathroom window, and made connections with a dray that took him to a Great Lakes steamer to ferry him to Canada, and freedom.[44] He remained in the British Northwest Territory for two years before returning to Chicago to receive a full pardon from the obliging court system. This kind of leniency encouraged widespread graft among public officials. The experience of the Police Commission convinced the sharpest thinkers that it would be useless to resurrect another board. What was needed, they thought, was meaningful Civil Service reform, already in force in certain municipalities.

As an adjunct to the ward bosses, the police became the first target of the lay reformers and well-meaning government people who naively assumed that Civil Service was the end-all to corruption. The movement toward a citywide law began with Mayor John Hopkins, a Democrat who sought to milk whatever favorable publicity he could gain for his reelection bid. In 1894 he appointed a blue-ribbon panel headed up by John W. Ela, president of the Chicago chapter of the Civil Service Reform League, to consider similar laws already adopted in Boston, Brooklyn, and Cincinnati. The committee's most important proposal was to recommend the merit system of selection. Political pulls would be curbed, the committee reasoned, since aspiring applicants to the police department would be forced to take competitive exams. Promotions would be based on seniority and achievement. A patrolman would not be permitted to take the sergeant's test until he had spent two full years on the force. Members agreed that the average police officer should be well acquainted with city geography, possess reading and writing skills, and be able to solve at least simple arithmetic problems. The first examination was administered to 1,600 men from Inspector Nicholas Hunt's and John Fitzpatrick's divisions at the West and South Division High Schools on January 2, 1895. Most of the men had little difficulty, and some finished in less than 18 minutes. The successful new applicants were placed on an eligible list in order of merit.[45]

The final report, prepared by Ela with assistance from John Hamline and Harry Rubens, was signed by the mayor and Chief Brennan on December 12, and referred to the City Council for its vote. Said Brennan: "I have just finished reading the report and the best thing I can say is that I have signed it and thus go on record as heartily in favor of its provisions."[46] In the City Council, it met with angry resistance from the "gray wolf" factions. The aldermen realized that passage of any Civil Service law would curtail their patronage and influence in their respective wards. Ela's proposal to create a citizen's board to act as the final authority over policemen brought up for disciplinary action seemed to Alderman John McGillen of the powerful finance committee to be a new version of an old, and bad, idea. "Must it be said of Chicago that she is advancing backward by trying to reestablish another board?" he said, recalling the failures of Klokke, Sheridan, and Reno 20 years earlier. He added, somewhat sardonically, that "very few fair-minded citizens believe that any systematic wrongdoing prevails in the department. We do not believe that any malfeasance in the department has ever been tolerated in the city of Chicago."[47]

The motion to suspend all action to create a citizen's trial board and establish a local version of merit selection was passed by a 38–18 margin. The *Tribune* seemed delighted that Mayor Hopkins's version of Civil Service failed. As an ardent foe of "Hopkinsism" the paper was anxious to see this Democratic version of Republican legislation pending in the state house be defeated. This suggests that the *Tribune* believed the principle of merit selection would be distorted by the Democrats and passage of the Republican version would help boost the chances of its candidate for mayor, George Swift.

On March 20, 1895, the Civil Service Reform measure for Illinois municipalities was signed into law by the governor, contingent upon local approval by popular referendum. Among the modified provisions of the bill was the power vested in the mayor to appoint three commissioners for terms of one to three years. The examinations that would be be administered to each applicant was of greatest concern to the nervous members of the department. To assuage the fears of the men, 150 policemen and firemen were sent out to the precincts to build popular support for Civil Service before the city election on April 2. The police were uneasy about the exams, and a rumor that if they were dropped from the force they would not be eligible for reinstatement for five years.[48] Another problem was the 90-day period between the passage of the referendum and the actual time the law would take effect. There was nothing in the measure to stop the mayor from dismissing his political opponents in that time.

These concerns were addressed by six representatives of the Civic Federation who spoke to the men in the station houses. They were told that exams would be given only to new applicants, and if a man was dropped from active duty he would be allowed to take the test to gain readmission. Regarding the 90-day interval, John Ela's answer was deliberately evasive: "The mayor has had that power for 20 years and if Civil Service was defeated he would have it not only 40 to 90 days more—but for years to come."[49] Further, both candidates for mayor—Democrat Frank Wenter and Republican George Swift—had gone on record as saying that no man would be dismissed for political reasons during the grace period.

The Republicans in the legislature used some strong arm tactics to ensure that the police lobby groups in Springfield were powerless to influence the "fence-straddlers" against Civil Service. They warned that if it were to be defeated, another bill that would reduce pension benefits for retiring policemen would surely be passed.[50] Before it finally came up for a vote there was much arm-twisting on both sides. Commissioner John Hamline resigned in disgust when Mayor Hopkins stated that he was going to restore to active duty the 77 men who failed the first Civil Service test.

Civil Service was finally approved by Chicago voters by a convincing margin of 45,606 votes. Swift was easily elected, and incumbent police Chief Michael Brennan submitted his resignation even before the mayor had had time to select his cabinet. Swift, following the lead of previous Republican mayors, selected a leading Chicago businessman to run the affairs of the Police Department. John Badenoch was a former school board member, and an influential member of the grain exchange. However, he had no prior connections with police work, and did not feel legally or morally bound to the promises made by John Ela several months earlier. On May 8, 1895, General Order no. 13 was posted in the squad rooms across the city. Five hundred and eighty-seven men, including 210 second-class patrolmen hired for duty during the Pullman Strike and 110 substitute police, were discharged. Badenoch's motives for making such a radical reduction in the size of the force were not entirely political. The city finances were again in a sorry state, and his wholesale dismissal was in line with a recommendation made by the comptroller, who determined that the payroll had to be reduced by 500 men to meet the appropriation.[51] To meet these ends division inspectors were ordered to submit lists of expendable personnel. According to Badenoch, "I told them not to allow politics to have anything to do with their recommendations. Fitness as a policeman alone was to be the standard. Officers with bad records and who were incompetent were the ones looked for."[52]

Not content with purging the rank-and-file, Badenoch issued a second General Order three weeks later that set back the course of reform to create a real political vendetta between Democratic and Republican officers. Some of the most powerful and experienced men in the department were retired or demoted in rank, including Inspector Lyman Lewis, who was released with full pension, and Joseph Kipley, who was not.

The second group of dismissals was clearly an act of political spite and an attempt on the part of Badenoch to rid the department of men who might conspire against Mayor Swift. Among the officers let go was Thomas Kane of the Seventh District, a relative of the former mayor. Captain Walter Jenkins of the Sixth

District was a Republican, but to save his job he performed various pre-election tasks for Hopkins. For this, he was reduced to the rank of lieutenant.

The release of 600 men (the largest on record up to that time) before the Civil Service Law took effect clearly shows that the Republicans who paid lip service to the doctrines were as culpable as the Democrats for perpetuating the spoils system in Chicago. In his report to the City Council for 1895 Chief Badenoch boasted that the department had been taken out of politics once and for all. But there were some angry former officers with long memories who would not accept the outrage passively. Sol van Praag, a former state representative and close ally of Alderman Coughlin and Kenna, pandered to this ill feeling. He helped organize a body of men into the Star League, to be used for political purposes. Carter Harrison, Jr., promised them justice and their old jobs back in return for their support during his 1897 mayoral bid. Then, in one of the most riotous elections in Chicago's history Harrison easily defeated Republican Nathanial Sears. Star Leaguers were said to have plundered the streets of the Levee lighting bonfires and tipping over barrels in their wake.[53]

For all his manipulations on behalf of the Swift administration, Badenoch was probably a better man than the incoming superintendent, Joseph Kipley. During the traditional swearing-in ceremony, in which the departing official handed over the star of office, the belt, and the club to the new superintendent, Kipley chose to violate conventional decorum by using the occasion to tongue-lash Badenoch. He reminded the former chief that he had never forgotten what it was like to be retired after a long and distinguished career in the service.[54] Badenoch stood by silently, and when he asked Kipley if his carriage driver might retain his job during the upheavals, the new chief said nothing.

Kipley, whose brother Henry was a frequenter of pool rooms, promptly issued General Order no. 14, which can be construed as the Democrats' revenge. One hundred and fifty-eight men were let go in the first wave of dismissals. Completing his work four months later, Kipley issued General Order no. 32, which eliminated all the men hired between May 1895 and April 1897—exactly the time that Swift and Badenoch occupied their offices. He said in his defense, "I am simply carrying out my promises made during the campaign to correct the injustices done Democratic policemen by the Republican administration."[55]

The result, of course, was a demoralized and betrayed police force that was oblivious to Civil Service reform. By the time the afternoon papers hit the streets containing the names of the discharged men, many officers had simply walked off their beats to return to the station house to hand in their stars. Others abandoned street crossings to take a drink in a friendly saloon or lounge in a cigar store. Still others utilized the patrol boxes to phone in their resignations.

The Civil Service laws gave the mayor the legal means to carry out these politically inspired job terminations. It was the mayor's prerogative to remove at will the Civil Service commissioners he judged to be incompetent or inefficient in their duties. Following his election, Harrison removed two Republican com-

missioners for what he called "neglect of duty."[56] They were replaced by
Democrats, and by this change the mayor gained the power to appoint 50 department heads, including the assistant superintendent of police and the divisional
inspectors, which the Republicans claimed were protected by Civil Service. The
construction of the law, as liberally interpreted by Harrison and his supportive
commissioners, was that the mayor could also appoint captains and lieutenants,
a view upheld by the City Council, which had tried unsuccessfully to kill Civil
Service altogether. An ordinance was passed that exempted captains from classified service, thereby permitting many objectionable officers to return to the
ranks.

Rigid examinations, promotions based on ability rather than influence, and an
end to the practice of dismissing men for political reasons were the ideals rather
than the reality of the 1895 Civil Service Act. Nine years later, the City Club of
Chicago commissioned Alexander Piper, former deputy commissioner of the New
York Police Department, to conduct an independent investigation into the affairs
of the department. Had Civil Service finally cured the lingering abuses?

The evidence accumulated by the committee proved that after a decade of
Civil Service, discipline was still lax and the department was still very much
embroiled in partisan politics. Before the final report was handed over to Charles
Crane of the City Club, Detective Louis Grossman of the committee tipped off
the press about what could be expected: "The police of Chicago are piano
movers, bums, cripples, janitors, ward healers—anything but policemen."[57] In
the same article, he reported, "They have no respect for the law, and they depend
upon their pull with the alderman to get them out of trouble."[58] One hundred
men were cited for "their bad habits and utter lack of desire to serve the city
properly." The department carried on the payroll, according to Piper, a full 300
to 400 men who through age or physical disability were incapable of performing
active duty. Seventy-six out of 95 patrol sergeants assigned to supervise patrolmen on the beat were past the age of 40.

It was the patrol sergeant who was held most accountable for the existing
conditions, since it was his responsibility to make sure the neighborhood was
secure and the men were in the streets. Piper cited 68 instances of men loitering
in saloons while on duty.[59] The captains were quick to defend this dubious
practice, saying that the valuable exchange of information between a barkeep
and an officer was essential if the police were to keep on top of things in the
neighborhood. Harrison promised his support: "The responsibility for the shirk-
ing of work by the men on patrol lies with the sergeants. It's their duty to look
after this precise thing and it is evident they have not attended to it." Piper did
not confine his criticisms to the front line officers, however. He toured the station
houses and filed the following report about one of the worst in the city.

Nineteenth Precinct, March 3, 1905, 6:30 PM

Captain Clancy present and in command. Lieutenant also present. Civilians behind the
desk smoking. Sergeant in shirt sleeves. At roll-call men stood in slouchy positions and

talked to each other while orders were being read. House fairly clean. Men's bunks were not neat. Not sufficient number of men to properly care for the precinct. Cellar in disgraceful condition, partly due to the taking care of tramps who used old paper for bedding which is a menace to the safety of the house on account of fire, and to the health of the men in the station.[60]

Twelve commanding officers were cited for dereliction of duty, including two divisional inspectors, Patrick Lavin and John Wheeler. The practice of "hiding the star" was still a problem. This was given immediate attention by Chief Francis O'Neill, who issued a star-shaped badge with the city seal and number inlaid in the metal later that year.[61] No longer could the wearer scrape off the enamel to avoid detection. The tradition of loaning police stars to influential friends of the department to secure free admission to sporting and theater events was another practice that was ended by O'Neill, who accepted the dreary findings with resignation: "Every man knows how to manage a women until he gets married. I had some of those ideas myself until I got to be chief, and then, like the man who gets married, I found out."[62]

Frank O'Neill was the author of five source books on Irish folk music. He was happiest in the company of other men who shared his fascination with old Gaelic tunes. Once a week the chief joined three other officers at the home of Kate Doyle to play the pipes, flute, and fiddle, and analyze some of the 1,800 pieces of music in his collection.[63] Kate Doyle once worked as Carter Harrison's governess, and her intervention allegedly helped secure O'Neill's appointment as superintendent in 1901. The internal strife and endless political intrigues of police work held no special appeal for Francis O'Neill. He was an honest cop— a rare quality for the time. Alexander Piper sympathized with his plight: "He has not the proper assistance. He has not a sufficient number of men by fully 2,000 to take care of this great city."[64]

The real failure of Civil Service rested with the mayor, who removed the commissioners at will. Mayoral appointments ensured that the Police Department and other civic agencies would be controlled by partisan commissions. In the first 20 years of mandatory Civil Service in Chicago, only two commissioners bridged a mayoral change to serve out their full terms.[65] Old ways die hard. The understanding that political appointees would work for the good of the party was just too deeply ingrained in the minds of the politicians for any law of this nature to have lasting impact. The notion of Civil Service was repugnant to Mayor Harrison, and he said so many times. But he was the one man who might have possessed the power to strictly enforce the laws. Instead, Civil Service became a means to an end—the continuity of the ruling machine.

Notes

1. Robert M. Fogelson, *Big City Police* (Cambridge: Harvard University Press, 1977), p. 14.

2. Roger Lane, *Policing the City: Boston, 1822–1883* (Cambridge: Harvard University Press, 1967), p. 252.

3. James Richardson, *The New York Police: Colonial Times to 1901* (New York: Oxford University Press, 1970), p. 104.

4. *Chicago Tribune*, March 28, 1861.

5. Joseph Kirkland, and John Moses, *History of Chicago*, vol. 1 (Chicago and New York: The Munsel Co., 1895), p. 258.

6. Undated newspaper clipping, John D. Shea scrapbooks, the Chicago Historical Society Collection. Appointed to the force on October 2, 1873, Shea's career spanned 30 years. He traveled a beat with Joe Kipley for several years before moving on to the detective department.

7. *Chicago Tribune*, June 9, 1864.

8. Ibid., June 14, 1864.

9. Ibid., June 21, 1864.

10. Ibid., December 18, 1864. The case involved two detectives, James Webb and Robert Kenney, who arrested two men on a charge of larceny. The complainants were advised that they would have to pay $128 to the detectives, who would "square" matters with Justice of the Peace Thomas B. Brown—who had previously served as a police commissioner. Turtle, it was alleged, approved this scheme to receive a kickback. In a similar case, James Whitelow was arrested on December 14 as a Union Army deserter. Turtle threatened to return him to the front lines unless he surrendered a gold watch that had been reported missing at a dance.

11. Ibid., December 28, 1864. Wentwoth ran the gauntlet for Turtle during his term as police commissioner. He voted in favor of allowing the chief to retain certain fees and gifts he had received while in the discharge of his duties. This scheme was in violation of the city charter.

12. *Chicago City Council Proceedings*, 1868, p. 388.

13. See the *Chicago Tribune* account for August 3, 1873, for a case involving a police officer caught in a web of entanglements. The policeman in question was summoned to Bridgeport to arrest a man who had beaten his wife. The officer found the man walking aimlessly outside his home. He asked the police officer to step inside to help resolve the matter. Then the wife beater told the officer that unless he could produce a suitable warrant he could not be arrested. The policeman was ordered out of the house by the man, but the wife protested and begged that her husband be taken in. The officer consented, whereby blows were exchanged. When Commissioner Sheridan learned of these events he suspended the officer. Friends of the policeman petitioned Superintendent Washburn for redress. He countermanded Sheridan's original order, arguing that a commissioner had no power to suspend an officer without the formality of written charges.

14. Perry Duis, *The Saloon: Public Drinking in Boston and Chicago, 1880–1920* (Champaign: University of Illinois Press, 1983), p. 165.

15. Ibid.

16. Ibid., p. 12.

17. *Chicago Tribune*, August 17, 1875.

18. Duis, *The Saloon*, p. 137.

19. *Chicago Times*, January 23, 1873.

20. *Chicago Tribune*, January 7, 1889. Before his death in 1915, John Condon was a major force in horse racing and off-track betting. He was an early backer of Mike

McDonald before buying up a string of midwestern racetracks, including the Harlem Park located outside Chicago. In his youth he worked as a barber.

21. *Chicago City Council Proceedings*, 1868, p. 387. Roger Plant testified to the committee that he paid at various times to Captain Hickey an aggregate sum of $600 as part proceeds of profits for bailing people out of the Armory Jail.

22. *Chicago Tribune*, March 7, 1872.

23. For a review of Sheridan's "shortcomings," see the *Tribune*, August 13, 1872.

24. Ibid., December 6, 1872.

25. Ibid., February 2, 1873.

26. Ibid., February 4, 1873.

27. *Chicago Times*, January 30, 1873.

28. Ibid., January 31, 1873.

29. *Chicago Tribune*, March 27, 1873.

30. Ibid., July 19, 1873.

31. Ibid. After Sheridan called Washburn a "dirty dog," the chief replied, "There is no blackguard like an Irish blackguard." Born in Waterford, Ireland in 1826, Sheridan was active in nationalist politics, fighting on the side of Smith O'Brien. He fled Ireland in 1848 at the point of a British gun, settling in Chicago in 1856. He was elected alderman from the Fifth Ward seven years later. As a member of Colvin's People's Party he easily defeated Mike Hickey for South Division police commissioner in 1869. When he completed his storm term of office he returned to the City Council as alderman in 1876.

32. *Chicago Tribune*, August 3, 1873.

33. Ibid., November 30, 1873. The Irish nationalists were not pleased with the elective slate. The only cabinet member from their ranks to join Colvin's administration was Dan O'Hara, city treasurer.

34. Ibid., June 26, 1876. See also Rudolf Hofmeister, *The Germans of Chicago* (Chicago: University of Illinois, 1976), pp. 159–60.

35. *Chicago Tribune*, July 8, 1876.

36. Ibid., June 27, 1875: "When the multitudes of underlings in all these departments is considered, one may gain some approximate idea of the desperate game which Rehm and Colvin are playing. Three thousand votes with their influence politically is what the stakes approximate."

37. Ibid.

38. *Chicago City Council Proceedings, 1874–75*, p. 252.

39. *Chicago Tribune*, September 16, 1875. Marshal Dunlap was permitted to appoint men of "suitable" character to the position of special policemen, but the position did not carry with it a salary or the rights and privileges of a city officer. All regulations and ordinances regarding the transfer of sergeants, lieutenants, and captains issued by the marshal first had to be approved by Jake Rehm.

40. Quoted in Page Smith, *America Enters the World* (New York: McGraw-Hill, 1985), p. 74.

41. The First Precinct Arrest Book, January 1875 to June 30, 1885, Chicago Historical Society Manuscript Collection. Each arrest was recorded by hand listing the name, nativity, and occupation of the detainee, along with the nature of the complaint and the manner in which the case was settled.

42. Samuel Walker, *A Critical History of Police Reform: The Emergence of Professionalism* (Toronto: D.C. Heath & Co., 1977), p. 86. Also, the *Chicago Tribune*, March 23, 1895, for a review of the duties of the police matron. The younger Harrison appointed

the first Chicago policewomen on August 2, 1913. These women were invested with full arrest powers and were deployed to the city's amusement parks, public beaches, and juvenile courts to attend to runaways, truancy, and incidents of delinquency. See the *Literary Digest*, August 23, 1913, p. 271.

43. *Chicago Tribune*, December 16, 1881. Walker omits any mention of the Chicago Convention in this study. The available evidence suggests that the National Police Association, organized by McGarigle, predates the National Chief's Association.

44. Richard Lindberg, *Chicago Ragtime: Another Look at Chicago, 1880–1920* (South Bend: Icarus Press, 1985), pp. 61–70. McGarigle remained in exile in Banff for two years, where he joined the community choir and directed a theater group. He returned to Chicago on May 30, 1889, after striking a deal with State's Attorney Joel Longnecker in London, Ontario. He paid a small fine to the court and returned to private life unscathed.

45. *Chicago Tribune*, January 3, 1895.

46. Ibid., December 12, 1894.

47. Ibid., December 21, 1894. Concurrent with the motion to create a local version of Civil Service was the proposal to legislate funds for an independent committee to investigate police corruption. It was spearheaded by a reform-minded group of aldermen interested in copying the methods of New York's Lexow Committee, which uncovered a staggering network of graft and kickbacks in the city boroughs. Alfred S. Trude, who counseled Mike McDonald and received his funds, was retained as legal counsel for the Kerr Committee but the aldermen refused to appropriate the necessary funding to launch the investigation.

48. Ibid., March 29, 1895.

49. Ibid.

50. Ibid.

51. *Chicago Times-Herald*, May 8, 1895. This paper had recently been sold to Herman H. Kohlsaat, who shifted its traditional Democratic affiliation toward a more broad-based orientation.

52. *Chicago Tribune*, June 1, 1895.

53. Herman Kogan, and Lloyd Wendt, *Lords of the Levee: The Story of Bathhouse John and Hinky Dink* (New York: Garden Grove, 1944), p. 169.

54. *Chicago Times Herald*, April 17, 1897. Before the Democrats arrived in City Hall to claim the spoils, Chief Badenoch told 19 Republican candidates for the lieutenant's exam to report to City hall on March 2 for the physical. Under the existing rules of Civil Service any officer who passed the test could not be put off the force. Any politically inspired promotions the new Mayor Carter Harrison cared to make would have to come from the eligible list of the next lower rank—where 19 loyal Badenoch men were certified by Civil Service.

55. *Chicago Tribune*, June 20, 1897.

56. Ibid., April 24, 1897.

57. Ibid., March 2, 1904.

58. Ibid.

59. Report of an "Investigation of the Discipline and Administration of the Police Department of the City of Chicago" (City Club of Chicago, March 17, 1904), p. 6. Patrol sergeants were responsible for the abuse of Regulation no. 53, which prohibited the police from entering saloons while on duty.

60. Ibid., p. 39. Captain Clancy commanded the Hyde Park Station in Nicholas Hunt's Division. The conditions described in the report were fairly typical for the times. For

years police stations were "safe houses" for vagrants who were sheltered and fed at city expense. During periods of high unemployment and economic recession their numbers swelled appreciably. In 1899, for example, 114,115 homeless persons were given shelter in the police stations. With the opening of the Municipal Lodging House in 1901 the burden of caring for the homeless no longer rested solely with the police.

61. *Report of the General Superintendent to the City Council (1904)*, p. 4.

62. *Chicago Tribune*, March 31, 1904.

63. Charles Winslow, *Biographical Sketches of Famous Chicagoans*, vol. 3 (unpublished, Chicago Public Library Collection), p. 1078.

64. Report on "Discipline and Administration," p. 4.

65. *Chicago Police Problems*, (Champaign: University of Illionis Press, 1931), p. 49.

4

The Rule of the Club: Policing the Labor Strikes

Violence and lawlessness in Chicago were pervasive, despite the assurances of a dozen police chiefs who held office during the last quarter of the nineteenth century. The larger failures of the department to enact meaningful reforms were often obscured by the glow of favorable publicity that the police received for suppressing labor strikes and dispersing union meetings.

The pace of industrial growth and the disparity between wealth and poverty created a permanent, displaced urban underclass prone to acts of violence against individuals and the society at large. The labor troubles that swept the United States following the Civil War were never so drastic, so violent, or so malicious as they were in Chicago. The methods employed by the police to put down the rebellion were excessive and wanton, often reflecting their own ethnic prejudices against "foreigners." And this was the paradox of the police and their relationship to the working classes. Nearly a quarter of the force consisted of men born in Ireland. They shared the immigrant struggles with the Germans, Italians, and Bohemians living in close proximity. Many of them worked in the blue-collar trades and suffered the same exploitation from the factory owners, before they embarked on a career of law enforcement.

It would be understandable, therefore, if the police exhibited compassion for the working men during times of economic unrest, but this was simply not the case. Many of the frontline men realized that the quickest way to advance through the ranks was to attract publicity by the free use of the club. As John Bonfield explained to the mayor in 1885, "I am doing it in mercy of the people. A club today to make them scatter may save use of the pistol tomorrow."[1]

The perception that the leaders of the trade unions were somehow less than 100 percent American because of their foreign language newspapers and heavy accents often guided police conduct. Strikers were "agitators—no different from thieves, killers, and pimps. At issue in the post-Civil War period was the eight-hour workday. In May 1867, the state legislature recognized the eight-hour movement, but left it up to the private sector to determine its rightful course of action. When the manufacturers of the city refused to shorten the day, the trade unionists took to the streets. Mobs set fire to buildings on the North End, and random groups of workers confronted police with clubs and knives outside the factories.

Individual officers carried Army Colt revolvers, the usage of which was optional. The hickory club was the only weapon employed by the police, who continued to show restraint. This did not last, as polemics and angry rhetoric replaced reason in the 1870s and 1880s. In 1877 a devastating railroad strike began in Camden Junction, Maryland. It spread across the Ohio Valley until it reached Chicago in late July, when switchmen walked off the Michigan Central line in protest of management's decision to cut wages $10 a month. They were joined in sympathy by other skilled workmen and the leaders of the radical Social Democratic Party. Trading on the mercantile board ceased, and money due Chicago commission men on shipments remained frozen in the East. The police were called in to restore order to the stricken city.

Michael Hickey's small and untrained forced failed to quell the disturbances in a peaceful way. During the recession years preceding the strike, the size of the force had declined by 12.9 percent. Five hundred and seventeen men were scattered across the city but only 250 could be spared for riot duty at any given time.[2] Recognizing the shortcomings of the force, Hickey hired 300 "strike" policemen, to be paid out of public funds. These men were, for the most part, adventurers, vagrants, and soldiers of fortune. They were not by any stretch of the imagination qualified to end a bloody strike which had already claimed a dozen lives. Mayor Monroe Heath was a Republican of good intentions, but his advice to Hickey to exercise restraint went unheeded. Hickey was primed for action, and he had the support of the press in back of him. The *Chicago Tribune* declared "Red War" on one of its front pages.[3] The chief summoned to his headquarters one of the labor men, and gave it to him straight: "Parsons, your life is in danger. I advise you to leave this city at once. Why, those Board of Trade men would as soon hang you to a lamppost as not."[4]

Albert Parsons chose to remain in Chicago, but he was slugged and beaten by several men who followed him from police headquarters to the *Chicago Tribune* building. Peaceable meetings were broken up with ruthless abandon. As one newspaper observed, "Blessed club law ruled. Many innocent men were pounded but they brought it on themselves."[5] The most serious outrage by police against the strikers was the Turner Hall raid on July 26. An assembly of tradesmen were singled out for harassment by 15 to 20 of Hickey's riot police. "Get out of here, you damned sons of bitches," they screamed as they descended on the hall. One man was shot through the head, and a score were wounded by gunfire. As the men ran for the exits, they found their paths blocked by the police who clubbed them as they went by.

The injured workers belonged to the Association of Joiners who were holding a planning meeting. They brought suit against Hickey and the Chicago Police Department, and secured a favorable verdict. Hickey was reprimanded for his brutal, unprovoked tactics. Order was finally restored, only after President Rutherford B. Hayes ordered six companies of the Twenty-Second Infantry to Chicago from their posts in the Indian territory.

When the issue of Hickey's retention came up for a vote in July 1878, the press recounted the highlights of his scandal-plagued career, but little was said about his conduct during the riot. The *Tribune* chided the Democratic press for bringing up "old rumors that everyone had forgotten."[6] The council seemed to remember, however; they voted him out of office by a 22–11 margin, thus ending once and for all his connections with the department.

Captain Valorious Seavey, who commanded a battalion of riot police on the West Side, replaced Hickey. When he arrived at police headquarters to assume leadership of the department, he horrified his staff by climbing into his office through an open window that fronted the alley.[7] The white-faced police officers assigned to headquarters explained that this was a very bad omen, according to a long-standing superstition in the department that the preceding police chiefs took very seriously. To enter through an alley way or a window would mean that some personal tragedy would befall him. In Seavey's case this was certainly true: he served less than a year. Illness took his life early in 1879, and Superintendent Joseph Dixon filled out the remaining months of his term. Described by Allan Pinkerton as the "world's greatest detective" for his part in cracking the Gumbleton murder case in 1870, Dixon played into the hands of the businessmen by introducing paramilitaristic regimens into the scant training methods in use at this time. Dixon appointed himself "Lieutenant-Colonel" of the "regiment." He redesigned all of the officers' uniforms to bring them in line with contemporary U.S. Army fashions. Shoulder straps indicated the wearer's "rank." Of greater concern to the nervous members of Chicago's ruling elite was the protection the police could provide if another riot broke out.

To this end, 500 breach-loading rifles that were ordered by Seavey arrived in the station houses when scarce funding finally became available. The men marched in close order drill with the muskets, and learned how to operate a cannon that had been paid for by a private subscription of members of the Citizen's Association. Meanwhile, state legislators passed several restrictive laws to prohibit bodies of working men from parading with arms without the consent of the authorities.

Dixon's plan to create a military police force was dashed by Mayor Harrison in 1879. The Republicans were driven out following the city election, and the new superintendent was gruff old Simon O'Donnell, an 18-year veteran who sent the notorious safecracker Paddy Guerin to jail, after he knocked off the

Galesburg Bank. O'Donnell was not leadership material, however. He was better suited to run a small precinct, and he said so. In regards to the strikers O'Donnell was in favor of a policy of conciliation. This partly explains his demotion back to the 12th Street Precinct in 1881.

During the Austin Doyle administration (1883–85) the free and unrestrained use of the billy club characterized the police response to labor strikes. In June 1885, the streetcar conductors of the West Division walked off the job in sympathy with 15 members of the Benevolent and Protective Association who had been dismissed for union activity. After the company hired strikebreakers to run the cars, violence broke out along Madison, Halsted, and Lake Streets. Governor Altgeld, who was no friend of the traction interests, traced the blame to Captain John Bonfield, who "indulged in brutality never equaled before or since."[8]

Bonfield kept the trains running, usually at the point of a gun or a swinging baton. By the time he joined the police department at the advanced age of 41, Bonfield was a failed businessman who had already lost a grocery store and a fertilizing company to his creditors. Within a year of joining the force he was promoted to lieutenant, and a key position within McGarigle's Detective Force. It was not such a remarkable turn of events as it appeared: his brother Joseph was Mayor Heath's corporation counsel, and his other brother was a bailiff in the criminal court.

Bonfield's task was to protect the drivers who stood in the exposed portions of the streetcars. Waiting on the corners were gangs of rock-throwing men interested in overturning the cars as they rumbled noisily down the streets. The captain instituted an unpopular curfew and those who violated it were taken to the Des Plaines Street station and locked in one of the basement cells. At the corner of Madison and Western one afternoon, a group of bystanders who were waiting for an express wagon to take them to their downtown jobs were set upon by Bonfield and his men. A pedestrian named John Schulkens later sued Bonfield for $2,000 as a result of the facial lacerations he suffered from one of the policemen.[9] Alarmed by these events, Mayor Harrison asked for an accounting. "The backbone of the strike is broken, Mr. Mayor," Bonfield said. "The wholesale arrests we have made have dampened the enthusiasm of the strikers and their friends."[10]

Bonfield's work during the streetcar strike earned him praise—and condemnation. The merchant class sang his praises, while groups of bitter workers vowed to lynch him from the highest lamppost. When Austin Doyle retired on October 15, 1885, to accept a position from the grateful president of the street railway, Bonfield asked his friends to plead his case to the mayor. Harrison was faced with a dilemma. His friends in the neighborhood wards would just as soon see Bonfield dead as in the superintendent's office. But the mayor was anxious not to lose his support from LaSalle Street. Being the adept politician he was, Harrison selected Frederick Ebersold, a Bavarian war hero who fought alongside of Sherman at the battle of Shiloh, to take over for Doyle. Ebersold was a Republican, and thus acceptable to the businessmen. He was German, which placated a large voting constituency that had lately felt isolated from power. But it did not please Bonfield, who assembled a cabal of police officers whose sole intention was to undermine the new chief. This conflict divided the department into two feuding camps, just as the Haymarket bomb was thrown.

The Haymarket Affair

North of the Chicago River along Banks and Astor Streets resided some of Chicago's wealthiest citizens eager to copy the lifestyle of Bertha Honore Palmer, the grande dame of society. The burgeoning Gold Coast was showing signs of life. It had been nothing more than a swamp until Potter Palmer determined that Prairie Avenue on Chicago's fashionable South Side could not endure as a safe haven for the city's social movers. Palmer and his kind settled into the North Side, where they were uncomfortably close to the unwashed masses that lived in Shantytown a few miles to the west. They entrusted their well-being and the lives of their children to Captain Michael Schaak, the rotund burgomaster of the North Division whose hatred of the working classes matched Bonfield's.

Schaak was the caricature of an age. Posturing, defiant, self-assured, his bravado and bluster was exceeded only by that of Thomas Byrnes of New York. He was said to be familiar with every back alley and gaming house in his division. Born in the Grand Duchy of Luxembourg in 1843, Schaak became a policeman in 1869. Before that he worked in a Cairo, Illinois brewery as a night watchman. From the time he joined the police until his death in 1898, he claimed to have never taken a vacation. Police work was his life, and chasing down criminals and anarchists was his only joy. Within five years Schaak was credited with 865 arrests.[11] Using techniques that would not stand the scrutiny of the modern criminal justice system, Schaak solved several of the most infamous murder cases of the late nineteenth century. One of them occurred two days after he was promoted to captain of police. The date was August 23, 1885, less than nine months before the Haymarket Riot.

The body of a Polish immigrant woman named Anna Kledziec was found in the kitchen of her Southport Avenue home. She had been beaten to death by a blunt object, and robbed of her jewels and some cash which she had hidden in the furniture. All the police had to go by were the ashes of some burnt letters found in the stove. Impatient with the progress of the regular police assigned to the case, Schaak initiated an independent investigation with two of his young protégés—Michael Whalen, and a former streetcar conductor named Herman Schluetter, whom Schaak had hired two years earlier. They worked the case day and night, finally tracing the crime to Frank Mulkowski, who was the paramour of Kledziec's stepmother from Poland.[12] The motive was jealousy, with a dash of greed thrown in for good measure. Schaak was able to identify Mulkowski as the killer only after he had dressed up the man's sister in one of his old top coats and had a photograph taken. The picture was circulated in the Polish ghetto, and the killer was identified by a neighbor of Anna Kledziec. Then other people came forward to testify that the deceased woman's jewelry was being fenced in the neighborhood.[13] Based on this evidence, a conviction was secured and Mulkowski was sent to the gallows. Schaak meanwhile pronounced the entire detective department under Ebersold "incompetent." He would later write, "The department was rent and paralyzed with the feuds and jealousies between the chief and the subordinates. This too was at a time when the people of Chicago were in a condition of mind bordering on panic. It is charity to say no more. He [Ebersold] had neither a proper conception of his duties nor the ability to perform them."[14] He failed to add that Ebersold's undoing was largely the work of the ambitious clique that was rebuffed by Mayor Harrison: John Bonfield, Drillmaster John Fitzpatrick, Captains Alexander Ross, George Hubbard, and Michael Schaak.

A decade's worth of labor troubles reached a crisis level at the McCormick Reaper Works. Schaak and Bonfield were keenly aware of Ebersold's "soft" position concerning organized labor. They played to the fears of young Cyrus Hall McCormick, who was determined to bust the unions in his father's company at all costs. The winter of 1886 was a bitter one. There were numerous strikes and armed clashes between labor and capital culminating in the lockout of 1,482 employees at the Reaper Works on February 16. McCormick had identified the leaders of the Molder's Union through the reports submitted by agents of Allan Pinkerton assigned to the shops.[15]

Sensing the efforts of his subordinates to discredit him, Chief Ebersold placed 350 policemen at the McCormick works along the Black Road—a dangerous stretch of highway between Blue Island Avenue and the plant—to protect the strikebreakers from assault. This squad accounted for roughly one-third of the entire force, a surprisingly large contingent, given that the area to be policed encompassed roughly two miles.[16]

Ebersold may have been reacting blindly to a situation that was not as bad as it seemed. The presence of such a large body of police naturally invited hostility from the locked-out union men. On March 2, there were shooting incidents well into the night between police and strikers. A labor meeting was raided by police, and in the affray four men were killed.[17] On May 1, a large assembly of tradesmen marched peacefully down Michigan Avenue. The next day trouble flared up again at the McCormick Works. The Lumber Shover's Union had asked August Spies, the editor of the labor newspaper *Arbeiter-Zeitung*, to address several thousand men outside the factory. At 3:30 that same afternoon, the scabs that McCormick had hired exited the plant. They were given the afternoon off, perhaps as a demonstration of their employer's benevolence. The strikers rushed the gates to harass the scabs, despite Spies's pleadings to the contrary. The scabs were driven back into the factory under a hail of stones and shards of broken glass. Two police officers phoned the Hinman Avenue Station for assistance, and a detail of men under the direction of Simon O'Donnell arrived to quell the disturbance. Estimates as to the size of the force vary. Since each station house numbered less than 75, it seems unlikely that the actual figure exceeded 50.[18]

As groups of rioters surrounded his wagon, O'Donnell lashed them freely with the whip and fired a volley of shots into the crowd. Round after round of ammunition was discharged by police, even after the streets appeared to be clear of men. In the shots that were exchanged only one man was killed, and there were six reported injuries. But Spies fled the scene before he could accurately assess the casualties. He rushed back to the newspaper office to pen the fateful editorial that urged the working men into action. The circular read: "Workingmen to Arms! Your masters sent out their bloodhounds the police. They killed six of your brothers at McCormick's this afternoon."[19] A compositor added the word "revenge," and this was viewed by the state as a conspiratorial document for the events that followed.

The angry rhetoric of the labor newspapers first came to the attention of the police in 1884, when they began printing instructions concerning the proper usage of dynamite and street fighting tactics against management. Spies later argued that stories about bombs and the making of explosives first appeared in the *Chicago Times* and the *Chicago Daily News* to arouse popular opinion against the strikers.[20]

The incendiary nature of the labor pamphlets was the result of an ideological split between the leaders of the Socialist Labor Party (SPL) and a more radical faction known as the International Working People's Association (IWPA). The 2,500 active members of the IWPA were followers of Johan Most, who published his philosophy in the German-language newspaper *Die Freheit* on July 15, 1882.

I follow four commandments. Thou shalt deny God and love truth. Therefor I am an atheist. Thou shalt oppose tyranny and seek liberty. Therefor I am a Republican. Thou shalt refute property and champion equality. Therefore I am a communist. Thou shalt hate oppression and foment revolution. Therefore I am a revolutionary. Long live the revolution![21]

The fear of an armed confrontation with crazy foreign anarchists stockpiling guns in Chicago weighed heavily on the minds of many ordinary working people who lacked the convictions of Spies, and the desire to take their disputes into the streets. The call to arms printed by Spies on May 4 did not succeed in generating the positive response he had hoped. A respectable, but certainly not overwhelming, crowd of supporters turned out for his talk in the Haymarket Square (an open area on the western fringe of downtown Chicago where whole-sale meat, produce, and dry goods were exchanged) that evening. Mayor Harrison issued a permit to IWPA members, thinking that nothing would come of it. But Inspector Bonfield heard about "some bad work" that night, and ordered 600 police reserves to the West Chicago, Harrison, and Central Stations in anticipation of a city-wide riot.

However, there is no record of any additional police build-up in the vicinity of the sensitive Black Road. Earlier in the day, a crowd of 3,000 surrounded Sam Rosenfield's drugstore at 18th and Center Streets because Rosenfield was believed to be a police spy. A small detachment of men led by Simon O'Donnell drove the frenzied mob away, but curiously, O'Donnell did not post a guard. The mob reformed to plunder and loot the store and a nearby saloon.[22] Had Bonfield in fact seen to it that the police response was deliberately casual?

The movement of men between stations on May 4th suggests that the police manipulated events for reasons known only to Inspector Bonfield. When the Spies revenge circular was shown to Ebersold he dismissed it as unimportant, but Bonfield added 100 more men to the Des Plaines Station. The area these men would be assigned to protect was less than a third of a mile long and normally was under the jurisdiction of just 73 officers.

The Haymarket rally began at 8:30 PM. A crowd estimated to be between two and three thousand strong milled about the square, but was directed to move toward Des Plaines Street because Spies feared that the police would use the excuse of blocking streetcar traffic as a pretext for dispersing the meeting. The police later contended that this was part of a conspiracy to lure them into a narrow pocket that would allow the bomb thrower a clearer shot at the men, while affording a greater chance of escape.

Spies called the meeting to order, and when he did not see Albert Parsons present, he sent out Rudolph Schnaubelt to find him.[23] During the course of the evening Mayor Harrison dropped by. Satisfied that all was well, he visited Bonfield at the station to inform him that the reserves could all go home. Bonfield was not pleased with this. Throughout the evening he had been receiving reports from Detective Louis Haas, who mingled in the crowd to gauge the mood of the speakers. Other officers who were in the station chided Bonfield for being soft on the reds. "The trouble there is that these anarchists get their women and children mixed up with them," he replied, according to one eyewitness. "And we cannot get at them. I would like to get 3,000 of them in a crowd without their women and children. I would make short work of them."[24]

Several more detectives were sent back to the rally, and their reports convinced Bonfield to make a move. He was absolutely certain the Haymarket meeting was the prelude to a city-wide "revolution" that was to begin that night. Bonfield had confided to the mayor that he personally knew of a sinister plot to blow up some Milwaukee and St. Paul railroad houses. At 10:20 PM Samuel Fielden began his wrap-up. At that moment, Bonfield ordered the detail to fall in behind the station on the double.

Officer Herman Krueger of the Fourth Police Precinct, speaking as a former soldier, made the suggestion to Bonfield that the company surround the mob and converge on the demonstrators. Bonfield, vociferous as ever, dismissed the idea as impractical, saying that the mob "would run like hell" when the police arrived. The three divisions were commanded by five lieutenants and a sergeant. The rear detail barely had time to fall in when Bonfield ordered them to move out. He was in such a hurry to break up a meeting that was about to end that his men barely had time to adjust their belts and weapons as they trotted into formation. The police marched in columns covering the span of the street. By this time the crowd had dwindled to less than 300. It began to drizzle.

The police detail halted three paces from the wagon just as Captain William Ward spoke the words to Samuel Fielden that would etch his name in the history books: "In the name of the people of the state of Illinois, I command this meeting to disperse." He repeated the directive one more time. Fielden replied, "We are peaceable." Then a luminous object was thrown from a vestibule near the corner of Randolph and Des Plaines Street. Sixteen people later testified that they saw the bomb in flight but a positive identification of the thrower could not be made. The police commenced firing and in the bedlam that followed it was never clear who was shooting at whom. Lieutenants Martin Quinn and James Steele led a charge against the mob, but many of the police were running helter-skelter among the crowd and the chances of wounding one of their own was great. Inspector Bonfield, who was not in the first column of casualties, ordered a ceasefire. The force of the blast knocked much of the detail to the ground and in their haste to respond it is likely that many of the wounded men were injured by shots fired from their own service revolvers.

As Patrolman Mathias Degan of the Lake Street Station attempted to walk away, he collapsed and died as a result of bomb fragments severing his artery. He was a two-year veteran, appointed during the 1884 recruitment drive. Of the six other officers who died in the next ten days from shrapnel wounds, only Thomas Redden of Lake Street had more than two years on the force. Interestingly, none of the stricken officers were in supervisory positions. The remnants of the police column straggled back to the Des Plaines Station, where they were attended by parish priests before the doctors could arrive. Bonfield poked his head into the squad room and inquired about the well-being of the wounded. Officer Krueger, who stood within three feet of Fielden when the bomb landed, glared at Bonfield. This veteran army officer, who once rode with the ninth Cavalry at Fort McKavitt, Texas, reminded the inspector of his earlier warnings. "Well, this is plain murder!" he screamed. "If you were an army officer you would be cashiered!" Herman Krueger survived his wounds and went on to become alderman of the 15th Ward when his police career ended.

In a state of madness, the police set out across the city to arrest any suspicious characters in sight. They lacked a plan of action at this point, but thought it was a good idea to raid the headquarters of the *Arbeiter-Zeitung*. However, the office was deserted. Mayor Harrison asked for an account of Bonfield's actions on that fateful night. In a letter dated June 1, 1886, the inspector defended his decision to send the men out.

At different times between 8:00 and 9:30 officers in plain clothes reported progress of the meeting and stated nothing of a very inflammatory nature was said until a man named Fielden or Fielding took the stand. He advised his hearers to throttle the law. It would be as well for them to die fighting as to starve to death. He further advised them to exterminate the capitalists and to do it that night. Wanting to be clearly within the law, and wishing to leave no room for doubt as to the propriety of our actions, I did not act on his first reports, but sent the officers back to make further observations. A few minutes after 10:00 the officers reported that the crowd was getting excited and the speaker growing more incendiary in his language. I then felt to hesitate any longer would be criminal on my part, and then gave the order to fall in, and our force formed on Waldo Place.[25]

Bonfield theorized that the bombing was the work of the *Lehr und Wehr Verein* (Study and Resistance Group), an armed precision unit that had recently been forced underground by the authorities. What Bonfield had started, Captain Schaak was determined to finish. On the morning of May 7, he asked Ebersold's permission to head up the investigation, promising to leave no stone unturned. "With your permission I will work this case and all there is in this case," he said. "You will hear from me soon, but if you should not hear from me in three months do not ask for me."[26] The cloak-and-dagger dramatics of Schaak seem ridiculous today, but there were people who took him very seriously as he painted a picture of impending anarchism in the city of Chicago. In 1889, he published an entertaining but preposterous retelling of the Haymarket Affair, with a special emphasis on the history of social revolutions and how he personally thwarted the one about to occur along the banks of the Chicago River. At one point, Schaak quotes a prominent businessman who proclaims: "I think you are the world's greatest detective."[27]

But first he had to crack the case, and to do this he recruited his favorite plainclothes men: Herman Schluetter, Michael Whalen, Michael Hoffman, Jake Loewenstein, and John Stift. They were instructed to report through his office only, because Schaak did not trust Ebersold or his crowd. These men arrested dozens of known socialist sympathizers, and they seized a large amount of paraphernalia in the meeting halls of the IWPA. The police under Ebersold and the detectives reporting to Schaak bumped heads time and again, but ultimately failed to identify the real culprit. The two men who might have tossed the bomb into the police ranks slipped right through their hands. Suspect number one was Rudolph Schnaubelt, a member of the IWPA and a brother-in-law of Michael Schwab, one of the men later condemned to death by the state. Schnaubelt was a machinist by trade, in the employ of Fred P. Rusback.[28] It has been conclusively proven that he was present at the Haymarket meeting, for it was Spies who sent him out to locate Parsons. During the trial he was positively identified by M. M. Thompson, a dry goods clerk at Marshall Field's, who claimed that he observed Spies and Schnaubelt standing together near the mouth of the alley shortly before the bomb was thrown. There is little credence given to Harry Gilmer's testimony that he saw Spies hand the bomb to Schnaubelt. But the suspect's movements and the actions of the police raise some interesting questions.

Schnaubelt was arrested at 224 Washington Street by officers Palmer and Cosgrove, who were assigned to Bonfield's detachment working out of the Central Station. At the station he admitted that he was present at the rally, and

Figure 5

Michael Schaak, inspector of the "Nord Seide" and author of *Anarchy and Anarchists*.
(Deckert)

stood near the wagon until a half-minute before the bomb was thrown.[29] Notwithstanding these admissions, he was ordered released by Ebersold. Schaak later claimed that Schnaubelt lingered in the police station until someone forced him out the door. A week later, detectives Stift and Whalen arrested him again, but they were told to "lay off" by Palmer. Later, the police paid a call on Fred Rusback, who said that Schnaubelt finished his work at the shop and left without collecting his paycheck.[30] That was the last anyone ever saw of him in Chicago. He was indicted by the grand jury, but by this time had left the country. From time to time, various people claimed to have seen Schnaubelt in Los Angeles, Nicaragua, and Sweden. A report from Teguciagalpa, Honduras in 1895 listed Schnaubelt as being mortally wounded in a saloon fracas.[31]

For years people were convinced that Schnaubelt was the bomb thrower, but the eyewitness accounts of Gilmer and Thompson were shaky. The real mystery is why the police seemed determined to let him flee, when other men were seized and tortured into false confessions. Ebersold personally interrogated Gustave Stange, who was arrested for possessing several Remington rifles and labor pamphlets. The chief told the press that he had convincing evidence that Stange was the miscreant who killed the policemen, but no one had ever heard of this man before or since. It seems unlikely that Ebersold was party to any conspiracy, but his actions regarding Schnaubelt were inconsistent with the treatment given other prisoners incarcerated at the Central Station.

There is little doubt today that the real bomb thrower was a member of one of the radical labor groups operating in Chicago. The fragments of the bomb were identical to the kind that was manufactured by Louis Lingg, who committed suicide in his jail cell shortly before the scheduled date of the hangings. Perhaps the culprit was George Meng, a Hegwisch farmer who attended the 1883 Pittsburgh Congress, which outlined the course of action for the IWPA. Meng was never implicated by the police, and his identity was unknown until 1985, when Dr. Adah Maurer revealed to historian Paul Avrich that her grandfather (Meng) was the actual bomb thrower.[32] In a letter to Avrich she recalled stories her mother used to relate about a man named Rudolph who was hiding out at the Meng farm during the police dragnet. George Meng died in a saloon fire in the early 1890s, a pathetic, embittered old man who probably resented the fact that no one in Chicago considered him important enough to question him about the bombing.

Meanwhile, Schaak planted spies among the laboring men. He recruited mysterious informers in the dead of night, and generally succeeded in creating deeper divisions with his superiors at police headquarters. Ebersold ruefully asked, "Are you the chief, or am I?" Schaak accused the superintendent of keeping company with Clark Street drunks, and behaving in an unacceptable matter.

By May 27, 31 indictments were presented to the grand jury. The police raided ten labor halls and 17 saloons, and had arrested over 200 people. Forty-five families were paid money by the police in exchange for their testimony, and many others were coerced into giving false evidence. The wheels of justice turned, and in the end, four men gave their lives. It is doubtful that any of the Haymarket martyrs had direct knowledge of the actual bomb thrower, or would have sanctioned the killings. But on November 11, 1887, August Spies, Albert Parsons, Adolph Fischer, and George Engel were dropped to eternity in the courtyard between the jailhouse and the court. Sitting next to Ebersold, Schaak whispered, "The law is vindicated." The chief, who would go to his grave with nagging self-doubts about his own conduct during the affair, agreed: "The anarchists will understand that they cannot do as they please in this country."[33]

And so it was. For a short time, Schaak and Bonfield basked in the glow of public favor. They were heroes and their exploits were retold in the dime novels and pulp tabloids of the day. Grateful Chicago industrialists contributed $31,371.50 to the Benevolent Association, and a matching contribution to the families of the slain patrolmen. The railroads, which had felt the brunt of the most serious labor agitation of the decade, chipped in $10,759; young Cyrus Hall McCormick, whose actions caused the Haymarket tragedy, put in a meager $250.

The police who gave their lives in this tragedy were to become forgotten martyrs. Their memory was kept alive for a generation, but when the last of the Haymarket veterans passed away—Officer Frank P. Tyrrell on February 11, 1947—all that remained was a statue that became a symbol of police repression to student activists of the 1960s. The infamous statue—the first monument to the police in the United States—was designed by Frank Batchelder of St. Paul, Minnesota in 1889. It was paid for by Richard T. Crane and dedicated in the Haymarket Square on May 4, 1889. The officer depicted represents Captain William Ward, raising his hands seconds before the bomb was flung. In fact the model was Patrolman Thomas Birmingham, who was also in uniform that fateful night. Thousands of people who came to Chicago to preview the 1893 World's Fair desired to see the Haymarket monument and hear the story. Tom Birmingham was detailed to escort them, and explain the tragedy as he understood it. Many of these tourists wished to buy a drink for the handsome policeman, and gradually Birmingham—a temperant man before he joined the force—became accustomed to the spirits. He died destitute in the County Hospital on September 26, 1912, after spending his last six years alternating between the Oak Forest infirmary and the indigent ward in Chicago.[34]

The policemen who were assigned to the six companies that night organized a Veteran's Association which gathered each May 4 to swap stories and recall old times. They met in the squad room of the Des Plaines Station, from which point they marched into the square to honor their fallen comrades. In the early years the veterans talked freely of the riot, and offered theories about the circumstances leading up to the moment that the bomb was thrown. But with each passing year they spoke less and less of it. They held together, though, in spite of the ravages of old age. As the Haymarket police entered their eighties, the reunion was held only when the weather was favorable. In the last few years it was abandoned altogether.

The upkeep of the statue was traditionally the responsibility of the Veteran's Association, but following the death of Captain Tyrrell it fell into neglect and decay. It was a tired symbol of a forgotten age, ignored by all but a few students of the period and a handful of politicians. In 1950 the last link to the Des Plaines Street Station ended when the old building was razed and the police who were assigned there were transferred to the Monroe Street detail.

In the late 1960s, radical student groups bombed the statue twice, forcing an angry Mayor Richard Daley to move it to police headquarters. It was an ignoble epitaph. Today the statue is on permanent display at the police training academy, but the concrete base at Haymarket collects graffiti—and abuse—from people who fail to understand that the statue memorializes not a corrupt police regime but seven working men whose aims were similar to those of Spies and Parsons— to create a better life for themselves and their families. The cause and the deed, fortunately, did not slip from memory.

The Aftermath of Haymarket

The Haymarket Affair became a symbolic event for the worldwide labor movement. Its influence on future generations was profound. One can only wonder how different future events might have been if a weak-willed superintendent and a petty, vainglorious bigot had not figured so prominently in police matters.

The 1877 railroad strike and the Haymarket Riot of 1886 exposed the weaknesses and corruption that permeated the department. In both cases the police responded to an industrial dispute with needless violence and brutality when restraint and good sense might have saved some lives. The police were at their very worst usually when the leadership of the department had succeeded in demoralizing the rank-and-file.

In 1894, minus the disruptive influence of Schaak, Bonfield and their respective cliques, the police demonstrated that they were capable of maintaining order, even when events seemed uncontrollable. Pullman, on the city's far South Side, was built as a company town for the workers hired to construct sleeping cars for the railroads. Behind the tenements, and invisible to most, people crowded together in narrow quarters to share one faucet. Low wages, escalating rents, and an intolerant attitude toward the workers seeking to organize a local chapter of the American Railway Union were the real issues of the 1894 Pullman strike. The acts of violence against the workers were committed by federal deputy marshals pressed into service by the government. The Chicago police arrested a number of Deputy Marshals for various charges, including arson, burglary, and assorted acts of violence against Pullman residents.[35] In his annual report

Table 2
Nationality of Pullman Workers, 1894

Nationality	Number of Workers
American	1,796
Scandinavian	1,422
German	824
British & Canadian	796
Dutch	753
Irish	402
Latin	170
All others	161
	6,324

Source: William H. Carwardine, *The Pullman Strike* (Chicago: Charles Kerr & Co., 1973), p. 98.

to the City Council, Superintendent Michael Brennan did not deny that his men sided with the aims of the union.

To the charge made that the police sympathized with the strikers, I would say that such is probably the fact. Most of the police as well as most of the troops [ordered in by President Cleveland] came from the same class of society from which the working men come, and their sympathies were naturally with the men who were striving to better their condition.[36]

This was a marked departure from police attitudes toward the Haymarket "anarchists," who were perceived to be outside the mainstream of acceptable behavior because of their political beliefs, manner of dress, and ethnic identity. The Pullman community was composed of U.S.-born wage earners who were largely apolitical in their attitudes toward the civilian authorities (see Table 2). The fact that many of the striking workers belonged to patriotic societies like the Grand Army of the Republic (GAR) and Daughters of the American Revolution may have also worked to their advantage.

The Teamsters' Strike of 1902

Fair and unbiased in his dealings, Francis O'Neill recognized the shortcomings of untrained, special policemen hired for strike duty. In 1902 he broke established patterns by refusing to hire these men to enforce order during the stockyards/Teamsters' strike. By special order of the superintendent, the police were directed to arrest anyone carrying a concealed weapon, including the private security guards retained by the meat-packing companies.[37] But the police assigned to duty in the yards were loyal to one master—Inspector Nicholas Hunt, who commanded for the better part of 25 years. White-haired Nick Hunt was an ambitious and powerful adversary who happened to belong to the Republican Party (O'Neill was a Democrat). He owed his allegiance not to the chief, whom he considered a downtown caretaker, but to the gambler James O'Leary and the packing town magnates who helped make him a wealthy man. His personal fortune was estimated to be a quarter of a million, and he owned a string of flats along Indiana Avenue; not bad for a poor Irish immigrant who landed in the streets of New York at the age of 14 without family, friends, or money.[38]

Hunt was there when the wealthy meat packers needed someone to put down the growing threat of the Teamsters' Union. When O'Neill refused to allow special policemen to accompany the drivers of the freight wagons as they made their rounds, Hunt found a few of his own men who would do the job. When the Teamsters threatened to get the upper hand, Hunt had the top leaders imprisoned without bail or legal counsel. He proudly boasted that this was the decisive element of the "battle"—and the Teamsters could all go home after this.[39]

Innocent bystanders, including many women who were standing on a sidewalk near the factories, were beaten unmercifully. The Teamsters' Union and the Chicago Federation of Labor sent delegations to Mayor Harrison to protest, but Hunt explained that the use of "sluggers" against the police necessitated his actions. There was probably some truth in this statement, but it is clear that Hunt was out to smash the strike at all costs. The police made 200 arrests during the strike, although only a few were fined. Mayor Harrison was anxious to placate the angry union men, and he recommended that the pending charges be dropped. The 1902 strike was a prelude to more labor problems in the packing industry, which came to a head just two years later in another walkout. Again, Nicholas Hunt was at the vanguard of the police columns. Hunt's work earned the praise of the industry moguls, but censure from the unions. His clear biases were not groundless. The grateful meat packers were said to have contributed vast sums of money to his personal account, and his job was saved when the boys downtown decided to retire him. In time, though, his greed and personal arrogance finally got the best of him.

The scandal that discredited Hunt and ultimately led to his dismissal involved a number of highly placed officers in the Hyde Park Station, including Captain Patrick Lavin, a man who was personally trained by the inspector. One of Lavin's men, Officer Patrick Mahoney, was accused of complicity in a jewelry theft at Bernard Hagamann's South Side store on August 30, 1901. Two expert safe-blowers named James Clark and Thomas Barry were supplied with the necessary tools to crack Hagamann's safe by Officer Mahoney. Some $9,000 worth of precious jewels were reported missing to the police, which afforded Lavin an excellent chance to solve the mystery and earn a promotion for himself. This was the sorry conclusion that Chief O'Neill reached just before he retired from public life to take up farming.

When the details of the robbery hit the papers, Mahoney made a name for himself by promising to bring the offenders to justice, based on the sworn statement of an "informant." The unnamed man suddenly fled to Missouri, which aroused the curiosity of the state's attorney. Special police were sent out to track down the informant, and when he was located, he revealed the identity of the two safeblowers. Before the police wagon finally led them away to prison they revealed Mahoney's role in the affair. The policeman took the fall, but remained silent about Lavin's involvement in the robbery. While in jail, Mahoney's family was taken care of in a lavish manner, which led to a second investigation in 1905.

Lavin was called before the grand jury when all the facts came to light. The incoming police chief, John Collins, was a Democrat. Before the grand jury had time to act on the complaint, he summarily dismissed both Lavin and Hunt from the force on August 11, 1906. The action was taken not because the men were accessories to a crime, but rather as a way to clean out a Republican stronghold on the South Side; Collins had traced some unfavorable election publicity back to the Hunt-Lavin clique. "I didn't know a thing about it," Hunt told waiting reporters as he left the chief's office. "It's either you resign or you are suspended. That's all that was said. I had no warning that there were any charges against me. There was no preliminary investigation that I knew of."[40]

Hunt sat it out for exactly one year, long enough for Chief Collins to run afoul of the law himself. Over his signature, orders were issued to patrolmen to distribute campaign literature for Mayor Edward Dunne in his bid for reelection in 1907. He instructed officers detailed to polling places to exclude anyone from the building guilty of "disorderly conduct"—in other words, Republican precinct workers. By law, only the election judge was permitted to make this decision, and the policeman was there to carry out his orders. Collins's difficulties were further compounded by a $2,600 slush fund that he had raised for the mayor's personal use.[41]

When the Republicans were returned to City Hall that spring, Mayor Fred Busse and Chief George Shippy restored Hunt to active duty—exactly one year to the date of his "retirement." Shippy proceeded on the theory that Hunt was outside Civil Service and could not have been legally discharged by Collins. The Hyde Park community, at least those residents not associated with the "blind pig" saloons, gambling joints, and traveling handbooks, were incensed. "I believe that Chicago is taking a step backward in the reappointment of such a man," complained Arthur Barrage Farwell, a community activist. "Personally, I regret the actions of the police—how deeply you would realize if you knew what I have gone through in the last 17 years."[42]

Returning to his comfortable second-floor office at the Hyde Park Station, Hunt was surrounded by a roomful of well-wishes and favor-seekers. Bouquets of American Beauty roses lined the walls. "Now what the devil is this?" he muttered under his breath as he took a closer look at the cryptic inscription on one of the most beautiful pieces in the room. It read "Rejuvenesance"—and it was signed by J. Ogden Armour, the heir to one of Chicago's largest and most respected meat packing families.[43]

Notes

1. Richard C. Lindberg, *Chicago Ragtime: Another Look at Chicago 1880–1920* (South Bend: Icarus Press, 1985), p. 15.

2. David Johnson, *Policing the Urban Underworld: The Impact of Crime on the Development of the American Police: 1800–1887* (Philadelphia: Temple University Press, 1979), p. 117. The city police were assisted by 8,000 volunteers in putting down this disturbance. The volunteers included 600 Civil War veterans enlisted in the "Veteran's Corps." Postal workers, Pinkerton agents, the Gun Club, and a company of Board of Trade employees rounded out the brigade.

3. *Chicago Tribune*, July 25, 1877.

4. Lindberg, *Chicago Ragtime*, p. 9. This scenario has been repeated in a number of secondary sources, including William Adelman's *Haymarket Revisited* (The Illinois Labor History Society, 1976). Whether Hickey actually threatened Parsons in this manner cannot be verified with certainty.

5. Howard Barton Myers, *The Policing of Labor Disputes in Chicago: A Case Study* (Ph.D dissertation, University of Chicago, 1925), p. 124. The police believed that roughness in dispersing a crowd during the early stages of a strike was excusable on the grounds that it might discourage more extreme violence later on.

6. *Chicago Tribune*, July 18, 1878. As the traditional spokesman of the Republican Party, the newspaper looked past the more sordid episodes of Hickey's career, reminding the City Council that "nothing has been brought out against him in the present effort to defeat him, except some scandal several years old which he may fairly said to have outlived."

7. John J. Flinn and John Wilkie, *History of the Chicago Police* (Chicago: The Policeman's Benevolent Association, 1887), p. 205. Seavey was confirmed by the City Council by a 32–2 margin. They ignored an anonymous communication that told of Seavey's early life as a traveling circus barker selling ornamental jewelry. During his short term as police superintendent, Seavey introduced the Morse telegraph to the department. He hired five operators to oversee the operation of the system.

8. Myers, *Labor Disputes*, p. 150.

9. Lindberg, *Chicago Ragtime*, p. 14.

10. Ibid.:"The police were so brutal under the leadership of Bonfield that Captain Michael Schaak felt constrained to write a letter condemning his actions as "brutal and uncalled for." See Myers, *Labor Disputes*, p. 151.

11. The Schaak obituary, *Chicago Times-Herald*, May 18, 1898. The captain was a 33rd-degree Mason known to his associates as the "burgomaster of the nord seid." His success in solving burglaries, murders, and garrotings were considered unparalleled in nineteenth-century Chicago police work.

12. *Chicago Daily News*, August 23–30, 1885. It took Schaak three days to identify Mulkowski, who had served a prison sentence in Poland for murder prior to his arrival in the United States.

13. *Chicago Tribune*, August 30, 1885.

14. Lindberg, *Chicago Ragtime*, p. 187.

15. Myers, *Labor Disputes*, p. 152.

16. *Report of the General Superintendent to the City Council (1886)*, p. 41.

17. *Chicago Times*, March 2, 1886.

18. *Superintendent's Report, 1886*, p. 41. Henry David claims the size of the police detail numbered 200, but it is unlikely the police could have assembled a force of this size in such a narrow time frame.

19. Myers, *Labor Disputes*, p. 154. Spies ordered the word "revenge" deleted, but several hundred of the circulars escaped the printer's office.

20. Carl Smith, "Cataclysm and Cultural Consciousness: Chicago and the Haymarket Trial," *Chicago History* (Summer 1986): 46. "Did not these monopolists bring about the inception of this language?" Parsons asked at the trial.

21. Bruce C. Nelson, "Anarchism: The Movement Behind the Martyrs," *Chicago History* (Summer 1986): 11.

22. *Chicago Daily News*, May 5, 1886. The incident at Rosenfield's drugstore is rarely discussed by historians in the context of Haymarket.

23. Lindberg, *Chicago Ragtime*, p. 23.

24. Ibid., p. 25. Barton Simonson, a traveling salesman, visited the Des Plaines Street station early in the evening and overheard this conversation.

25. John Bonfield to Frederick Ebersold, June 1, 1886. Edward Steele papers, Chicago Historical Society Manuscript Collection.

26. Michael J. Schaak, *Anarchy and Anarchists* (Chicago: F. J. Schulte & Co., 1889), p. 188.

27. Ibid.

28. See the *Chicago Tribune*, June 6, 1895, for an account of Schnaubelt's movements before and after the bomb was dropped.

29. Ibid.

30. Ibid.

31. Ibid.

32. Ibid., November 14, 1985; April 27, 1986. Policeman John Bernett claimed to observe the bomb thrower. He described the man as standing 5'9" and wearing a mustache. The description fits Meng but at this late date judgments are purely speculative.

33. *Chicago Tribune*, November 11, 1887. The police feared that a city-wide revolution was going to break out on execution day. A squad of 300 men armed with bayonets and revolvers ringed the court house and jail. Reserves were pressed into duty in the surrounding German communities.

34. Ibid., September 27, 1912.

35. Myers, *Labor Disputes*, p. 245.

36. *Report of the General Superintendent to the City Council (1894)*, p. 16.

37. Myers, *Labor Disputes*, p. 358. O'Neill ordered that the municipal ordinances forbidding private security guards from bearing arms be strictly enforced. During other strike periods the police usually overlooked this violation.

38. *Chicago Tribune*, August 11, 1906. Hunt worked in Hyde Park as a common laborer before joining the village police in 1871. He progressed through the ranks until he was appointed inspector of police in 1890. In 1911 he left the force of his own accord to organize a private detective agency with George Shippy and Charles Dorman—two other officers who had fallen out of favor.

39. Myers, *Labor Disputes*, p. 363.

40. *Chicago Tribune*, August 11, 1906. q.

41. Captain John Collins of the Warren Avenue Station was a political crony of Mayor Edward Dunne, and a sworn enemy of Nick Hunt. Prominent in Clan-Na-Gael circles, Collins concentrated his gambling raids against Jim O'Leary. His term ended in scandal

and disgrace when he designated police attorney Frank Comerford to serve as the cashier for the Dunne election campaign. The $2,600 slush fund went to William O'Connell, commissioner of Public Works. When the Civil Service Commission became suspicious, Collins falsified police ledgers and destroyed sensitive departmental data to hide his political work.

42. Ibid., August 7, 1907.
43. Ibid.

Close Up on the Chicago Police: Fingerprints Doom a Murderer

In the fall of 1910 a failed house thief named Thomas Jennings made history of a dubious nature—all because he left for work without taking along his gloves. It turned out to be a fatal mistake. Jennings was a black man, the first American sentenced to death based solely on fingerprint evidence.

Jennings was a two-time loser, first convicted of burglary in November 1906. He was sent to the Joliet Penitentiary and was paroled three years later. He was returned to prison the next year for a house burglary in suburban Harvey, Illinois. On August 3, 1910, the gates of the state pen swung open for the last time. The parole board seemed satisfied that he could make a good accounting of himself. Instead, he targeted the residence of Clarence Hiller for a holdup. At 2:00 AM on September 19, 1910, Jennings scaled the back porch of the Hiller place and entered a second-floor bedroom, where his shadowy outline was observed by one of the young daughters who was awakened by a noise. The girl screamed, alerting her father, who was employed by the Chicago Rock Island Railway as a freight office clerk. Hiller grappled with the intruder, but lost his balance. The two men tumbled down the stairs into the parlor where Jennings pulled a revolver and fired two shots into Hiller. The man was dead in seconds.

Jennings fled through the front door and down Vincennes Avenue. He was intercepted by three police officers from the South Englewood Station who were curious about why a frightened black man would be running through a white residential neighborhood at that late hour. "I'm going to the streetcar stop," he explained, but the officers were not satisfied with this, and searched him. The murder weapon was found in his pocket, but the police had no way of knowing, of course, that it had been used in the commission of a crime. They decided to take him into the jail and book him "on suspicion"—a common practice in those days.

Captain Michael Evans of the police identification bureau was called out to Englewood to review the evidence at the Hiller place. He recognized Jennings as a parole violator. Since no one other than the dead man had actually seen the murderer's face, it was up to Evans to see if there were any telltale fingerprints around. Three were found on the back porch railing and they matched those of Jennings. "If he had worn gloves that night he entered the Hiller home, I don't think he would have been convicted," explained Detective George Porteous. Porteous was a pupil of Alphonse Bertillon, a junior file clerk in the Paris Préfecture of Police, credited with inventing the earlier system of prisoner identification.

Jennings was tried and convicted of murder on November 10, 1910. His defense attorney bungled the case and probably sent his client to death by demanding that Evans conduct another fingerprint test before the jury. It turned out that the courtroom print on a piece of paper matched the one on the railing, to the lawyer's disbelief. Jennings was later given a stay of execution by Governor Deneen, but it was only temporary. He went to the gallows several months later, establishing a new precedent in jurisprudence.

Fingerprinting techniques were known to ancient Chinese but not introduced in the U.S. until an Englishman named Edward Henry demonstrated their practical application at the 1904 St. Louis World's Fair. Sir Edward showed that the impressions taken from the inside bulb of the first joint of each of the ten fingers were as individual as a photograph or signature. One immediate advantage to policing agencies was the tremendous reduction of paperwork and file maintenance. Bertillon photographs and measurements took up miles of space in the city police stations, and were a filing nightmare for the clerks sent to retrieve a particular case history. However, fingerprints could be made on a 3" x 5" index card. Bertillon was an imprecise science; fingerprinting was not. And while measuring instruments were costly, a fingerprint set could be purchased for $6 in 1922.

Michael Evans introduced the Henry system to Chicago on January 1, 1905. Within a year, 2,533 prints were taken and by 1907, nearly 40 percent of all criminal identifications were made using this method. Bertillon, which had served a useful purpose for nearly a quarter of a century, was scrapped by most law enforcement and penal institutions by 1920 in favor of Sir Edward's system.

5

The Triangle and the Star:
The Cronin Case

The struggle to free Ireland from British rule was an issue that united all strata of Irish immigrant society. Prominent businessmen John M. Smythe and Francis Agnew, a wealthy contractor, were among the local leaders of Clan Na Gael, a secret oath-bound society dedicated to establishing home rule in Ireland.[1] Clan Na Gael was organized in New York in 1867 as a splinter group of the Fenian Brotherhood. Named for Fianna, the legendary band of Celtic warriors, the brotherhood raised hundreds of thousands of dollars to purchase arms and equipment for the eventual overthrow of the British landlords.[2]

In 1866 the radical Fenians rebelled against the conservative leadership, much the same way as the IWPA had split with the Socialist Labor Party. The Clan Na Gael men committed themselves to the same principles as the radical Fenians—the movement of guns, explosives, and money to Ireland. By 1877, a decade after its founding, Clan Na Gael numbered 11,000 members.[3] The first Chicago "camp" was founded in 1869 but the Clan did not attain peak growth until after 1871. From 1881 until the Cronin murder of 1889, which sent many of its members into hiding, Chicago was the foremost center of radical Clan activity in the United States.

Clan Na Gael members living in Chicago were deeply involved in the local ward politics. The Democratic Party was comprised of a number of Clan members who dispensed jobs and patronage to members of their local community. One of them was Dan O'Hara, who served as city treasurer under Mayor Colvin. He used his influence to secure an appointment for Alexander Sullivan as director of the Board of Works.[4] Sullivan was a former political reporter who joined the Clan in 1875. He was elected national chairman in 1883, and was the recognized leader of the radical faction that sent the dynamiters and hired assassins to terrorize Britain. Indeed, he exerted considerable power in Democratic circles even though he never ran for elective office. In return for his endorsement of Carter Harrison's mayoral bid, he was permitted to appoint several of his friends to the Police Department.[5] Sullivan did not enjoy the support of the moderate faction, led by Dr. Patrick Cronin, a North Sider bitterly opposed to Sullivan's high-handed tactics.

After a lengthy power struggle in 1884, Cronin was expelled from the Clan on charges of internal treason. Sullivan engineered the charges and had personally selected the tribunal that adjudged Cronin guilty. One of the resolutions adopted by the 1881 Convention was to vest control in an executive board of five, with three constituting a quorum. This came to be known as the "Triangle." Cronin disavowed Sullivan-style politics, but he failed in his attempt to block Sullivan's election to the post of executive director. Cronin charged that $111,000 had been misspent on an ill-fated bombing foray in the British Isles.[6] The sinews of war were furnished on a grand scale. Twenty-three dedicated, anonymous operatives were sent to England to commit acts of violence in the country. They were supplied with new identities and told to live under cover until the time was right. Before they so much as stepped off the boat in Liverpool, however, they were seized by the British authorities who seemed to have a direct tie-in with Clan Na Gael. The Triangle was convinced that there was a spy in their midst, and they were right. His name was Henry LeCaron, a city employee, who was one of four British agents planted in the United States to infiltrate the Clan. Detective Dan Coughlin of the East Chicago Avenue Station, a member of Camp no. 20, accused Cronin of being an intimate of LeCaron, after the spy's real identity was established.[7] In accordance with rules established in Dublin, Cronin was put on trial by a committee of seven. He was convicted and sentenced to death on what later proved to be a trumped-up charge. Fittingly, it was Coughlan who drew the lot to carry out the death sentence. Dr. Cronin was last seen in his office on May 4, 1889. Eight days later his mutilated corpse was found in a catch-basin in suburban Lake View.

The disappearance and murder of one of Chicago's most prominent physicians shocked and outraged the community. The investigation was handled by Captain Schaak, whose personal negligence in the matter nearly allowed the guilty parties to slip away. Schaak refused to believe that Cronin was missing, even after ten days.[8] The first clue to the existence of a murder conspiracy was provided by a Clark Street livery man named Patrick Dinan, who told Schaak that it was Coughlan who had rented the carriage that carried Cronin to his death. The rig had been summoned by an employee of the O'Sullivan Ice Works. Cronin was asked to accompany the driver to an industrial accident, but was instead driven to a cottage owned by a Swede named Carlson. After a fierce struggle with his abductors, Cronin was subdued and murdered.

The two men who rented the cottage from Carlson, Martin Burke and Patrick Cooney, went on trial for murder along with Coughlan and the ice-man O'Sullivan. After a lengthy inquest, the trial started on August 30, 1889, and it was riveting front-page news for nearly three months. Michael Schaak professed to know very little about the personal background of Detective Coughlan. He could not say with any certainty where the man even lived.[9] Coughlan had been hired, Schaak explained, because he was a former miner from Leadville Colorado, and was an expert on explosives. These talents served him well during the height of the anarchist hysteria, which was more to Schaak's liking than a murder case with ominous political overtones. The morning after the murder Schaak told the court that he had no knowledge of Coughlan's whereabouts. As a member of the detective squad, Coughlan was accustomed to showing up for the 9:00 AM rollcall with the rest of the day left to himself. After Dinan related his story to Schaak, the captain brought the matter before Detective Coughlin, who explained that a friend of his brother had paid him to secure the carriage. This seemed good enough for Schaak, who then ordered Coughlan to bring this man into the station for questioning.

Working with Coughlan was Michael Whalen, a 19-year veteran of the police force who was a key member of the Haymarket detail assigned to Schaak. He was also a 16-year Clan member, and a first cousin of the ice-man Patrick O'Sullivan.[10] Whalen's brother lived in the same rooming house with the O'Sullivan family, and it was his business card that was given to Dr. Cronin as the pretense to lure him out to Lakeview.

Officer Whalen later testified that he was unaware of the sinister nature of Clan Na Gael. It was his understanding that it was merely a "social and literary" club.[11] On the witness stand he contradicted Schaak's sworn testimony by claiming to have observed the captain conversing with Coughlan directly in front of the station the night Cronin disappeared. When he told Schaak about a chance meeting that occurred between Coughlan and the man commissioned to hire the rig, he dismissed it as "unimportant." This occurred after Schaak ordered the detectives to bring the man in.

It is likely that Whalen not only had direct knowledge of the events leading up to the murder of Cronin, but also that he helped conceal evidence. The conduct of Schaak and other policemen detailed to the East Chicago Avenue Station suggests that they feared the reprisals of Alexander Sullivan. He no doubt realized that cooperation with Sullivan was necessary if he was to remain a fixture in this Irish precinct with strong ties to the Clan Na Gael.

If Schaak engineered a coverup, at least one officer assigned to duty in this district took the case a little more seriously. John Kunze, one of the scapegoats of the trial, testified that Herman Schluetter attempted to beat a confession out of him in the basement cell of the Halsted Station lockup. Schluetter promised that justice would be swift unless Kunze admitted to driving Cronin to the Lakeview cottage.[12] Burly Herman Schluetter had little regard for Clan Na Gael or the lot of Irish politicians that fell into lock-step behind Alexander Sullivan. His career was on the rise and he no longer felt the need for Michael Schaak's personal indulgence. Throughout the investigation and trial Schluetter turned his back on his former mentor to closet himself with Superintendent Hubbard, who had implicit confidence in his detective abilities. Regarding his old ally Schaak, Hubbard was chagrined. "It has bothered me a great deal—his negligence in this business," he explained. "It has bothered me to understand it because previous to that he had always been a thorough officer who was conscientious in his duties."[13]

The first Cronin trial ended on December 16, 1889, amid charges of jury-packing and bribery by Clan Na Gael members. Finally a guilty verdict against Coughlan, O'Sullivan, Burke, and Kunze was returned—but only after the jury had deliberated for 48 straight hours. John Culver was the only jury member to hold out for an acquittal. The *Chicago Herald* speculated that he was on the Clan's payroll although the charge was vehemently denied by his family and at least one member of the prosecution team.

All of the convicted men except Kunze were sentenced to life in prison. A curious sidelight to the affair was the deaths of O'Sullivan, Patrick Dinan, and John Beggs, senior guardian of Camp no. 20. Each of these men passed away within four weeks of each other while awaiting the Supreme Court's decision about whether they would be given a new trial. O'Sullivan died in his jail cell on May 5, 1892—three years and one day after Dr. Cronin. Dan Coughlin was granted a second trial which commenced in December 1893. After three months of vague and often contradictory testimony, Coughlan was acquitted on March 8, 1894. The decision was hailed as just by the Irish community. On the grave of Martin Burke, who had also died in prison, someone placed a wreath of lillies bearing the inscription, "Vindicated."[14]

Repercussions

The Cronin case was more than a sensational murder of a well-known local celebrity. It laid bare the deep ties and integration of Irish radicalism into all aspects of city government. The *Tribune* estimated that there were at least 500 Clan Na Gael men in Cook County in 1889 who held positions of responsibility in city agencies.[15]

Superintendent Hubbard was not happy with the outcome of the first trial. He was particularly vociferous in his criticisms of the court system that had allowed a band of murderers to get away with their lives. Within a few weeks of the trial Hubbard removed five policemen who were also members of the Triangle on the grounds that their treachery had played into the hands of the defense. Detective Barney Flynn disposed of a set of knives that he found in the possession of Dan Coughlin, which seriously damaged the prosecution's case.[16] Michael Whalen was discharged for little more than guilt by association.

The chief was a Connecticut Yankee of Irish-Protestant descent who freely punished Clan sympathizers for the extreme embarrassment they had brought down on the department in the aftermath of Haymarket. Captain Schaak's career ended on a bitter note when he was asked to remove himself from the East

Chicago Avenue Station so that his protégé Herman Schluetter could take his place. The former streetcar conductor had benefitted from the Cronin case, much to the consternation of Mike Schaak, who wanted to play down the affair. Schluetter realized early on that Schaak could no longer serve a useful purpose in the advancement of his career, so he skillfully played up to Hubbard and State's Attorney Joel Longnecker, who wanted to make examples out of the defendants and thereby restore credibility to the Republican regime.

Mayor Dewitt Creiger agreed that changes were necessary, but was not convinced that Hubbard was the man to carry them out. Once again, the city administration went outside the department to locate a successor who might be acceptable to the power brokers of commerce, industry, and civic reform. Such a man was Frederick Marsh, President Grover Cleveland's personal choice for U.S. marshal of the Northern District of Illinois. In a letter to Marsh, Creiger outlined the objectives that needed to be established if the department was to be put on a course of reform.

Intelligence, integrity, and industry constitute the tripod of a safe police force. And so the reputation and usefulness of the police department of our city will materially depend on the zeal and diligence with which the members of it obey their instructions and devote themselves to their exacting and important duties. I desire that you issue such general orders.[17]

Marsh turned the department upside down, moving lieutenants and captains across the city like a skilled chess master. He divided the city into five divisions, with an inspector fully responsible for maintaining property, stations, and discipline in each district. Thirty-four new precincts were added within the city boundaries, and for the first time captains and lieutenants were expected to drill their men in the city ordinances and police rules at least once a week (see Table 3).[18]

The changes were designed to check Clan Na Gael influence and fortify the position of the superintendent. Superintendents' directions were largely ignored by the captains and lieutenants, who permitted outsiders to dictate policy making. Interestingly, George Hubbard was assigned to the North Side neighborhoods in which Clan members exerted the greatest influence. He continued to receive the advice and counsel of Herman Schluetter but within a month the new reorganization plan threatened to come undone as a result of senseless saloon killing.

Schluetter and two companions were waiting for a streetcar outside of Vogelsaang's Madison Street restaurant one bitterly cold January day when they decided to go in for a quick drink before heading home. Vogelsaang's was a popular hangout for Chicago's German community. Schluetter did not expect to find any Clan Na Gael men inside, but standing at the end of the bar was Alderman John McCormick of the 23rd Ward, accompanied by Red McDonald and Bob Gibbons. McDonald was put off the police force in the wake of the Cronin trial,

Table 3
Chicago Police Department, 1890 Reorganization

First Division (First, Sixth Districts)

Inspector	Years of Service	Known Political Affiliation
Frederick Ebersold	23	Republican

Precincts	Location	Size of Detail
First	Harrison & Pacific	93
Second	22nd & Wentworth	62
Third	Cottage Grove Ave.	54
Fourth	144 35th Street	53
Fifth	35th Street	58
Sixth	Archer & Deering	36

Second Division (Seventh, Eighth, Ninth Districts)

Inspector	Years of Service	Known Political Affiliation
Nicolas Hunt	*18	Republican

Precincts	Location	Size of Detail
Seventh	Halsted & 47th St	65
Eigth	State & 50th	30
Ninth	Lake & 53rd	45
Tenth	Wentworth & 54th	45
Eleventh	Grand Crossing	23
Twelfth	S. Chicago & Commercial	30
Thirteenth	Hegwisch in Hyde Park	8
Fourteenth	Front & 115th (Kensington)	19
Fifteenth	38th & California	18

Third Division (Second District)

Inspector	Years of Service	Known Political Affiliation
Simon O'Donnell	28	Democrat

Precincts	Location	Size of Detail
Sixteenth	Maxwell & Morgan	81
Seventeenth	Halsted & Canalport	44
Eighteenth	Hinman & Paulina	52
Nineteenth	Hinman & Paulina	52
Twentieth	Lawndale	(Assigned to 18th)

Source: *Report of the General Superintendent to the City Council* (1890). See also the *Chicago Times*, January 21, 1890. The five division inspectors totalled 112 years of experience. The provisions of the 1887 Pension Bill permitted an officer with 20 years of experience to retire with half-pay if he had attained the age of 50. O'Donnell, Ebersold, and Hathaway, three of the oldest men on the force, did not wish to retire of their own accord. When McLaughery replaced Marsh as superintendent, he retired each of these men with full pension. The yearly salary of a police inspector was $2,800—which was roughly $2,300 more than an average worker could expect to make in 1890. See the *Chicago Times*, January 12, 1890.

*Nicholas Hunt spent the first 18 years of his career with the Hyde Park Police until the village was annexed in 1889.

Table 3 (continued)

Fourth Division (Third, Fourth Districts)

Inspector	Years of Service	Known Political Affiliation
Amos Hathaway	26	Democrat

Precincts	Location	Size of Detail
Twenty-First	Lake & 43rd	29
Twenty-Second	DesPlaines & Waldo	100
Twenty-Third	Lake & Paulina	63
Twenty-Fourth	Warren near Western	60
Twenty-Fifth	Chicago near Milwaukee	85
Twenty-Sixth	North Ave. & Wright	34
Twenty-Seventh	North Ave. & Milwaukee	51
Twenty-Eighth	Milwaukee & Attrill	31
Twenty-Ninth	Irving Pk. & Milwaukee	25

Fifth Division (Fifth, Tenth Districts)

Inspector	Years of Service	Known Political Affiliation
George Hubbard	17	Republican

Precincts	Location	Size of Detail
Thirieth	Chicago, near Clark	85
Thirty-First	Larrabee & North	48
Thirty-Second	North Halsted St.	48
Thirty-Third	Sheffield & Diversey	32
Thirty-Fourth	Addison & Halsted	28

Cadre: (1) General Superintendent; (1) Secretary; (5) Inspectors; (50) Lieutenants; (52) Patrol Sergeants.

and Gibbons was a local organizer for the North Side Clan. The three man shared a common hatred of Schluetter and other German police men who worked up the Cronin case. Alderman McCormick in particular felt the sting of Schluetter's methods. His brother's saloon had been raided by the captain and he had been denied a renewal of his liquor license. This stemmed from the sworn testimony of a prosecution witness, who told of McCormick's attempts to hire an assassin to kill Dr. Cronin. Gibbons was a member of Camp no. 20 and a popular figure among the immigrant Irish.

"When I see Schluetter, I see Schaak," the alderman thundered across the room. "Schaak stole himself rich and if it wasn't for that gray bearded —— I would put you in the Bridewell!"[19] Schluetter whispered something in German to one of his friends just before they turned toward the exit and a waiting streetcar. McCormick however, was primed for a fight. He strode across the bar until he was inches from Schluetter, who had said nothing to this point. McCormick said, "I have dirty words in my mouth for you, but there will be no trouble tonight," and flicked the stub of his cigar into Schluetter's face, which was a red flag for Nicholas Petrie, a bystander on intimate terms with the captain.

Again Schluetter attempted to walk way, but McCormick disengaged himself from Petrie to renew his taunts, saying, "That's what I think of you!"[20] Gibbons rushed to McCormick's defense, and in the scuffle that followed Schluetter discharged a bullet into his lung. When the news reached Mrs. Gibbons, she immediately swore out an arrest warrant for Schluetter. Her husband was removed to the nearly hospital, where his condition was listed as critical. He lingered for three more days before succumbing to his wounds on February 1, 1890. An anxious crowd of friends and well-wishers gathered outside the Gibbons home while an unnamed county official promised retribution. "The end of this thing hasn't come yet," he said. "Henceforth Captain Schluetter's life is in imminent peril. Don't think the hatred against him is confined to the Market Street crowd [as it had been referred to]. There are officials, policemen, politicians, tradesmen, and many others whose feelings the general public knows nothing, but who are the friends of Gibbons and his friends."[21]

Chief Marsh assigned a young assistant corporation counsel to help Schluetter in his defense. The up-and-coming young lawyer had arrived in the city just three years earlier, but Schluetter adjudged him to be too "green" to handle a case of this magnitude. The lawyer was Clarence Darrow, and he was dismissed in favor of the old and respected firm of Mills and Ingham.

A large crowd attended the formal inquest into the matter, including the angry widow, whose gaze never wavered from Schluetter. The jury was composed entirely of men born in the United States who had no ties to the German or Irish communities. They returned a verdict of acquittal, agreeing with Schluetter's attorneys, who contended that it was a simple case of self-defense. Alderman McCormick, who had supplied Gibbons with a job as tender of the Erie Street Bridge, was not present for the hearing or available for comment.

In deference to public opinion Schluetter was moved out of the Chicago Avenue Station and sent to Central Detail, where he served for a time as the custodian of records. Lieutenant Charles Koch of Lakeview, who was supported by the Clan, took his place.

Schluetter suffered no recriminations at the hands of Clan Na Gael. In fact, the decade of the 1890s witnessed his ascension to the post of assistant super-intendent. He was considered to be the toughest, but most honest cop on the force—a claim with which many laboring people would gladly take issue with. In 1897 he cracked a baffling murder case in which a 52-year-old German immigrant named Adolph Luetgert killed his young wife and then dissolved her remains in a sausage vat filled with deadly potash and arsenic. Schluetter's detectives pieced together the smallest shreds of evidence that tended to prove Luetgert's guilt. The police found 50 bottles of mineral water on a shelf in the sausage factory. By lifting the bottles, the detective squad noticed rings of dust where they had sat. Luetgert claimed at the time that he had sent the night watchman out to purchase bottles of water, which could only have been a device to get rid of him.[22] Sifting through the ashes in the cauldron, a gold ring that belonged to Louisa Luetgert was found. In Schluetter's opinion, this was enough to secure a conviction. The captain appeared at the sausage maker's door on May 17, 1897, to lead him away to jail. As the two men walked past a throng of spectators, several children repeated a grisly little rhyme that was gaining popularity in the North Side German community where Luetgert peddled his sausage.

Old man Luetgert made sausage out of his wife
He turned on the steam, his wife began to scream
There'll be a hot time in the old town tonight!

It was never conclusively proven that the fragments of bone were actually those of Louisa Luetgert, and it took two lengthy trials for the state to secure a guilty verdict. Adolph Luetgert died in prison, and up to the very end he maintained his innocence: "She'll come back. You'll see!"[23] As it turned out, she never did.

Schluetter's work on this case earned him a national reputation and placed him beyond the reproach of his critics. The Gibbons affray was a dead issue by 1897. Years later, interviewers were hard pressed to get Schluetter to explain just what happened at Vogelssang's that night. He lightly brushed it off and would not elaborate. To his way of thinking it was an unfortunate occurrence that mirrored the sentiment of the times.

Irish nationalism provided a cultural and social identity to many of the foreign-born policemen. By virtue of their status in the community the cause provided self-respect, comradeship, and the cohesiveness that made police work not so much a job but a fraternal brotherhood. But their real responsibility to the city was often blurred by involvement in a political struggle that had little relevance to the common good. Years later one policeman received quite a chuckle when he replied to a Civil Service examiner that in his view the *real* duty of an officer was to free Ireland.[24]

Notes

1. Michael Funchion, *Chicago's Irish Nationalists: 1881–1890* (New York: Arno Press, 1976), p. 125. Support for Clan Na Gael cut across all segments of Irish immigrant society including the church. According to Ellen Skerrett in "The Catholic Dimension," in Lawrence McCaffrey, et al. *The Irish In Chicago* (University of Illinois Press, 1987), many of Chicago's ecumenical leaders, including Archbishop Patrick Feehan, openly supported radical Clan activity. Feehan was an intimate of Alexander Sullivan.

2. William D. Griffin, *The Irish in America* (New York: Scribner's, 1981), p. 145.

3. Funchion, *Irish Nationalists*, p. 127.

4. Ibid., p. 45. In August 1881 Sullivan was appointed chairman of the Clan Na Gael executive committee.

5. Michael Funchion, "Political and National Dimensions," *The Irish In Chicago*, p. 74.

6. Funchion, *Irish Nationalists*, p. 103. Cronin sided with John Devoy of New York, who demanded Sullivan's ouster from the executive council. From May of 1881 until November 18, 1885, 29 men were arrested on British soil and sent to prison for terms ranging from seven years to life. See Henry M. Hunt's *The Crime of the Century: The Assassination of Dr. Patrick Cronin* (Chicago: H. L. Kochersperger, 1889), p. 66.

7. *Chicago Tribune*, June 5, 1889.

8. Hunt, *Crime of the Century*, p. 204.

9. *Chicago Tribune*, June 5, 1889.

10. Coughlan's first partner on the force was Jake Loewenstein, who was suspended for his part in the North Side fencing ring that sold the personal belongings of incarcerated prisoners. See Chapter 6.

11. *Chicago Times*, February 4, 1894.

12. Ibid. Kunze was later found guilty of manslaughter and was sentenced to three years in prison.

13. *Chicago Tribune*, June 12, 1889.

14. Ibid., March 12, 1894.

15. Ibid., June 25, 1889. It was estimated that there were 14,000 Clan members nationwide. Their influence in the court system was pervasive. When William McGarigle went on trial in 1887 for embezzling county tax money, the foreman of the jury was P. V. Fitzpatrick, a 22nd Street bookseller who was also a Clan member. Fitzpatrick's influence was important in securing a guilty verdict against McGarigle, a Protestant Irishman.

16. Ibid. Coughlan left Chicago after the trial but ran afoul of the law in 1911 when he was convicted of jury tampering. He died in South America, fugitive from justice.

17. Ibid., June 10, 1890. Chief Marsh was appointed U.S. marshal in 1885 by President Grover Cleveland, who couldn't decide between two other prominent Chicago law enforcement officials—William McGarigle and Sheriff Jacob Kern.

18. Ibid.

19. Ibid., February 1, 1890.

20. Ibid.

21. Ibid., February 2, 1890.

22. Edward Baumann and John O'Brien, "The Sausage Factory Mystery," *Chicago Tribune Magazine*, August 3, 1986, p. 18. See also in Albert Halper, ed., *The Chicago Crime Book*, "The Luetgert Case," Matthew W. Pinkerton, (New York: Pyramid Books, 1969) pp. 203–217.

23. Baumann and O'Brien, "Mystery," p. 18. Luetgert died of natural causes in 1900. Attorney Lawrence Harmon, who represented the sausage maker in his second trial, was convinced his client was innocent. He spent $2,000 of his own money tracking down Louisa. In 1920 he went mad and was committed to an asylum.

24. *Chicago Times-Herald*, December 12, 1894.

6

Gambling and the Police

Mike McDonald was a figure to be reckoned with in the seamy underworld of Chicago politics and gambling. Unlike the gang of pre-Civil War gamblers who nervously ran their penny-ante faro games from the second-floor storerooms along the wharf, McDonald, the Hankins brothers, John Corcoran, and Thomas Foley were not content with merely bribing public officials. They sought the means to control them through their own involvement in local politics.

These men drifted into Chicago sometime during the Civil War for the same reasons as the southern blackleg. Wartime business conditions were good. Copperhead sentiment was rife, and the threat of war reaching this northern metropolis was minimal. There is little known about the movements of Foley and Corcoran before they settled in Chicago, but the Hankins brothers opened a lavish Clark Street gambling resort after winning a law suit against a stagecoach firm.

The early career of Mike McDonald is illustrative of the path a clever nineteenth-century gambler might have followed. As a boy growing up in Niagara Falls, New York, he was apprenticed to a bootmaker but this trade held no special fascination for him. Tired of the work, McDonald left home to take a position with the Michigan Central Railroad as a "train butcher"—a boy who sold confections and magazines to passengers commuting between cities. By 1860 his finances permitted him to relocate to Chicago where he continued to work as an itinerant train concessionaire in the employ of John R. Walsh.[1]

During these years McDonald made a significant amount of money which permitted him to purchase controlling interest in the bar at the Richmond House Hotel. Among his other business holdings was a wholesale liquor distributorship, which put him in contact with the powerful, politically connected German brewers. One of these men was Anton Hesing, publisher of the *Staats-Zeitung*. Hesing bolted the Republican Party to back Harvey Colvin's mayoral bid in 1875, and later that fall he ran for county treasurer on the "Opposition Party" ticket, a German-Irish coalition party formed in 1874.

Hesing counted on the warm support of McDonald and his crowd. The *Tribune* reported that in return for John Corcoran carrying the 20th Ward for Hesing, he was to be rewarded with an appointment as circuit court clerk. To McDonald, Hesing offered to support John Appleton, the gambler's handpicked candidate for the county board.[2] Tom Foley, who ran a saloon, had won a billiards tournament and owned a piece of the Chicago White Stockings baseball team. He was asked to run for clerk of the superior court but ultimately lost out in the party caucuses. Foley, Corcoran, and McDonald cemented their alliance and agreed to work together to elect only the candidates favorable to the gambling and liquor business.

By 1873 McDonald was firmly entrenched as Chicago's leading purveyor of dice and cards. That year he opened the Store, a deluxe downtown gambling emporium with a first-floor cigar store and saloon, adjacent to a popular eating establishment known as Chapin and Gore.

It was all here for the traveling "drummer," or commission man: an elegant dinner at Chapin and Gore, brandy, cigars, and the latest gossip from the sporting world at McDonald's saloon, topped off by an evening of friendly wagering on the second floor. To gain entrance to the club the gambler had to first knock on the door and be recognized by a black man in a waistcoat and cummerbund who knew all the visiting sports.

The room was elegantly furnished with the most expensive antique oak furniture available from the Tobey Company of Chicago. Above one of the stud poker tables were two signs: "Poker, Limit $5.00" and "Open at 9 AM." Two faro tables were always in use, accommodating 15 to 20 men at a time. The stakes ran high. Few, if any, of these men engaged in idle banter while seated at the poker table or drawing cards from the faro box.

Down the street were the various "dinner pail" gambling houses that catered to less affluent gamblers who needed encouragement to lay down the coin. Above the continuous click of the ivory chips at the Hankins resort could be heard the cry of the "capper:" "Come, come, gents! Play up! Room for all. Chance for all! Only a nickel a try!" Around the "buzzard table," the favored game of the Civil War veterans, a band of ragged men wagered their meager earnings while the capper described the action. "Pair of fours and an ace also low—wins. Eleven and high wins! Three aces—grand raffle—$180 for $1.00. That was your chance, gents!" The penny-ante games of Hankins and a score of independents were allowed to operate only after joining the McDonald "trust" and paying a monthly stipend for the privilege. McDonald commanded an army of bunko men who worked the lobbies of the Sherman House, the Grand Pacific, and a half-dozen train stations that carried thousands of transients in and out of the city each week.

The bunko man dressed with elegance and taste and was never suspiciously loud or showy. His voice was cultivated and his fine manners often deceived the Granger elements in town to sell their produce or livestock. These bunko artists foreshadowed the activities of the "handbook" operative popular in the Levee after 1900. What they offered to the syndicate was incremental income, which typically ranged from 15 to 20 percent of the take, and important local gossip.[3] The traveling bunko man made it his business to know which out-of-town banker had just checked into a lush downtown hotel, or which western cattleman was looking to spend some money in a game of poker. Armed with this information McDonald was able to make his necessary contacts through "Kid" Jerry, California Jack, and Harry Lawrence, thereby developing the reputation as the man to see in Chicago.

Cooperation with McDonald meant increased profit for all in a relaxed environment. The bunko men had nothing to fear from the police courts, which routinely suspended sentences following the testimony of favorable witnesses secured by McDonald on their behalf. Even the mayor once appeared as a friendly witness for McDonald when he was dragged into court for one of the few times in his celebrated career. On March 7, 1882, McDonald, along with James C. Gore, proprietor of Chapin and Gore's restaurant, and the illustrious Potter Palmer, were indicted for keeping a gaming house. Palmer had maintained a small place just two doors down from the Store.[4]

When Mayor Harrison was summoned to the stand, he stated that he had called on McDonald numerous times, and had visited the Store to advise him against harboring large numbers of idle men in the building. The mayor went on to say that he was satisfied with McDonald's assurances that he was no longer connected with the business. "Gamblers are disreputable people," McDonald said to the mayor. "And I don't want anything to do with them. Oh sure, I may loan some money to those fellows from time to time, but that is it."[5] When asked about a southern boy who complained of losing vast sums of money at the Store, Harrison replied that if a Kentuckian wasn't sharp enough to save himself from a tinhorn, he wasn't going to help out. Privately, McDonald returned the lad's money and by the time the case reached Judge Joseph Gary's courtroom, the boy had suffered an alarming loss of memory. Palmer, McDonald, Gore, and a number of small-time gamblers walked out of the building acquitted on all charges.

Usually, events never got this far. The proprietors of the gambling dens received protection from police raids or, at the very least, some advance notice of their arrival. After losing a substantial amount of money in Al Hankins's resort at 134 Clark Street, a coal merchant named Robert Law complained to Superintendent William McGarigle about the crooked nature of the game. Law secured a warrant and presented it to the chief at City Hall. McGarigle promised justice, and a return of the swindled money.[6] Law received the strictest assurance that his confidence would be maintained and there would be no leaks. Later that evening George Hankins appeared at the Law residence asking if some accommodation might be reached. "I know nothing about that," Law said.

"You do know all about it, Mr. Law," the gambler shot back. "If this raid

Table 4
Gambling Arrests: 1875–76

	Keeping a Gaming House	Inmates of a Gambling Resort
1875	17	391
1876	46	480

Source: *Report of the General Superintendent to the City Council*, 1877.

is allowed to go on, it will ruin my business and I can't afford to have that happen.''[7] Hankins peeled off six one-hundred dollar bills and gave them to Law.

Politics and Gambling

The ominous specter of McDonald hung over the city like a pail. He packed the County Board with his supporters to gain influence in state and city government. These commissioners invented the word ''boodle'' as they parcelled out tax money to contractors friendly to the board. A court house was constructed but the cost overruns on the job depleted the treasury. The private contractors, who were eager to land fat city jobs, routinely paid ''commissions'' to the board which were attached to the invoice. This boodle money was skimmed by the board members, many of whom owed their livelihoods to McDonald.

In 1879 McDonald supported Congressman Carter Harrison, an old friend from the West Side, for mayor of Chicago. Business conditions were not good for the syndicate. Outgoing Mayor Monroe Heath proved to be hostile to the gamblers despite the presence of an old ally in the general superintendent's office—Mike Hickey. Ironically, the number of gambling arrests rose during the two years of the Republican regime (see Table 4).

Harrison seemed willing to give the Irish and Germans what they wanted all along—the right to patronize a saloon and lay down a friendly wager. A Republican businessman named Abner Wright did not share these views, and he lost the election by 5,000 votes amidst charges of vote-stealing by the Democrats. Wagonloads of repeaters—men paid to vote twice—were driven from precinct to precinct on behalf of Harrison.[8] Acting Superintendent Dixon was told of these charges but chose not to investigate. Harrison's election was a foregone conclusion, and Dixon wisely decided to look out for his own neck before the new mayor decided to swing the spoils axe. The 50 detectives assigned to the polls made no arrests. Candidate Wright complained that ''ballots must have been put in by the handful. It is a physical impossibility for that many people to vote [57,000] in the manner in which voting was done.''[9] An examination of the voter turnout in the traditional Democratic strongholds shows that more people went to the polls than in 1878 (Table 5). Years later the city reporters who were

Table 5
1879 Democratic Mayoral Vote by Ward

Ward	1878 Democratic Vote	1879 Democratic Vote
Fifth	806	2,609
Sixth	659	1,345
Seventh	1,239	2,269
Eigth	1,648	3,006
Ninth	690	1,547
Tenth	751	1,004
Fourteenth	1,014	1,613
Fifteenth	916	1,100
Sixteenth	948	694
Seventeenth	643	1,611

Source: *Chicago Tribune*, election returns, April 3, 1879.

around in the days when Mike McDonald rolled the dice were unanimous in the opinion that it was election larceny, pure and simple.

McDonald's next foray into elective politics occurred in the fall of 1882 when he slated William McGarigle to run for Cook County sheriff despite Mayor Harrison's stern admonishments. At stake was the continuation of McDonald's gambling empire and the wholesale buying and selling of justice. In Chicago, almost anyone could be bailed out of jail and McDonald was the one to see. He figured in every type of bail bond, providing recognizance for offenses ranging from assault to keeping a gaming house, or selling liquor to the intoxicated. In just one month in 1882, McDonald supplied bonds to 66 offenders in the lower courts and 21 appeal bonds.[10]

The professional bondsman realized a quick and easy profit, especially if the offender who left the money with him was compelled by law enforcement officials to flee the country. Then, if the judgment on the forfeiture was not pressed against the bondsman, that same person made a clear profit. Police courts were little more than "justice shops" in which the judge, the policeman, and the bondsman could receive a dollar a head for releasing a gambler on a "straw bail." It was a system in which everyone came out ahead. The police could make money on the side, while satisfying the reformers and the press that their intentions were good. The arrested individual need only pay two or three dollars to secure a release, and the judge, who spent many long and tedious hours behind the bench in a grimy police station, was richly compensated for his time.

The scheme was simple. To save the various bail bonding rackets, all McDonald needed to do was place his men in the sheriff's office and then guarantee that bail bonds could be sold on short notice and easy terms with acquittal on any charge at greatly reduced rates. McGarigle had demonstrated his willingness to cooperate regardless of the mayor's wishes. McDonald bankrolled the campaign and stood proudly alongside the candidate on the dais of the athletic halls and public meeting places in Chicago. Here, the local gamblers and saloon keepers who did business with the "trust" were expected to kick in $500. And on election night, two hours after the polls had closed, McGarigle was still listed as a 2–1 favorite. However, in a stunning upset the Republican Seth Hanchett won by 4,900 votes.[11] It was a shocking setback for the gambler boss, whose own "trust" was in apparent revolt. John Dowling, one of Mc-Donald's earliest backers, defected to the Hanchett camp because of his personal antipathy toward McGarigle, an Irish Protestant opposed to the Clan Na Gael.[12]

After 1885 McDonald pursued more legitimate endeavors as a way of gaining social acceptance for himself and his growing children. His principal backers at the Store were forced to go their own ways. Charles Winship, a quiet, well-mannered chap, carried on the trade for a few more years before opening a livery business on Michigan Avenue. Cliff Dohority saw greater opportunity in the horse tracks and left the "green cloth" trade behind. The nature of public gambling was changing. McDonald meanwhile purchased a lavish brownstone on Ashland Avenue for his wife Mary, down the street from Carter Harrison. But Mary soon became bored in her gilded palace. She took off with an actor named Billy Arlington, but returned to Mike just a few months later, only to bolt the nest for a Catholic priest. Mike, a failure in love, took up with a showgirl named Dora Feldman but she was even less faithful than Mary. Just when it seemed that he had found happiness with a woman half his age, McDonald discovered one day that Dora—one of the Famous "Flora-Dora" Sextet of the 1890s—was carrying on with a 15-year-old boy. Her jealous obsessions for this feckless youth, whom she indulged with money and gifts, drove her half mad.

In a rage she shot and killed the boy, Webster Guerin, on February 21, 1907. Mike McDonald spent his remaining fortune keeping Dora off death row, but in the end it proved to be a terrible strain on the old man. He died on August 9 of that same year, from what many people believed to be a broken heart.[13] With Mike dead, Dora and her three stepsons battled for control of the estate. No one had given a second thought to preserving the memory of McDonald, until the aggrieved parties placed a personal notice in a Chicago evening newspaper to save face with their neighbors on the boulevard.

The undersigned requested the executors to erect a monument to the memory of Michael C. McDonald and wish it understood by his friends that through no fault of theirs it has not been done. Dora, Guy, Cassius, and Harold McDonald.

The West Side Scandals of 1889

With the McDonald syndicate breaking up, organized gambling in Chicago became more decentralized. Instead of one syndicate controlled by a broker who dispensed police protection in exchange for a percentage of the house, the gamblers were free to cut their own deals as they saw fit. By 1889 the remnants of the McDonald trust scattered across the city to establish independently on the

South, West, and North Sides. George Hubbard began his second full year as superintendent in 1889. He presided over the department in one of its most turbulent years. The city annexed the surrounding communities of Lakeview, Hyde Park, Jefferson, and a portion of Cicero. Police jurisdiction stretched across 170 square miles with an additional three new precincts. Appropriations for new stations and additional men to police these areas were slow in coming, leaving Hubbard to wonder how to deploy his reduced forces. Just when the department was at its lowest ebb in the wake of the Haymarket affair, a Democratic newspaper seized the opportunity to launch a startling broadside against Bonfield and Schaak.

Weary of the endless harangues about anarchy in the city, the *Chicago Times* began a month-long probe into allegations that the two police captains used their offices to shield gambling and vice on the North and West Sides. Whatever the paper's true motives, which Schaak considered purely political, the exposé was blunt, revealing, and profound.

Serious charges were leveled at Bonfield and his "Parisian" methods of police work. In the words of Patrick Tyrrell, an esteemed seven-year veteran who infiltrated counterfeit rings and solved some of the decade's most unusual murder cases, "Bonfield has no claims of ability fitting him for the place, only that he is a malicious bigot. There is no record of any important case that he has ever worked up except to hunt ignorant anarchists and create a scare about them."[14]

During the time of the Haymarket trouble Bonfield and Captain William Ward permitted a shady bail bond shark named John Brennan to construct a saloon on police property adjacent to the Des Plaines Street Station. He came to know most of the officers who stopped by for a drink, and familiarized himself with their neighborhood beats. Brennan began a bonding racket that catered to the streetwalkers picked up by the police in their nightly rounds. Brennan was permitted to examine confidential arrest records and to make the rounds of the basement lockup. With notebook in hand he moved from cell to cell asking the women if they had the necessary four dollars to secure bail.[15] He sometimes accepted jewelry or credit from girls who were short on cash. Those who refused to comply with this scheme faced incarceration in the city Bridewell.

On the North Side Schaak used his influence in other ways. Watches, dresses, jewelry, and a silk shawl belonging to the fianceé of one of the Haymarket men were among the items that had been deposited by Schaak at the home of his partner Jake Loewenstein. His residence became a clearing house for impounded merchandise. When the prisoners were released, they were frequently told their property had been lost.[16] Mabel Loewenstein, the estranged wife of the detective, pressed her husband and Schaak for an accounting; she was subsequently placed under arrest. These and other sensational stories about police wrongdoing were spread across the front page of the *Times* for three weeks.

Bonfield ranted, raved, and finally did the only thing befitting a man who felt the noose getting tighter around his neck. He arrested city editor James Dunlop and the newspaper's principal owner James West on a charge of criminal libel.

The two newsmen were locked in a cell at the dingy Harrison Street Station alongside drunks, vagrants, and thieves. Mysteriously, there were no bondsmen to be found, so West and Dunlop remained in their cells all day.

The West Side exposé, the gifts that Bonfield received from certain gamblers and "madames," and the details of the Schaak-Loewenstein fencing ring finally forced the mayor and Chief Hubbard to act against their two old friends. Mayor Roche suspended—but did not remove—the pair from the force. He stated that he believed the evidence did not allow him to make that kind of determination. It would take several more months and the Cronin trial before Bonfield and Schaak were put off the force.

Bonfield severed his formal connections with the Police Department after this affair, but was called back to head a special detail to maintain order at the 1893 World's Fair. Later he formed his own private detective force, but a business failure threw the company into bankruptcy. Schaak remained flamboyant to the end. During another Republican administration he was able to secure reappointment to the force, with an official correction of the record entered after his name. Schaak had beaten the blasphemous reporters after all. The two men died five months apart in 1898. Several months before he passed away, Schaak declared that he had a premonition of his death. He turned over all of his files to a subordinate and returned to his home to await his death.[17] It came on May 18.

The *Chicago Times* eulogized both men as credits to their city and the Police Department. Their work on the Haymarket case was discussed only in the most glowing terms, with no mention of the events of 1889, which the paper had played up when it was still a Democratic organ. There was a very good reason for this. Within a year of Schaak's suspension, James West was forced to sell the *Times*. He had been found guilty of the felonious over-issue of 1,250 shares of company stock and was off to jail to begin serving a five-year sentence. His partner Joseph Dunlop founded the *Chicago Dispatch*, which prefaced the gospel of free silver and Bryanism in the 1890s. Dunlop made an enemy of many powerful men in Chicago. When he crossed the line of propriety in the kind of advertising he ran in his sheet, Herman H. Kohlsaat and others had him jailed for two years as a smut merchant. Not even Dunlop's friend Potter Palmer could save him. What happened to these two editors illustrates a fundamental principle of newspaper reformers: Throw the rascals out of office, but first make sure they work for the other guy's party.

Racetracks, Handbooks, Poolrooms, and the Police

The traditional games of the riverboat gambler—stud poker, faro, and craps—were eclipsed in popularity by horse racing as the century drew to a close. Since the end of the Civil War, the newspapers had provided information to their readers about the horses, trainers, and racing moguls. Important East Coast gamblers like John Morrissey took an active interest in the sport. In Chicago Mike McDonald was the principal owner of the Garfield Track. His backers included "Blind" John Condon and "Prince" Hal Varnell, one of the indicted county commissioners in the 1887 McGarigle-boodle Case. By 1905 there were only 30 tracks open in the United States but these were controlled by four competing associations: the Jockey Club, the Western Jockey Club, the Pacific Coast Jockey Club, and the American Turf Association. Within these associations were the race tracks, which fiercely competed with each other for choice dates and the City Hall protection so necessary for their survival. These associations worked to keep the sport "clean" in the public's eyes. However, presence of bookmakers at the tracks was not only permitted, but encouraged by the owners as a continuing source of illegal revenue.[18] Total attendance at the various tracks numbered six million by 1905, with an additional return on investment to the bookmakers of $15,500,000.[19]

The astonishing popularity of horse racing in the last quarter of the nineteenth century is due to several important factors. Betting at the tracks was legal, and handicapping a pony offered a greater chance of a payoff than faro. Society placed its stamp of approval on the "sport of kings" by turning out for Derby Day, an annual event at Chicago's Washington Park that attracted some of the city's most prominent citizens.

Technological advances allowed gambling patrons to place their wagers at betting parlors, thanks to the telegraph line that connected all the major tracks in the country to a central switchboard. The racing "wire" was developed by the Ditmus Company of New York, but in 1899 Western Union offered more competitive rates for providing the hookup to the poolrooms—which were often the back rooms of a cigar store or saloon.

The new breed of gambler was less ostentatious than McDonald or Jack Haverly. He was often content to run his string of poolrooms within the narrowly defined boundaries of his ward, at least until his territoriality was threatened by interlopers. The political allegiance of the emerging gamblers like Jim O'Leary and Mont Tennes was dependent on the relative strength of the local ward organization or their valuable links to a powerful police official like Nicholas Hunt.

Jim O'Leary was a rising star in the Chicago underworld of 1900. He was the son of Catherine O'Leary, who was forced to raise her shirt-tail brood in the squalid section of the town of Lake. The family lived a day-to-day existence on South Wallace Street after Catherine's Chicago neighbors drove her from the family's South Side home. Her cow had allegedly kicked over the lantern that started the Chicago Fire. The O'Learys were social pariahs, and the boys did little to change this image. Her brawling, hard-drinking son Con "Puggy" O'Leary murdered a woman, and wounded his own sister on a South Side prairie one night when they refused to give him a dollar to buy a pail of beer.[20]

Jim O'Leary was less prone to violence, and he carved his niche by getting to know the "right" people in the Stockyards District. In the early days of his career he opened a lavish saloon and bowling alley across the street from the transit house of the Union Stockyards. His income was derived from the western cattlemen who delivered their stock to Chicago, and then stopped by O'Learys for entertainment. Like so many other gamblers of the day, Jim O'Leary eliminated dice and cards in favor of the quickest payoff from the racing wire services provided by John Payne.

After Western Union was barred from the race tracks in 1904, Payne organized the National News Company and Interstate News Company to dispense race results by leasing long-distance phone wires from American Telephone and Telegraph. He then sold this service to local gambling interests such as Mont Tennes, whose switchboard in Forest Park funneled race results to 200 poolrooms and handbooks in the city. The handbook, though certainly not indigenous to Chicago, enjoyed a popularity there unrivaled by New York, perhaps due to the determination of Mont Tennes to establish himself as the rightful heir to the McDonald throne. While this never came to be, Tennes was the largest operator of the handbook—or traveling poolroom—in the city. As Josiah Flynt observed, "To play the ponies in a poolroom you have to go to the room. To play the ponies in a handbook, the handbook comes to you."[21] Tennes subscribed to this theory and soon found himself the king of the North Side handbook.

After he covered the entire North Side with an army of handbook men, Tennes bought the Payne service for the purpose of supplying his poolrooms with information about odds, scratches, and race results. Not content with being a mere client, he had ambitions of becoming Chicago's sole provider. He waged a war of intimidation against the Payne Company in 1911, prompting one company official to complain that "we are fighting Tennes fairly but he insists on having the whole thing and seems to want a renewal of the gambling war."[22]

From time to time there were sporadic outbreaks of warfare between three rival groups. In 1902 the first of these wars broke out when O'Leary violated an agreement reached in 1901 which decreed that the respective syndicates would not attempt to gain an upper hand at the racetracks. O'Leary stood alone against two powerful gambling combines operating within the city at this time. Charles "Social" Smith and Harry Perry were former "policy" men who plied their trade at carnivals and agricultural shows before making the big time. Later they forged an alliance with "Bud" White, owner and operator of the floating poolroom known as the *City of Traverse*.

Tennes aligned himself with Aldermen Kenna and Coughlan of the 1st Ward, who looked out for the interests of John Condon and Tom McGinnis. O'Leary's clout came from the office of Nicholas Hunt, and Captain William Clancy, commander of the Hyde Park Station. Clancy's daughter Gertrude later eloped with James Patrick O'Leary, Jr.[23]

On May 30, 1902, arsonists torched the grandstand of the Hawthorne Park Racetrack at which the Smith-Perry combination operated a handbook. The finger was pointed at O'Leary, who had his own money tied into a track located in Roby, Indiana. A year later, agents of O'Leary set fire to a can of oil underneath the stands at Washington Park. While the gamblers doused the flames, Nicholas Hunt stood idly by, unwilling to put a stop to the destruction.[24]

During the racetrack war of 1902–3 the Smith-Perry forces had at their beck and call the Chicago Constabulary, a private policing agency headed up by Dickie Dean and John Ryan, frontier shell workers and con men once employed by Mike McDonald. Ryan's constabulary used axes and shotguns to batter down the gambling dens of Tennes, O'Leary, and the independents not belonging to the "trust." The constables drove spikes into lead-sheathed cables carrying telephone wires to the poolrooms and thousands of other, more legitimate, customers of Chicago Telephone.[25] The company threatened Tennes with a cut-off if the raids were not stopped. As events escalated, the *Chicago Daily News* took the mayor and the chief to task for permitting a lawless band of hired detectives to do their job.

The trust gamblers call out the police one day. The anti-trust gamblers call out the police another day. There is no attempt on either side to disguise the fact that it is a fight to determine which set of gamblers control the city, or that part of the city which may be controlled by the influences that do not always make for food. Our Mayor [Harrison] is in Yellowstone. Our chief-of-police [O'Neill] is composing melodies; all the rest of them are afraid to move lest they move the wrong way. And so the gamblers are compelled to settle the matter between themselves.[26]

The Smith-Perry trust was the ultimate loser of the gambling wars. The Chicago Constabulary was legislated out of existence in 1906. In a final effort to gain city wide influence over the handbooks and poolrooms, agents of the combine tossed 40 dynamite bombs into the storefronts and private residences of the Tennes and O'Leary syndicates. Tennes, Condon, O'Leary, Alderman John Rogers, and Pat O'Malley saw their property destroyed, but remarkably, not one life was lost. Murder was never considered a solution to the problem in those days. The bombs were planted in the buildings during the late evening hours, or when they were thought to be deserted. The police had all kinds of theories, but as usual, none of them had any credence. Herman Schluetter thought it was the work of the Black Hand, hired by former employees of the *City of Traverse*.[27] A grand jury investigated the matter but the gamblers maintained a wall of silence.

Hostilities eventually ceased, but only after a pre-election deal had been struck between Tennes, the Democratic organization in the 1st Ward, and the Republican mayoral candidate Fred Busse. In return for 12,000 votes Busse agreed to four conditions:

1. The license of Bud White's boat, the *City of Traverse*, would be permanently revoked.
2. Aldermen Kenna and Coughlan would be allowed a free hand in the 1st Ward without Republican interference.
3. Inspector Hunt and Captain Lavin, who were acceptable to the gamblers, would have their suspensions lifted.
4. A "business as usual" approach—minus Smith-Perry—would continue under Busse.[28]

Busse was elected. Hunt and Lavin were returned to their old districts, and the *City of Traverse* was put out of business on July 10, 1907. The boat was sold to the Graham and Morton Line, which used it for lake Michigan excursions.

The Police Response

The poolroom and the handbook were vigorously suppressed for a time by Herman Schluetter's "flying squadron," composed of an elite group of detectives not unlike the special detail assigned to smoke out anarchists during the Haymarket troubles. The flying squad's jurisdiction extended across the city, so it was relatively free of the coercive tactics of a local alderman or politically connected gambler. Without this parasitic relationship between politician and gambler, the squadron diligently closed down some of the largest handbooks in the city, including Mont Tennes's "clearing house" at 823 Larrabee Street. Schluetter's men scaled a telephone pole and broke through the windows to smash the switchboard and scratch sheets spread across the tables. One newspaper even published the phone number of Mrs. Herman Schluetter, inviting gambling "widows" to call with their stories about the evils of wagering.[29]

With imagination and daring Schluetter's men used various disguises and gimmicks to infiltrate the gambler's lair. Once, the gambling detail uncovered a crap game inside a closed bank vault. When the occupants refused to surrender to police, Schluetter sprinkled red pepper under the crack of the door. In a few minutes a horde of choking, wheezing gamblers stumbled out of the vault and into the paddy wagon.

Schluetter's good intentions were often at odds with the interests of the city administration. Sensitive to divided opinion about gambling, Mayor Carter Harrison took a neutral stance. In a 1904 speech he warned reformers of the consequences of enforcing an unpopular blue law: "Now, if your reformers want the same kind of thing, all you have to do is insist on a return to the blue-law regime which preceded the Colvin administration."[30] Harrison was a pragmatist. He understood it was folly to try to close down every Chicago handbook or dancehall, but privately he counted on the warm support of the gamblers.

In the South Side 7th Ward, 36 handbooks were running wide open. They were controlled from the saloon of Edward Brennan, Democratic committee member and local organizer for the campaign to reelect Harrison. Brennan saw to it that Jim O'Leary's suspended liquor license was restored by the mayor with the understanding that $40,000 would be funneled into the preelection war chest by the O'Leary faction. Everybody came out ahead because the mayor and O'Leary were reconciled, and Brennan was assured that Nick Hunt's raiding party would not be making any unannounced visits.[31]

After the election Schluetter's duties were "rearranged." The men detailed to the gambling squad were sent back to their precincts, with responsibility for existing conditions returned to the police inspectors. Said Schluetter: "I cannot cover the whole city. It is the duty of the patrolmen on the beat to report gambling

Figure 6

When Herman Schluetter is on the job, the gamblers flee the city (lower box), but with John McWeeney on the trail (top), the "Gambling Crusade" is more illusion than reality, 1911. (Deckert/McCutcheon)

places and the duty of the commanding officers to see the offenders prosecuted."[32] Of course, this was never done willingly. "Hello there, what's become of your raiding brigade?" chuckled Mont Tennes over the phone wire one afternoon.[33]

When the flying squad was reorganized and permitted to carry out its duty without official interference, the sporting fraternity was compelled to seek alternative arrangements. In 1906 the *City of Traverse* sailed into Indiana waters when conditions became unfavorable within the city limits. A "Gambler's Special" run by the Lake Shore Railroad conveyed the nervous sportsmen directly to the South Chicago pier. Sometimes these men disguised themselves as fisherman to avoid the watchful eyes of the gambling squad covering the train station. A year later, when the detail disbanded again, total gambling arrests dropped from 5,603 to 1,561.[34]

The effectiveness of the special squad illustrated the clear need for a separate branch of police to handle gambling and vice matters. There was little, if any, chance for this to become a reality during the Busse administration (1907–11). For superintendent, the mayor chose Inspector George Shippy, a second-generation policeman who earned his stripes guarding the private residence of State's Attorney Julius Grinnell during the Haymarket affair. " I will not tolerate open gambling in Chicago," Chief Shippy vowed. "I will lock up every capper I can find."[35] These were fighting words, no doubt, but there was a hollow ring to them when Shippy refused to reactivate the flying squad. " I do not intend to have my men climb on roofs and cut telephone wires," he added.

Attention was soon diverted from the worsening gambling conditions in a new effort to purge Chicago of its anarchists following an attempt on the chief's life on March 1, 1908. A young Russian Jew named Lazarus Averbuch followed Shippy's carriage to his North Side home. As Shippy entered his residence he was accosted by Averbuch who shoved a blank envelope into his hand. Sensing some danger here, the chief lunged at the man. Shippy's son tried to intervene but Averbuch's pistol discharged into his chest. The anarchist was shot five times by Shippy, and twice more by his son. This was the first time in police history that anyone had attempted such a desperate act. Emma Goldman was among the 300 suspects brought in for questioning as the police tried to piece together evidence that this was part of a far-flung conspiracy to assassinate the city's top leaders.[36] It turned out that there was no plot after all. Averbuch was a member of small group of anti-Catholic extremists that had its origins in Denver. It was an isolated act of a madman, and disappointing to the police, who received their most favorable press during times like this. The dead man was buried in Potter's Field against the objections of his sister. Later, with the help of Jane Addams the body was finally relocated to the Bohemian Cemetery on the Northwest Side.

As a result of the "shot heard 'round the city" Shippy took an extended medical leave. His doctors advised him to get away from it all for a while. He chose instead to try to recover in northern Michigan. When there was no immediate improvement, Shippy resigned on August 5, 1909. The various rest cures did not work, for the chief suffered from the ravages of unchecked syphilis. He was adjudged insane by a team of doctors and carried away in a straightjacket to a private institution in Kankakee. He died a week later from a condition that the press described as a "brain disorder."[37]

The Nature of Police Corruption

Lazarus Averbuch lived on the near West Side, teeming with poor Russian Jews by day, but at night a saturnalia of vice and crime. Cocaine addicts with miserable blank stares shuffled in and out of Adolph Brendecke's drugstone on Sangamon Street for their daily fix, issued discreetly under the counter for 25 cents a bag.[38] Between Morgan and Green Streets Mike "de Pike" Heitler ran a white slave racket under the watchful eyes of Inspector Edward McCann, a bull-necked, rough-hewn policeman whose greatest joy was playing cribbage in the back room of the Des Plaines Street Station.[39] A small gold cross was affixed to the front of his vest, for McCann was a man of God who tried to instill in his nine children the Christian virtues. "I'd say I was glad to be suspended and have a chance to stay at home and play with the kids," he said in reply to State's Attorney John Wayman, whose unrelenting crusade uncovered the truth about McCann.[40]

For months McCann exacted tribute from the highest gambler bosses to the lowliest streetwalker. Protection money was delivered in a leather satchel in accordance with instructions given to Louis and Julius Frank, two of Heitler's men. The price of doing business on the West Side in 1909 rose to $550 a month, a sum that the criminal panders finally refused to pay. With his money McCann purchased a stable of prized race horses. "If I had been grafting I wouldn't have driven so many people out of business," he said, failing to add that only the rebellious elements who refused to pay up were banished from the district.

McCann was indicted by a grand jury, convicted, and sent to the Joliet Penitentiary on September 24, 1909. It was one of the hardest-fought cases in the court system up to that time. Wayman based his case on the testimony of West Side underworld figures, which raised some doubts about McCann's guilt or innocence. After the prison doors slammed shut the friends of the inspector circulated a petition urging the governor to grant executive clemency. Thirty-thousand people, including church leaders, settlement workers, businessmen, and former President Theodore Roosevelt, who had served for a time as police commissioner of New York, affixed their signatures to the document. Colonel Roosevelt cited McCann's sterling record *before* he was sent to the West Side as a reason for an official pardon.

Indeed, the scorecard, at least on the surface, showed more hits than misses. Since taking over as inspector of the West Side District in March 1908, McCann was credited with abolishing dozens of immoral houses, the return of 200 errant girls to their parents, curtailment of the cocaine traffic, enforcement of the 1:00

AM closing, and the regulation of concert halls and the five-cent theaters that screened lewd and suggestive movies. Social worker at Hull House lauded McCann for his efforts, and municipal judges, juvenile officers, and church officials marveled at the clean-up of the Des Plaines District.

"Don't give me all the credit for the work," McCann protested. "It's the men. They know I'm behind them and they do the work. I'm behind them because I know the right men are behind me. I will say this: the day of the man with the pull has passed at this station. I'm not allowing poor ignorant foreigners to be robbed by grafters who say they have a pull." McCann, like so many other powerful police officials, was able to pick and choose his partners in the vice club. When the indictments were handed down and the inspector went off to jail, there were hundreds of city officials and church reformers who chose not to believe that such a fine man could be guilty as charged. Thus, with an eye toward saving McCann's police pension, Governor Charles Deneen commuted the sentence just 30 days before his retirement benefits were scheduled to expire.[41] The Republican state's attorney had sent to prison a man of his own party, an uncommon event in those partisan days. He was roundly criticized from all quarters, while McCann was perceived to be a hero who had been railroaded by an ambitious politician. It was a disturbing setback for the reformers, who counted on the elected officials to uphold the will of the court system and punish wrong-doers.

With greater power vested in the district inspectors, two predictable forms of police corruption surfaced: arrangements and events. The illicit money and gifts that McCann received over a period of months was an ongoing arrangement. The short-term, single acts of corruption, such as the one-time payoff given to 15 officers assigned to Comiskey Park on Labor Day, 1911, can be thought of as an event.

Eyewitnesses charged the police with accepting $50 bribes from a gang of sidewalk bookies betting on the Gotch-Hackenschmidt wrestling match inside the ballpark. In both instances, external factors stimulated the detection and punishment since the police, either through their own inertia or because of direct influence from the chief, seemed unwilling to initiate an internal investigation.

These two unrelated incidents of police malfeasance suggest that the department could not satisfactorily manage its own affairs unless the proper internal controls were in place. In direct contrast to the police, the Chicago Fire Department remained relatively free of scandal from the time the City Council took the budgetary responsibility away from the Police Commission in 1874 until 1903, when a Civil Service probe revealed some illegal hiring practices. From 1879 until his retirement in 1901, the Fire Department was run by Chief Denis Swenie, a blunt, hard-working administrator who feared no political reprisals. The firefighters were, in the words of Mayor Harrison, "Denny's boys."[42] One reason Swenie was able to maintain the department on a stable, efficient basis was his ambitious plan to create a unit within the rank-and-file to guard against corruption. In 1880 the Department of Inspection was organized and Chicago profited from an honest, capable Fire Department.[43] Not until 1960 and the reform superintendency of Orlando W. Wilson was such a mechanism put in place in the Police Department. Without these necessary controls the police of the late nineteenth century and early twentieth century were essentially reactive in their response to a public outcry.

In a tongue-in-cheek article the *Chicago Tribune* outlined for its readers the painful details of the "Chronology of a Comedy."[44]

1. A few individual citizens complain of a certain abuse to their nearest precinct station.
2. The police tell the citizens to mind their own business and not to be so ready to overburden an already overworked department.
3. Citizens write to newspapers.
4. Police begin to sit up and take notice.
5. Mayor Harrison is interviewed.
6. Chief O'Neill becomes talkative on the subject.
7. Police show many signs of life.
8. Inspectors, captains, and lieutenants begin to talk and promise to do things.
9. Police, spurred to activity, make many arrests. The story is printed on the first page of the newspaper.
10. "Something doing every minute" is the screaming farce. The "great awakening" of the official conscience of the city of Chicago.
11. Police watch the papers carefully.
12. Then some big news event crowds the crusade off page one.
13. Fewer arrests are made.
14. Crusade retreats to the back part of the paper.
15. Requiescat in peace.

This sequence of events, written in 1904, could apply to any major police investigation over a period of 75 years: agitation, followed by a period of reform, and then a return to pre-scandal levels of corruption. Following the 1911 wrestling match and the flagrant way in which the gamblers flaunted the police, Mayor Harrison appointed three Civil Service commissioners to begin a six-month investigation into the department, focusing on charges that there was collusion between the sporting fraternity and the police. "There have been so many rumors and charges circulated, that I have decided they should be investigated," Harrison said.[45] The mayor was a foe of Civil Service, and he may have had an ulterior motive in calling for an investigation. "Every commanding officer with one exception is under the merit system," he said, "and it would be perfectly proper for the Commission to investigate." He was perhaps looking to see if the Commission had arrived at the same conclusion he had formed years earlier, that Civil Service had not improved the efficiency of the department or its ability to police gambling.

The Commission conducted a three-month probe into alleged police connections to organized gambling, concluding:

- that there is, and for years has been, a connection between the Police Department and the various criminal classes in the city of Chicago
- that a bipartisan political combination or ring exists, by and through which the connection between the Police Department and the criminal classes referred to above is fostered and maintained
- that to such connections may be charged a great part of the inefficiency, disorganization, and lack of discipline existing in the department
- that aside from such connections, inefficiency also arises through faults of organization and administration
- that the Police Department as now numerically constituted can enforce any reasonable regulation in regard to gambling, crime, and other form of vice, if honestly and efficiently administered, as well as perform all other routine police duty[46]

The 1911 Civil Service Report, like all other police investigations, stated the obvious. The men were still drinking in saloons while on duty, though one area of improvement noted by the Commission was the creditable appearance of the uniformed personnel.

Regarding gambling, there was personal jealousy and antagonism toward the Schluetter gambling squad. Any special assignment of this sort invariably led to suspicion and jealousy by those who were not a part of the inner circle. But in the case of the "flying squad," gamblers were frequently provided notice in advance of its arrival.[47]

Protection money was paid to the inspector, captain, or local politician based on the number of "tables" in play. Generally, this fee was $50. Each game had four to six "boosters," known in the trade as "cappers." They received $5.00 a day. One or more games had a collector or outside man who received the money won by the cappers. This person returned the money to the gamekeeper.[48]

The gamblers showed amazing determination to keep the game going, even when the "lid" was officially on. A typical gambling nest at 68 W. Chicago Avenue was first raided September 27, 1911, but all the players escaped. They moved the game from the lower floor to the upper floor, but were driven out. Next, they moved into a flat on Rush Street. Following another raid, operations were shifted to a barn fronting the alley, then back to the original base of operations, and finally to a location at 1013 Dearborn.[49] Part of the problem in closing down a handbook of this sort was the policeman's own attitude concerning gambling. A man born in the city slums who received only a grade-school education probably did not share the same moralistic views about wagering as a clergyman or Gold Coast reformer. The perception of the seriousness of the crime was frequently a determinant in the police response. An assassination attempt on the chief or the murder of a patrolman elicited a much stronger feeling in the station house than a traveling handbook.

The reorganization of the department was a consequence of the Civil Service Commission's final report. Policing authority was divided between three deputy commissioners but, regrettably, the gambling squad was taken away from Schluetter and assigned to William Schubert, an intimate of Mont Tennes. Responsibility for moral issues such as prostitution and movie censorship was given over to the civilian deputy, who was to report vice conditions directly to the chief (Figure 7). The idea was to separate the crime-fighting organization from the more delicate vice issues. Traditionally, vice and gambling squads carried the greatest potential for graft.

Chief John McWeeney summed up the prevailing attitude toward civilian meddling in police work as a "big joke": "What does the smartest judge or lawyer know about police work? Think of putting a civilian in to run coppers! This is just what you would expect from a bunch of wise guys."[50] However, McWeeney was grossly ignorant of the true conditions. He told the Civil Service commissioners that there existed a card index in each station house listing the names and addresses of all streetwalkers in the precinct. Thirty-six lieutenants were called forward, but only one man knew of the existence of such a file.[51] Reports crossing his desk from the divisional inspectors were inaccurate and certainly unverified. The revised Book of Rules, published in O'Neill's time, required the inspector to visit the stations once a week. When asked about this, one inspector proudly recalled that he had been out to see his captains once or twice in the previous three months.

Metellius L. C. Funkhouser, a former major in the Illinois National Guard, was appointed second deputy on March 13, 1913. He issued seven controversial reports between January and October 1913 that described ten police precincts as being "wide open."[52] In defense of his inaction McWeeney drafted a strongly worded letter to the mayor citing his years of valuable frontline experience in such matters, and protesting that no morals squad had the right to tell him how to control vice. John McWeeney was a man of the streets. He owned a saloon, and he enjoyed the support of "Hot Stove" Jimmy Quinn in the North Side wards.

Mayor Harrison, whose tolerance of gambling and vice was slowly ebbing, decided to vest greater control in Funkhouser's office by assigning five policemen to him with full arresting powers. Without a vote of confidence from the mayor, McWeeney had no recourse but to step down. He submitted his formal resignation on October 24, to be replaced by James Gleason, who took a more conciliatory view of the morals squad.

During the waning years of the Harrison administration (1913–14), gambling conditions stabilized across the city because Mont Tennes consolidated his holdings at the expense of his rivals. John Condon passed away in 1915. Jim O'Leary turned to other business interests, and the Smith-Perry combination faded from view. The number of Tennes handbooks increased significantly once Bill Schubert was installed as head of the gambling squad. Schubert had failed a Civil Service exam, and tipped the scales at an unacceptable weight, but he "had it

Figure 7
1911 Plan of Reorganization

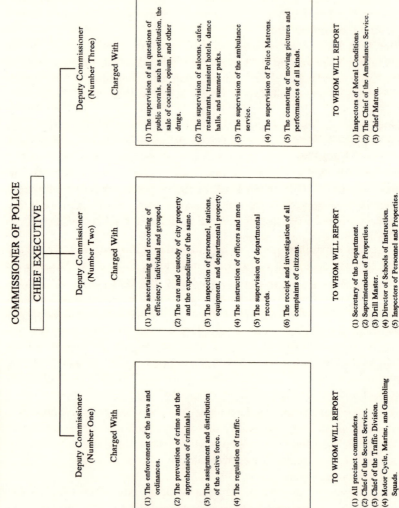

COMMISSIONER OF POLICE

CHIEF EXECUTIVE

Deputy Commissioner (Number One)

Charged With

(1) The enforcement of the laws and ordinances.
(2) The prevention of crime and the apprehension of criminals.
(3) The assignment and distribution of the active force.
(4) The regulation of traffic.

TO WHOM WILL REPORT

(1) All precinct commanders.
(2) Chief of the Secret Service.
(3) Chief of the Traffic Division.
(4) Motor Cycle, Marine, and Gambling Squads.

Deputy Commissioner (Number Two)

Charged With

(1) The ascertaining and recording of efficiency, individual and grouped.
(2) The care and custody of city property and the expenditure of the same.
(3) The inspection of personnel, stations, equipment, and departmental property.
(4) The instruction of officers and men.
(5) The supervision of departmental records.
(6) The receipt and investigation of all complaints of citizens.

TO WHOM WILL REPORT

(1) Secretary of the Department.
(2) Superintendent of Properties.
(3) Drill Master.
(4) Director of Schools of Instruction.
(5) Inspectors of Personnel and Properties.

Deputy Commissioner (Number Three)

Charged With

(1) The supervision of all questions of public morals, such as prostitution, the sale of cocaine, opium, and other drugs.
(2) The supervision of saloons, cafes, restaurants, transient hotels, dance halls, and summer parks.
(3) The supervision of the ambulance service.
(4) The supervision of Police Matrons.
(5) The censoring of moving pictures and performances of all kinds.

TO WHOM WILL REPORT

(1) Inspectors of Moral Conditions.
(2) The Chief of the Ambulance Service.
(3) Chief Matron.

Source: Final Report: Police Investigation. An Inquiry Conducted by the Authority of His Honor, Carter Harrison, Mayor, September 5, 1911 to March 7, 1912.

in right" with Carter Harrison after raiding the gambling strongholds of Roger Sullivan and Billy Skidmore, two City Hall opponents.

Gambling would never be alleviated, of course. In time, it would come under the control of a more ruthless crime syndicate less concerned about human life than the "Mustache Petes" of 1907. But as the first decade of the twentieth century came to a close, there was some optimism that the police were at least beginning to put their house in order. Significant reforms in the criminal court system helped break the power of the bail-bonding rackets that had flourished near Central Headquarters and the outlying precinct stations. Before 1906, locally selected police justices handled most of the routine cases brought before them, including gambling and prostitution. Police justice appointees were usually ward healers who extended a wink and a nod to the handbook and policy kings that appeared before them. They were particularly good at circumventing the law. A policeman's own ignorance of the city statutes, or claims of entrapment, were frequently cited as reason for releasing a gambler from jurisdiction. The bail-bonding racket in which the justice, the bondsman, and the street cop divided up the money was curtailed in 1906, when Chicago became one of the first cities in the country to adopt the municipal court system for both criminal and civil cases.[53] This unified court system required appointees to be licensed attorneys with a minimum of six years' experience.

LeRoy Steward, former postmaster of Chicago, replaced George Shippy as superintendent in 1909. Fair-minded and honest, Steward reduced the workload of the patrolmen by introducing the eight-hour day in August 1909. He opened the first formal police training academy in October 1910 at the Shakespeare Station. Men were drilled in license law, traffic and health rules, and the departmental regulations. "We are going to inculate in the minds of the police a new sentiment with reference to their duties," Steward said. "It is a fact that the making of an arrest is a small part of the average patrolman's duties. We wish to avoid making an arrest if the peace can be conserved by intelligent handling of a situation by the patrolman on the beat."[54] Steward represented a glimmer of hope in a city oblivious to the broad social changes of the Progressive Era. But unfortunately, that's all it was—a glimmer.

Notes

1. Charles Winslow, *Biographical Sketches of Famous Chicagoans*, vol. 4 (unpublished, Chicago Public Library Collection), p. 1587. *Chicago Journal*, August 8, 1907.

2. *Chicago Tribune*, October 16, 1875.

3. Ibid., August 1, 1875.

4. Richard C. Lindberg, *Chicago Ragtime: Another Look at Chicago 1880–1920* (South Bend: Icarus Press, 1985), p. 51. *Chicago Tribune*, April 18, 1882.

5. Ibid. McDonald testified in court that he ended his connections with the gentlemen of the green cloth in 1873 or 1874, when he severed his dealings with Harry Lawrence and Morris Martin. While his battery of crack defense attorneys (including Alfred S. Trude) looked on, McDonald listed his place of business at 176 Clark Street—the Store.

It was known to all as M. C. McDonald & Co. Until December 10, 1881, he resided on the third floor of this establishment with his wife and children. The adjoining rooms were rented to transients. In March 1882, he moved his family into a spacious brownstone on the corner of Ashland and Harrison—not far from the mayor.

6. Ibid., December 31, 1881.

7. Ibid. See the accounts of futile gambling raids conducted by Elmer Washburn on December 1, 1872. Bags of checks, bushels of cards, and dealing boxes were carried out to the street by police but the gamblers had fled the premises minutes before the squad arrived.

8. Ibid., April 3, 1879.

9. Ibid. A socialist candidate named Ernest Schmidt received 11,829 votes. It is doubtful that these extra votes would have affected the Wright campaign. The elder Harrison's widest victory margin in his various mayoral races was 11,000 votes over Eugene Cary in 1883. See Claudius Johnson, *Carter Harrison I: Political Leader* (Chicago: University of Chicago Press, 1928), p. 288.

10. *Chicago Tribune*, April 18, 1882. Mark Haller, "Historical Roots of Police Misbehavior in Chicago," *Law and Society Review* (Winter 1976): 308–10. Police justices received a salary from the city and remitted the fines they imposed on gamblers and prostitutes to the city treasury. However, if a justice was assigned to a night court he was allowed to keep a portion of the fees as compensation for working the late evening hours. This encouraged the police to conduct nighttime raids in the red-light districts. The bail bond money from a mass arrest could net everyone a tidy profit.

11. *Chicago Tribune*, November 16, 1882.

12. Michael Funchion, *Chicago's Irish Nationalists: 1881–1890* (New York: Arno Press, 1976), p. 49.

13. Lindberg, *Chicago Ragtime*, p. 73. Dora received one-third of McDonald's two million dollar estate. The balance went to charity and the local hospital.

14. *Chicago Times*, January 8, 1889. Tyrrell was reduced to the rank of ordinary patrolman and ordered to walk a beat in the "terror district"—Simon O'Donnell's 12th Street Precinct—after embarrassing Bonfield during a burglary investigation.

15. Ibid., January 6, 1889. A one-time member of the city police force, Brennan worked as a house detective at the Grand Pacific Hotel, earning $50 a month. The *Daily News* first investigated Brennan's bonding racket in September 1885, but nothing came of it.

16. Ibid., January 4, 1889.

17. See the Schaak obituary, *Times-Herald*, May 19, 1898.

18. Josiah Flynt, "The Poolroom Vampire," *Cosmopolitan Magazine* (February 1907): 368–69. The racing associations circulated a black list preventing an owner, jockey, trainer, or horse who had been barred from one member track from running in another. "Why," exclaimed one racing man, "they have to keep the public believing that racing is on the square. If they didn't have these rules and regulations there would be all kinds of crooked work and the suckers would get tired of going against the knife."

19. Ibid.

20. *Chicago Tribune*, August 24, 1885. On her deathbed Mary O'Leary Scully refused to divulge the whereabouts of the assassin—her brother—to the police.

21. Flynt, "Poolroom Vampire," p. 371.

22. Lindberg, *Chicago Ragtime*, p. 180.

23. Richard Griffin, "Big Jim O'Leary: Gambler Boss 'iv th' Yards," *Chicago History*

(Winter 1976–77): 214. Also, Josiah Flynt, "The Men Behind the Poolrooms," *Cosmopolitan Magazine* (May 1907): 643. According to this account a certain justice of the peace in the Stockyards Court would occasionally place a bet at O'Leary's place. When the pony won, O'Leary refused to cash the ticket because he said it did not reach him before the post. The next day several of Nick Hunt's men raided the place and arrested everyone in sight. A raid of this nature was little more than an irritation to O'Leary, who once employed a press agent to "work" the Chicago papers.

24. Lindberg, *Chicago Ragtime*, p. 180.

25. Flynt, "The Men Behind the Poolrooms," p. 647. Ryan was originally a house burglar before he joined "the wrong arm of the law." He organized the Cook County Constables into a business partnership, serving the gambling trust with alacrity.

26. *Chicago Daily News*, August 30, 1903.

27. Lindberg, *Chicago Ragtime*, p. 192. A pair of dynamiters named Elihu Rosencranz and Ed Kelly were arrested on September 7, 1907, but the evidence against them was purely circumstantial. Kelly escaped the police by slipping a revolver out of one of their holsters at the Armory.

28. Charles Edward Russell, "Chaos and Bomb Throwing in Chicago," *Hampton's Magazine* (March 1910): 307–20.

29. The Herman Schluetter scrapbooks at the Chicago Historical Society contain hundreds of newspaper accounts of gambling squad raids from 1903 until 1908.

30. *Chicago Tribune*, March 29, 1904.

31. Ibid., May 4, 1904. Harrison went so far as to permit Brennan to situate a polling place in a well-known Madison Street cigar store with a handbook attached to the rear of the building.

32. Ibid., July 24, 1905.

33. John Landesco, *Organized Crime: Part Three of the Illinois Crime Survey* (Chicago: University of Chicago Press, 1929), p. 56. In that same year, 1905, Chief O'Neill optimistically reported that the "aggressive and persistent warfare raged against gambling has reduced that fascinating form of law breaking to a minimum. Iron doors and fire proof vaults proved no barrier to muscular officers armed with crow-bars and hammers"; *Report of the General Superintendent to the City Council* (1905), p. 26.

34. *Report of the General Superintendent to the City Council* (1908), p. 10.

35. Four years earlier Chief John Collins told reporters the same thing upon assuming office: "Gambling in this town has been a disgrace. Men are waylaid on their way home from work and solicited by barkers and touts. We can drive every damned one of them out of Chicago." See the *Tribune*, July 28, 1905.

36. *Chicago Daily Journal*, March 1, 1908. Averbuch's motive was apparently revenge. Earlier in the week Shippy denied Emma Goldman permission to address a meeting of Averbuch's antic-clerical society. The police believed that Averbuch drew the "lot" to kill Shippy and that the mayor and the chief of detectives were next on the list.

37. See the Shippy obituary, April 14, 1913, *Chicago Tribune*.

38. Honest McCann or foxy McCann? The *Tribune* could not decide; See issue of August 1, 1909.

39. Ibid.

40. Ibid.

41. Ibid., May 4, 1911.

42. Carter Harrison, *The Stormy Years* (New York: Bobbs-Merrill, 1935), p. 109.

43. Perry Duis, "The World's Greatest Fireman," *Chicago Magazine* 4 (May 1978):

p. 230. Lawrence Sherman, *Scandal and Reform* (Berkeley: University of California Press, 1978), pp. 42–44, 254–55. Sherman identifies "arrangements and events" as the two predictable forms of police corruption, each occurring at regular intervals. They differ only in the sense that internal detection by the police is more effective in the long run than an outside agency in uncovering the evidence after the fact.

44. *Chicago Tribune*, March 24, 1904. The "Chronology of a Comedy" followed up on the police efforts to enforce the anti-spitting ordinance.

45. Ibid., September 6, 1911.

46. *Final Report of the Police Investigation: An Inquiry Conducted by Authority of His Honor the Mayor*. Details of the Vice Investigation, Departmental Analysis, Reorganization Plan, Conclusions, and Recommendations, p. 42.

47. Ibid., p. 11.

48. Ibid., p. 12.

49. Ibid., p. 9.

50. *Chicago Tribune*, October 24, 1913.

51. Lindberg, *Chicago Ragtime*, p. 145. McWeeney was part-owner of a downtown saloon called the Delaware. Also, Final Report of the Police Investigation, p. 14.

52. *Chicago Tribune*, October 10, 1913.

53. *Report of the General Superintendent to the City Council (1906)*, p. 6. The Municipal Court System went into effect in Chicago on December 3, 1906. Chief Collins appointed Frank D. Comerford to the newly created post of police attorney. He supervised the gathering and preparation of evidence in felony cases, representing the department before the municipal court. Comerford was later indicted for his role in the slush fund engineered by Collins to reelect Dunne. Immediately after establishment of the court, police arrests fell by nearly one-third (91,554 in 1906 to 63,132 in 1907.) Despite the optimistic outlook the ward bosses found new ways to control the court judges. In the 1920s the judges frequently took time out to canvass the local wards on behalf of their political benefactors. See Mark Haller, "Historical Roots," *Law and Society Review* (October 1976): p. 309.

54. *Chicago Tribune*, August 15, 1909. As postmaster of Chicago, Steward applied military methods to a branch of city government notorious for its patronage abuses and political infighting. New carrier stations were established and a revised street numbering system, in place in 1909, was Steward's brainchild. In another civic project of note Steward began the process to fill in the shallows east of the Illinois Central tracks, resulting in the creation of Grant Park. Steward was Busse's second choice for police superintendent; the position was first offered to Bernard J. Mullaney, departmental secretary. After considering the matter Mullaney decided that long-term job security was more important than temporary glory. He declined to accept because, as he explained, there was a family to support. "Who is Steward?" the rank-and-file asked. Nick Hunt, a perennial contender for the job was even more blunt: "You are not kidding me, are you? What's his name?" Steward began a long-overdue process of internal reform but his term ended when Busse left office. For Steward's position on the vice issue see "The Police and Vice in Chicago," *The Survey* 23 (November 8, 1909): 160–64.

Close Up on the Chicago Police:
The Armory Station—Home to
100,000 Desperate Characters

Shell workers, pyromaniacs, panel house thieves, confidence men, and murderers called it home—nearly 100,000 of them in 40 years. Chicago's Armory Station in the First Precinct was a testament to desperation, a reeking, sweating stone fortress that cast a long shadow over the Custom House Levee. There were actually two Armory Stations. The first one stood in the Market House Square near State and Randolph. It was a wooden clapboard structure, inadequate for the growing city's needs. In 1858 it was demolished and a larger police station was built at Adams Street and Franklin. Minutes before the Chicago Fire destroyed this building, Mike Hickey opened the jail cells to save the prisoners from instant cremation. When the smoke cleared, it was a pile of rubble. He secured temporary quarters in a wooden school building not far from where the last Armory was to be constructed.

The City Council appropriated $25,000 for the bricks, mortar, and steam fittings that built the infamous First Precinct Station house on a site formerly occupied by disease-ridden prostitution cribs. Medill renamed this section of Griswold Street, Pacific Avenue, hoping against hope that the sins of the past would be swept away in the flames and forgotten.

The presence of the largest and most imposing police station in the midwest had an opposite, undesirable effect. The forces of vice merely reclaimed their turf, building new gambling dens and prostitution parlors around the Armory, much the same way as the western homesteaders lived outside the walls of old Fort Laramie.

The police in the station and the criminals on the street formed a unique nineteenth-century subculture. Life was a trade-off and everything had its price.

During the wild and woolly days of the 1893 World's Fair it was not unusual for 300 men and women to be locked up in a single day. And as fast as they were brought in, they were provided their bail and were back on the streets, trailed by the bondsman counting his bills.

Hardened criminals outside the mainstream of acceptable Levee behavior had a more difficult time of it. Adolph Luetgert was photographed and measured with Bertillon devices before being led away to the interrogation room—or sweatshop—where Herman Schluetter grilled him for hours on end. He did not confess.

Lining the walls of the Rogues' Gallery, meticulously maintained for nearly 20 years by Captain Michael Evans, were the images of Chicago's criminal class. All but a few are forgotten today. One of them was the bank robber Eddie Guerin, who escaped from Devil's Island in a row boat only to be arrested in Chicago and sent to Harrison and Pacific. The French penal colony was no match for the thick walls of the Armory. Guerin remained secure in his cell until he was deported.[1] "Crooked Jaw" Johnny Green, "Little Louise," queen of the State Street shoplifters, and the sneak thief "Molly Matches"—who was really a man—often lounged on the soft side of a wooden plank in an Armory cell.

Chicago's first black patrolmen, Rodney Long and Johnny Enders, worked a beat out of the station in the late 1870s. The captaincy of the Armory was a stepping stone into the superintendent's office. Six Chicago police chiefs—Mike Hickey, Frederick Ebersold, Joseph Kipley, Francis O'Neill, John Collins, and George Shippy—commanded the Harrison Street Precinct at various times. Among the cub reporters sent here to cover the goings-on included Finley Peter Dunne (creator of Mr. Dooley), Brand Whitlock, James Keeley, Henry Barrett Chamberlin, and John Wilkie, who later headed up the U.S. Government Secret Service.

Reformers frequently dropped in to call on the chief, but their pleas were often ignored. This was, after all, a prison and not a country club, the police reasoned. William Stead and the English suffragete Sylvia Parkhurst pronounced the Armory a "reeking, filthy place, unfit in which to incarcerate a human being." It was that—and probably a lot more in its heyday.

That's why no one shed a tear when the wrecker's ball assailed its walls on June 27, 1911, to make way for a printing company. The Levee was long gone and there was no further need for an Armory Station. With its demolition a dubious landmark of those earlier times passed into memory. After another generation had come and gone, it wasn't even a landmark anymore.

Note

1. Eddie Guerin was one of the most famous criminals to roam the streets of Chicago. Born on the West Side, Guerin came to the attention of the police when he shot Detective Thomas Trehorn in a dispute over the affections of a woman. Following the shooting, Guerin fled to Allegheny, Pennsylvania, where he held up a bank. He was arrested, but

escaped from his jail cell. Then he robbed a commission house in Columbus, Ohio, but was pardoned because the courts took sympathy on him. He was just 18 years old. He returned to Chicago, where the police made things uncomfortable for him. He disappeared shortly after this, and the next anyone heard of him was a dispatch from Lyons, France, where he robbed the American Express office of $8,000. That was in 1901, and together with his girlfriend "Chicago May" Churchill, queen of the international female thieves, Guerin received a life sentence to Devil's Island. He served three years before slipping away from the French authorities in a row boat—the first person to accomplish this feat. Guerin's father wanted him to be a Chicago policeman but the boy had other ideas. His brother was employed as a tout on the *City of Traverse*. See the *Chicago Herald Examiner*, April 24–27, 1921.

7

A Juicy Tenderloin: Politics and Graft in the South Side Levee

Gambling, prostitution, the narcotics trade, and other forms of socially unacceptable behavior are consolidated in the wharf areas, rooming house districts, and industrial sections nearest the central business community. The vice operatives were assured of a dense but transitory population less inclined to take their problems to the police than the members of a residential neighborhood.

There has always been "segregated" vice in Chicago—from the time Wentworth pulled down the "Sand" houses with hooks and chains—to the trendy night spots along Rush Street where prostitutes mingle with young suburbanites and conventioneers in town for a good time. When threatened with public repression, vice merely scatters outward and then regroups.

In 1867 there were an estimated 1,300 prostitutes working the streets of Chicago. By the time William Stead arrived in 1894 to examine the existing conditions for his magazine *Review of Reviews*, that figure had risen to just under 10,000.[1] The most notorious of these nineteenth-century vice districts was the wicked Custom House Levee on the southern tip of the Chicago Loop near the Dearborn Street train station. It was a self-contained district of 37 houses of ill-fame, 46 saloons, 11 pawnbrokers, and one shooting gallery.[2] Within a block or two of the city's prestigious Union League Club, Carrie Watson and Vina Fields provided girls, liquor, and morphine from their high-toned resorts. Some of the girls who worked the resorts were lured by the pimps on the promise of fast money, good company, and relief from the tedium and drudgery of work in the factories and sweatshops of the city. "The recruiting grounds of the bagnio are the stores where girls are often cast, still unknown to sin, but in want and without shelter; in a word, places outside the Levee where distress and temptation stand ever-present as a menace to purity and rectitude. Behind every effort is a cause," Madame Dora Clafin told Stead. May Churchill Sharpe, "queen of the criminals," took a simpler, less dignified view of the old Levee: "The mere mention of the details of some of the circuses is unthinkable. I think Rome at its worst had nothing on Chicago during those lurid days."[3]

Into this cesspool of despair came Stead, the bearded English editor who thought the mere wave of his pen could change overnight the conditions of a half-century. Hank North's Clark Street saloon became his headquarters, in which he recorded the impressions of the vagrants and streetwalkers who lived there. For the residents of the Custom House Place, a good night sleep was often found in the basement corridor of the old Harrison Street Station, where rats and vermin competed for the precious space of the stone floor.

Stead's book, *If Christ Came to Chicago*, was published in the spring of 1894. Within two weeks, 100,000 copies were sold to Chicagoans anxious to read about the inner workings of their city. Like *Uncle Tom's Cabin* in another era, Stead's book aroused the consciousness of the people, but did not achieve the kind of results he believed were possible. He concluded that the city's administrators were hopelessly corrupt and that the conditions within the Levee were not only sanctioned but in fact *regulated* by the police, whose sworn duty it was to uphold the law.

The questionable resorts may be said to run, if not under the patronage of the police, at least with their cognizance. A friend of mine who made the rounds was personally escorted by a detective. When the police and the large wholesale houses and country cousins are in collusion to support unnatural crimes which the good people of Chicago fondly imagined only existed in the corruption of the later Roman empire, it is obvious that the moral reformer has a very uphill task before him.[4]

The detective force assigned to look after conditions in the Levee worked out of the Central Detail at the Harrison Street Station. The richest plum in the department was to be a plainclothes man in the "Tenderloin"—a phrase coined by a New York police captain who considered the enormous graft potential in these areas to be "filet mignon."[5]

The department was base, corrupt, and virtually independent of the superintendent. From the early morning roll-call at 8:30 until the detectives returned to the squadroom at 6:00, the men were on their own. A few mingled among the State Street shoppers in search of pickpockets while others guarded bank lobbies or patrolled the train stations looking for bunko artists. Those who did not receive a specific assignment from the lieutenant of detectives were given the choicest of all police jobs: to "freelance" the city and identify and apprehend the well-known criminals and thieves that were still at large.

The ambiguous nature of these assignments gave the Central detectives plenty of leisure time. Many frequented the saloons or gambling houses to while away the hours playing slot machines. During the summer months the number of arrests dropped significantly, indicating that the detectives had other things on their minds than police work (see Table 6).

Detectives and Clairvoyants

"Captain Jack," the name by which Jack Halpin's friends called him, capped off a 20-year police career with his appointment as chief of the detective bureau in 1911. In the next two years the "clairvoyant trust"—Captain Jack Halpin and his most skilled theif catchers—swindled hundreds of Chicagoans out of their life savings. The trust operated out of a flat on South Michigan Avenue, not far from other confidence tricksters and men of poor reputation who prowled the Levee for "pigeons." Here the rich and poor alike came to hear the sage words of "Professor" Robert L. Milton, who communed with the spiritual world about matters of the heart, inheritances, trusts, and all things green.

The mastermind of the clairvoyant racket of Chicago was Christian "Barney" Bertsche, a veteran of many such deceptions. Milton, whose real name was Frank Ryan, devised a payment schedule that satisfied the greed of the central detective bureau.

1. Monthly tribute during good business	$400
2. Monthly tribute during poor business	$300
3. Tipoff of sucker making a complaint	$25
4. Tipoff when warrant has been sworn out	$25
5. For arresting wrong man by mistake	$50
6. Contribution to funerals of detective friends	$25
7. Entertainment of out-of-town detectives	$50
8. Plain touches	$50 to $500

Municipal court records showed that when Halpin's men were given arrest warrants to serve on Ryan, they were actually handed to Eddie McCabe, a paid stooge who "stood the pinch." He would be taken to the bureau and booked as Professor Milton, minutes ahead of the arrival of the bondsman. In the morning McCabe would be dragged before the judge and the victim for a preliminary hearing. The "sucker," unable to make a positive identification, left the court scratching his head. Halpin's men would pat him on the back, and explain that they had done all they could.

When things became too hot in Chicago, Bertsche and Ryan took their act on the road to Kansas City, but soon returned—only to be picked up by State's Attorney McLay Hoyne's men. "During the year and a half that we operated here I was never taken to a police station or the detective bureau or court once. That's what I was paying money for. The coppers attended to the rest," explained Ryan.

As preparation for the greater tests ahead, Hoyne prosecuted Halpin for bribery

Table 6
Report of the Detective Bureau's, 1901

Months	Arrests	Sentenced to Penitentiary	Sentenced to Co. Jail, House of Correction, Reformatory	Fugitives Arrested in Chicago
January	217	3	17	5
February	219	2	14	6
March	211	2	17	7
April	263	5	9	4
May	223	12	13	9
June	204	2	15	6
July	129	4	8	11
August	151	1	1	10
September	133	3	5	7
October	151	4	9	13
November	159	5	11	5
December	194	4	2	10
	2,254	47	121	96

Recovered stolen property, including horses and vehicles: $113,887
Number of miscellaneous complaints investigated: 932
Number of warrants received and acted on: 934

Source: Report of the General Superintendent to the City Council (1901), p. 63. At the time of the Colleran investigation, there were 108 men detailed to detective duty in the department. Using the above table, we see that each man averaged roughly 21 arrests per year.

and conspiracy to defeat the ends of justice. At the trial Bertsche testified that three of Halpin's bravos—Lieutenant John Tobin, Sergeant W. J. Egan, and Detective J. F. Monaghan—tried to kill him outside the Rialto at Clark and Randolph one night in October 1914. "Self-defense!" Egan cried. He, like Chief Halpin, was convicted and sentenced to from one to five years in prison.

Halpin took his appeals to the state supreme court, but the conviction stood. With a smile on his face the captain resigned himself to his fate and went off to the Joliet Penitentiary in 1917, where he was greeted with warmest affection by Warden Zimmer, the brother of his first partner on the beat, Matthew Zimmer.

Less than a year later, on February 1, 1918, the gates of the pen swung wide open for Halpin. His friends and admirers awaited there with an automobile to take him to dinner with former Joliet Police Chief Harry DeMiller. The next morning Halpin went to work as the head of security for the Western Steel Car Foundry Company on the South Side. He worked there for years, and died a contented man in 1941. Halpin was 79 years old.

Certainly the same could not be said of Mrs. Mary Rapp, the Naperville woman who tucked $12,000—her life savings—into a satchel and headed to downtown Chicago to receive guidance from Professor Milton, who had advertised his special talents in the newspapers.

The Changing Nature of Organized Vice

By the time Stead arrived in Chicago, the era of the large, elegant gaming house owned and operated by Mike McDonald and others had been brought to a close. The gamblers dispersed into the neighborhoods, where the mobility of a handbook permitted them to reach a wider clientele. But organized gambling, as practiced by McDonald and, later, Mont Tennes, did not keep pace with the acceleration of other forms of vice, notably prostitution and drug usage. The openness that had characterized Mike McDonald's business dealings in the 1870s and 1880s was assumed by the proprietors of the sporting houses that dotted the Custom House before and after the 1893 World's Fair.

These were the men and women of Italian, Jewish, and Eastern European descent who were perhaps less concerned about maintaining image and gaining eventual social acceptance than the Irish famine immigrants had been a generation earlier. Wealthy vice lords like Ike Bloom, James Colosimo, Maurice Van Bever, Johnny Torrio, and George Silver owned the Levee resorts that were maintained by the famous madames Carrie Watson, Mary Hastings, and Victoria Shaw. While Bloom and his associates maintained the books, the women who recruited the girls became well known to the public because of their occasional charitable acts on behalf of the community and the extravagant lifestyles they maintained. "I'm really quite a noted character in my line," boasted Vic Shaw in 1949, as she recalled her torrid days on the Levee. "I was the pet of Chicago. They dressed me beautiful and took good care of me. Yeah, chicken, I had it once. Any one who knew me, knew I had it."[6]

Caroline Watson, whose name first turned up in the 1868 Comiskey investigation, staged an annual benefit ball for the relief of the homeless waifs living near the Levee, and to replenish the war chest of her two benefactors—Alderman John Coughlan and Michael Kenna. Stead's book publicized the exploits of Carrie Watson and her flock, but the vicious resort owners were not mentioned by name. Thus, the move to close the old Levee waned in the intervening years. Stead left Chicago, not to return for another decade. It was business as usual until Mayor Harrison and State's Attorney Healy seized the initiative in 1903, and drove them south to 22nd and Wabash. Altruism, and the desire to create a better downtown for people to live and work, had nothing to do with it. As Detective Clifton Rodman Wooldridge suggests, the commercial interests decided to reclaim the land for real estate development.

But it will soon be only a memory. The march of progress is not only consigning this Harrison Street station to the dead past, but it is driving the levee out of existence. Business men promoting gigantic commercial enterprises need the space occupied by the station and that used by disreputable houses adjacent to it for advancement of trade and in a few years their territory of depravity, immorality, and crime will disappear from the map of Chicago.[7]

The printing companies and bookbinding firms leveled the panel houses, opium dens, and disreputable saloons to make way for their towering office buildings while Van Bever, Colosimo, and the other Custom House people settled into a more favorable location south of 18th Street near the railroad tracks. The forces of vice, having been driven from their old haunts near the Loop, chased out the remaining residents of the fashionable Prairie Avenue district. Their insulated, secure existence was relegated to another era as the property was bought up by wealthy vice lords like Vic Shaw and her husband Roy Jones, who lived in splendor at 2906 Prairie—not far from Potter Palmer's first home. Real estate agents, who had witnessed a slow but steady decline in property values, welcomed the wealthy vice agents. So did the landlords, whose buildings had fallen into disrepair after the residents abandoned the neighborhood for the emerging north area.

In the next ten years, the city wrestled with what was essentially a moral dilemma. Pragmatic city officials like Carter Harrison and State's Attorney John Wayman believed that a segregated vice district was preferable to a wide open city. Church people like Dean Walter Sumner of the West Side Episcopal congregation decried the moral turpitude of the Levee and demanded its immediate closing. He was joined in this effort by Lucy Page Gaston of the Anti-Cigarette League, Jane Addams, and Arthur Barrage Farwell, a temperance advocate from Hyde Park.

Vice segregation in Chicago was more theory than hard reality. Despite police insistence that the names of prostitutes were maintained in card files in the station house, these woman frequently solicited business in adjacent neighborhoods and were often found in the better downtown hotels. The Levee became a haven for criminals, drug addicts, and fugitives. A network of tunnels was constructed underneath the sidewalk, which served as an underground railway for individuals fleeing the law, or escaping police raids. By 1910 conditions in the Levee deteriorated to such an extent that even its strongest supporters were forced to deal with it. In his memoirs, Mayor Harrison recalled the circumstances leading to his decision to close the Levee.

I have never been afflicted with Puritan leanings. I have always recognized the necessity of prostitution in such social organizations as have been so far perfected in this world of ours. Convinced of its inevitableness, I had permitted the then existing red-light territory to function. It was far from my idea, however, that the more notorious, the more luxurious of the houses should conduct branch institutions, succursales, in decent neighborhoods.[8]

The toast of Chicago's scarlet patch was, of course, the Everleigh Club located at 2131 Dearborn Street. Built in 1890 for $125,000 by Lizzie Allen and Christopher Columbus Crabb, the club was leased to Effie Hankins in 1895. When Lizzie died, Crabb then rented the floors to Ada and Minna Everleigh, two Kentucky beauties who fled their brutish husbands for a stage career. They arrived in Chicago in 1900 and opened their opulent bordello on February 2, explaining that they catered only to ''the best people''—politicians, show people, athletes, and visiting celebrities. Their uppity airs incensed the base elements of the Levee. When Nathaniel Ford Moore, scion of the Rock Island Railroad fortune, passed away from a drug overdose while staying incognito at the Shaw place, Victoria and Roy planned to move the body into the furnace of the Everleigh Club before calling the police. Their plan was thwarted by a girl who once worked for Ada and Minnie.[9] ''Nat Moore was a fine fellow,'' Vic Shaw told Captain William Cudmore, Levee police captain. ''He was here about a month ago with an actress, I think.'' Incidents of this nature shocked and outraged even the most sympathetic supporters of segregated vice—including Fred Busse, who owned a saloon and consorted with the underworld characters who did business with Edward McCann. During Busse's first term, Alderman Robert Buck, Mike Heitler, and Thomas Costello, a former crime reporter and ''bag man'' for the police, decided to shift the West Side Levee from its location on Sangamon, Green and Morgan Streets. Costello and Heitler had a monopoly of leases along Curtis Street, several blocks south.[10] Chief Steward heard of these plans, and put a stop to it. Heitler and Costello then moved into the expanding ''black belt'' along 31st Street where the political winds blew in a more favorable direction.

Busse allowed everyone enough room to conduct his business; there was certainly enough money in this business for all. But if they violated the acceptable decorum, an example had to be made of them. The church, as the guardian of social values, took up the cause. In 1910 Mayor Busse appointed Dean Sumner to head up the Committee of Fifteen, which published a blistering attack against the Levee, backing up its assertions with cold, hard data. Incidents of police misbehavior were documented, with the names of the offenders and the dates catalogued in a separate index. The Vice Commission concluded that the casual attitude of the police toward the law resulted in a widespread tolerance of prostitution, even in neighborhoods outside the Levee.[11]

The police found themselves in the crossfire of divided opinion. In one district, the police *regulated* the social evil instead of enforcing an inoperable, disregarded law. In yet another precinct, where vice was not as firmly entrenched, the police were expected to uphold the law vigorously and arrest anyone engaged in open pandering. Without a firm direction from the municipal government, police corruption was inevitable. Officers assigned to a district in which law-breaking was openly tolerated found an open invitation to dissipate.

Policing the Levee: Politics and Graft in the 1st Ward

Three vice rings formed the hub of the Levee graft wheel. The three syndicates identified in 1912 by State's Attorney MacLay Hoyne included the Colosimo-Torrio outfit, with connections to the Black Hand, the labor unions, and the saloon and restaurant trade; the Van Bever white-slave ring, which maintained close ties to Colosimo; and Charley Maibaum, owner of Buxbaums, an after-hours hotel to which the streetwalkers took their clients.[12] Operating outside the ruling syndicates were a score of independents, including Joe Grabiner and Harry Cusick (Guzik), who later became a top lieutenant in the Capone organization. The three rings were in direct competition with each other, but formed a tightly knit circle when threatened by the outside forces of reform.

None of the syndicates, no matter how organized, could have sustained a profit while remaining free of police interference without the support of the 1st Ward Democratic organization. According to John Landesco, "Hoyne revealed an astonishing array of precinct committeemen and captains of the 1st Ward holding jobs as bailiffs, jail guards, as well as in other capacities in the courts, the Sheriff's Office, the county treasurer's office, office of the county jail, and the Bridewell, especially where they can be of some help to the boys."[13]

The power of Alderman Kenna and Coughlin had grown steadily following the election of Mayor Carter Harrison II in 1897. The continuing alliance they formed with the new mayor served all parties well. During most of his terms in office Carter Harrison maintained a hands-off policy toward the red-light districts on the South and West Sides. In return for the votes of the saloon keepers, prostitutes, and the rest of the 1st Ward riffraff, Kenna and Coughlin had a say in the appointment of police inspectors and captains to their district. The fertile brain of Mike Kenna hatched new schemes to organize this mass of neer-do-wells into a stratified organization whose loyalty was unquestioned. Their support sustained Harrison in his own bitter fight against the rival Democratic factions controlled by Roger Sullivan and former Mayor John Hopkins. In 1911 Harrison won a narrow primary victory, but rather than see the mayor win a fifth term the Sullivan men crossed party lines to support a Republican who wielded the

Figure 8

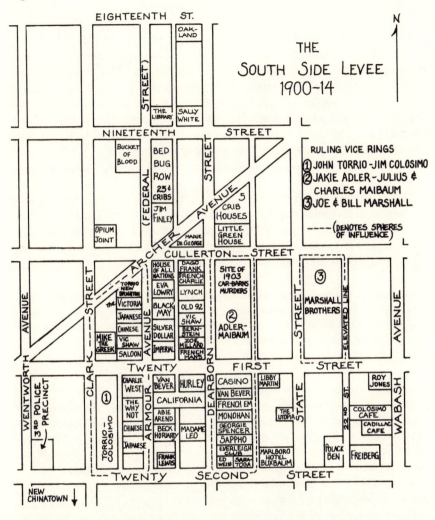

A map of the South Side Levee District. Three "rings" enjoyed autonomy in the "bad-lands" before the reform groups forced the gangsters to disperse into the outlying areas after 1914. (Deckert)

sword of reform—Professor Charles Merriam. But the 1st Ward came through again for a man they affectionately called "Our Carter," providing the margin of victory.

On election day, as previously on primary day, my oldtime friends in the 1st Ward, Hinky Dink and Bathhouse John, came through with flying colors. The flop vote, while it did not elect me, helped. My plurality in the 1st Ward was 3,647. Beyond a shadow of a doubt I owed my victory to the loyalty of the foreign nationalities backed up by the flop-house ballots of the 1st Ward. In politics you take them as they come.[14]

Machine politics was the handmaiden of Levee graft. The police entered into corrupt arrangements with the vice-keepers not only to supplement their incomes but because of the practical considerations involved. To refuse cooperation to a "friend" of the organization would invite a transfer "to the woods." According to Policeman William . . . "the Wrong Dick" Meadows, who arrested two women loitering in a Levee wineroom, the consequences did not justify carrying out the law. "The saloon was owned by two officers of my precinct," he said. "I was transferred way out in the country during wintertime. They would transfer me to a beat twenty miles from home. If I moved they would transfer me back again."[15]

Those officers who went along with the prevailing corruption worked with the bondsman and police magistrate to shake down prostitutes—an ancient problem in the red-light districts of Chicago. The inhabitants of a resort at 113 W. 21st Street paid a weekly stipend of three dollars, which was divided between the policeman and the bondsman. According to one woman,

The policeman had the habit of sometimes loafing 'round the entrance to the houses. When the owner saw them standing there, he knew what it meant and then he would send down a dollar or two by the porter who would slip it into the policeman's hand. The coin would always lubricate the knee joints and make walking the beat less irksome like.[16]

Scattered locations made it all the more difficult to get to the root of the problem. Superintendent LeRoy Steward issues 12 directives governing police conduct in the Levee, including an order to arrest all persons soliciting in the streets and in saloons. But as Steward admitted, "I could never place my hand on the patrolman, detectives, or officers who were responsible, though at one time I cleaned out the whole 22nd Street Station. I did not think that all the men were unreliable, but those who did the fixing were so thoroughly entrenched that it was impossible to find out who they were."[17]

Police corruption in the 1st Ward was systematic and ongoing despite the numerous personnel shakeups engineered by the mayor and superintendent. As long as the politicians interested in vice had a say in the selection of personnel, the appointment of a capable, honest officer was impossible. In 1911 Inspector John Wheeler and Lieutenant John Bonfield—son of the Haymarket police captain of earlier days—were accused of extorting $860 from the State Street resort keepers. Bonfield was the go-between—the man in the streets who collected the money each month from the dive keepers. "The inspector has to be taken care of, too," he said.[18] Wheeler's division encompassed the greater part of the Levee. The money was paid out in installments covering six months during which the dives were not to be raided. "Don't you accuse me of taking money from you," roared Wheeler, as he confronted his accuser in the office of Chief McWeeney. "If you make that charge against me on the witness stand I'll have you arrested for perjury and I'll send you to the penitentiary!"[19]

Captain Patrick Harding, who commanded the 22nd Street Station, added: "It's sort of an unwritten law that the inspector who has headquarters at the Harrison Street Station is directly responsible for conditions in that precinct."[20] When the mayor ordered Harding to padlock the doors of the Everleigh Club in 1911, the captain deferred action to Wheeler, who refused to see it through until Kenna and Coughlan had registered their protests to the mayor.[21] The order stood and Harrison indignantly ordered the removal of both Wheeler and Harding from the district.

This incident occurred shortly before the Civil Service plan of reorganization was pushed through. In its final report the Commission recommended the abolition of the inspector's office. The office had been created in 1890 to provide the superintendent with the counsel, assistance, and advice of trained senior officers who could provide first-hand reports of the true conditions in their districts. But as the Civil Service commissioners noted, "they are virtually independent commanders, frequently owing allegiance not to the general superintendent, but to the politicians most powerful in their respective territorial districts."[22] This was certainly true in the Levee and in Nick Hunt's South Side stronghold.

When the division inspector's position was eliminated, the Powers-Kenna-Coughlan crowd turned to their local captains to carry on the corrupt arrangements that existed before the measure was passed. Captain Harding was superseded by other officers willing to carry out the orders of Kenna and his lieutenant, Dennis "the Duke" Cooney. William Cudmore filled in for a time, and then late in 1912 Michael "White Alley" Ryan, whose son served as legal counsel for the United Police, settled into the 22nd Street Station with the approval of all the resort owners. A picture of Ike Bloom, owner of the notorious Freiberg's Dance Hall, was hung above his desk.[23] The names had changed but the results were still very much the same. According to Reverand W. P. Boynton, who urged the mayor to allow Deputy Funkhouser a freer hand in the vice clean-up, "It was a colossal blunder to have organized the police force for the purpose of regulating the morals of the city. The failure of the police is shockingly apparent."[24]

The Break-Up of the South Side Levee

After Mayor Harrison was elected to his fifth and final term of office in 1911, he pledged to uphold the policy of containment outlined by LeRoy Steward a year earlier. Vice in the Levee would be tolerated as long as it did not intrude into the surrounding communities south and west of 22nd and Wabash.

The closing of the Everleigh Club sent a clear signal to the Committee of Fifteen that the reformers need not settle for containment when it was possible to alleviate the district altogether. Early in 1912, 10,000 people marched down Michigan Avenue in support of an early closing of the Tenderloin. Led by attorney Carl Walderon, the Committee of Fifteen secured indictments against such Levee insurgents as Al Harris and Harry Cusick. Walderon sidestepped State's Attorney John Wayman, who was the victim of some malicious rumors involving his work for the Santa Fe Railroad. Before his 1908 election Wayman served as legal counsel for the rail interests, handling property litigation and other civil matters.[25] For a long time the railroads coveted the prized Levee real estate, which lay directly in the path of the southern terminals linking together Indiana, southern Illinois, and other eastern points. Between 1907 and 1909 the railroads quietly bought up $3,000,000 worth of property lying between Sixteenth Street and Archer Avenue, west of Dearborn.[26] They transferred the property to Chicago Title and Trust until the time was right for them to purchase the remaining lands.

The rail interests sought to build a spacious new passenger terminal to connect the Illinois Central (IC), the Western Indiana Line, and the Pennsylvania Road in one central location. If the remaining Levee houses could be knocked down, the property values of the empty land would depreciate, making their purchase a cost-effective, lucrative business venture for all. Virginia Brooks accused Wayman of being a party to this scheme, a charge to which he was very sensitive as his unblemished term of office was scheduled to expire at the end of the year. Wayman was a Greek scholar and a noted criminologist. His work on the McCann case crossed partisan lines. It is hard to imagine that he would have represented a special interest group in this way. His personal attitudes toward segregated vice mirrored those of other pragmatic city officials: that prostitution was not going to be eliminated with one simple brush stroke, and that it was better to contain it in a small section of the city. Stung by the accusations of wrongdoing he boldly declared that he would close the district for them, but challenged the reformers to keep it that way after his term expired in January 1913.

Whatever his true motives, Wayman moved quickly and resourcefully against the 22nd Street syndicates. Agents from the State's Attorney's office examined county torrens records for the names of the property owners. A network of holding companies, aliases, names of deceased people and third parties all but impossible to trace were listed as owners of the dives. Harrison B. Riley, president of Chicago Title & Trust, was subpoenaed by the grand jury to explain his company's involvement in Levee real estate. "It has been our policy to allow no improper persons to occupy property held in trust by us," he explained.

Working closely with Inspector William Dannenberg of the Morals Squad, Wayman closed down 518 resorts between September 26 and December 1, 1912.[27] This resulted in the forcible eviction of 1,000 prostitutes, whose cases were heard in the courtroom of Judge Kickham Scanlan. Scanlan kept the Criminal Courts Building open from 9:00 AM until 10:00 PM each day. By the end of November the red-light district was virtually empty.

Of all the people who figured prominently in the history of the Levee, Wayman was the least understood and probably the most tragic. He was boxed in by the do-gooders and reformers whose grasp was exceeded only by their reach. In the end he gave them what they wanted, but his challenge was a prophetic one. Changes in the city administration frequently affected the policy of vice repression, and with it conditions in the Levee. The election of Democrat McLay Hoyne as the new state's attorney was perceived to be a clear victory for the vice interests.

Following his unsuccessful gubernatorial bid in 1913, Wayman suffered a nervous breakdown. While recovering at his home at 6832 Constance he fired two shots into his chest. Some people said he was cleaning his gun, which accidentally discharged. Others maintained he was despondent over the directions his career had taken. Whatever the case, Chicago had lost one of its most outstanding public officials.

McLay Hoyne enjoyed the unflagging support of the 1st Ward Democrats because he did not consider the vice clean-up to be an immediate priority of the administration. Within a month of the official closing of the Levee, the wine-rooms, panel houses, and disorderly hotels cautiously reopened.

Major Funkhouser was the only official still interested in the issue after election day. With a staff of five men and a limited working budget he issued a series of reports to the mayor, which incensed the line officers who permitted the spread of vice in their districts. Thirty-six places were found to be open in the Levee despite the presence of plainclothes men. "It is apparent from the foregoing that the police of this precinct can stop the operation of these places if they so desire," Funkhouser stated.[28]

In the 22nd Street district, Captain Ryan resented the intrusions of civilian cops into his domain. "This district has never been clean and it never will be. We don't want no Dannenbergs around here," he snapped. "He uses stool pigeons and I won't stand for it."[29] Ryan, who replaced Harding, was described as "the chief of police" in the 1st Ward. "The Hink put him there, and the Hink and the Bath keep him there," the *Tribune* theorized. "He has been denounced as either notoriously corrupt or notoriously incompetent. But Funk-houser, Dannenberg, Gleason, and Hoyne himself cannot budge Ryan from that station," the paper continued.[30]

Despite charges that Ryan provided the resort owners with advance notice of Funkhouser's raids, this second Levee crusade, initiated in 1914, was taking its toll. "They're running us into a hole," complained Johnny Torrio, one of the young Turks in the Levee. "I'm gettin' tired of payin' dough to get a chance to run, and having these guys bustin' me and my friends every day or so, We got to take a couple of them into the alley and kick 'em up some. So's the others will wise up to the fact that they're not wanted around here."[31]

Tensions between the Morals Squad, the syndicates, and Ryan's men brewed in the Levee for months. Finally on July 16, 1914, a senseless shooting tragedy occurred that might have been avoided if the rival police factions had worked together for a common purpose.

The Levee Shootout and Its Aftermath

The Morals Squad had just completed a raid on the Turf, a saloon and bagnio located three blocks west of Wabash and 22nd Streets. Two of Dannenberg's special investigators, Fred Amart and Joseph Merrill, headed east on 22nd Street for what they thought would be a rendezvous with their boss. They were trailed by a heckling crowd of Levee characters, including a gunman named Roxy Venillo whom Johnny Torrio had brought in from Montana for some special "work." The two Morals officers encountered two of Ryan's detectives, John Sloop and Stanley Birns. A man in the crowd brandished a revolver at Amart seconds before a brick was hurled into the crowd. The man with the gun was thought to be Roxy Venillo, but it was not conclusively proven because the mob dispersed amidst gunfire and flying objects. Detective Birns was shot and killed by what the investigators later thought was a bullet from Amart's gun. While all this was going on Captain Ryan was walking with Detective Bill Schubert and Solly Friedman, who worked for Alderman Kenna. They were joined in front of Freiberg's Dance Hall by Jim Colosimo and his lawyer Rocco Stefano, where they observed the unfolding street riot. Curiously, Ryan made no attempt to disperse the mob or seek assistance from the precinct station even after being told of the disruptive behavior of the gathering. Later, Ryan was quoted as saying that the blame for the Birns shooting rested with the "green" Morals Squad who shouldn't have been there in the first place.[32] An autopsy of the body showed that Birns had been killed by a cartridge that was not standard police issue.

Roxy Venillo, who had been wounded in the fracas, was driven away from the scene of the shooting in an automobile owned by Maurice Van Bever. He fled Chicago, and was never brought to trial for his alleged involvement in the crime.

The shooting in the Levee forced an indifferent MacLay Hoyne to temporarily retreat from his policy of nonintervention. Under the direction of the state's attorney's office, the Levee was scoured for suspects, informers, and anyone who could shed light on the matter. Several men were arrested, including Colosimo, Van Bever, saloon owner James Leathers, and Policeman J. A. Carey of the 22nd Street Station. Gleason filed charges with the Civil Service Commission against Captain Ryan and three of his lieutenants who permitted the saloons to remain open after 1:00 AM.[33]

One focus of the commission was the question of why so many of Ryan's men were permitted to roam the district in plain clothes when police regulations stipulated that only detectives enjoyed that privilege. A witness testified that Ryan admonished his men to do their duty, but created difficulties for them when they tried to do so. One officer was praised for his efforts to keep people away from the resorts and was told that as a reward he would be allowed to do undercover work in street clothes. The next day he found himself assigned to duty in the western section of the precinct, far removed from the Levee.[34]

The plainclothes men received their orders directly from Ryan and were not

Figure 9

Four who shared responsibility for the shooting in the Levee, left to right: Mettelius C. Funkhouser, Detective Fred Amart, Chief James Gleason, and William C. Dannenberg. (Deckert)

expected to show up for the morning roll-call. Although 183 policemen were assigned to the 22nd Street substation, the number of detectives in this precinct varied depending on the situation. However, there were always more men than the police ordinances mandated.[35] In contrast, there were only six uniformed officers found in the district, even after the Birns shooting.[36] Departmental regulations called for a force of 50 patrolmen, with three assigned to each block.

Ryan maintained his absolute innocence: "I've raided till I'm thin in the face. And what good has it done? The places are left open. Anybody can move in. You raid again, and you find nothing. They move around from place to place and laugh at your back. And when you locate them, the judge lets them off with a light fine. If you think I'm having a picnic here, you're crazy," he said.

Chief Gleason transferred him to the West Lake Street Station, but the Austin community businessmen lodged an official protest with the mayor. They did not want a man of his unsavory reputation in their district. Ryan then submitted his resignation from the force for what he claimed to be medical reasons. Twenty-six interdepartmental transfers were made as a result of the Birns slaying. Captain Max Nootbar, a graduate of Heidelburg University and a former instructor at LeRoy Steward's police academy, was placed in charge of the district.[37]

Nootbar had the support of Mayor Harrison, who did not interfere with his plans to drive all the vagrants out of the district and enforce the 1:00 AM closing. Ike Bloom's dance hall, which had been the last impregnable fortress of the Levee, was closed, and Jim Colosimo's saloon license was revoked. For all purposes, the old Levee was finally closed. Carter Harrison paid the price for his betrayal of the vice interests in the 1915 mayoral primary: Aldermen Kenna and Coughlin shifted their allegiance to Roger Sullivan's candidate. In the primary Hinky Dink and Bathhouse delivered 6,105 votes to Robert Sweitzer, as compared with only 1,098 for Harrison.[38]

The combined efforts of the Morals Squad, the Committee of Fifteen, the mayor, and Captain Nootbar succeeded in driving the vice faction out of the 1st Ward. Two years after the Birns shooting Henry Hyde toured the old "badlands." The Levee was dark and silent, and the lavish resorts that dotted 21st Street, Dearborn, and Federal were empty, vandalized shells. Buildings that once rented from between $200 to $500 a month stood for a few more years before succumbing to the wrecker's ball and the railroad tracks that eventually lay in their dust. The Committee of Fifteen estimated that in its heyday, 1,200 houses and flats were used for immoral purposes in the district.[39] But what effect, if any, did the closing of the Levee have on commercial vice in Chicago?

The repression of vice merely scattered it across the city and into the suburbs. In their effort to hide from the vigilance of public repression, the vice interests invaded those regions where it could not be so readily detected as it had been in the old 22nd Street Levee.

The rival syndicates relocated to South Chicago, suburban Cicero, and Burnham, where 25-year-old Mayor Johnny Patton proclaimed his town wide open and ready for business.[40] Jim Colosimo and Johnny Torrio purchased the Speedway Inn on October 15, 1917, which became one of the first road houses to attain notoriety during Prohibition. Other 22nd Street bosses purchased property in the adjacent communities. "Jew Kid" Grabiner was hired to run the Speedway Inn; "Dago" Frank Lewis opened the Columbia Cafe on Ogden Avenue where he was joined by Ed Weiss. Victoria Shaw remained on the South Side, though, where she opened a luxurious call-flat on South Michigan Avenue. In the 1920s she expanded her business to venture into the lucrative narcotics trade, and occasionally hijacked a truck of whiskey coming in from Canada.[41]

The United States had become an increasingly mobile society. The automobile linked together city and suburb, making the locations on the fringe of the expanding city easily accessible from downtown. The taxicab driver could now serve the same purpose as the cadet-roper who formerly canvassed the train stations and amusement parks in search of prostitutes and male customers. The move to the suburbs simply meant that the social evils were even more decentralized than before and that much harder to suppress.

Notes

1. Walter C. Reckless, *The Natural History of the Vice Areas in Chicago* (Ph.D. dissertation, University of Chicago, 1925), p. 43.

2. Richard C. Lindberg, *Chicago Ragtime: Another Look at Chicago 1880–1920* (South Bend: Icarus Press, 1985), p. 120.

3. Ibid.

4. William Stead, *If Christ Came to Chicago* (Chicago: Laird & Lee, 1894), p. 160.

5. James A. Richardson, *The New York Police: Colonial Times to 1901* (New York:

Oxford University Press, 1970), p. 181. When Captain Alexander "Clubber" Williams was transferred to New York's most seedy red-light district he rubbed his hands together gleefully and spoke of having moved up from "salt chuck" to "tenderloin."

6. Vic Shaw, Chicago's parlor house queen, reflected on her life and times in this rare, published interview appearing in the *Chicago Tribune*, March 14–16, 1949. For another view of the Levee and its scarlet women see Charles Washburn, *Come Into My Parlor* (New York: National Library Press, 1934), pp. 123–24.

7. Clifton Rodman Wooldridge, *Hands Up In the World of Crime!* (Chicago: Stanton & Van Vliet, 1901), p. 308. This was the first of several books Detective Wooldridge published.

8. Carter Harrison, *The Stormy Years* (New York: Bobbs-Merrill, 1935), p. 308.

9. Lindberg, *Chicago Ragtime*, p. 138. Roy Jones was the second of Shaw's four husbands, and one of the early vice kings in the Levee. His saloon was the scene of one of the most lurid gangland slayings on April 7, 1914. James Franche, alias "Duffy the Goat," was a well-known local character who shot and killed an out-of-towner named Ike Henagow inside the Jones saloon. To save his liquor license Jones instructed his employees to tell the police that they had seen Henagow shot outside on the sidewalk. The newsmen had already poked holes through this story by the time Captain Ryan arrived. "The shooting could have happened in the city's best places," Ryan said. "I believe the man was shot out on the street." A stray bullet was later pulled from the wall—inside the dive.

10. *Chicago Tribune*, January 10, 1917. Known in the business as a "squeeze-in," Fred Busse's friend Costello made his money forcing himself on someone else's racket. During Thompson's reign Costello squeezed John "Kid" Warren out of the Riverview Teddy Bear concession. Warren had originally received exclusive rights to this business by virtue of a $1,000 campaign donation to Thompson. When Warren began making money Costello demanded a 25 percent protection cut. Warren rejected the demand, whereupon Costello used his clout to have the business shut down.

11. *The Social Evil in Chicago: A Report of the Chicago Vice Commission to His Honor the Mayor* (Chicago: Gunthrop & Warren Publishers, 1910), p. 160. This was the famous vice report that was censored by the U.S. Postal System in 1910.

12. *Chicago Tribune*, July 29, 1914.

13. John Landesco, *Organized Crime: Part III of the Illinois Crime Survey* (Champaign: University of Illinois Press, 1929), p. 30.

14. Harrison, *The Stormy Years*, p. 294. Voters were brought in from the Oak Forest Poor Hospital and from the Dunning Asylum to cast their votes for Harrison because these inmates were the most "perspicacious," according to Hinky Dink Kenna. See Herman Kogan and Lloyd Wendt's account of this election in *Lords of the Levee: The Story of Bathhouse John and Hinky Dink* (New York: Bobbs-Merrill, 1944), pp. 291–93.

15. *Chicago Tribune*, January 10, 1909.

16. *Chicago Journal*, July 23, 1914. Also: *The Social Evil In Chicago*, pp. 150–152, for additional accounts of police shakedowns in the 22nd Street Levee.

17. *Chicago Evening-American*, July 23, 1914.

18. *Chicago Tribune*, November 2, 1911.

19. Ibid., June 9, 1911.

20. Ibid., November 2, 1911.

21. Harrison, *The Stormy Years*, p. 310.

22. *Final Report of the Police Investigation* (1911), p. 28.

23. Lindberg, *Chicago Ragtime*, p. 160. When Nootbar took over at 22nd Street, the picture was thrown in the garbage—where it belonged.

24. *Chicago Tribune*, June 11, 1911.

25. Harrison, *The Stormy Years*, p. 303, for further discussion about the railroad's efforts to secure this property.

26. *Chicago American*, October 8, 1912.

27. *Chicago Tribune*, July 23, 1914. See also Washburn, *Come Into My Parlor*, pp. 216–17. Those with direct knowledge about the property owners of Levee houses were asked to swear out complaints in the municipal courts. The state law under which prosecutions were brought appeared under the heading of disorderly conduct.

28. *Chicago Tribune*, October 11, 1913.

29. Ibid., July 17, 1914.

30. Ibid., July 18, 1914.

31. Lindberg, *Chicago Ragtime*, p. 154. See also Humbert Nelli, *Italians In Chicago 1880–1930: A Study in Ethnic Mobility* (New York: Oxford University Press, 1970), pp. 150–51. Torrio was the hot-headed nephew of Jim Colosimo and heir apparent to the vice throne. When the situation calmed down Colosimo instructed Police Detectives Ed Murphy and Johnny Howe to offer Dannenberg a $500 a week bribe to "lay low." This gambit failed and there were physical threats.

32. Ryan was partially correct. Morals policemen, by the mayor's own admission, were men with less than two months on the force and not subject to Civil Service rules. Major Funkhouser later admitted that Dannenberg's raid was unauthorized by his office. *Chicago Tribune*, July 3, 1918.

33. Lindberg, *Chicago Ragtime*, p. 158.

34. *Chicago Tribune*, July 29, 1914.

35. Ibid., July 18, 1914.

36. Ibid., July 19, 1914.

37. For an intimate look at Max Nootbar, see Donald Culross Peattie's "The Most Unforgettable Character I've Met," *Reader's Digest* 20 (January 1944): 77–80. See also Thomas Reppetto, *The Blue Parade* (New York: The Free Press, 1978), pp. 200–1. Nootbar was a graduate of Heidelberg University. Before joining the Chicago police in 1896 he served as secretary to the U.S. consul in Hamburg, and as an aid to the Austrian government at the 1893 World's Fair.

38. Kogan and Wendt, *Lords of the Levee*, p. 325.

39. *Chicago Tribune*, January 11, 1916. The Levee today is an area very much in dispute. Portions of the land remain empty. The railroads have no further need of it as a passenger terminus, but the Sante Fe officials could not reach a suitable accord with community leaders from Chinatown for commercial and residential expansion.

40. Known as the "Boy Mayor," cocky, cigar-smoking jazz baby Johnny Patton was a member of the Torrio-Capone liquor syndicate in the 1920s. In 1918 Patton received $100,000 of stolen government property that had been consigned to the troops serving in France. The gang of thieves were provided safe haven in Burnham. They removed the supplies from box cars in the Calumet District. *Chicago Tribune*, July 20, 1918. See also Landesco, *Illinois Crime Survey*, p. 232.

41. *Chicago Tribune*, March 14, 1949. In 1928 Shaw was fined $500 for bootlegging. In 1931 she was named in a murder indictment involving a slain policeman. In 1942 Shaw was sentenced to a Dallas prison on a narcotics charge, but returned to Chicago after only 24 months.

8

The Triumph of Vice and Graft during the First Thompson Administration

William Hale Thompson, the scion of a wealthy Boston family, defeated the Democratic candidate Sweitzer and was inaugurated as Chicago's next mayor on May 15, 1915. As a youth growing up in Chicago Thompson had frequent altercations with the law. He was an unrestrained youth who spent much of his time brawling in Levee saloons when he wasn't playing football or water polo at the Chicago Athletic Club.[1] Politics for Thompson was an extension of sport. He loved the old-fashioned oratory, the revivalist flavor of the torchlight rally and the masculine camaraderie of the "back room." Bill Thompson entered the political field when the Republican organization was hopelessly split into factions loyal to Governor Charles Deneen, and those loyal to Congressman William Lorimer, popularly known as the "blond boss."

Thompson allied himself to the Lorimerites, and used their influence to secure election to the City Council in 1902. But he lost this base of support several years later when the normally supportive *Tribune* exposed the most powerful party leader as a bribetaker. In 1912, Lorimer was removed from his senatorial seat after it was revealed that he had accepted over $100,000 from Edward Hines, president of Chicago's largest wholesale lumber companies, in exchange for various considerations.[2]

Without an effective organization behind him, Thompson's elective prospects seemed dim. But he attracted the attention of Fred Lundin, a North Side Swede who began his life selling "Juniper Juice" to poor immigrants settling into the North Side ghettos near Belmont and Clark. Lundin the medicine man later served a term in Congress before returning to Chicago to supervise the Thompson mayoral campaign. He was a tireless worker, cutting political deals with progressive committee men and Harrison Democrats alike. Lundin turned the 1915 mayoral contest into a campaign of demagoguery that traded on the ethnic prejudices of Irish, Germans, nativists, and the 2nd Ward blacks, from whom Thompson found his greatest support.

The return of the Republicans to City Hall after a four-year absence did not mean a continuation of the reform measures that Harrison had pushed through in respect to vice and gambling. It simply meant that the power of the Democratic alliances—manifested in the ties between the ward office and City Hall—was curbed. Lacking the political clout of a Roger Sullivan or Bobby Burke, Thompson was compelled to make alternative arrangements with crime bosses like James Colosimo, who had valuable links to the emerging labor unions.[3] As a result, the crime syndicate, which was in utter disarray in 1914, consolidated its network in the coming decade. The wide open town returned, to the utter amazement of Hinky Dink and the Bath, while the single event of Prohibition unified the vice factions in a manner unknown in the times of Mike McDonald.

When the time came for Thompson to select his cabinet, Fred "the Poor Swede" Lundin scored a brilliant public relations coup. He arranged with W. N. Pelouse, the mayor' brother-in-law, a conference of distinguished business and civic leaders to assist in the selection process. The message to the voters seemed clear. Bill Thompson was one man who would not work out of a smoke-filled room. Nelson Lampert of the Fort Dearborn Bank extolled the career of Captain Charles Healey, and put his name in nomination for police chief. The choice of Healey seemed to affirm the mayor's farcical campaign pledge that he "would drive the crooks out of Chicago and make this administration memorable for the honesty of its officers."[4]

As captain of the Chicago Police Mounted Squadron Healey was considered to be the nation's leading expert on traffic management. In 1908 George Shippy appointed him to represent the department in its dealings with downtown merchants to resolve the dilemma of congested streets. Two years later he toured the capitals of Europe at the behest of the Association of Commerce to consider the methods employed by London bobbies in dealing with this increasing problem. Healey's task force led to the publication of the first set of printed rules governing traffic regulation. His work for the Association put him in touch with the LaSalle Street bankers, and this no doubt endeared him to Thompson.

"As the first and most important step in ridding Chicago of its crime I will close every vicious poolroom in the city," Healey promised. "Folktalk of driving the criminal from Chicago is not all that is needed. We have to strike first at the crime factories."[5] Despite these public utterances Healey went along with Thompson's plan to permit the "wide open town." Concerning the 1:00 AM closing, which had resulted in the revocation of Ike Bloom's saloon license, Thompson's Corporation Counsel argued that the law need not be enforced as long as intoxicants were not sold to the public after that hour.[6] Mayor Thompson quietly restored the saloon licenses of Bloom, Colosimo, and some of the "Black and Tan" resorts in the 2nd Ward. Captain Nootbar, who had been a thorn in the side of the Levee for nearly a year, was called before a trial board to answer charges that he had "harassed" black patrons in one of those cabarets. He was found guilty and sent "to the woods"—the Kensington District, far removed from the vice centers of Chicago.[7] Then Thompson considered ways to eliminate the Morals Squad, still commanded by Major Funkhouser. Phase one was a direct order from Healey to Funkhouser to desist from making any further vice raids. "The second deputy's office is authorized to investigate and report only on vice matters—not to make police raids," Healey explained.[8] In phase two the six investigators who were assigned to the Morals Squad were replaced by men loyal to the chief and generally not interested in vice clean-up. Funkhouser was undeterred. Then the City Council refused to appropriate additional funds for future vice investigations. The comptroller put things into clear perspective by saying that the administration "is trying to make friends. We have to have friends if we are going to build a machine."[9] The unnamed friends were the resort keepers, labor union racketeers, and gamblers.

The office of second deputy staggered with each new blow but continued to operate to the mayor' chagrin. For nearly six years the Morals Squad had weathered the shifting political winds in their task to rid Chicago of vice. Funkhouser was the target not only of Thompson but also of the church ladies who criticized him for his leniency concerning the movies that played in the city. In these days before the Hays Code, it was up to the local police agencies to impose censorship.[10] As the guardian of decency the major excised scenes of excessive violence, morbidity, and sexual suggestiveness. The movie producers regarded him as a puritanical blue-blood. Complained one irate trade journal, "Since Mr. Funkhouser began exercising divine right in Chicago, he has killed three times as many motion picture subjects as his predecessor."[11] He was dragged into court by the distributors of "Sins of the Sons," who charged him with lack of education, refinement, and good artistic means when he ordered the film shut down in Chicago.[12] Thompson took an opposing view, and replaced Funkhouser with a civilian panel that would more closely monitor lewd and lascivious scenes in the movies. His wrangles with the censorship board, filmmakers, and fellow officers in the department was carefully documented by acting Chief of Police John Alcock in June 1918. A full slate of 57 grievances against Funkhouser and Inspector Francis Hanna were brought to the Civil Service Commission with the hope that the Morals Squad could finally be brought under control if Funkhouser were removed.

Alcock was given extraordinary latitude in expressing what amounted to little more than opinion and hearsay evidence concerning the neglect of duty and general inefficiency with which Funkhouser was charged.[13] Alcock testified that before leaving for Florida to regain his failing health, Herman Schluetter had agreed that conditions in the second deputy's office were bad. After hearing about this, Alcock was asked if Funkhouser had ordered surveillance of the chief's home.

Q: Do you know of any other shadowing that was done on Chief Schluetter?

A: Yes. The telephone wire at his home was tapped.

On cross-examination Funkhouser's attorney demanded the statement be stricken from the record unless it could be supported in some way. Alcock replied: "I knew it was tapped, but I don't know who tapped it."[14]

The hearing was a classic Chicago whitewash, at least from the defense point of view. First, it was ruled that vice conditions in the city were not criterion for the judgment of a public official whose duties were to prevent immoral conditions. The defense had based its entire case on the fact that conditions had disintegrated following Funkhouser's suspension from active duty.[15] Then Charles E. Frazier, the new president of the Civil Service Commission, refused to hear arguments from reformers who were willing to testify to this fact.

After five weeks of hearings, the Commission ruled in favor of Alcock and ordered Funkhouser discharged from the force. He was judged guilty of 41 of the charges preferred against him. There was little doubt that the commission had acted in the best interests of the mayor. Percy Coffin, the former president of the commission, who had vacated his office to run for treasurer, was a regular attendee at Thompson election rallies, and was said to have provided 10,000 campaign workers with city jobs.[16] His successor was Frazier, who was rewarded by Thompson for his special handling of the Funkhouser case with an appointment as second deputy on September 18, 1918.[17] This promotion paved the way for Percy Coffin to be reappointed head of the Civil Service Commission. Alderman Otto Kerner described the newly appointed board as "victims of moral leprosy."[18] In a blatant, but not surprising affront to Hoyne and the Healey prosecution team, Frazier was sworn in as second deputy by William Luthardt, who had held Funkhouser's position on an interim basis. It was a case of the inmates taking over the asylum.

The demise of the Morals Squad—for it existed in name only after Funkhouser was removed—was the end of reform and the repudiation of the noteworthy recommendations of the 1911 Civil Service Commission. The true irony was the fact that the Commission, the intended agent of reform, had repeatedly served the mayor as his political steering device, both in 1897 and even more so in 1918.

The Motive for Revenge

The ouster of Metellius Funkhouser from the position of second deputy was punishment for what the mayor believed to be a politically inspired vendetta against his police chief, Charles Healey. In the guise of a reformer, Healey not only used his office to further Thompson's elective aims—there was nothing new about that—but was also the ringleader of one of the city's most notorious graft rings. Healey, Secretary William Luthardt, and Charles T. Essig of the Sportsman's Club of America were all indicted on October 23, 1916, for accepting payoffs from prominent gamblers. The indictments were the result of an investigation of police irregularity by State's Attorney MacLay Hoyne, whose interest in these matters was buoyed by the presence of a Republican in City Hall.

The Sportsman's Club of America had been organized in 1915 by Jim Pugh, who worked closely with the Lorimerites to elect Thompson. Hoyne charged the mayor with maintaining the club as a "clearing house" for graft payments. Lifetime memberships were parcelled out to Republican worthies for $100. The chief and one of the disciples, Morgan Collins, were listed in the membership directory along with Mont Tennes, Jim Colosimo, and Herbert Mills, president of the Mills Novelty Company, which manufactured slot machines for use in the company-owned arcades near the sleazy intersection of State and Van Buren.[19] Harry Seligman, one of Mont Tennes's lawyers, was legal counsel for the club.

Hoyne uncovered a letter written to Healey by Detective William P. O'Brien which described conditions at the Elite and the Schiller Cafes, two "protected" Black and Tan resorts in the 2nd Ward. Both were under the control of Republican State Senator George Harding and the city's first black alderman, Oscar De Priest. In return for their support in the black community their liquor licences had been saved. On October 9, Hoyne's men seized the vice reports and confidential documents submitted to Major Funkhouser by Francis Hanna, which spelled out in graphic detail the payoffs to leading Chicago policemen. Healey had filed away the reports without any official action. When the Morals Squad followed up their investigation with a raid, Healey called each of them in for an official reprimand.[20]

Thompson stood by Healey—the "white knight" of Chicago law enforcement—and punished the state's attorney by reassigning the men under his control to city precincts. "The chief has a clean bill of health as far as I'm concerned," Thompson said. "I am confident the people will resent Hoyne's actions at the election."[21] But in a surprising blow to the mayor, his candidate was easily defeated in the general election that fall. Following the campaign, Hoyne renewed his attacks against Healey, who continued to occupy office despite the pending indictment.

Hoyne assembled a new staff of officers and on January 8, 1917, he staged another raid—this time on the offices of Thomas Costello, where Costello was meeting privately with Mike Heitler, bondsman William Skidmore, and Lieutenant Martin White of the Lake Street Station. The arresting officers found four sealed envelopes in their possession with money totaling $1,000.[22] A green book was taken from White listing the names of the resorts that could and could not be raided. Those protected by Healey were designated as "the chief's place." One of them was Ike Bloom's Panama Cafe, which was reopened after $600 had been paid to Healey by Costello. The shifty Costello had been under surveillance for a month. Three times a week he made a delivery to the Healey residence, where he received his instructions.[23] Posing as newspaper reporters, Hoyne's raiders arrested the chief at his home after the evidence had been assembled.

Healey maintained absolute innocence, but was arraigned before Municipal Judge Mahoney and held on a $25,000 bond. The sinking fortunes of the administration required some gesture from the mayor, who finally withdrew his support of Healey. On January 11, 1917, Herman Schluetter was appointed superintendent after Healey submitted his resignation. Thompson's choice was a popular one. During the swearing-in ceremony, Schluetter received a standing ovation from the City Council. Public opinion demanded that someone of high moral fiber be selected, and what better man than Schluetter? Despite his rough tactics toward the labor classes, Schluetter's career was a distinguished one. He was effusive with the press, and would take the necessary steps to put his house back in order.

Meanwhile, the grand jury returned another wave of indictments against Healey, Skidmore, and Sergeant Stephen Barry on conspiracy charges. Heitler agreed to turn state's evidence in return for immunity. By September 17 a series of 13 true-bills had been returned. Charles Healey and his two confederates went on trial in Judge Joseph Sabath's courtroom on October 15, 1917. The case attracted the national press when Clarence Darrow agreed to represent Healey. This crusader for the underdog and champion of social justice was appalled by the criminal excess of the Thompson administration yet, paradoxically, he chose to represent two of the leading party hacks, Oscar De Priest and Fred Lundin, in their fight to escape a jail sentence.[24]

MacLay Hoyne assembled an army of 193 witnesses who testified to the graft money funneled to the chief's office and the wholesale transfer of police officers who interfered in the activities of the ring. Darrow's defense was brilliant, given the damning evidence presented by Frank Johnson, attorney for the prosecution. Billy Skidmore, the gambler and bondsman, was portrayed as an innocent in the hands of the wily Mike Heitler. Detective Stephen Barry was described as Chicago's greatest vice foe; however, he was hamstrung by Nicholas Hunt, who told him to leave Mike Heitler alone. Regarding the transfer of policemen, Darrow argued that Healey was merely carrying out the orders of the mayor, who was accommodating the wishes of his "supporters."[25]

Darrow stated, "In this trial I have seen vice, corruption, and infamy paid for and rewarded at the expense of my client—old, weary, feeble, and broken. I am free to confess that if I were mayor of this city, and knowing Healey as I know him now, I wouldn't make him chief of police. This man is a child in the hands of Costello."[26] Each day, weary, old Healey dragged himself into court wearing a tattered overcoat and workman's pants. It was a stark contrast to the slick, oily appearance of Skidmore and Costello. "Mr. Healey's appearance on the stand won the jurors," explained juryman Robert Beattie. "He appeared to be an honest, hard-pressed man. The jury considered well the fact that he had come from a sickbed to sit 90 days in a courtroom. Costello's word was no good against Healey."[27]

The "poor man" defense resulted in acquittal for Healey, Barry, and Skidmore. Costello turned state's evidence while Heitler languished in Leavenworth

Penitentiary for violations of the Mann Act. The *Tribune* reported that after the verdict was read Skidmore was barely able to contain his laughter.[28] Lamented Alderman Charles Merriam, a loser in his battle against machine politics, "Chicago is unique. It is the only completely corrupt city in America."[29]

MacLay Hoyne tried futilely to bring Healey back to court on other indictments, but upon the testimony of the state physicians, the charges were not prosecuted. The verdict sent a message that the town was again open to the gamblers, pimps, burglars, Black Hand extortionists, and influence peddlers, just as it had been during the balmy days of 1900 when Joe Kipley ran the department.[30]

Lawlessness pervaded the city. Liquor was sold to men in uniform in violation of a wartime prohibition. The road houses in the suburbs and cabarets in the 2nd Ward operated with minimal interference, and the smart guys in the streets knew whom to see for probation, paroles, and pardons. Out of the ashes of the scattered and defeated reform movements came the Chicago Crime Commission, organized to launch a frontal assault on this corrupt administration in league with the devil. Colonel Henry Barrett Chamberlin proposed a civic federation that would examine the origins of crime and its relationship to the police, the criminal justice system, and penology. These were the humble beginnings of the Crime Commission, which would attain greater significance in the coming decades.

By 1927 the graft of Charles Healey seemed small-time when compared with the real fortunes being made by the Capone syndicate in bootleg whiskey, numbers, and prostitution. Frank J. Loesch of the Crime Commission estimated that $260,000 of Capone booze money went directly into the Thompson campaign. The names of the members of the William Hale Thompson Republican Club read like a "Who's Who" of Chicago crime. The Commission assiduously reported these findings, but it is doubtful that anyone listened or cared.

Chicago and "the history of its reputation" rightfully begins with Mayor Thompson, who permitted Colosimo and, later, Al Capone to reunite the scattered vice elements into an all-powerful crime syndicate. The logical choice between reform and the urban political machine, which characterized the development of New York and other cities, was never a factor of Chicago life. The choice in Chicago seemed to be that between the individual ward machines and organized crime.

Notes

1. Herman Kogan and Lloyd Wendt, *Big Bill of Chicago* (New York: Bobbs-Merrill, 1944), p. 75.

2. Ibid., p. 77. For years, Lorimer made Illinois Republican governors. Born in Manchester, England in 1861, Lorimer sold newspapers from the same street corner as Hinky Dink Kenna when both men were lads. He went to Congress in 1895 and served three terms. Lorimer was elected to the U.S. Senate in 1909 by the Illinois legislature.

3. Colosimo organized the Street Sweeper's Union into a potent political machine. A number of his underworld associates, including Tim Murphy and "Dago" Mike Corrozzo, were top union officials. Murphy was a safecracker and gambling boss who owned a North Side poolroom before his foray in Union politics. In 1920 he ordered the execution of "Mossie" Enright, a labor slugger active in Chicago from the circulation wars of 1910 until John Wayman sent him to prison for the murder of Vincent Altman in 1911. (see Chapter 9). With Enright out of the way, Murphy obtained a charter from the American Federation of Labor (AFL) to organize 5,000 streetcleaners, teamsters, and garbage men into a union ostensibly controlled by Corrozzo. The syndicate-run labor unions also worked behind the scenes to elect Governor Len Small, a Thompson puppet indicted in 1921 for embezzling $600,000 that he had collected as state treasurer. Veteran labor slugger Walter Stevens and Michael "Umbrella" Boyle, business agents of the Electrical Worker's Union, bribed and intimidated a number of jurors in the Small case. As a result the governor was acquitted. In return Small pardoned 1,000 felons during his terms of office. Stevens and Boyle were in the employ of John Torrio. See John Kobler, *Capone: The Life and World of Al Capone* (New York: G. P. Putnam's Sons, 1971), p. 78; see also *Chicago Tribune*, May 18, 1920, for a review of Murphy's union connections.

4. *Chicago Tribune*, April 25, 1915. The mounted squad was introduced in 1908 after years of haggling with the City Council to appropriate the necessary funding.

5. Ibid., April 26, 1915.

6. John Landesco, *Organized Crime: Part III of the Illinois Crime Survey* (Champaign: University of Illinois Press, 1929), p. 37.

7. *Chicago Daily News*, October 27, 1917. Thompson's political boss in the 2nd Ward was George F. Harding, who demanded the removal of Nootbar for raiding several "black and tan" resorts after receiving reports of all-night carousing between white women and black men—to which the captain had taken offense. See Thomas Reppetto, *The Blue Parade* (New York: The Free Press, 1978), pp. 219–20, for Thompson's standing in the black community. Between 1915 and 1919 the percentage of black policemen doubled. He also saved the 2nd Ward station from closing.

8. *Chicago Tribune*, April 28, 1915.

9. Landesco, *Illinois Crime Survey*, p. 34.

10. Kathleen McCarthy, "Nickel Vice and Virtue: Movie Censorship in Chicago: 1907–1919," *Journal of Popular Film* 1 (1976): 45–46. Chief Shippy assigned ten policemen to the five-cent theaters to be on guard for "blood and thunder" violence, and films depicting lewd and suggestive behavior. If the police uncovered some impropriety in the films, the theater owner faced revocation of his amusement license; See *Tribune* accounts, April 15 and May 6, 1907.

11. McCarthy, "Nickel Vice and Virtue," p. 45.

12. *Chicago Tribune*, October 21, 1917.

13. Ibid., June 25, 1918. See also "Turning Chicago's Police Crisis," *The Survey*, January 20, 1917. Schluetter was appointed Superintendent on January 12, 1917, in the wake of the Healey payoff scandal; this was yet another instance of a highly regarded German career officer replacing a discredited Irish police official, a disturbing but certainly discernible pattern during this period. Schluetter visualized the formation of an expanded, autonomous morals division independent of the city police. His plans never went past the discussion stage because nervous exhaustion, complicated by other undisclosed ailments, forced him to take an extended leave of absence beginning in November 1917. He passed away a year later.

14. Ibid., June 26, 1918.

15. Ibid., July 19, 1918.

16. Kogan and Wendt, *Big Bill of Chicago*, p. 132.

17. *Chicago Tribune*, September 18, 1918. Funkhouser landed on his feet. He eventually secured an appointment to the Chicago Crime Commission.

18. Kogan and Wendt, *Big Bill of Chicago*, p. 133.

19. Ibid., p. 145.

20. *Chicago Tribune*, October 24, 1916.

21. Ibid. "Chicago's Police Scandal," *Literary Digest*, January 27, 1917, p. 179. Hoyne served as state's attorney from 1912 until 1920. Until the advent of the Republican Thompson administration he showed little interest in vice matters. After inauguration day in 1915, he stood up and took notice. Hoyne targeted the Sportsman's Club for his first investigation. Dive keepers and gamblers joined the club, Hoyne asserted, to receive immunity from Healey's police raids. Although the club had collected $100,000 for lifetime memberships, it had 80 outstanding judgments against it in municipal court. See Landesco, *Illinois Crime Survey*, p. 34.

22. *Chicago Tribune*, January 10, 1917. Skidmore ran a handbook in the rear of his saloon at California and Madison. Formerly a Harrison man, he defected to Roger Sullivan's wing of the party in 1907, raising a staggering sum of $1,000,000 while serving as purchasing agent for the Democratic National Committee. Skidmore went on to become the foremost political fixer in Chicago during the years of the Kelly-Nash machine in the 1930s.

23. Ibid. Typical payoff sums ranged from $40 per week up to $150. The "chief's place" was reserved exclusively for Healey. Thus, Costello, Skidmore, and Heitler could not share in the payoff. Other saloons were split three ways; see Landesco, *Illinois Crime Survey*, p. 35.

24. Arthur Weinberg and Lila Weinberg, *Clarence Darrow: Sentimental Rebel* (New York: G. P. Putnam's Sons, 1980), p. 272. While Darrow may have been a champion for the oppressed, he also took time out to defend a variety of powerful underworld figures including Mont Tennes, who was called before Judge Kenesaw Mountain Landis in 1916 on a gambling indictment.

25. *Chicago Tribune*, November 16, 1917.

26. Ibid., January 12, 1918.

27. Ibid., January 13, 1918.

28. Ibid., January 14, 1918.

29. Kobler, *Capone*, p. 64. Hoyne's police investigation was not the only one in progress at this time. The Civil Service Commission under the stewardship of Percy Coffin brought charges against several officers at the Warren Avenue Station for allowing the dives to remain open all night. This prompted another proposed reorganization. A modified version was passed without the three deputy commissioners, against recommended procedure. The superintendent remained the figurehead of the department; see Landesco, *Illinois Crime Survey*, p. 36.

30. By the mid–1920s, the modern crime syndicate spearheaded by a younger, more ruthless set of gangsters was firmly entrenched in Chicago and firmly behind Bill Thompson, whose motto was "America First, Last, and Always." Such underworld luminaries as John Torrio, Jimmy Mondi, Mike Heitler, and Jack Zuta carried memberships in the Thompson Republican Club, while some of the old Levee characters like Jake Guzik, Dennis Cooney and others slipped back into the city to open up shop along South Michigan Avenue; see Chapter 9.

9

The Guns of Chicago: The Police, Prohibition, and the Crime Syndicate, 1921–31

Prologue: New Year's Eve, 1919

At the stroke of midnight on the last day of the year, a 16-year-old boy named John Walstrom stumbled into the Warren Avenue police station. His face was ashen and he suffered painful, violent convulsions. The boy's father explained to the desk sergeant that his son was not the kind to take a drink, but it being New Year's Eve and all . . .

John Walstrom passed out on the floor. A police van took the stricken boy to the county hospital, but he died before he could tell the detectives where he purchased the contaminated liquor. It was the thirty-second wood-alcohol death reported to the police in less than a month. The police had no leads.

Meanwhile, the New Year's celebration was in high gear at all swank downtown hotels. At the Congress bleary-eyed celebrants quaffed cocktails in casual defiance of a wartime prohibition that would become the law of the land in just 17 days. At Hinky Dink Kenna's saloon, the largest, tallest beer schooner in the midwest, measuring 18 inches in height, was in use for the last time. ''The tub of suds will never foam again,'' lamented the bartender. The expensive leaden glassware was carted off to the basement. As an afterthought Kenna decided to send one to the Chicago Historical Society as a curio of a lost age.

Satisfied that his police would keep matters in hand, Chief John Garrity retired for the evening. ''I visited a few of the cafes and so far as I could see it was a lawful and orderly celebration. Everyone was happy, as they should be on such an occasion,'' he said.

Earlier in the day, "Colonel" Garrity, the mayor's unknown soldier, filmed a public service announcement that was flashed across the screens of the city movie houses.

John Barleycorn is a very, very sick man. His chances for recovery are remote. His stock in trade is in the hands of the government. Many people are trying to imitate him by making false booze. Don't drink it. Death will be your reward!

On the eve of Prohibition Herbert Hoover pronounced the Volstead Act "a great social and economic experiment noble in motive." Humorist Will Rogers offered a more realistic view of the matter: "If you think this country ain't dry, just watch 'em vote. If you think this country ain't wet, just watch 'em drink. You see, when they vote it's counted. But when they drink it ain't."[1]

National Prohibition, years in the making, was to become the national obsession. In tracing the social ills of the nation to demon rum, the Anti-Saloon League and the Women's Christian Temperance Union drafted resolutions and lobbied the halls of Congress with the righteous fervor of an old-fashioned Chautauqua meeting. These modern-day Carrie Nations opened an office directly across the street from the Capitol building. They convinced the powerful industrialists that levels of productivity among the working class were intrinsically tied to clean living and sobriety. To the police they promised empty jails and lower crime rates. Medical people were advised to close down all the alcoholics' asylums. There would be no further need.

In 1907 Georgia set in motion a sequence of events leading to the Volstead Act when the state passed the first prohibition law. The Bible-belt states of North Carolina, Tennessee, Mississippi, West Virginia, and Oklahoma quickly followed suit. A rural grassroots, Protestant movement with no practical application in the teeming ethnic centers of the north was about to become law and the Democratic bosses with deep ties to the liquor trade deeply resented the intrusion. "The south never has respected the amendment proclaiming the Negro equal. More than 83,000 stills have been confiscated in the south. Why should the south tell us to respect the Eighteenth Amendment?" complained Alderman Anton Cermak, who tried in vain to effect a repeal in 1922.[2]

Chicago had wrestled with the temperance issue before. The reputations of two sitting mayors were forever besmirched when they tried to enforce the ill-conceived and unpopular Sunday closing laws. Phase one of the Volstead Act, prohibiting the manufacture of hard liquor, passed into law on July 1, 1919. Commenting on the level of cooperation he expected to receive from the Police Department and the drinking public, District Attorney Charles Clyne predicted that "Chicago is a law-abiding community and will comply with the dry law to the letter. If, however, there should be a violation, the law will take its course just as the same in a counterfeiting case." Clyne positioned 175 agents across the city to assist the police in upholding Senator Andrew Volstead's folly—no easy task in a town that boasted an annual production of 180,000 barrels of beer a year from one brewery *alone*.

The last of the legal beer and wine disappeared from the shelves of the stores on January 16, 1920. Chicagoans persevered. The Eighteenth Amendment permitted the manufacture of various cereal beverages for medical and industrial use. Chicago's ration of whiskey was 35,000 pints, promulgated by the prohibition director for Illinois and his superiors in Washington. The city's 2,000 druggists were allotted 100 gallons of whiskey and wine every three months from heavily guarded federal warehouses near Chicago. This meant to the ethnic Germans, whose culture was tied to beer and *gemutlichkeit*, that they could purchase their favorite beverage from a druggist twice a month—provided of course that they could produce a doctor's prescription.

A cottage industry was born. Skilled penmen sold forged prescriptions to the highest bidder, or openly collaborated with crooked physicians. Fake permits were much easier to obtain. The prohibition officer used a rubber stamp to place the name of the authorizing agent on all permits. The officers who used the permits were required to affix their initials directly over the stamp upon issuance.[3] The trick was to bribe a friendly prohibition agent to secure a permit. Corruption in the early days was rampant. When the government recruited men less inclined to take bribes, people began producing their own revenue stamps. However, it was difficult to replicate one of these stamps. The government printed them with a series of wavy dots in an irregular pattern. The fake stamps invariably depicted vertical rows and were obviously counterfeit.

Booze could also be obtained from unscrupulous druggists who sold cheaply manufactured wood-grain alcohol when their three-month quota ended. The rot gut variety could be purchased directly from the "alky-cookers" along the Madison Street corridor. The police estimated that there were 100 stills operating on every block of the 19th Ward. Public service announcements and political posturing by the chief and the state's attorney's office failed to stem sales of the deadly "coroner's cocktail." Finally, a blue-colored dye was injected into industrial alcohol at the urging of Cook County Coroner Peter Hoffman.

Robbery was another quick and easy way to secure liquor from a drug store. Sometimes the "stick-up" was a put-up job, staged by an unlicensed druggist in order to secure additional quantities from the government on appeal. Each burglarized drug store owner was required to appear before a hearing officer who determined the legitimacy of the claim. If the claim was found to be in order, a replacement supply would be sent from the warehouses.[4]

Everybody tried to make some sense out of Prohibition. In the beginning the prevailing wisdom held that it was every man for himself. The criminal gangs were primarily engaged in labor racketeering, numbers, the slot machines, and suburban prostitution. Old-fashioned gang lords like Jim Colosimo were fat and secure in what was left of the old Levee, while others looked to the future and realized that a new day had dawned.

Crime in Chicago, 1920

Younger men, criminal upstarts of the underworld, seeking admission to the realm seized upon Prohibition to establish reputations and build fortunes. Mindful of the fact that Big Jim Colosimo seemed more interested in his young musical protégé Dale Winter than in running his rackets, Johnny Torrio cautioned his boss that unless the syndicate acted quickly, the bootlegging profits would be taken over by punks. These punks included Dean O'Bannion, "Spike" O'Donnell, and Frank Ragen, who had his own personal army of union men and City Hall payrollers.

It was estimated that there were 1,313 gangs in Chicago during the 1920s.[5] The largest, most vicious street gang of them all was first organized as the Morgan Athletic Club in 1902. Six years later its members changed the name to Ragen's Colts to honor their street-wise, politically ambitious boss. Shrewd, cunning, and utterly ruthless, Ragen turned a ragged bunch of Irish and German pool hustlers into skilled politicians and labor sluggers. Ragen was elected a Cook County commissioner. He doled out patronage and maneuvered his thugs with the acumen of a field marshal, although he never campaigned for election. Sometimes he failed to show up for board meetings. He argued with fellow board members incessantly, thereby delaying crucial votes for hours. The *Tribune* railed against Ragen's antics in its editorial columns but it did little good: his reelection was a foregone conclusion.

Ragen had powerful friends in the blue-collar trades, one of whom was "Big" Tim Murphy, a towering bully with an affectionate smile. He rose to prominence in the railroad union on the strength of fists and gunplay. He was so formidable that he organized the gas workers and was the real power behind the street-sweeper's union fronted by his Italian satrap, Mike Corrozzo. Smiling Tim appointed Ragen the nominal president of the Meter Reader's Collector's and Biller's Union while he pocketed a portion of the dues to keep his pretty wife and young daughter in luxury.[6]

With Ragen's Colts providing the muscle ("Hit me," said Ragen, "and you hit 2,000!"), Murphy had the necessary firepower to wage war against Maurice "Moss" Enright, one of the elder statesmen of the union wars who challenged him for supremacy of the Chicago Federation of Labor in 1920.

"Vote for Tim Murphy—he's a friend of mine!" Murphy's campaign slogan was familiar to every dues-paying member in the union. Meanwhile, the police kept score as the bodies were carried off to the morgue one by one. The labor unions—and not Prohibition—was viewed as the bigger prize during the first few months following passage of the Volstead Act. Between 1911 and 1920 the unions were up for grabs. Twenty-three men lost their lives in the various labor wars. Most were petty hoodlums engaged by the ward healers to slug and intimidate rivals at election time.[7]

Others, like Moss Enright, had powerful friends in state government. Convicted of murdering a rival in 1911, Moss was sentenced to life imprisonment.

Two years after his arrival at Joliet, he was pardoned by Democratic governor Edward Dunne.[8] Enright returned to Chicago to live—and die—by the gun. On a cold winter's day in February 1920, Moss pulled his automobile up to the curb of his South Side home. He exited the car, no doubt anticipating a quiet evening at home with his wife, when suddenly a late model Chalmers pulled noiselessly alongside his vehicle. At a distance of eight feet the gunman discharged 11 blasts from a sawed-off shotgun into Moss. Enright reached for a pistol concealed in his inner coat pocket but it was too late. He collapsed in the bloody snow while his wife watched the unfolding drama from the front porch. Moss Enright became the first of the important gangland "hits" of the 1920s.[9]

The killer was Vincenzo Cosmano, a Black Hand extortionist and foreman of a streetsweeping gang working in Bathhouse John Coughlan's 1st Ward. The cops fingered James Vinci, an Italian chauffeur who happened to drive the getaway car. The execution had been planned for weeks by Tim Murphy, who refused to turn over a portion of the dues to Enright in exchange for Enright obtaining the original charter for the gas workers. When Enright made known his intention to reveal the names of politicians who accepted graft from Murphy, the hit was ordered.

"D'ya know, I don't believe in enmity," Murphy told the police when he was arrested. "If I want to punch a man in the nose I'll do it myself—then shake hands with him after we fought it out."

It was noble sentiment, to be sure, but Murphy, Cosmano, and "Dago" Mike Corrozzo were compelled to sit in jail while State Attorney MacLay Hoyne made Vinci the fall guy. To wring a confession out of Vinci, Hoyne employed the third-degree "sweat," a favorite tactic of the Chicago police in those days. Deprived of sleep and struck by blows to the face, according to defense counsel James Barbour, Vinci finally confessed to being the getaway driver the night of the murder.

The prosecuting attorney was James "Ropes" O'Brien, a flint-eyed, no-nonsense mouthpiece who earned his nickname because of the number of men he had sent to the gallows. This time, though, the evidence was shaky and the motives of the state were dubious. Corrozzo and Murphy planned and carried out the murder but they languished in the city jail. Vinci, devoid of any political connections, faced the hangman. The powerful labor leaders had also secured the best defense money could buy at that time: Clarence Darrow, Stephen Malato and Francis Walker. Realizing that delays meant the loss of witnesses, Darrow was granted extensions from the court because of "other matters" he had to attend to. Hoyne agreed to the arrangement. He seemed in no hurry to bring Murphy and Corrozzo to trial, possibly because of the Black Hand threats he had been receiving in the mail.

On May 23, 1920, Vinci was sentenced to 14 years in jail. Carl Sandburg, then a young *Daily News* crime reporter, asked Deputy Superintendent John Alcock if he thought the gang killings were going to cease in the face of police vigilance. "Well, I think they're getting fewer," Alcock replied. "There's only one thing to do if a murderer is found. Take a life for a life. If the murderer is young and it's the first offense, why, that's a little different.''[10]

Murder, burglary, extortion, and assault had spiraled in the city since 1918.[11] Chief Garrity lauded the efforts of his police, who had stepped up the war on crime. The number of felony cases filed in 1919 increased by 3,000. In 1919 76,793 persons were arrested for violations of the city ordinances.[12] Yet there were fewer felony cases held in the criminal court in 1919 than in the previous year. Of the 76,000 arrests, fewer than 22,000 violators were fined or held guilty of the charges. ''The police arrest thousands and are unable to substantiate charges brought.'' explained Chief Justice Harry Olson of the municipal court. ''It is a terrific waste. The increased activities of the police, the roundups and what-not result in the long run in waste.''[13]

Garrity's romantic vision of a law-abiding city was not shared by everyone. Growing disenchantment with the chief prompted a six-month investigation into the affairs of the department by a committee of maverick aldermen determined not to surrender to Mayor Thompson or be pigeonholed by his stooge Fred Lundin.

Following the Healey disgrace Thompson attempted to appease the reformers by naming Herman Schluetter to the top job. When Schluetter passed away in 1918 the position passed to First Deputy John Alcock on an interim basis. The mayor waited 11 months before naming a permanent successor. The usual candidates passed in review. Friends of Nicholas Hunt cited their man's loyalty to the party and years of experience in police affairs. For his part in bringing down Major Funkhouser, Percy Coffin's name was circulated as a likely candidate.

The guessing game, the intrigues, and the endless moves and counter-moves continued for weeks. Thompson smiled and said only that the next chief would be free of all political pulls.

Bill Thompson had no intention of appointing a competent, single-minded administrator to clear up the entangling alliances with the ward politicians. Instead, he turned to Bill Cooke for the answers. Cooke was a wealthy South Side paving contractor who was a lackey of the blond boss, William Lorimer. When the boss faced expulsion from the Senate on charges of bribery and malfeasance in 1911, it was Thompson and Cooke who were the first to raise money to defend the honor and good name of Lorimer. Thompson, Gus Nohe, Ernest Magerstadt, and Billy Cooke organized a singing quartet that travelled the state to drum up support.[14] At the end of each speaking engagement, Thompson and company lapsed into a boozy rendition of ''Illinois''—comic buffoonery in the first degree.

That was 1911. A decade later the buffoons controlled the political destiny of the city and dispensed patronage as they saw fit. Bill Cooke decided the job of police chief should go to John Garrity, former colonel of the 2nd Illinois Regiment. He was a strutting martinet in breeches, wholly unsuited to command the second largest police force in the United States and one plagued in recent months by simmering racial tension.

Playing checkers and cards with the firemen in the Curtis Street Station was Garrity's consuming passion. For 30 years he dropped by to swat flies and swap lies with the firemen, after marching his men up and down the floor of the West Side Armory.[15] "I hope to inculate the military idea of implicitly obeying orders into the members of the department, from the man on the beat up to the highest officials. I alone am to be captain!" he said.[16]

Within eight months of his appointment in 1918, the discipline he had promised the city was shattered in the midst of Chicago's bloodiest race riot. Garrity's failure to address racial problems within the department directly contributed to the events of July 1919.

Chicago's growing black population supported Thompson at the polls. They were bitterly disappointed when the mayor failed to move quickly to protect the lives and property of South Side black people living in fear along Cottage Grove Avenue.

The riot began at the 29th Street beach when five adolescent boys crossed the invisible line separating the white and black bathing areas. They had steered a raft dangerously close to the white swimmers. From the beach a white man later identified as George Stauber began throwing rocks at the boys playing on the raft. For one deadly second their attention was diverted—long enough for a rock to strike 14-year-old Eugene Williams, who collapsed into the water. Eyewitnesses summoned Officer Dan Callahan to the scene. They pointed out Stauber to Callahan, but he refused to act. When the indignant black men took matters into their own hands, the white swimmers rushed to Stauber's defense. Callahan fled down 29th Street pursued by a gang of black people. The riot was on.

A week of terror followed. Caught in the crossfire of Chicago politics, Garrity did nothing; meanwhile, a contingent of black leaders asked the mayor to petition Governor Frank Lowden for help. "Our police can handle this," Thompson told them. "They're in full command." Captain Michael Gallery candidly told the mayor what was on Garrity's mind—the chief was reluctant to speak candidly, aware that Thompson and Lowden were on less than social terms. "The militia must be called and the entire South Side put under martial law," Gallery said.[17]

The predominantly white police force was obviously in sympathy with the rioters, who desired nothing less than the complete destruction of the black neighborhoods. Two weeks before hostilities broke out, three black patrolmen assigned to the Wabash Avenue Station had been suspended for brandishing a pistol at one of the white officers who had denied them access to the whites-only dormitory.[18]

Garrity deployed much of his 3,500-man force along Cottage Grove Avenue and Wentworth, two north-south streets that effectively separated the black neighborhoods from the Irish-German neighborhoods—the bailiwick of Ragen's Colts, the Aylward Club, the Dirty Dozen, and other defenders of the white race. The Colts entered the affray much the same way as they played football at Normal Park, with their dukes up and geared for action. Under the cover of darkness they assaulted black men working in the downtown hotels and the neighborhoods left unprotected by the police cordon. Streetcars were stopped by Ragen vigilante teams in search of blacks to assault.

Alderman McDonough of the South Side urged Garrity to mobilize 2,000 special policemen for riot duty, as worried city hall officials contemplated the consequences of having deployed the troops too thinly. Garrity and the mayor remained firm until rumors began to circulate that the ramshackle tenements of the black areas were to go up in flames. Six thousand guardsmen were sent in by the governor. The mayor had suffered his first serious reversal, and suddenly things weren't quite as jolly in City Hall.

By August 8 the rioting had ended, leaving 34 dead—20 blacks and 14 whites. Hundreds more suffered injuries. Thompson threw the guardsmen a party, marching them down Michigan Avenue like returning war heroes. They just wanted to go home and leave the police work to the so-called professionals.

Garrity's timid, inept handling of the police during the riot was excused temporarily. State's Attorney MacLay Hoyne presented the grand jury with 17 indictments, all of them involving black men. The prevailing opinion at the time exonerated the police and the entire white race for their part in the riot. Had not the rioting been started by a criminal band of black men who warehoused guns and ammunition in their social clubs?[19]

The grand jury expressed amazement that the state's attorney had been so lax in prosecuting the Colts or any of the other social and athletic clubs. Meanwhile, Garrity reinstated Officer Callahan, who had been temporarily suspended for negligent conduct. "It wouldn't take much to start another riot and most of the white people are resolved to make a clean-up this time," Garrity said.[20] The black population of Chicago had replaced the German anarchist as the policeman's worst enemy in the 33 years since Haymarket.

Placated by a vague promise from the governor that their grievances would be addressed, and cowed by a growing belief that the police were unwilling to protect them from the white gangs, Chicago's blacks retreated behind a wall of stony silence and compliance to the system. The police, for all purposes, would not be confronted with this issue again for the next 45 years.

The City Council considered the riot in different terms. The police had failed to quell a civil disturbance, regardless of its cause. A police committee, which had been formed two months earlier by an anti-Thompson faction led by Aldermen Guy Guernsey and Walter P. Steffen, stepped up its investigation. Guernsey in particular was interested in framing a reorganization bill that might put the police on par with several progressive departments on the East Coast. Their intention was to remove able-bodied administrators and place them on the street patrolling the crime-ridden South and West sides, while at the same time eliminating overhead. This would be accomplished by abolishing the jobs of a dozen captains and closing down stations that had long outlived their usefulness. The graft-ridden detective bureau, a political cesspool since the days of Joe Kipley, was to be done away with under the Guernsey plan. "Any alderman who doesn't vote for this ordinance—which would put 350 policemen to traveling a beat who are now tucked away in jobs which can be eliminated—is voting to protect the thugs and criminals of Chicago,'' Guernsey said, but his ordinance quickly came under fire by the machine regulars who caught their first whiff of it shortly before Christmas 1919.[21]

''It's as bad a botch as the 1911 police ordinance, which was the worst piece of police legislation ever passed by the City Council,'' complained Percy Coffin, who pulled the patronage strings in his role as president of the Civil Service Commission.[22]

The politicians did not like it because the elimination of a dozen captains and several obsolete police stations would drain their political influence. The rank and file resented Guernsey's ordinance for two reasons. Another intruding civilian was attempting to tell a copper how to do his job, and, more importantly, the chances for promotion to headquarters and a safe desk job were being further curtailed.

Clearly, the bill would have to be blocked by the mayor's floor leader in the council, black Alderman Louis Anderson. Thompson circled the wagons and mustered the support necessary to defeat the measure. But the mayor was frustrated and angry with Garrity whose penchant for complaining was exceeded only by his general unwillingness to provide solutions. The chief was called to the carpet by the mayor and given his instructions. ''Present something constructive to me and quit criticizing if you expect my support in reorganizing the department,'' Thompson said.[23]

With hat in hand Garrity returned to his desk to frame an alternative reorganization bill, one that might appease the police committee but not upset the status quo by relinquishing control of certain key precincts and wards to the silk-stocking crowd.

Of course, something this important could not be entrusted to the mayor's indolent, whining chief. The Garrity plan was drawn up by Percy Coffin and Charles Ward, a former secretary of Lorimer's who wrote Thompson's campaign speeches. The new ordinance preserved the detective bureau by giving the chief the right to appoint a captain from the rank and file. Before the plan was considered by the council, Garrity and Coffin had already decided on James L. Mooney for this job; Mooney was one of the captains targeted for dismissal under the Guernsey measure.[24]

For five years the mayor and most of the top officers had sought the elimination of the second deputy's office, which was responsible for moral standards. Funkhouser was long gone and now it was time to do away with the post itself. Second Deputy Charles Frazier was promised an appointment to assistant corporation counsel by the mayor. Since taking over for Funkhouser in 1918 he had performed his duties well, by the mayor's own estimation. He kept his mouth shut and had not issued any inflammatory vice reports that would draw attention to the wide open conditions in over two years. ''The ordinance is a much more comprehensive piece of work than the so-called Guernsey ordinance recommended by the police committee," said Coffin. "We believe it will help the chief materially in his fight on crime."

Honesty and impartiality was needed here to curb the graft, pull, and spoils. What the Coffin-Ward-Garrity measure did to remedy the three evils was to return even greater power to the administration—unlimited power. The Guernsey faction realized that its bill would soon die on the floor. These advocates assumed a different attitude, that maybe it would turn out to be a good thing after all. By giving the mayor all he asked for, let *him* then shoulder the responsibility for its failure. If Thompson was correct in saying that the Guernsey proposals would not work in Chicago, there was no alternative but to approve a plan that would satisfy those most responsible for law enforcement. This was the strange logic that motivated the council to pass a watered-down version of the Garrity measure on March 11, 1920. The Thompsonites lost out in their attempt to create three deputy commissionerships, but succeeded in their original intention of gaining absolute autonomy over the Police Department. Still Garrity was not placated. "I might as well quit before I start," he moaned. "However, I am a soldier and I am not trying to dodge the issue." Garrity promised to "make good" or quit. Said Alderman Anderson: "I still think he should do it in the event that he fails to do the things he said he would."[25]

Chicago teetered on the edge of a criminal abyss. Until 1920 the city was regarded as an upstart on the prairie, a cocksure, youthful town. Larceny was its soul. The activities of the gaslight-era gamblers were not so much crimes in themselves as the expression of a town in its misspent youth. Chicago was never innocent. It was less so in 1920, the start of a ten-year orgy of murder and mayhem unprecedented in U.S. cities. The perception of the city changed in the 1920s. The left bank of Chicago, populated by Carl Sandburg, Ring Lardner, Ben Hecht, and all the other artists and writers who breathed cultural life into the city, was eclipsed and then buried by 1931 when Thompson was finally voted out of office. In the interim the city acquired its reputation as a syndicate town. There might have been a chance if the City Council had the wherewithal to draft a police bill with some teeth, independent of the mayor and his toadies. "Clean up or get out!" the mayor said, and Deputy Alcock ordered a dragnet. In a loud pleased voice Alcock replied, "All in jail, or most of them." For a few weeks the city would be quiet. Then the guns began to fire.

Killer or Killers Unknown

Everybody went to Colosimos, both for the danger of it and for the thrill of it. In the dim early morning hours when everyone else was in bed, the intersection of 22nd and Wabash was aglow. The sharp calls for taxis and chauffeurs could be heard until dawn. The area rivaled opening night at the Lyric Opera, for the magnetic sense of being. Stars of opera and boxing—the two loves of Big Jim's life—made it the favored rendezvous for both the elite and the lowbrow. Particularly after 1914, when the truly dangerous Levee characters had been scattered to the four winds, Colosimo's Cafe attained celebrity status. Colosimo was a patron of the opera. He held season tickets to the Lyric and made it a point to travel to New York once a year to visit his friend Enrico Caruso, who maintained a suite of rooms at the Knickerbocker Hotel.

Caruso was a patron of Big Jim. So was Clarence Darrow, George Ade, Barrett O'Hara, and half the City Council. In the early days Colosimo and his wife Victoria ran a bawdy house, protected by Hinky Dink Kenna and Bathhouse John Coughlin. The internationally famous restaurant of future years was a sleazy, underworld honkytonk populated by the likes of "Izzy the Rat" Buchowski, "Jew Kid" Grabiner, and the denizens of the old Levee two blocks west.

Prostitution was Big Jim's first step up. He opened his dive at 21st and Armour Avenue and named it, appropriately enough, the Victoria.[26] Prior to this time he was a humble Italian "white wing," carrying pails of water to the immigrant section hands in the railroad yards west of the Levee. He had brains and ambition, and came to know other Italians who also wanted to move ahead in the system. These included Anthony D'Andrea of the 19th Ward, "Dago" Mike Corrozzo, and Republican ward committeeman "Diamond" Joe Esposito who also fancied himself a bon vivant. Soon they were no longer hod carriers. They organized the streetcleaner's union, and made it a political force to be reckoned with. The brothel business was always lucrative, but distasteful to gangland social climbers. Colosimo preferred to let Torrio run the dive and the two gambling houses within a block of the restaurant. To his former associates in the Levee, Jim had taken on the airs of a society swell. He was soft, and he wasn't listening to reason.

Torrio was patient with his uncle. Since leaving New York's Five Points in 1909, Torrio had shielded Big Jim from those who sought to do him harm, or try to muscle in on the racket. While not a violent man himself, Torrio employed violence when necessary. In 1910 the Camorra sent Big Jim a death threat. The author of the anonymous letter was "Sunny" Jim Cosmano.[27] A conference was arranged in Little Italy between Torrio and the leaders of the Camorra. A payment of $10,000 was demanded but Torrio angrily rejected their threats. Later that night the three Camorra men were ambushed as they walked under the Archer Avenue subway below the Rock Island tracks. Two died instantly. The third victim was rushed to the hospital where the surgeons worked hard to save his life. The police summoned Colosimo to shed some light on the matter, but the Italian refused to say anything. When Big Jim appeared the dying man opened his eyes and made a mysterious sign with his fingers. "Jim Colosimo! Traitor!" he said. Big Jim, his face ashen, said nothing. But Cosmano had learned a lesson; he made his peace with Big Jim and retracted his demand for payment.

For the next ten years Colosimo lived in the shadow of the Black Hand. Always insulated, always protected by Torrio and the politicians in City Hall, Big Jim lived a life of uneasy security. After Prohibition the situation slowly changed. Torrio had run the resorts and taken the police heat for over ten years. A fear of the federal authorities, coupled with the natural inclination to be a little more conservative when there is something to be conservative with, led Colosimo to resist Torrio's efforts to build a booze syndicate with Joseph Stenson, who owned two breweries.[28] The territories were already being carved up. Frankie McErlane, called the "most brutal gunman who ever pulled a trigger in Chicago," supplied the neighborhoods west of the stockyards with beer manufactured in Joliet. Dion O'Bannion's gang was firmly entrenched in Little Hell, a seamy urban ghetto north of the Chicago River once occupied by law-abiding Swedes and Germans but now a source of crime and gang activity. Dean was a choir singer and owner of a State Street flower shop. Combining sentimentality with a cold-blooded talent for cracking safes, shooting up saloons, and busting the heads of rival labor leaders, O'Bannion had risen in a few short years to become boss of the North Side.

His gang cut across ethnic lines. Samuel "Nails" Morton was a Jewish gangster who won the Croix de Guerre for gallantry in the field of battle during the war. In the little floral shop Morton educated O'Bannion about the potential of national prohibition. They forged liquor permits and removed 5,000 gallons of booze from the Royal Drug Company while six uniformed policemen looked on. When the last of it had been loaded onto the trucks the police blew their whistles and cleared the street of traffic so that the truck might drive away unimpeded.[29] It was the first great hijack of Prohibition and it was all the more reason for Torrio to grow impatient with the old don, his opera records, and his pretty 24-year-old mistress, Dale Winter.

The winsome young songbird from Grand Rapids, Michigan had been with Colosimo since 1915. He provided her with voice lessons from Octave Dua, Victor Arimondi, and Desire DeFerre. Flo Ziegfeld offered her a bit part in one of his shows, but she turned him down so that she could be near the man she loved—Big Jim Colosimo.

Jim's wife Victoria had seen him through the lean and hungry years. If Torrio had protected him from his enemies in the streets, Victoria had protected Big Jim from himself. And now it had all come down to this. The offended wife was granted an uncontested divorce on March 31, 1920, receiving over $45,000 of Colosimo's money.[30] Two weeks later he wed his young girlfriend in a private ceremony at West Baden, Indiana. Two weeks after that Dale Winter Colosimo was a widow.

In the annals of the Chicago Crime Commission, the slaying of Jim Colosimo on May 11, 1920 was the fourth unsolved "hit" of the year, and the twenty-sixth since the agency began keeping track of such murders in 1919.[31] As Chicago murders go, this one was masterful. There were no witnesses, no gun play, and only one fingerprint left at the scene of the crime. The police were not able to link it to any of the usual Levee hangers-on.

Big Jim was gunned down in the vestibule of his cabaret at 4:25 PM. The place was deserted except for two cooks, a pantryman and a waiter preparing for the

5:30 table d'hote. It was his custom to check the cash receipts in the night manager's office. Colosimo went to his telephone to call his lawyer and bondsman Rocco de Stefano but was unable to make a connection. Walking through the east doors of the cafe, he lingered for a moment in the north room. A few seconds later the pantryman heard two sharp reports. He thought a tire had been blown on a passing automobile. Colosimo's body was found in semi-darkness near the Wabash Avenue entrance.[32]

Within a half-hour the streets of the old Levee were jammed with curious onlookers. The top brass of the Police Department, including Chief Garrity, Deputy Alcock, and James Mooney of the detective bureau, considered it important enough to drop everything in order to grill the four employees. Coroner Peter Hoffman and an attending physician examined the body. Colosimo's clothes were arranged in a normal position, suggesting that he might have known the killer. Then Dr. Cunningham glanced about the main dining room. There was a place set for one person who had evidently just finished a meal. The cream pitcher was wet on the sides. The lone diner who paid a call on Colosimo's that afternoon had sipped a glass of apricot brandy, and scrawled a cryptic message on a blank order check. "So long, vampire. So long, lefty."[33]

There were plenty of motives and lots of suspects. Colosimo had received another Black Hand threat as recently as September. The police did not discount the possibility that someone in the Camorra—possibly Mike Corrozzo locked in a jail cell when the bullets were fired—might have ordered the killing. More likely, it was Victoria Colosimo's trigger-happy brothers out for revenge. Joseph and Jose Moresco were arrested and held by the police but released for lack of evidence.

The police were stymied, even after two witnesses testified that they had seen two men, both dressed in dark suits, fleeing the cafe minutes after the shooting. One of them was a short, squat Italian. The police showed the witness a photograph of Frank Razzino, an old-time Black Hand member who had threatened Colosimo in 1907. The witnesses were unable to make the identification. The books were closed on the Colosimo murder, even as new suspects emerged. Who really killed Big Jim? Years later Al Capone allegedly told the playwright Charles MacArthur that he had pulled the trigger that day, on orders of Johnny Torrio.[34] Capone was new to Chicago in 1920. He was a punk from Broadway and Flushing Avenue in the Williamsburg section of Brooklyn. Capone was only ten years old when Torrio was summoned to Chicago, but his name was well known to the Levee vice lord.

The Colosimo funeral set the standard for years to come. Two 20-piece bands were hired, and the list of pallbearers, both active and honorary, was a virtual blue book of Chicago politics, arts, business, and crime.

Levee Characters

George Silver, saloon owner, pimp

Ike Bloom, dive-keeper, white slaver

Mike "The Greek" Potson, gambler, bootlegger (took over Colosimo's)

Patrick O'Malley, saloon owner, gambler

Mike Merlo, Mafia/Black Hand

Ike Roderick, bondsman

Anthony D'Andrea, 19th Ward alderman candidate, Mafia

Rocco de Stefano, gangland lawyer

Aldermen

Michael Kenna, 1st Ward, D

John Coughlan, 1st Ward, D

Dorsey Crowe, 21st Ward, D

George Maypole, 14th Ward, D

John Powers, 19th Ward, R

James Bowler, 19th Ward, D

Timothy Hogan, 4th Ward, D

John Toman, 34th Ward, D

Joseph Kostner, 34th Ward, D

Judges of Chicago

John Caverly, Municipal Court, D

Bernard Barasa, Municipal Court, R

John Prindiville, Municipal Court, D

John Irwin, retired

State and Federal Politicians

John J. Griffin, state senator

Francis Borelli, assistant U.S. attorney

James P. Brady, state senator

J. Rainey, Congressman, Chicago, D

Arts and Entertainment

Giacome Spadoni, Chicago Opera

Titta Ruffo, Chicago Opera

Francisco Daddi, opera

Johnny Torrio and the Catholic Church were noticeably absent from the proceedings. Torrio was not listed among the mourners, and may in fact have already begun the groundwork for his new criminal order. The Chicago archdiocese decreed that Colosimo could not be buried in consecrated ground. A Presbyterian minister, assisted by Alderman Coughlan, delivered the sad eulogy. When it was over the long funeral procession wound its way down Wabash Street past the restaurant. A moving truck full of flowers was trailed by a parade float left over from a week earlier. An advertisement on the side bore the inscription "U-Auto Ride."[35]

The death of Big Jim closed out the rule of the "Mustache Petes," the first-generation Italian crime bosses who confined their activities to the boundaries of the neighborhood. The Black Hand was active in Chicago before the turn of the century. In a copyrighted story *Chicago Tribune* newsman Jack Lait claimed that the ominous sounding name was a journalistic invention, given credence by a veteran Chicago police officer who had spent his last years confined to a desk at a West Side precinct.[36] He took a fancy to a young reporter (possibly Lait) who was trying to manufacture a story while assigned to the dreary police beat. A murderous plot involving a letter bearing the imprint of a hand, coupled with the mysteries and intrigue of Little Italy, was good grist for the evening papers. According to Lait it was a cute piece of fiction—in the beginning. The veracity of the story is doubtful, but after 1900 the kind of extortion practiced in the Italian 19th Ward and in Little Hell was a fact of life and the police were powerless to stop it.

The word "Mafia" is a derivative of the Arabic *maafir*, the name of a tribe of Arabs who settled in Palermo, Sicily before the Middle Ages.[37] The Sicilian peasants adopted the customs of the nomadic tribe, integrating the name into everyday language. When the French were massacred in Palermo on Easter Sunday, 1282, the townsmen described their brave defenders as the "Mafia." In 1417 this secret band of guerrillas absorbed another society of local origin, the Camorra.

The Mafia first appeared in the United States in 1861. An Italian dramatist named Rissoti wrote a parody of prison life entitled *La Mafia*. When the critics asked what the term meant, Rissoti told them it referred to the unique prison argot between inmates and guards. Giuseppi Esposito established the Mafia's first branch office in the United States. Fleeing from the Palermo police he emigrated to New Orleans in the 1880s, where he organized his gang into a cohesive unit. When Police Chief David Hennessey led a campaign to drive them out of his city, he was killed. The attending publicity drew nationwide attention to the Mafia. Eleven Mafia men connected with the Hennessey assassination were executed by New Orleans vigilantes in 1891.

By the 1920s Chicago had become the next major theater for the Mafia. Membership was enlarged; alliances were forged with cooperative members of other ethnic groups. Frank Ragen demonstrated a willingness to work with Torrio and his young lieutenant, Al Capone. On the far South Side the O'Donnell gang bided its time, awaiting the release of "Spike," who had been ruminating about his future from a private cell in the Joliet penitentiary. In 1917 Spike was convicted of robbing the Stockman's Trust and Savings Bank. Frustrated by the judicial system, O'Donnell exerted some political influence with various local legislators. Soon Governor Len Small was beseiged with requests for an official pardon. The O'Donnell gang watched and waited; they would not cross Torrio at this point.

Of greater interest to Torrio were the West Side Gennas, a bootlegging, alky-cooking family of Sicilian killers who controlled the powerful Unione Siciliane through their ally Mike Merlo. The six Genna brothers—Sam, Vincenzo, Pete, Mike, Angelo, and Tony—embodied the immigrant success story since their arrival in Chicago in 1894. Father Genna was a railroad section hand from Marsala, doing the best he could to feed his hungry brood in the midst of the American Depression. He died, leaving his six boys to fend for themselves in the tough 19th Ward ruled by the hated Irishman Johnny Powers.

The Gennas improvised. Black Hand extortion against other Italians kept a roof over their head, and afforded them a chance to invest in more lucrative businesses. They opened a blind pig saloon in a dry district, engaged in the famous olive oil-importing business—a favorite Mafia front in the old days—and established ties to the ward bosses. Anthony, a.k.a. "Tony the Gentleman," was the political fixer in the family, *consigliere*, and society pretender. He maintained a suite of rooms at the Congress Hotel where he entertained his girlfriend, Gladys Bagwell from Chester, Illinois, in regal style. Angelo Genna built the family bootlegging business long before the other gangs gave it a passing thought.

Angelo was the youngest Genna, and the first to die. Before he fell under the blazing guns of O'Bannion, Angelo organized hundreds of peasant Sicilians in the West Side slums bordering Taylor Street into the nation's largest still. Using a formula invented by their brother-in-law Henry Spingola, the Gennas hired neighborhood people to cook the corn-sugar alcohol in their kitchens and bathrooms; the alcohol would later be sold at greatly inflated prices to the speakeasys and restaurants. The liquor was of dubious quality. Some of it was toxic, which accounted for the high number of wood-alcohol deaths in 1920.

To give the illegal and dangerous booze an authentic look, the Gennas substituted coal tar dyes and fuel oil for added flavoring. To expand their output the Gennas and their fellow bootleggers across the city maintained a rendering plant—not unlike a distillery. The good booze acquired through hijacking, by false permit, or brought in from out-of-state breweries could be augmented by "watering". A quart of good whiskey would be added to an equal portion of water and grain alcohol. The essence of bourbon, tripled in quantity, returned a tidy profit to the gangs.

The alky-cookers of the 19th and 20th Wards were paid $15 a day, a princely sum to a class of people who had known only poverty and deprivation since arriving in the United States.

Angelo Genna oversaw the creation of the booze empire. Police protection was available to the highest bidder, and for the moment the Gennas possessed the fattest wallet. With palms outstretched, Captain William Russell's detail at Maxwell Street received $10 to $125 per man each month. Payday was the end of the month at 1022 Taylor Street. A procession of police both in and out of uniform stopped by to receive their take. Sometimes they brought with them lists of new men in the district—and their badge numbers, should they decide not to play ball.

"It was such a common thing," recalled Patrolman Abner Bender, who was assigned to the Italian quarter in 1922. "I never went asking for it. It came as a matter of course. I tried to do my job but the whole thing was so rampant. Nobody wanted to take Saturdays off because on Saturday you just drove up in front of a place, and someone came out with an envelope. They threw it in the car and you drove away."[38]

The Gennas consolidated their political ties in the 19th Ward with armed attacks against Johnny Powers' henchmen, who still maintained firm control of the political destiny of the community. Paul Labriola was a municipal court bailiff and Powers point man in the Italian quarter. For ten years he was precinct captain and political fixer for the hated Irish—an unpardonable treason in the eyes of Anthony D'Andrea who had run unsuccessfully for alderman against Powers.

On a gray March morning in 1921 Labriola left his home near Congress and Halsted. Fifteen feet from his doorstep he was set upon by five D'Andrea gunmen. He said a few words to his assailants, and there was a discharge of heavy caliber fire. One of the gunmen was Angelo Genna, who ensured that Labriola would not recover. He leaned over the body and discharged three more bullets at point-blank range before driving away. Young Angelo was considered the least violent of the terrible Gennas. The real killer in the family was Mike, which should have given the O'Bannionites reason to pause.

Angelo Genna was brought to trial for the slaying of Labriola. For lack of witnesses, a verdict of not guilty was returned. Torrio made his peace with the Gennas and attempted a reconciliation with the defiant North Siders. There was enough profit potential in the liquor trade of all the gangs, he reasoned. His mild-mannered approach could not be construed as cowardice. The muscle of the Gennas, the political connections of Frank Ragen, and the remnants of Big Jim's former vice coalition presented a strong, unified front that was too much even for tough Dean O'Bannion. These were the humble beginnings of the Chicago syndicate—the most omnipotent, kill-crazy crime family in the United States.

The $200,000 Whiskey Ring

Chief Garrity was no David; that much was certain as 1920 came to a close. The Goliath of crime became Chicago's most serious social problem. The killings, burglaries, and Black Hand threats continued through the summer with a new wrinkle. Liquor was arriving in Chicago in box cars and out-of-town trucks on a daily basis. The small-time forgery of medical prescriptions and permit stamps gave way a new underworld technique: the hijack. Mike "de Pike"

Heitler, out of jail and back in business following his conviction for violating the Mann Act, engineered the famous "coup de hooch," which set the Prohibition standard for years to come.

Morris Gidnich, a minor character on the West Side who sold sacramental wines for a living, provided Heitler with the liquor permit. The flabby, aging pimp turned bootlegger sent the permit and a bank draft for $31,000 to the Old Grand distillery in Louisville, Kentucky for the purchase of 1,000 gallons of whisky to be shipped by rail to Chicago. The word was out on the streets that a big carload of liquor was soon bound for Chicago. Robert Perlman and "Mannie" Greenburg were two of Heitler's associates from the old days on the West Side. They took the orders, guaranteeing a return on the investment of nearly $200,000.

The cargo arrived at the Gresham Station near 83rd and Vincennes on the South Side on September 30, 1920. In the dim light of lanterns and moonlight, 30 men worked feverishly to unload the cases of liquor from the box cars into awaiting trucks. Chubby fisted, corpulent Heitler and at least 20 uniformed and plainclothes policemen were identified by eyewitnesses. They stood idly by, drinking from flasks opened on Heitler's command.

The trucks pulled out of the yard, but they did not get far. The saloon-keepers who attempted to cart away their illegal booze were stopped before they reached the outskirts of the loop by Heitler's *own men*, who hijacked the entire load. The lid stayed on for exactly one month, but the cheated saloon-keepers did not remain quiet for long. Heitler was pressed to repay the money, and "Billy" Weinstein, owner of the Clark Street dining room, confessed to the U.S. attorney that he had "fixed" the deal with the police.

For months rumors and allegations circulated that the entire police force was "wet." In May, just ten days after an assassin's bullet felled Big Jim, a motor truck containing a shipment of liquor had been expropriated by four detectives assigned to duty at the Maxwell Street Station. "The incident is closed. The merchandise will be returned," promised Captain Russell. The matter ended there.

"Chief Garrity should clean up the Police Department and make the town safe for its citizens or resign his job," said Alderman Guernsey, renewing his attack against the police. With the city wetter than ever, a grand jury was summoned to investigate the now famous "coup de hooch." Heitler surrendered to federal authorities on October 27. Wild rumors circulated in the hall that his confession would link every top politician and police officer from the mayor on down. However, this was not the case; Heitler was tight-lipped and uncooperative. Garrity was subpoenaed by the grand jury, but under instructions from the corporation counsel he refused to surrender the statements given by the 11 indicted rum-runners.

Significant in the Garrity subpoena were the words "to testify." Federal statutes decreed that persons testifying before the grand jury gained immunity from prosecution. Without Garrity's knowledge the mayor revoked the license of Colosimo's and Ike Bloom's cabaret on 22nd Street. The conspicuous raid against the two Levee nightspots had little to do with the pending indictments, and everything to do with partisan politics. Aldermen Kenna and Coughlan had brought the ward into line behind the Democratic ticket in the November election. "I don't care what favors you may be getting from City Hall. You must be right with the ticket and the vote in your precinct will tell the tale," Kenna told his precinct captains who preferred breaking with the mayor than with the aldermen. When Thompson heard the news he dispatched Lieutenant James MacMahon to the cabarets. Before he died, Big Jim was a trusted 1st Ward precinct captain. Now Bloom picked up the fallen mantle for the Kenna democracy.

A battery of police officers including James Mooney appeared before the grand jury. The district attorney had no luck in coaxing a confession out of them, while Heitler and his co-defendants produced a series of witnesses who swore to a perfect alibi. The "million dollar" defense team headed by Clarence Darrow and Weymouth Kirkland down played the seriousness of the crime. "The government tells us that anarchy and Bolshevism will follow the uncurbed violation of this law," sneered Darrow.[39]

In his summation Assistant District Attorney James R. Glass put the matter in perspective by reminding the jury that "this case is the first real test of the government's ability to fight the whisky game." The verdict did little to affirm the validity of the Prohibition laws. Heitler and five of the original defendants were convicted. Their prison sentences were light, but of greater concern was the vindication of the police. Over 20 officers were named by the grand jury in the first wave of indictments. Only Detective Sergeant George Harris was prosecuted, and he was later acquitted.

Heitler's star was on the wane. His influence in criminal circles, like that of Colosimo, was of another era. The Torrio syndicate had little use for him and therefore it mattered little that he faced another stretch in Leavenworth. The booze caper merely provided the emerging syndicate with a useful lesson on beating the government at its own game. In disgust, Major A. V. Dalrymple resigned as supervising Prohibition agent of the central department. In his final report he accused the mayor, the police, and top administration officials of blocking his every move to enforce the dry law. In less than a year he destroyed 2,500 working stills, and confiscated $4,000,000 worth of booze—a record that even Eliot Ness would be hard pressed to duplicate. Dalrymple had tired of the politics and the endless shams. He entered the booming Texas oil business.

Though technically absolved of wrongdoing by the courts, the Garrity police continued to stumble. Charges were filed against the department by John A. Carroll, president of the Hyde Park State Bank, for bungling the capture of bandits who made off with $272,000 worth of securities. "To my way of thinking, banker Carroll bungled his attempts at capturing the bandits much worse than the police did," Garrity said.

Thompson's patience had finally run out. Returning from a vacation to West Baden, Indiana, the mayor summoned Garrity to his office on November 10,

1920, and ordered him to resign with haste. He reminded the chief that the probation period had ended, and since the Guernsey ordinance had been defeated in the council, crime conditions had not improved. Garrity, who should never have been appointed in the first place, was understandably chagrined. His undoing was his zealous desire to please the mayor at the expense of upholding the laws.

In naming a successor Thompson was compelled to appoint a man without regard to politics, a plan he had found successful two years earlier when Herman Schluetter replaced Healey. The mayor decided the job should go to 36-year-old Charles Fitzmorris, a former newspaper office boy who had served as private secretary to both Carter Harrison and Thompson. Fitzmorris became Chicago's second youngest police chief. Good fortune, practical common sense, and a talent for navigating through the changing political climate of Chicago made Fitzmorris a success story at 29.

Born in Fort Wayne, Indiana, his career got off to an early spectacular start when he won a trip around the world in 1900. The contest was sponsored by William Randolph Hearst's *Chicago American*. When he returned he joined the paper as an office boy. He got to know Mayor Carter Harrison while covering the City Hall beat, and in 1911 he was appointed private secretary.

Fred Lundin decided that the young, impressionable Fitzmorris might be able to do Thompson some good in 1915, when Harrison was in political eclipse. He not only bolted to the Thompson camp; he also brought with him the only certified list of registered Democratic voters, which proved invaluable to Lundin and his campaign strategists. During the 1919 race riots Fitzmorris made a name for himself by touring the South Side no-man's-land with National Guard officials. While Garrity continued to falter, Fitzmorris built his case with Thompson. For weeks he actively campaigned for the job, presenting ideas and alternatives that Garrity had not even considered. Fitzmorris enjoyed a reputation as a maverick and the reform elements were anxious to give him a chance to make good. The Chicago Crime Commission promised its support while the City Council approved the nomination unanimously.

"In making this appointment I am giving you absolute authority over the Police Department," Thompson promised. To the reporters he added: "Charley's the boss. What he says, goes!" News of the surprise appointment caught the City Hall boys off guard. Fred Lundin, who had been consulted by the mayor, threw up his hands and said, "Well, I am not in politics, you know."

Within 72 hours Fitzmorris began issuing sharp directives that hinted at the most ambitious shakeup in years. Three objectives were outlined.

- To break up all existing cliques, systems, and understandings that militate against police efficiency and permit patrol sergeants and operators to cover up laxity and take care of their buddies

- to give a new deal at the detective bureau with a chief of detectives in charge who has picked his own staff and can therefore be held strictly responsible for results

- to reduce special details to a minimum and thereby put more men on the job of crime fighting. Under the new arrangement the auto squad, anarchist squad, payroll, bomb, and burglary details were eliminated for an all-out assault on crime.

Fitzmorris believed somewhat naively that shaking up the department was the best way to bring the men into line and would thereby result in greater productivity. To meet these ends he transferred every patrol sergeant in the city, and brought to the forefront a new cadre of officers who would guide the destiny of the police department for the next ten years. The political rottenness of the detective department was given immediate attention. Chief Mooney, who had effectively stonewalled the grand jury, was demoted to lieutenant and assigned to the apolitical department of identification. Lieutenant Michael Hughes, who had been in the department since 1897 and was twice wounded in gun battles with criminals, was given responsibility for the detective force, which was reduced from 100 chairwarmers to just 25. Fitzmorris gave Hughes a blank check to run the bureau as he saw fit—an irony, given the fact that he was the first cousin of Judge Robert Emmett Crowe, one of the chief's most strident opponents. In turn, Hughes appointed Lieutenant William "Shoes" Schoemaker to serve as his assistant. Shoes made a good name for himself at Des Plaines Street, where he held the denizens of the West Side Levee in check.

Deputy Alcock, relegated to obscurity by Garrity, was entrusted with the responsibility of drafting a merit system that would reward efficiency and punish those officers who were lax or negligent in the performance of their duties. Fitzmorris received City Council support for his plan to imprison all armed robbers for life, whether it was their first conviction or not. Alderman Anton Cermak, the most powerful Democrat in the City Council, pushed for immediate adoption of the measure.

Alderman Joseph Kostner attached a provision to the bill that would have rewarded any police officer who killed a robber in cold-blood with an automatic promotion. Fitzmorris and the council were whipped into a state of frenzy.

Within a week the raiding parties were dispatched across the city and hundreds of low-level gamblers and pickpockets were rounded up. Commenting on the prospects of ending crime through tough measures, the *Tribune* recalled that "methods of dealing with crime to date have been largely a failure. An experiment with what practical men consider more practical measures certainly is worth making." The bill to reward the police based on the number of thugs killed in the commission of a crime was doomed to failure. The prospect of a trigger-happy police force that had been branded just two months earlier as thoroughly demoralized and unfit to protect the good people of Chicago was just too much to swallow.

The chief's reorganization plan and commitment to reducing violent crime yielded some practical results during the first 58 days of his reign. With the cooperation of the Civil Service Commission, 31 slackers were dismissed for insubordination and inefficient work. Criminal arrests were up 30 percent from the corresponding period a year earlier. The detective bureau under Schoemaker captured first place in the monthly efficiency ratings for December, with 550 arrests and $33,000 in recovered property. It was an enviable beginning, but there was much work left to be done.

Satisfied that he had cleansed the department of its rotten apples, the mayor summoned 1,000 captains, lieutenants, sergeants, and senior patrolmen to a special ceremony in Orchestra Hall to laud them for their achievements. Likening the war on crime to a football game, Thompson reminded the men that teamwork was the key. "Let's leave this building a team, each man helping his fellow to protect the people we serve!" Thompson chortled. "Go get the crooks!"[40]

Caught up in the spirit of the pep rally, Fitzmorris seized the podium: "Mayor Thompson is the best friend the Police Department ever had!"

The Failure of Prohibition to Prohibit

The era of good feeling lasted all of three months. As the spring alderman election approached there was more bomb throwing and gunplay in the 19th Ward between Powers and D'Andrea. The new state's attorney was Robert Crowe, a master of power politics. A member of John Wayman's staff while in his early thirties, Crowe's rise in Republican politics was mercurial. In 1919 he became chief justice of the criminal court; at 38 he was the youngest man ever to serve in this capacity. In the fall 1920 election Crowe received a strong mandate from the voters. He polled over 200,000 more votes than the Democratic challenger Michael Igoe, who had waged a mudslinging campaign. Eager to establish his independence from the Thompsonites while at the same time playing to the Chicago press corps, Crowe advertised himself as the worst enemy a criminal ever had.

The year 1921 was not a good one for Fitzmorris. For eight months Crowe swiped at the chief, Governor Len Small and his liberal system of pardons and paroles, and the Thompson judges sworn to uphold the wide-open town. In September Judge Joseph David of the superior court slapped a $100 fine on the chief and sentenced him to five days in jail for contempt of court. The second worst enemy a Chicago criminal ever had made it known that in his view the courts were derelict in their duty when convicted murderer Carl Wanderer was let off with a 20-year prison sentence.

Fitzmorris was not whistling in the wind on this issue. As a part of Crowe's scheme to build an organization independent of Thompson, he set out to enlist the support of a dozen well-known judges of the higher courts, the 4,000 members of the Chicago Bar Association, and the anti-vice advocates in the Committee of Fifteen.

Since there could only be one really big name crimefighter in Chicago, Crowe spent the first months engaged in guerrilla tactics against Thompson's young Galahad. A postwar recession had swelled the ranks of Chicago's unemployed. With more than 100,000 idle men in the streets, there was a significant decrease in burglary and larceny in the first quarter of 1921, as compared with the similar period under Garrity. Henry Barrett Chamberlin of the Chicago Crime Commission compared the numbers to other metropolitan areas and concluded that under Fitzmorris, Chicago was the only city to show a downward trend in winter crime. The personnel changes and the vigilance he had shown in going after notorious vice rings had paid off handsomely—at least on the surface.

The vexing issue of Prohibition was another matter. Since the Heitler indictments the police were still knee-deep in the booze graft. Corruption extended from the city into the counties. In January Ralph W. Stone, Illinois Prohibition director, admitted that his office was bereft of honest men. "I know that graft exists in my office," he said, recalling that crooked agents were in the habit of placing liquor permits for blacklisted dealers on his desk for authorization.

Fitzmorris echoed the larger failure of Prohibition when he admitted to the press on September 25, 1921, that his police were as lax as the federal authorities in curbing the traffic in liquor: "Reports and rumors reaching me indicate that 50 percent of the men on the Chicago police force are involved seriously in the illegal sale or transportation of liquor." He estimated that a full 2,500 men were implicated in bootlegging, and took strong measures to ensure compliance with the federal laws. Charges were preferred against Lieutenant James Van Natta of the Irving Park District for aiding and abetting a bootlegging ring in his district. Fitzmorris revealed the existence of a slush fund raised by officers at the South Side Deering District to pay for the legal defense of three sergeants facing federal indictments. The station was commanded by Captain Michael J. Gallery, a bitter foe of Fitzmorris, who was called to task in January for his failure to "clean up." From behind closed doors the angry shouts of the chief could be heard by other anxious officers lining the corridors. "The chief is young but not to be monkeyed with," said one. When Gallery emerged from the meeting he explained that it was "just a little misunderstanding about the failure of some of the men to pull on time. There's mighty little about the department the chief doesn't know."[41]

What Fitzmorris didn't know was that eleven members of Gallery's command were protecting one South Side bootlegger. "This department alone cannot enforce the government laws controlling the sale and distribution of liquor any more than it can enforce the laws governing counterfeiting," Fitzmorris said, admitting that the federal government needed to take a more active role if Prohibition was going to prohibit.

At the same time the chief issued the second major transfer order in six months, moving 800 men to new precincts. Captains Gallery, James Madden, and William Russell were moved out of their districts, an open acknowledgment that these men had done little to chase out the rum thieves in their command. The *Tribune* noted that if these men could "thrive in cahoots with bootleggers and rum runners, they might thrive in association with yeggmen and second story workers."

The police boundary map was redrawn, thus affecting nearly every precinct in the city. With a stroke of the pen Fitzmorris closed the North Halsted Station,

Figure 10

CLAMPING IT DOWN

Prohibition was barely two years old when this cartoon appeared in the *Herald & Examiner*, December 19, 1921. As quickly as the "lid" went down, there was usually someone within to quietly take it off. (Deckert reproduction)

but opened three new ones at Woodlawn, Hudson Avenue and West North Avenue. In attempting to deal with violations of the Volstead Act, Fitzmorris was guided by the mistaken belief that it was up to the government to establish policy and enforce the laws, with his men acting in a supporting capacity.

The intention henceforth would be "to make Chicago so dry that a sponge can be wiped across it without picking up a drop of liquor," explained Fitzmorris as he outlined a bold new policy of enforcement. Raids, arrests, suits to enjoin property owners, and the revocation of licences were the weapons placed in the hands of the police by the new dry order. From his office in City Hall—two miles from police headquarters—Fitzmorris was satisfied that he had acted decisively and with dispatch. All that remained was for the commanding officers in the precincts to carry out the new directives. Given the decentralized nature of policing and the day-to-day administrative tasks of City Hall, the best Fitzmorris could hope for would be minimal compliance, and cooperative noninterference from the state's attorney. His admission that half the force were bootleggers provided Robert Emmet Crowe with the necessary firepower to launch an all-out frontal attack on the chief's unguarded flank.

A Political Bird of Passage

The effectiveness of the chief was tied to the captains and deputy commissioners who were the "eyes and ears." If they succumbed to bribery and influence peddling, any hope of cleaning up vice and crime was lost. Behind his desk in City Hall Chief Fitzmorris spent his days greeting a retinue of party hacks, reporters, and members of various citizens' groups. They shared one thing: a hope that Fitzmorris would grant them a special favor.

His day typically began at 9:00 AM, sometimes earlier if there was a full calendar of interviews, public appearances, and meetings on the docket. The mail—whatever was left after the department secretary had sifted through it— was reviewed by the chief. With responsibility for police records, statistics, financial, and purchasing, the secretary was an integral player in the bureaucracy. An effective administrator could shield the chief from the reams of paperwork and the imposing questions of City Hall reporters.

Before ten o'clock the parade began. Business agents of a traveling circus would stop by to inquire about the possibility of 50 uniformed men providing free security during a week-long carnival. It would be explained that such-and-such a committeeman gave his blessing. The request is granted, and the agent is grateful.

An alderman who serves on the powerful City Hall Finance Committee enters the office. Certain enterprising businessmen in the ward resent the intrusions of the police into their activities. Lately, the cops have made things hot, and these businessmen have been known to contribute to the mayor's reelection campaign. The chief smiles wanly, and reminds the alderman that if the law is to be upheld and respected it must apply to everyone. The alderman, somewhat miffed by this affront, excuses himself. The slight will be remembered at year's end when the chief goes before his committee with budget requests for the coming year. Then perhaps the well-intentioned young crimebuster will understand that Chicago politics means trade-off and compromise.

Outside his door the anteroom is filling up fast. The usual assortment of bailbondsmen, street hustlers, and reporters with credentials seek admittance. They have gotten past the outer office by virtue of rank and privilege: numbered pass keys.

The chief will pick and choose among the hangers-on. Some will get discouraged and leave; others will wait all day. An office holder who dispenses patronage in the ward presents the chief with a fist full of traffic citations issued to his constituents. It is a serious matter, explains the cloutster. Unless they are dismissed right now his power and influence in the ward will become suspect, and that could have serious consequences in the spring primary. With a wave of his finger the chief motions the politician out of his office. The tickets will be slipped into the secretary's envelope and properly disposed of.

Next comes a police inspector who presents his findings. Graft has been uncovered on the North Side that would support formal charges. The accused has some political connections that could impact the balance of political power in the ward. The chief will have to weigh carefully his options on this one.

By now the noon hour has arrived. The commissioner leaves his office and must fight his way past the milling throng in the corridor. He says a few words to key people he recognizes. He pretends not to hear the rest, for they will still be there when he returns. In the company of one of the deputies he exits the hall and takes his lunch at a nearby eatery where the subject rarely deviates from police topics.

When he returns the gentlemen of the press are greeted cordially, but with an air of aloof diffidence. They want to talk about the Wanderer case—a sensitive subject with the chief—but he issues an innocuous statement that will be reprinted in the afternoon papers. The reporters know more about the latest developments in criminal court than the chief. It is a cat-and-mouse game he has played with them for years.

The chief scans the incoming teletype tape, and the reports submitted by the divisional commanders. It is the only connection he has with the men in the field. The reports are studied carefully before the Board of Strategy convenes— the last, but most important piece of business of the day.

Before the real police business commences he must deal with a censorship case—one of the most disagreeable tasks facing a commissioner who must assume the guise of art critic and be damned for it. The manager of a local art house complains that a policewoman closed him down because his movie contained sexually suggestive material. "What is art?" screams the manager, whose business has fallen off. Since the elimination of the post of morals inspector, the chief has become the final arbiter of public decency. He is the court of final appeal. The theater remains closed in this instance.

The anteroom is all but empty, clearing the way for a serious, frank discussion between the chief and his immediate subordinates: the deputy, the chief of detectives, and certain captains. A wide variety of issues are raised. Opinions are supported by facts. The men in the field present the chief with an imposing array of statistical data for the preceding 24 hours. He takes a few moments to scan the reports before commenting.

Invariably the topic reverts to morale and discipline, the bane of 30 other men who once occupied the hot seat. He must carefully balance the political consideration—represented by the army of office holders who visited him that afternoon—with the needs of the community and the demands of the reformers. It is a dangerous tightrope to cross, with no margin for error. The allegations of malfeasance are resolved by the drafting of the transfer order. The chief can hope that the collective wisdom of these men, coupled with his own instincts, will result in a police reorganization that will please the public with minimal damage to the delicate balance of power in the wards.

By now it is early evening. The meeting ends and the commissioner leaves his office. He realizes that his career will end if the election is lost, if not sooner. The men he has tried to placate today will not remember him five minutes after he cleans out his desk for the last time.[42]

The State's Attorney's War

"Fitzmorris is the best chief Chicago ever had!" said the unabashed Thompson. With this vote of confidence the mayor sequestered himself at Fred Lundin's farm for a working holiday, unaware of the alley-sniping going on between Crowe and Fitzmorris. Events reached a head on October 29, 1921, when the state's attorney sent six raiding squads into the gambling strongholds to illustrate the point that the wide-open town was fact—not myth—in Chicago. When news of the clandestine raids reached the downtown offices, Captain Patrick Lavin, a holdover from the Harrison days, was summoned to Fitzmorris's office. He had just been handed a jury summons to appear before the grand jury to explain why vice was intolerable in the central district. The indictments followed the roundup of 150 prisoners taken in the afternoon raids. "If I must not only conduct a prosecutor's office but a police department as well I shall do so until I have cleaned this city," sniffed Crowe, whose motives were purely political.

The Chicago press corps was puzzled over the apparent schism in the ranks. The attack on the Fitzmorris regime flew in the face of the warm, energetic support he had received from various civic agencies. At the outset of his term Crowe had pledged political unity and the cooperation of his office in the war on crime. It was the least anyone could expect since it was the duty of the police to catch the crooks and the responsibility of the state's attorney to prosecute them. "The police department is in a better position to stand an investigation than the state's attorney's office," Fitzmorris snapped, adding that in his opinion there were plenty of arrests but few prosecutions. Of the 150 gamblers and pimps brought in, all but five were released; and for those men facing arraignment, Billy Skidmore, Sam Cohen, and Izzy Lazarus waved bail bonds in the face of Crowe.

The feud had all the earmarks of a classic Chicago donnybrook. Crowe accused Fitzmorris of tipping off the handbooks and whorehouses of impending state's attorney's raids through an operative—Captain Lavin. The embattled chief reverted to a familiar tactic, one used by Charles Healey in his battles with MacLay Hoyne in 1917. He withdrew the 27 police officers assigned to the state's attorney's office. The detail was supervised by Sergeant Thomas O'Malley. He was suspended and charges against him were brought before the Civil Service board for adhering to the orders of Crowe and not Fitzmorris. It was the privilege of the chief, and he exploited his position. "I will not have police officers carrying out raids for ulterior motives," Fitzmorris said.

In City Hall the aldermen began choosing up sides. John Jontry of the 3rd Ward asked permission from the upper echelons of the Thompson camp to address the full council about the matter. He said he would demand the chief's immediate resignation. Jontry and other likeminded aldermen had been insulted "too many times" when they had gone to his office to transact "business." It was an interesting dilemma that faced Thompson as he raced back from Lundin's retreat in West Baden to put out the firestorm. When he arrived in City Hall on Monday morning the mayor expressed amazement: "I left Friday and the chief and the state's attorney were good friends. I came back and found things as they are. I'm still trying to find out what it's all about."

Thompson was hard pressed to find any fault in the way Fitzmorris had conducted police business. To back down from his earlier support would mean that he sanctioned the political brinkmanship of the state's attorney. Working quietly behind the scenes, Thompson tried to effect a reconciliation. Lundin strategists were first dispatched to the office of Alderman Jontry, who was told in no uncertain terms to shut up. When asked whether he intended to go to the floor in search of the chief's scalp, Jontry said: "I've postponed it. I was afraid the public would think I was butting in."

Crowe said the matter would not rest until Sergeant O'Malley was reinstated and a formal apology issued from the chief's office. It was hardly a face-saving gesture, but there were signs of a thaw. Thompson drafted a letter reminding Crowe that his landslide election might not have been such a landslide after all, if not for the patronage army the mayor placed at his disposal.

For his part, Fitzmorris backed down from earlier statements that disclaimed Crowe's contention that the city was wide open. He told police captains that when raids were followed by convictions, the convicted men would thereafter have their cabaret licences revoked. "The town is cleaner now than in years and this order will help keep it that way," he said, as he boarded the train for an old-fashioned political hegira in West Baden.

To the victor belonged no spoils, only the satisfaction of knowing that he had been sustained in his job for a few more months. Following Thompson's lead, the City Council turned down Robert Crowe's request for a separate and independent police force. Charles Fitzmorris was no great visionary, but neither was he incompetent. The city murder rate—perhaps the most accurate barometer of true crime conditions—was the lowest it was going to get. After 1923 the gangland killings began to mount.

Fitzmorris's record as a crimefighter during his short term of office was an enviable one, given the rapacity of the Thompsonites. Fitzmorris was independent to a point—understanding that results are achieved through delicate negotiations and compromise. With the pack of scoundrels occupying the City Council at this time, it was not always possible or even desirable.

He was a skeptic of Prohibition who preferred to allow the government to enforce the laws. The chief's critics accused him of running a wide-open town, but the record later showed that a degree of toleration was preferable to vigorous suppression.

The political winds of Chicago shifted in 1923, and Fitzmorris was not one to go down with the ship. Two of Thompson's closest allies—Governor Len Small and Fred Lundin—were implicated in major scandals. The rift between the mayor and the state's attorney played into the hands of the Democratic reform element, which rallied behind Judge William Dever of the superior court. Thompson prudently withdrew to lick his wounds and plot his strategy for 1927.

It was entirely conceivable that Mayor Dever would have retained Fitzmorris as police chief when he assumed office in April 1923. The chief had, after all, been a loyal Democrat for many years prior to 1915, and there was not the residue of Thompson scandal attached to his name. Instead, Fitzmorris chose to enter the private sector, in the employ of George F. Getz, a coal millionaire and well-known supporter of Thompson. It was a job that carried with it a hefty salary, which sustained Fitzmorris until 1927 when he made his grand comeback with Big Bill as city comptroller.

A Dollar's Worth of Protection

William Emmett Dever was a sheep in wolf's clothing, a reformer thrust into the mayor's office by "Boss" George Brennan who desired party unity in the wake of Republican scandal and growing uneasiness with Thompson. He easily defeated Arthur Lueder, the city postmaster slated by party regulars in what was viewed as a "throw-away" election. Dever accomplished many things in four short years; school reform and great public works projects were begun, and the city took a step in the right direction to solve the perplexing issue of municipal ownership of the traction companies. It was a record most mayors could be proud of, but William Emmett Dever went down in flames—the embodiment of "Paddy" Bauler's old adage that "Chicago ain't ready for reform."

He promised the voters something new: clean government. To achieve this end he focused on the crime situation, which was probably not as bad as he had painted it during the campaign. Fitzmorris's policy of passive resistance to the bootleggers resulted in fewer gangland slayings but widespread violation of the Prohibition laws. Dever personally opposed the Volstead Act, but he was sworn to uphold the laws at the risk of losing political support. To German ethnics who merely wanted to drink a glass of beer on Sunday he said that he wanted to promote respect for the law and protect the public from the poison of wood alcohol. Beyond that, he hoped that the law would be modified in time. "I have never pretended to be and I am not a prohibitionist," Dever said, setting forth the tone of his administration. "It is true that I am trying to make Chicago a place of law and order."

Ultimately it was action and not words that counted. Harrison was a law and order man. So was Busse. And who could forget Thompson's promise to drive all the crooks out of town? With this mayor, though, crime was no laughing matter. Accordingly, he appointed Captain Morgan Collins, commander of the sensitive East Chicago Avenue Station, a Republican bailiwick since the days of Mike Schaak. The bipartisan nomination was greeted with a mixture of surprise and concern. Maybe this mayor was serious after all.

Collins was a distinguished line officer who had been with the department since the horse and buggy days of 1888. His period of service was interrupted only once, when Joseph Kipley fired all the Republican policemen in 1897 to settle scores with John Badenoch. Collins, who lived on the North Side, aspired to be a doctor. He studied at the Bennett Medical College but never received a degree. What he learned about forensics proved invaluable during key murder investigations.

When he showed up for work on April 17, the usual throng of well-wishers stopped by, pledging their support to the chief in his huge task of guarding the peace and security of the city of Chicago and urging him not to pay too much attention to the high hats who would tell him how to do his job. Mayor Dever, who paid more than lip service to this element, saw it differently: "Collins, there's a dry law on the nation's books. This town will immediately become dry. Tell your captains I will break every police official in whose district I hear a drop of liquor is being sold."

But first was the perfunctory reorganization. Captain Patrick Lavin, who commanded the powerful three-legged throne of traffic, central, and the South Clark Street District, was ousted in favor of Patrick Kelleher. Kelleher had a guardian angel of his own in City Hall: Municipal Court Bailiff Dennis Egan, who kept Paul Labriola on the payroll until D'Andrea gunmen cut him down. Mindful of the dangers of giving a politically connected captain too much power, Collins split up the central detail between three men: Kelleher, Charles Larkin, and John Martin. With an eye on efficiency Chief Collins scanned the duty rosters of all the precincts. Two hundred sergeants who were assigned to the station houses were returned to the streets to travel a beat. The order effectively eliminated the "soft snaps." "The people of Chicago are entitled to a dollar's worth of protection for each $1 of the $11,000,000 they pay annually for the support of the police," he said.

The direct line of accountability was established between the captains and the chief's office. Policemen were told to disregard the orders of politicians and other influence peddlers. These first directives issue to divisional captains set the tone for the next four years, forcing the entrenched booze syndicates to make accommodations. Collins proved to be a worthy and zealous adversary.

The Torrio mob attempted to buy him off in the usual way. They offered him $1,000 a day to allow deliveries of bootleg whiskey into Chicago. Collins called the reporters in and told them, "Some policemen are taking $5 to look the other way when a beer truck passes. How long will it be before they're taking $100 to look the other way when a murder is being committed?" The ante was upped to $100,000 before he sent a squad of blue coats into the Levee to padlock the doors of the Four Deuces, where Torrio and Capone ran their operations.

In January 1923 there were 6,565 legal "saloons" selling nonalcoholic beverages. By the first quarter of 1924, 2,100 licences had been revoked and another 2,500 bars were compelled to close permanently.[43] Collins hit hard and with a vengeance. He sought the means to enter restaurants and the private homes of the West Side alky cookers. In a celebrated incident that drew criticism from the blue-nosed *Tribune*, Collins seized a mother of two for operating a still. Vicious gangster or neighborhood moonshiner, it made no difference to Chicago's top cop.

The raids, the crackdowns, and the seemingly incorruptible nature of Collins caught Torrio by surprise. Threatened by "Spike" O'Donnell's boys on the South Side and "Nails" Morton and Dion O'Bannion on the North, the former kingpin of the Levee took a vacation to Italy, where he purchased a villa for his mother. It afforded him time to reevaluate his shaky position. When he returned in March 1924 he began the long anticipated ingress into neighboring Cicero, which offered temporary shelter from the storm. The town was controlled haphazardly by the West Side O'Donnells; Eddie Vogel, boss of the slot machine racket for nearly 25 years; and Eddie Tancl, a native son who achieved minor fame in the boxing ring before turning to crime. The mayor was Joseph Klenha, who, like Johnny Patton in Burnham, eagerly welcomed the incursions of gangsters into his suburb as long as they brought with them their cash. The town stood on the outskirts of Chicago, and it was populated by hard-working Bohemians and Slavs who appreciated beer as much as the Germans and Italians. Cicero was a natural and the Torrio gang members were prepared to go to war to claim it for their own. But first Johnny Torrio had a piece of business to transact with O'Bannion. The North Side Sieben Brewery had churned out thousands of barrels of illegal beer since the Prohibition law went into effect. The original owner, Bernard Sieben, was no longer affiliated with the business. He leased the malting plant to a holding company listed in the city records as Mid-City Products. Sieben was on the payroll as a consulting "engineer," receiving $200 a month.

Joseph Stenson and his brother Ed, pre-Prohibition beer suppliers to the flophouses, masterminded the take-over of Sieben Brewery and the South Side Manhattan Brewery in June 1920 when the syndicate organized their business. Over $25,000,000 of working capital was invested in the project and it yielded a tidy return estimated at $50,000,000. The Stensons maintained an elegant suite of downtown offices and dined regularly at the Chicago Athletic Association. The Stensons were members of that class of wealthy privileged men who enjoyed the companionship of gangsters. O'Bannion, "Two-Gun" Louis Alterie, and Johnny Torrio managed the brewery and took the heat until Stenson had the good sense to get out before he jeopardized his social ranking and his life.

When internecine warfare threatened to upset the peace, Torrio made accommodations. O'Bannion exploited his position by violating existing trade agreements and showing blatant disregard for the West Side Gennas—especially after Angelo refused to pay a $30,000 gambling debt to the Irish North Side boss. O'Bannion demanded satisfaction, and prevailed upon Torrio to make sure that Genna paid up. The truth was that Torrio no longer exercised that kind of influence over the murderous West Siders. Because of this quarrel the shaky partnership begun in 1920 between the Irish and the Italians collapsed on May 19, 1924, near the loading dock of the Sieben Brewery at 1470 Larrabee Street on the North Side. O'Bannion communicated his bogus intention to "quit the rackets," offering his Sieben interests as a sign of good faith.

The deal was to go down on May 19, when an armed convoy of 14 trucks loaded with 4 percent beer was to depart the brewery. A retinue of gangland heavyweights, including Torrio, Alterie, O'Bannion, and Hymie Weiss, oversaw the loading of the booze trucks. Three policemen from the Hudson Avenue Station, Joseph Sonnenfeld, Charles Hurst, and Joseph Warszynski, stood guard for the beer-runners. Suddenly a police raiding party showed up at the doorstep of the brewery. It was personally led by Collins and Deputy Chief Matthew Zimmer. Collins promptly removed the stars from the three officers, whose sole duty was to ensure that no trucks left or entered the yard. If there was treachery in O'Bannion's heart, he was at least temporarily forced to endure the humiliation of being remanded over to the station for booking. Arraigned before Commissioner Herman Beitler, Torrio pulled out $7,500 from his pocket, which made his bond. James Casey, who listed his residence as the Tremont Hotel, posted $5,000 on demand. The mysterious Mr. Casey turned out to be Daniel O'Connor, a Democratic heavyweight who coordinated the Illinois campaign for presidential aspirant William McAdoo. O'Connor was a business agent of Torrio's who cabled Torrio $3,000 when the gang boss visited Milan. A little black book bearing his handwriting was seized by Collins. In it were the names of police sergeants targeted for bribery offers. It was a disappointing discovery but a major triumph for the dry forces: disappointing because O'Connor wielded considerable influence for the *proponents* of the Volstead Act, and a success because a fistful of indictments was returned by the grand jury as a result of the largest, most successful police raid against the bootleggers to date.

Collins proved that he was not kidding when he said he would uphold the dry laws. A large measure of credibility was restored to the department, and the syndicate was thrown into disarray. Five police captains were removed from their posts, including James Madden and James McCann, son of the old West Side Levee boss-cop of bygone days. Captain Kelleher was called to the carpet and told to clean up or risk dismissal.

In gangland the consequences were equally far-reaching. For several months Torrio seethed and fumed at what he believed was O'Bannion's duplicity. To compound the outrage O'Bannion made light of the incident, bragging to his friends: "I guess I rubbed that pimp's nose in the mud all right." Torrio, Capone, and the South Side contingent made an alliance with the Gennas against their common enemy—Dion O'Bannion.

The leader of the North Side mob was born in "Kilgubbin," an Irish section located between Division Street and the Chicago River. O'Bannion hustled newspapers in the loop, bringing his boyhood friends into the business: George "Bugs" Moran, Earl "Hymie" Weiss, and Frank and Pete Gusenberg. They formed a United Nations of Crime, unified in their common hatred of the Italians who were quickly supplanting the Irish and Western Europeans in the ethnic pockets of the near North Side of Chicago. Little Dean was a bright cheerful lad who attended St. Dominic's school during the week and served as an altar boy on Sunday. When he was twelve a streetcar struck him in the LaSalle Street tunnel. His lacerated leg never completely healed, leaving him with a noticeable limp.

"Gimpie" O'Bannion got to know the downtown crowd when he worked as a singing waiter at McGovern's Chop House near Clark and Erie. By the time Prohibition was in full swing he made use of these connections to buy protection during the many booze hijacks.

He bought into the Sieben Brewery, which distributed illegal beer, and the Cragin Products Company, which manufactured the denatured alcohol necessary to produce the booze. From Maxie Eisen's saloon on Roosevelt Road, O'Bannion, Weiss, Alterie, and a former policeman named Warren Lavin threatened to corner the market in Chicago. The situation was a grave one for Torrio and the Gennas, but they could not move against O'Bannion as long as Mike Merlo, first president of the Unione Siciliano, refused permission. Merlo urged moderation and restraint. He had ties to both of the quarreling factions and was not anxious to see an outbreak of war. But Mike Merlo suffered from cancer and was not expected to live to see the new year. Sensing imminent danger, Dean O'Bannion kept two pistols near the cash register of his State Street florist shop, which he purchased with William Schofield in 1922.

On November 8, Merlo died, leaving the all-powerful Unione Siciliano in the hands of Angelo Genna. Dean O'Bannion, unaware that the Genna-Torrio forces were planning his murder, went about his business preparing for the Merlo funeral. The same men who signed his death warrant directed $100,000 worth of business his way—the cost of the floral arrangements to bury Mike in style. From Al Capone came an order for $8,000 worth of flowers. It was a busy weekend of work for O'Bannion. The Armistice Day orders were coming in, which required Schofield to remain out of the shop. On Sunday night a caller phoned the shop saying that someone would stop by the next day for the Merlo floral wreaths.

The next day O'Bannion remained in the shop, clipping and grooming his American Beauty roses, while the porter Crutchfield cleaned and swept the showroom. It was 11:30 AM. The remaining customers exited the shop, and then the phone rang. "This is Bill," his partner said. "I'm out at Mount Carmel Cemetery fixing up the graves for Armistice Day. Can you stay until one?"

"Sure," was O'Bannion's reply. Three swarthy Italians entered the front door. They wore brown overcoats and were smooth shaven, according to the description later given by Crutchfield. From the rear of the store O'Bannion emerged. "Hello, boys, you from Mike Merlo's?" Dean extended his hand to greet the taller man in the middle, whom he might have known. There were six shots, fired in rapid succession. O'Bannion crashed to the floor as the killers made their exit through the front entrance into a dark-colored, nickel-trimmed Jewett.

Within minutes Mike Hughes, Captain Schoemaker of the Detective Bureau, and Assistant Attorneys John Sbarbaro and William McSwiggin arrived to question the witness. All three had more than a passing interest in the death of Dean O'Bannion. McSwiggin was the son of a Chicago police sergeant who had deeper ties to the West Side O'Donnell's, sworn to drive Torrio-Capone beer-runners out of Cicero. Sbarbaro owned a funeral home patronized by gangsters on all sides of town. With the inquest out of the way, Sbarbaro drew up a contract with O'Bannion's widow for the most lavish, gaudy funeral the city had ever seen—minus the blessing of the church, of course. Father O'Brien at Holy Name Cathedral first made Dean an altar boy, but refused to bury him in hallowed ground when he was gunned down in his flower shop.

At the Chicago Avenue Police Station O'Bannion gangsters milled about the entrance way, awaiting the arrival of key witnesses. Their hip pockets bulged with concealed handguns; their attitude was defiant. Mayor Dever wondered who was really in control. It certainly wasn't the police: "It is time to decide which element in Chicago is going to control."

Embarrassment and humiliation compounded the state of open lawlessness. As the hundreds of mourners filed slowly past O'Bannion's casket a published report crossed Collins' desk, describing a testimonial banquet that was held for the fallen gangster two weeks earlier at the Webster Hotel. In attendance that night were six police lieutenants, and Chief of Detectives Michael Hughes. It was not known whether Hughes contributed to a general fund to purchase a diamond studded, platinum watch for O'Bannion. Dever demanded an immediate investigation, but for the moment Collins stood behind Hughes whose crime fighting record was impressive. The detective chief explained that he believed the banquet was to be given in honor of Jerry O'Connor, secretary of the Theater Janitors union, and that County Clerk Robert Sweitzer was to be in attendance. "As soon as he entered the banquet hall and recognized a number of characters whom he had thrown into the detective bureau basement a half-dozen times, Chief Hughes knew he had been framed," Collins said.

Framed or not, Mike Hughes was ousted by Dever with Collins's silent blessing. The usual platitudes were offered by the mayor and the chief, who pointed to Hughes's declining health. "I'm as well and as fit as I ever was, Hughes replied. The real reason he was out and Schoemaker and John Stege were in, according to Hughes, was the axe wielded by party boss George Brennan: "I wouldn't stay on under the current administration if I had to take a job shoveling the streets! They had been wanting to get rid of me since Dever became mayor. But until now they didn't have the nerve."

To placate party loyalists who inwardly fumed against the Thompsonites that were retained in the administration, Dever offered the head of Hughes on a platter. If not the chief of detectives, Collins would have sufficed. Following the November election and the O'Bannion fallout, top Democrats closeted themselves in French Lick, Indiana to rectify this situation. "Never in its history," said one politician, "was the Police Department so closely hooked up with the underworld as it is today." Of course, no one of that generation was present when Mike McDonald and his henchmen wielded the big stick, so judgments offered by the political bosses were premature. But neither had the city encountered so much open gunplay in so short a time.

The call went out for Collins's dismissal. Forgotten were the brewery raids, and the chief's pledge to uphold all laws, something he had sincerely tried to do since taking office in 1923. "If Collins were the man for the job, he would have used the bureau to smash these syndicates of gunmen and policeman," said one politician. Dever sustained the chief, but ordered wholesale raids against all vicious resorts and liquor flats. Nightly raids were staged in the old South Side badlands. The war on gunmen could only be partially successful as long as the gangs were able to retreat beyond the city limits in Cicero. When a gangster was shot, a big holdup staged, or a policeman killed in the line of duty, the perpetrator needed only to seek refuge in the village whose cottage industry was vice. The bootleg beer was a superior variety, since it was shipped in on a daily basis from Johnny Torrio's own brewery in West Hammond, Indiana. The busiest saloon in the whole wet town was Eddie Tancl's place at 48th and Ogden, and it was the magnet that drew the O'Bannionites and the Torrio men into Cicero. Tancl, who once killed a man in a semiprofessional boxing match, operated his saloon with the full support of Mayor Klenha and his crooked police chief Theodore Svoboda. When federal agents descended on the place, there was usually a tip-off. "When the cops and agents come out here after hours all the time to get drunk of course they tip us off," explained a Cicero bartender.

The majority of the saloons bought their beer from Torrio, with Tancl stubbornly refusing to bend a knee to the new master. This was a costly mistake. The former boxer was shot down in his own saloon by Myles O'Donnell a few days after Dean O'Bannion went to meet his maker. There was little Collins could do to eradicate vice outside his jurisdiction. The responsibility belonged to the state's attorney and the Cicero police, both of whom talked a good game but did nothing. "Every saloon and disreputable joint in the county is going to be closed," Crowe promised. "It's the end for liquor, beer, and vice."

There were limits to what the police could do in the face of an escalating murder rate. Collins was quick to point this out, but his political opponents maintained he was being hoodwinked by the police captains in the districts, who wielded more power and influence than the chief.

Expert observers of the police maintained that deteriorating conditions resulted from the "scatteration" policy of Dever and Collins. Under Fitzmorris the emphasis had been on public safety, and the prevention of violent crime. His intention had been to sweep the city for lone gunmen, rapists, and stick-up men who would threaten the peace of the neighborhood, and to make the streets safe for an unescorted woman to walk home late at night in peace. Prohibition and organized vice were relegated to secondary status. This policy reflected the traditional views held by the big-city police departments of that time.

Dever took a more active role in day-to-day policing than his clownish predecessor. His dictum to "uphold all laws" was carried to the letter by Chief Collins. The effects of the "closed-town" policy were closely observed by other large cities confronted by wholesale violation of the Volstead Law. After two years the results were none too encouraging. In the four years following the passage of the Prohibition law, nearly one-third of all Chicago murders remained unsolved. Out of 991 killings, the assailants were unidentified in 365 cases. For the first ten months of 1924 the figure was 105, or 34 percent.[44]

Gangsters killing gangsters was something Chicagoans accepted with weary resignation. But when the crimefighting organization was faced with a major murder investigation outside the criminal fraternity, the public expected and demanded action. The failure of the "scatteration" policy was best illustrated when Mike Hughes set out to solve the disappearance of 14-year-old Bobby Franks on May 21, 1924.

The quiet, dark-haired youth was the son of Jacob Franks, a retired millionaire who made his fortune by quietly buying up parcels of Chicago real estate and then converting it into saleable property. His son attended classes at the South Side Harvard School, a private facility for the scions of Chicago society and business. At 5:15 PM young Franks was seen near the corner of 47th and Ellis Avenue. He started to walk south on Ellis to go home when he was abducted by two men in a car. That was the last anyone saw of the boy alive. The next morning a special delivery letter arrived at the Franks home on South Ellis Avenue demanding $10,000 in unmarked fifties and twenties. The letter was typewritten on two sheets of paper.

In the wake of the gangster bloodbath of recent months, the opportunity had at last presented itself for the Chicago police to make a clean breast of it, employing all available means to solve this sensational case and redeem its soiled image.

The police first learned of the disappearance of Bobby Franks at 2:00 AM, when the worried father paid a call on the detective headquarters to see Schoemaker or Hughes. An acting lieutenant named Robert Welling was in charge. Jacob Franks, in the company of former City Corporation Counsel Samuel Ettelson, discussed the matter at length. Fearing that the attending publicity might drive the kidnappers to murder, Ettelson urged Franks to wait until morning before taking further action. Deferring to the judgment of this former Thompson appointee, Welling decided not to say anything about the matter to his superiors. Nothing was entered into the police blotter. It was as if the whole meeting had never occurred.

The next morning, just as the ransom demand was arriving at the Franks household, the lifeless body of Bobby Franks was fished out of a muddy culvert under the railroad tracks between Wolf Lake and suburban Hyde Park. Death was the only certainty, for the Chicago police had no clues when at last they began their investigation. "After a hard day's work on the Franks mystery, I am convinced tonight that it was a plain case of kidnapping for ransom, not a case of a victim of perverts," Hughes theorized. The Franks home was circled by police, who had reason to suspect that a kidnapping gang planned to abduct the eldest daughter Josephine. Two mysterious letters—one sent to Collins, the other to Mr. Franks—convinced the police that a "moron" was loose in the city. All known sexual deviates were rounded up as a precautionary move. Thomas Gilfoyle, a former policeman emerged as the first suspect and was hustled off to detective headquarters where he was grilled by Hughes.

Ten days passed before the real killers were identified. Neither Hughes nor State's Attorney Crowe were major factors in fingering Nathan "Babe" Leopold and Richard "Dickie" Loeb as the kidnappers. The two wealthy University of Chicago students killed the boy for the thrill of it, and then lingered in the neighborhood to lend encouragement to the police, the reporters, and state's attorney employees during the investigation. Two reporters from the *Chicago Daily News*, James Mulroy and Alvin Goldstein, found the typewriter used by the killers to write the ransom note. Assistant State's Attorney Berthold A. Cronson obtained a confession from the pair and then announced to the shocked, disbelieving city that the case was closed.

Bob Crowe stole all the credit, and then agreed to a backroom deal with wily old Clarence Darrow in the dining room of the Germania Club on Clark. The state's attorney was eager to send the boys to the gallows, but Darrow vowed a fight to the finish, pointing out that if his clients pleaded not guilty, the trial could drag on for months. The cost to the state would run in excess of a million dollars. It was agreed: Loeb and Leopold would enter a guilty plea in return for their lives. Darrow would later say that he caught the state by surprise, but in Chicago, nothing is left to chance.[45]

Clarence Darrow emerged as a national figure for his brilliant courtroom stand against the death penalty, and all the police had to show for it was another missed opportunity. The handling of the Loeb-Leopold case reflected the larger failures of the mayor's police policy. By attaching a greater emphasis to vice and Volstead instead of traditional crime prevention, the efficiency of the force was seriously undermined. Strong vigilance and suppression had a reverse effect, apparent to even the most dewy-eyed reformer by 1927, the close of William Dever's term of office.

At the outset of the administration Morgan Collins promised "full jails and a populous morgue." To his surprise, he found out that in Chicago the jails will not stay full. Collins galloped full speed into the judicial windmill, his lance cut to the quick by Judge Joseph David of the superior court, who reminded his zealous friend that "the writ of habeas corpus is a most sacred right 700 years old." David resented the chief's implication that crime could not be properly punished by "rubber stamp" judges. "The chief of police issues an edict to pick up everybody," he said. "The next day hundreds of humans—many, if not all innocent—fill the jails. Yet they fume to newspapermen about habeas corpus judges."

When this tack didn't work Collins issued a famous "shoot-to-kill" order and then outfitted high-power persuit cars with a special open top that allowed police officers to engage in running gun battles during wild chases down Chicago streets. During the Collins years the Torrio forces were scattered to the city's perimeter, but quickly regrouped and attained a virtual stranglehold over organized crime. It can be said that Al Capone came of age during this reform administration— an irony that Bill Thompson could point to with some pride. How much better off was Chicago with a dry reformer in the mayor's chair? Not very much.

The Downfall of Dever and Decency

Word for word, insult for insult, Mayor Dever was no match for the demagoguery of William Hale Thompson. In the emotionally charged mayoral campaign of April 1927, William Dever emphasized the unprecedented public works projects initiated in his term. He pointed with pride to the clean record of his administration, not one public official had been censured for malfeasance. His achilles heel was, of course, the dry issue. "When I'm elected, we will not only reopen places these people have closed, but we'll open 10,000 new ones!" Thompson thundered. "Dever and Decency" was attacked broadside by Thompson's "America First" theme. The real enemy was the King of England, who was in league with Dever's school superintendent William McAndrew to propagandize the children of Chicago.

Throughout the campaign Thompson polarized the black neighborhoods against Dever. The Collins police, according to Big Bill, were "cossacks," who disrupted Thompson campaign rallies in the black wards. Robert Crowe, having mended his fences with Bill Thompson, accused Dever of trying to foment a race riot to effect a favorable outcome in the election.

Clean government is what the people want, Dever answered in his characteristic low-key style. To the mayor's assertion that Chicago was safer than it had been in years, Thompson took out a full-page advertisement in the *Chicago Tribune* to refute the claim. The *Tribune*, which threw its support behind Dever, published the diatribes without comment or reply.

Mayor Dever says he is satisfied with crime conditions in Chicago.

Thompson points to the fact that the insurance companies have DOUBLED their premiums on burglar insurance during Dever's term. When Charles C. Fitzmorris was chief of police under *Thompson* the crooks were run out of Chicago. Although there are 7,000 policemen in Chicago, Dever has none of them walking beats to protect your homes and your lives. The city is overrun with morons and other vicious elements. The papers teem with accounts of murders and other horrible lawlessness. *Thompson* pledges himself to change these conditions and make life and property once again secure in Chicago.[46]

The syndicate's money was with Thompson. Al Capone was said to have personally contributed $250,000 and the services of his army of gunmen to the candidate's disposal. Since 1925, when Johnny Torrio escaped Chicago with his life after being riddled by O'Bannionite bullets, Capone sat atop the booze and vice empire. As election day drew near, Capone's headquarters at the Metropole Hotel was converted into campaign central. The gangster's domain was populated by key members of the Thompson Republican Club, whose shining stars included the pimp Jack Zuta, Dan Serritella of the Unione Siciliano, and soon-to-be-appointed city sealer, and the 20th Ward Ellers. Morris Eller was to become city collector, and his son Emmanuel a judge of the superior court. These men engineered a secret slush fund and supplied "floaters"—men paid to vote twice—in the 1st, 2nd, 3rd, 4th, and 5th Wards. Typical payoffs from operators of policy wheels and illicit saloons ranged from $100 to $600 a week, with a total return to the Thompson campaign coffers of $1,000,000.

Chicago braced for its wildest election yet. In Grant Park the day before the vote, Deputy Chief John Stege instructed seven members of the detective squad on the proper technique of loading and firing the Thompson submachine gun, a deadly new weapon capable of firing 1,500 shots a minute. The machine gun was perfected by General James Thompson of New York—no relation to Big Bill, although many of his staunchest supporters were well acquainted with its amazing power. Bullets from the Thompson submachine gun had already claimed the life of Assistant State's Attorney William McSwiggin outside a Cicero dive in 1926. "We designed that gun for law enforcement and military usage," explained Colonel M. H. Thompson, son of the inventor. "Machine guns, bulletproof vests, and bulletproof automobiles for the beer-runners. God knows what we'll come to!" sighed "Shoes" Schoemaker. It was a changing world.

Chief Collins detailed 250 auto squads to cover the city, with one patrolman assigned to each polling place. Any suspicious car was to be pulled over to the curb and its contents searched. The "trouble spots" designated for added police surveillance included the South Side black wards, and the syndicate-infested North Side precincts. These elaborate preparations were not really necessary, because Al Capone had sent the word out to "lay low." Frank Loesch of the Chicago Crime Commission, it is said, prevailed upon the gang leader to permit clean elections. Capone was touched by this gesture and was anxious to reciprocate.

Chicago gangsters—at least from the Capone camp—kept a low profile during the waning hours of the campaign. Chief Collins continued his policy of rounding up all known gunmen, focusing his efforts on the North Side, where "Bugs" Moran refused to make the same peaceful guarantees.

On April 4, shortly after ransacking the offices of Alderman Dorsey Crowe—a Dever supporter—Vincent "Schemer" Drucci was arrested near Wacker Drive and Clark. The "Schemer" was the eyes and ears of the North Side mob. The dark-haired gangster had served O'Bannion and then Hymie Weiss faithfully since the lean and hungry days when they earned their daily bread cracking open bank safes. After rising to preeminence in the rackets, Drucci dogged Al Capone's tracks. In early March he took a Pullman to Hot Springs, Arkansas to assassinate the vacationing Capone. Like most of the O'Bannion-Weiss-Moran plots to kill the big fellow, this one also ran awry. Drucci slipped into Chicago, quietly. Whatever acts of vengeance Capone might have planned never reached fruition. A Chicago police detective named Dan Healy shot and killed Drucci in the front seat of the police squad car after the gangster lunged for his shoulder holster. "You're a punk copper!" Drucci said, echoing the words of another Chicago hood of note, Joe Saltis, with whom Healy had recently tangled on the South Side.

The death of the "Schemer" was ruled accidental, but his widow sued the city and the Police Department. The funeral of Drucci was another showy event observed by thousands of Loop officeworkers. Defeated alderman candidate and mob gunsel "Dingbat" O'Berta led the mourners. A U.S. flag was draped over the silver and aluminum casket, which was conveyed from Municipal Judge Sbarbaro's undertaker's parlor on Wells Street.

The other casualty of the election, hardly noticed by many of the worthies in attendance at the "Schemer's" funeral was Mayor Dever, who lost by 83,000 votes. To the outside world it was a shocking repudiation of the principle of clean government. To thirsty Chicagoans, it was the price of doing business. The Dever defeat was reflected in the ethnic wards. His support had badly withered in the German, Italian, Polish, and Czech communities. The game was really lost in the black neighborhoods, where the mayor garnered only 7 percent of the vote.

After 39 years in the Police Department, Collins chose to go down with the ship. He was the first superintendent to complete a full four-year term of office, and he left with no regrets. "I have faced the hardest job of any police chief in Chicago," he said. "The Prohibition law and the racketeers that exist in its violation presented a problem that no other police chief in the history of the world had to face."

The 61-year-old chief left behind an enviable legacy. Despite the gangland mayhem that could only get worse before it got better, there was not a hint of scandal during his term. During the Collins era the city health department drew attention to the deplorable sanitary conditions at several crumbling nineteenth-century police stations. The cell block of the Des Plaines Street Station was "clearly in violation of the ordinances and as maintained is a nuisance and a menace to health," according to one published report. Sixteen prisoners were packed in each of the larger cells, which allowed less than 50 cubic feet of air space for each prisoner. At Stanton Avenue 29 men were crammed like sardines into four cells. These conditions were nothing new. With a limited operating budget they could not be renovated as quickly as the health department wished. Bad plumbing, deteriorating masonry, poor ventilation, and myriad other problems plagued the district commanders and contributed to declining morale. There were 40 precinct stations in use when the Collins term ended in 1927; 19 were built before the turn of the century. Morgan Collins oversaw the acquisition of three new properties—District 9, "East Side"; District 13, "Morgan Park"; and District 16, "Chicago Lawn"—and the preliminary work for a new headquarters building began in 1924.

The new building occupied nearly a square block on South State Street and 11th Avenue. It was the first step to rid the city of squalid, disease-ridden police stations that had long outlived their usefulness. During a 1924 inspection of detective headquarters at 179 LaSalle Street, City Health Commissioner Dr. Herman Bundesen declared that he would order the facility abandoned. "It is not fit for a dog," he snapped. The five detention cells in the basement were designed to accommodate ten persons. During a weekend sweep of the Levee it was not uncommon for 150 to 200 persons to be jammed in the narrow space. All this changed when Central opened in 1928.

The 15-story structure was hailed as a marvel of the decade, a fine example of what a city could do if politicians could reach a consensus. The Central Station was approved by public referendum and financed through bond issues. It was a major step in modernizing a big-city police department still wedded to nineteenth-century concepts. Design flaws were scrupulously avoided by the architects and engineers who consulted with Deputy John Stege on the layout of the plant. Facilities included automatic telephone switchboards, a movie projection room for the film censor, a floor a cells accommodating 2,500 prisoners, two floors for the detectives' department, and several courtrooms. Speeder's court, the morals division, and other special branches of the municipal court were allotted space in a building that blended smoothly into the urban tapestry. The absence of window bars made the police headquarters resemble any other office building in the neighborhood. Chief Collins could begin his retirement with a measure of pride: the new building was to be his legacy. "In my four years I have worked harder, I think, than any of the other 6,000 men in the force," he said. The old bromide was certainly true, at least in the case of Chicago's top Prohibition cop. He worked to become, and not to acquire.

A City's Shame

Michael Hughes was returned from political exile to guide the department during the third and final Thompson administration. In the months before he made his triumphant return to the hall, Hughes headed up the county highway patrol for Sheriff Charles Graydon, a syndicate lackey appointed by the Thompson forces to replace Paddy Carr, who died before he could collect his first paycheck. Graydon permitted the slot machine racket to flourish in suburban road houses in unincorporated Cook County and the distant suburbs north and northwest of Chicago. "You can't operate slot machines and gambling unless you have the word to go from the state's attorney and the sheriff's office," explained Roger Touhy, a powerful independent who operated outside the Capone interests in the northwest suburbs. "Otherwise you couldn't possibly keep the slot machines up for a day or two."[47]

Touhy's man in the sheriff's office was Matt Kolb, who was assigned to Hughes's uniformed patrol. When the newspaper boys began snooping around the county, reliable Kolb would alert the cafe owners to button up until the storm passed. Kolb was killed in a Morton Grove tavern on October 17, 1931, by Al Capone when the big fellow became jealous of his relationship with Touhy.

The spread of vice, bootlegging, and gambling into the far reaches of the county mirrored the outward push of a generation of thrifty immigrants who saved their dimes and nickels during the prosperous 1920s. The decade gave rise to the "bungalow belt" in the northwest corridor of the city—low-cost, sturdy housing for Germans, Poles, Swedes, and Lithuanians. Dever's crackdown, coupled with this steady and impressive growth, encouraged Capone to expand beyond Cicero. Roger Touhy and his brother stood in the way. The Touhys entered the booze racket in 1921, operating out of a small garage near Hoyne and Madison Streets on the West Side, where they got to know the cop on the beat—Dan "Tubbo" Gilbert. Tommy Touhy and Tubbo became good friends. A year earlier, in 1920, Gilbert was one of the police officers questioned in the Mike Heitler "coup de hooch" hijacking. The strapping, wiry police officer was naturally sympathetic to private entrepreneurs engaged in the booze trade. As the Touhy sphere of influence continued to widen in the 1920s, Gilbert's star was also in ascendancy, hitched as it was to the rum-runners.

By 1923 Gilbert was a sergeant in the Cragin District near Grand Avenue and Leclaire. One afternoon Touhy and his partners were moving a truck through the district, believing that everything had been squared with the police. Personal friendships aside, Gilbert had the truck stopped and impounded to the station. Roger Touhy dropped by the 27th Ward Democratic club, where he reminded Gilbert that the truck was loaded with near-beer. Always willing to accommodate, the police sergeant accompanied Touhy back to the truck and apologized profusely for the oversight. He had several patrolmen help the gangsters load the barrels back into the cab. Pulling his old friend aside, Gilbert whispered, "I don't care what kind of beer comes in this district, it has got to be a fin a barrel, or no beer comes in this district."[48]

The price was exorbitantly high; a single barrel cost the Touhy gang $12. Why so much, Roger wanted to know. Gilbert reminded him that this was Tony Hartford's district. Hartford was a former polo player who also owned a saloon on North Avenue. Of greater importance to Dan Gilbert was his political connections. Tony Hartford was a perennial candidate for the state legislature. Gilbert was a shrewd operator, smart enough to know which side of the bread was buttered in his district. In 1926 he was promoted to lieutenant, and was named a district captain at West Chicago a few years after that. Dan Gilbert was a bright, young up-and-comer, someone the syndicate kept a watchful eye on as the years passed.

Mayor Thompson was sworn in on April 13. He slapped his new chief on the back and offered these encouraging words: "Go get 'em, Mike! Drive the crooks out in 90 days!" The 56-year-old police chief smiled wanly. He was not in the best of health and the rigors of office would prove to be too much in the end, but he promised to give it his best shot: "When the crooks are convinced we mean business, some of them will volunteer to get out of town. I will do everything possible to put them in jail where they belong!" There was one problem: some of the worst crooks were doling out city contracts and raping the municipal treasury.

The expert hand of Charles Fitzmorris, the new city comptroller, guided the appointment process. Fitzmorris saw to it that his former cronies who had been shelved by Collins were brought back to preeminence. John Alcock was elevated to deputy superintendent. For the past four years he had been assigned to a simple desk job in the stenographer's office. John Stege and "Shoes" Schoemaker were demoted in this latest shakeup. They were good men, dedicated crimefighters who earned impressive records, but were temporarily put out to pasture because of their loyalty to the ancien regime of Dever. Stege, the corpulent, bespectacled detective chief, had received three creditable mentions for meritorious police work in a career dating back to 1910. In 1926 he arrested Joe Saltis for the murder of Johnny "Mitters" Foley, a rival beer baron. Saltis was the highest-ranking Chicago gangster to go to trial up to that time. Suddenly, key prosecution witnesses disappeared. The jury was bribed and intimidated, and Saltis walked out free. He filed a $100,000 libel suit against Stege for calling him a gangster, but it was thrown out of court. Refusing to be corrupted by the mob bosses, Stege went about his business until the Thompson Civil Service sharks stripped him of his star in 1927 for allegedly falsifying applications for new patrolmen. The superior court quashed the charge and castigated the Commission for what was considered to be little more than harassment. The incorruptible Schoemaker was another foe of the vice lords, ever since his young daughter had allegedly been imprisoned in a brothel by a Levee pimp. Schoemaker and Stege, like Dever, were political exiles after April 1927.

The gangsters crept back into Chicago after sniffing the air and finding that the lethal fumes of Deverism had blown away. Al Capone established headquarters at 22nd and Michigan and graciously accepted the mayor's invitation to greet the visiting Italian aviator Francesco de Pinedo when he landed his hydroplane near Grant Park. Capone stood proudly alongside the Italian consul, several municipal judges, and officers of the Sixth Air Corps. When asked about the necessity of having Chicago's most notorious citizen in a line of dignitaries, the police explained that the threat of anti-fascist demonstrators required a "mediator." There were no reports of violence as syndicate torpedos roamed the crowd.

Hughes took the machine guns out of the hands of the police and returned the revolvers and rifles to the uniformed personnel, believing this to be a good first step in reducing street violence. "They are too hard to turn off, and before that can be done some innocent parties are likely to be hurt," the chief said. Hughes neglected to inform the gangsters of his concerns, as the guns continued to blaze even though a sympathetic mayor was in office.

Judge Sbarbaro's undertaking parlor did a box-office business, especially during the "war of Sicilian succession" waged over a five-year period. The O'Bannionites believed that if they were to succeed in the rackets, control of the Unione Siciliane was essential. Capone was an outsider—born on the mainland of Italy and therefore unable to make a move without the president's blessing. And since he was not of Sicilian descent, he could not be president himself. The North Side gang failed miserably in trying to kill Big Al, but they fared much better in eliminating the Capone flunkies occupying this sensitive office.

Angelo Genna, successor to Mike Merlo, was shot to death by O'Bannion's avengers as he steered his roadster down Ogden Avenue on May 26, 1925. Mike "the Devil" Genna was the next to fall. Weiss, Drucci, and Moran enticed "Samoots" Ammatuna to help them get John Scalise and Albert Anselmi, two hired hit men they believed to be responsible for putting O'Bannion in his grave. Amatuna, who was about to succeed Angelo Genna as president of the Italian Union, pretended to go along with the scheme to flush the two killers out into broad daylight. He told Weiss to position himself near Congress and Sangamon Streets, and to be ready. Meanwhile, "Samoots" tipped off Mike Genna well in advance, so the hunters themselves became the hunted. In the volley of gunfire, "Bugs" Moran and "Schemer" Drucci were badly wounded. They were lucky to escape with their lives.

Genna, Ammatuna, and the two intended "victims" drove to the South Side, and safe ground. Near 47th and Western the speeding gangsters were spotted by four detectives driving an unmarked Ford car. The police maneuvered their vehicle into the south-bound lanes to give chase. At the wheel was Harold Olson of the 20th District. He was assisted by Patrolmen Charles Walsh, William Sweeney, and Michael Conway. Near 59th Street a large truck got in the way of Genna. He slammed into a telephone pole, but amazingly, none of his passengers was hurt. They jumped out of the car with their guns blazing. Walsh and Olson were killed instantly, and Conway was wounded, while hundreds of onlookers took cover. Sweeney returned their fire from behind his squad car before the riot squad arrived on the scene. Genna fled in a panic to the rear of a building at 5941 Artesian Avenue. He was winged in the leg, and bleeding profusely when Sweeney cornered him in the basement. Mike "the Devil" died from his wound in the ambulance. Scalise and Anselmi, who were not widely known to police at this time, boarded a streetcar and tried to blend in with the commuters. A dry goods storeowner named Edward Issigson flagged down a passing patrol car. Sergeant Michael Stapleton boarded the rear platform to arrest the two killers. At detective headquarters they were recognized as one of the many suspects brought in for interrogation during the search for O'Bannion's killers.

The attorneys for Scalise and Anselmi, who could not speak a word of English, argued that their clients did not know their pursuers were policemen and therefore had broken no laws, inasmuch as they were defending themselves from attack. Officer Sweeney appeared for the prosecution despite threats to his life and property. Unknown bombers planted a device in front of his home, blowing out the porch and front parlor in order to dissuade him from testifying.

The jury declared Scalise and Anselmi guilty. They were sentenced to 14 years for the first murder. A second trial, held in March 1926, resulted in an acquittal. By this time a $100,000 defense fund had been raised among the gangsters. Undaunted, the defense team, headed by that noted mouthpiece William J. Ahearn, was pleased by the final outcome. In December the Supreme Court reversed the decision of the first trial, holding that if the men were guilty the verdict was a "mockery of justice." Free to kill again, Scalise and his partner walked out of the Joliet Penitentiary after serving less than nine months. Detective Olson's aging mother expressed bewilderment; so too did the city and the state. If gangsters could go free after murdering policemen, what did that say about the powers of law enforcement in this country?

The murder of these two officers was a relatively isolated event. The booze gangs of the 1920s generally avoided armed confrontations with police. Of the 91 slayings of police officers between 1921–29, only Walsh and Olson could be described as crime syndicate victims. In October 1923, Office Lawrence Harnett was gunned down in Little Italy during a moonshine raid on one of the Genna-run stills. However, the killer was Joe Montana, an alky-cooker and not a gangster. In 1928, 13 Chicago police officers lost their lives in random acts of violence, the highest annual rate in the decade. Nine of these men were killed by bank robbers and house-breakers. Police officers who patrolled the streets in the roaring twenties were more likely to die of natural causes than at the hands of Prohibition gangsters.

This is not to suggest that the police were immune to physical threats. In 1928 another bombing war commenced in Chicago between rival gambling factions headed by the millionaire "newsboy" Frankie Pope, "Dago" Lawrence Mangano on the West Side, and Louis Barsoti on the North. In January the residence of former Police Chief Charles Fitzmorris was bombed. Nobody was hurt, but Fitzmorris decided that life and limb were more important than his job as city comptroller. He stepped down in July, remaining closed-mouthed about the mysterious affair.

There were more unsolved bombings over the winter and summer. Chief of Detectives William O'Connor received death threats in the mail, and Captain Luke Garrick's home on Summerdale Avenue was almost destroyed by a dynamite bomb in September. The infant daughter of his son-in-law was buried in the debris. "Chicago is still sitting on a volcano—that is clearly demonstrated by the bombing of Captain Garrick!" thundered Frank Loesch of the Chicago Crime Commission. "The combine of criminals and politicians still exists, despite all the work done by the special grand jury."

Garrick had been muzzled by Hughes for much of his term. After William Russell took over in August, the dour but honest captain was transferred to the old Des Plaines Street Station to serve notice to Larry Mangano, whose deluxe gambling emporium, the Minerva Club, had been on the "protected" list for nearly a year. Judge Joseph B. David of the superior court issued an injunction in August 1927 that effectively blocked the police from conducting raids on the Minerva even if they wanted to, which wasn't likely. Hughes's extreme reluctance to bother the powerful West Side gambler was understandable. John F. Tyrrell, a powerful figure in the Crowe-Thompson juggernaut, served as Commissioner Hughes's private attorney. The nattily dressed lawyer was frequently seen driving around Chicago in a $7,000 automobile when an average family sedan cost several hundred dollars. Tyrrell's law partner was John Higgins, whose most influential client was "Dago" Mangano. The Garrick bombing was the last in a series, and Mangano was the last of the gangsters to be harassed by police raids in 1928. The various Capone factions had sent Thompson a message that he did not take lightly. In November 1927 Thompson ordered Hughes to slam the lid down on the gamblers in order to curry the favor of the goo-goos (good government) who had so viciously assailed him for his syndicate connections during the election. Henceforth, the mob would be shown every consideration. City Sealer Dan Serritella and First Assistant Corporation Counsel James Breen were the mayor's "liaisons" to Capone. They were the real powers controlling police activity in the Loop and the outlying areas. And they alone made sure that the police conformed to the "open-town" policy.

During the bombing epidemic Hughes promised to deliver the felons to justice, following the destruction of Charles Fitzmorris's and Dr. William Reid's homes. "When we go after our men [the suspects], we'll get them," he said. "You may be sure these bombers won't be handled with kid gloves." Earl Macoy, president of the Employer's Association of Chicago, wasn't sure about the chief's true motives, however. "The bomb squad of the Chicago police force was organized to ferret out the culprits of the bomb depredations," he said. "The only thing the bomb squad does is to measure shattered plate glass windows so that the insurance companies are not charged for too big a glass."

"Go get 'em, Mike!" Thompson had chortled from the campaign dais. Less than a year after the mayor uttered these immortal words, Mike Hughes, who must have done a few things right during his long career, was squeezed out by rival factions within the organization. The mayor waited until Hughes's friend and protector from the early days, Charles Fitzmorris, stepped aside before making a move.

Although he personally liked Hughes and probably was sincere when he called the aging chief "the greatest thief catcher Chicago had ever seen," Thompson acquiesced to Corporation Counsel Samuel Ettelson, who had emerged as the second Fred Lundin during the waning years of the mayorality. Fitzmorris and Ettelson were bitter opponents. Now with dapper Charlie out of the way, Ettelson was free to maneuver the apostles around the board. From his bed at the Murphy Hospital, Hughes signed his resignation papers, but refused to shift the blame. "I wasn't forced out and I am as much a friend of Mayor Thompson today as I was the day he appointed me," Hughes said.

With Ettelson now calling the shots, the decks were cleared for Deputy Commissioner William Russell, who had been publicly criticized years earlier by Fitzmorris for tolerating gambling and bootlegging. This latest shake-up brought to the commissioner's chair a closed-mouthed, secretive administrator who enjoyed the company of reporters, and members of the sporting fraternity. As a newly arrived immigrant from County Clare, Ireland, Russell joined a Gaelic football league. He was a rough and tumble fellow who acquired refinements as he grew older. One of them was golf. When reporters caught up with him on the links to advise him of his appointment, Russell's chauffeur told them that he could not be disturbed.

The new chief presided over a department that had reached an absolute nadir in its ability to apprehend felons, stop the booze traffic, and suppress gambling. The rank-and-file was demoralized by low pay, endless political entanglements, and the failure of the municipal court to prosecute felons. In 1927 there were 19,842 felony charges filed but only 6,560 defendants were bound over to a grand jury. Skillful criminal lawyers more often than not were able to secure reduced sentences for their clients by advising them to plead guilty to misdemeanor charges. In that same year felony courts were waived in 1,773 cases and pleas of guilty were accepted in their place.[49]

The municipal courts were scattered across the city in various police stations. Top gangsters brought in to answer charges needed only to call their bondsman in order to avoid spending the night in jail. "The people have got to know the hell of a fight we're having with the gangsters and politicians," said John Stege. "They've got to understand how tough it is for a policeman to find judges who will stand up under political pressure."

The message that crime pays filtered down through the ranks. In December 1928, a policeman assigned to the personal staff of Deputy Commissioner James L. Mooney inadvertently bared the corruption of the system through a series of letters written to his girlfriend, who introduced them as evidence in a breach-of-promise suit.

On August 24, Patrolman Howard Cleveland communicated the happy news to Ruthie Broderick, a cabaret singer, that he soon expected to be in the money.

You remember me telling you that I would soon have a job where I would be making good money and everything would be roses for you and me? Well, I now have that job and have had it for a week. I am working out of Deputy Commissioner Mooney's office of vice and gambling.

He added somewhat ominously:

No, I did not go to see the Malone fight. I don't get a chance to go any place right now. We have a new chief of police and he is tightening up on everything so it is up to us to close everything before the squads from his office do.

The new chief was William Russell, appointed on July 26, 1928. Like all other Thompson appointees to this office, Russell had been given his marching

Figure 11

The gunners, millionaire beer runners, and opulent bootleggers seem mysteriously successful in getting mercy and delays from the courts.

But when they get to fighting among themselves there is no mercy and no delay.

The courts, the police, and the bootleg gangs were all in it together, according to this November 12, 1924, McCutcheon drawing. (Deckert/McCutcheon)

orders. Drive the crooks out of Chicago! By September 7, the heat was off, as conditions in the precincts began to loosen up.

Well honey, things are beginning to look a little better in Chicago. It looks like things may be open up a little since the mayor got back. I got connected with one of the big bosses of the gambling outfit on the northwest side and was made some promises if things opened up a little. We haven't been quite so active as we may have been.

Two days later Cleveland rested his heels on Chief Mooney's desk to write another "love letter."

Well baby, there isn't anything new here. I sat in the captain's office all yesterday listening to the Cubs ballgame over the radio and last night after I was through with work my old partner Buck and myself went over in the Des Plaines Street District and got a still. But as usual, it belongs to the mob that we got a monthly consideration from: $10. It seems as though everything I run into belongs to a syndicate. Well, the old saying is keep on trying. I may connect with a good thing someday.[50]

When the letters were presented by the plaintiff's attorney, Harry X. Cole, Officer Cleveland was transferred to the West Chicago Station where he was forgotten about. Whether the two reconciled their differences and found the pot of gold at the end of the graft rainbow is a matter of speculation.

There were more embarrassments awaiting Russell as the old year drew to a close. Seven years after Fitzmorris astounded the city by announcing that half the force was involved in the rum trade, the situation appeared not to have improved one iota. The day before a grand jury probe submitted another damning report to the city about police inefficiency, detective Thomas Geary, who was attached to the Hudson Avenue station on the near North Side, was shot and killed in a saloon owned by Democratic State Representative Lawrence O'Brien. Geary had just gotten off duty when he stopped at the Wells Smoke Shop for a quick drink with the boys. O'Brien was an old-line politico who earned his livelihood in the liquor trade. He was a cordial host and his bartender Henry Mullarkey served up the beer as fast as the boys could quaff it. At one time he had worked as a policeman but was discharged in 1921.

Geary, who shouldn't have been there in the first place, quarreled with Mullarkey about the Irish homeland: Catholic versus Protestant, separation or union. The burning issue, which had concerned Chicago police for many years, resulted in the death of the patrolman after Mullarkey reached across the bar and snatched Officer Edward Johnson's holstered gun. He fired two shorts into Geary's brain.

Despite numerous raids, the saloon enjoyed protection since it was the favored watering hole of the city politicians. Chief Russell demoted Captain George De Mar, who commanded Hudson Avenue. It was the first of a massive series of transfers that were announced two days later, on December 1, 1928, following the final report of the grand jury.

Russell escaped condemnation this time, but only because he was new to the job. The blame for open gambling and vice was shifted to Hughes, the "friend and protector of the syndicate." Transcripts of three separate meetings between Russell and his deputy commissioners revealed that the chief had warned his subordinates to clean up the city—orders that were blatantly ignored. "It is apparent to this jury that intolerable and shocking conditions must have been known to the commanding officer of every district where such conditions exist." The jurors issued three strong recommendations:

1. That radical changes be brought about in the Police Department such as the metro-politan police force with the elimination of the county highway department and the continuation in office of the commissioner of police for a definite period of years instead of a change with each new administration.

2. A drastic change in the Civil Service Commission in order to free it from any political influence and the decrease in the number of commissions from five to three.

3. That the new state's attorney and his staff carry the investigation to a conclusion and indict those responsible for conditions that have prevailed.

The latest grand jury report reflected a growing uneasiness with Thompsonism, best illustrated by the stunning defeat of Robert Crowe in the April primary by Judge John A. Swanson, who was personally sponsored by the Charles Deneen faction of the Republican Party. The senator was an eloquent spokesman for the law and order advocates, allied as he was to the disenfranchised Lorimerites.

Robert Crowe had built a patronage army within the patronage army. At least a dozen well-known judges, the 4,000 members of the Chicago Bar Association, and even certain bluebloods belonging to the Committee of Fifteen endorsed Crowe for reelection.

The real test of the viability of the organization was in the precincts, and here Thompson's support was withering. What sustained the Republicans in the 1920s was the party's uncanny ability to forge bipartisan alliances with the Brennan Democrats. Fred Lundin and Bob Crowe were masters of this useful tactic. Now they were both gone, leaving the mayor to stand by himself. For expediency the county Democrats played ball with the Republicans while Boss Brennan slowly mended the fences between the warring Carter Harrison-Roger Sullivan factions. The two old patriarchs were throwbacks to the silk-hat era of Chicago politics, yet their influence was still considerable. It took Brennan nearly a decade of behind-the-scenes maneuvering to unify the party into a cohesive force. George Brennan and Tony Cermak, his floor leader in the City Council, were poised to recapture City Hall through attrition, while destroying the Cook County Repub-licans in the process. It had taken years of humility and retrenchment before the Chicago "Tammanys" were in a position to shove Big Bill over the precipice. Now with Crowe out of the way—one of the most powerful and venal politicians of his day—the Democratic kingmakers were ready to take over.

In principle they stood for the same things as the Republican mayor. Prohibition was the evil of the land. Vice and gambling could be put to good use, and effective political machines were built by the patronage system. The Brennanites understood the realities better. The coming "machine" was better equipped to muzzle the power of the gangs, and did not require their help to win on election day. This was a lesson Bill Thompson never learned. In 1929 Chicago's shame became the nation's.

The Clark Street Massacre

On the eve of the Volstead Law's ninth anniversary, Henry H. Curran, president of the Association Against the Prohibition Amendment, was asked to comment on the achievements of the drys to date. "We are also blessed," he drawled, "with speakeasys, hooch on the hip, bubbling vats and stearning stills in the kitchens in the land, a bumper crop of drink drys and an interesting transformation of the churches of yesteryear into the town halls of tyranny of today."

Dour-faced Herbert Hoover, about to assume office as the nation's thirty-first President, fulfilled a campaign pledge by naming an impartial panel to survey the pluses and minuses of Prohibition. The loss in revenue and lives was staggering. By its own estimate, the government had spent $300 million to enforce the law. Two-hundred moonshiners and big-city bootleggers were shot down in their tracks by trigger-happy Prohibition agents, and 269,584 persons—most of them small-time criminals—were sent to jail for a cumulative total of 26,613 years. And still the flow of illegal liquor from Canada continued without interruption.

In Chicago it was business as usual for the warring booze gangs. The police continued to be hounded by new grand jury revelations of rampant graft, which were beginning to filter through the halls of Congress. Senator Deneen brought the crime conditions before his colleagues, asking for and receiving financial help to clean up the city. The good senator had never drunk from the same political trough as the mayor. There was nothing to be lost, and everything to be gained by painting a bleak picture of the true conditions in Chicago. It was common knowledge that the police were a part of Thompson's dwindling patronage army, and the state's attorney belonged to Deneen. But then, Deneen did not require Swanson to assess his men a membership fee like the mayor did. Each of the 5,000 members of the Chicago Police Department paid $10 a piece to line the coffers of Big Bill's "America First" organization.

Chief Russell responded to the incessant criticism by transferring 339 men from their old haunts. Bob Crowe's special detail was returned to the streets and a new flying squad, reminiscent of Herman Schluetter's legendary gambling detail, was created to deal with burglary and petty larceny. A "major crime bureau" was formed to log case histories sent in from the outlying stations. Captain William Killeen of the Austin District was given day-to-day responsibility. He reported to John Stege who was back in good graces now that Hughes had been shipped out. The major crime bureau did not wait long for its first case.

In December 1928 Al Capone boarded a Pullman bound for Miami, where he was to soak up the sun and to plot the demise of former safecracker Bugs Moran. Moran had risen from obscurity to challenge the big man for supremacy, not only in the liquor trade, but for internal control of the corrupt labor unions, the police, and the aldermen. In the bloody 20th Ward, which encompassed

O'Bannion-Moran turf, the North Side gang sponsored Martin Krass as its candidate against the Capone man, William Pacelli, who was handpicked by Boss Morris Eller, now on his way to jail to begin serving a sentence for conspiracy. If Capone was to gain a foothold on the North Side, political control was essential.

The Moran gang had killed every president of the Unione Siciliano to date: Tony Genna, "Samoots" Ammatuna, Tony Lombardo, and on January 2, 1929, Pasquilino Lolordo was fatally shot in his North Avenue apartment by a trio of killers while his wife finished her ironing in the back room. The widow tentatively identified Joe Aiello as one of the gunmen. In his zeal to ascend to the presidency of this organization, Aiello had fallen into bad company. To achieve his goals he recruited the Moran gunmen to murder Lolordo, whose brother Joseph had served as Tony Lombardo's "bodyguard" when he was shot down in the Loop in 1928.

To settle old scores, Capone ordered Jack McGurn to lay a trap. For weeks he staked out the Lincoln Park area, recording every movement of the Moran gang. Through intermediaries, the Caponites rented rooms at 2135 and 2119 North Clark where a quartet of spies kept close watch on an undistinguished red brick warehouse across the street. The building was the S-M-C Cartage Company, which advertised shipping and packing services. Inside, the former garage had been converted to a liquor depot for the Moran gang.

On the morning of February 14, 1929, Al Capone was entertaining prize fighter Jack Sharkey and Dade County Solicitor Robert Taylor at his Palm Beach estate. A black Cadillac touring car outfitted to look like a police squad car emerged from a rented garage in the back of Wood Street. There were five men inside: two dressed as police officers, and three wearing long overcoats and fedoras. Tucked under their outer wear were sawn-off shotguns—known as "sawyers" to members of the underworld—and the deadly Thompson submachine guns.

The vehicle proceeded north on Wood to Webster Street, then east to Clark, where the driver made a right-hand turn. It was shortly after 10:20 AM when the Cadillac pulled in front of the garage at 2122 Clark. A teen-age boy named George Brichet observed the five men as they alighted from the police wagon. Each carried a large "box-like" contraption wrapped in newspapers. The boy thought he was about to see his first police raid.

Inside, seven Moran man were lolling about the garage awaiting a shipment of whiskey that had been hijacked on Indianapolis Boulevard in Whiting two weeks earlier. The load of liquor—with an estimated value of $10,000—was to be delivered to Pete Gusenberg that morning with a promise of payment when it was retailed.

Suddenly, the intruders entered. They ordered the gangsters to line up against the wall. Believing that it was little more than a routine police shakedown, James Clark, Albert Weinshank, Peter and Frank Gusenberg, Adam Heyer, a mechanic named John May, and Dr. Reinhart Schwimmer—who had abandoned his practice in order to spend all his time with the Moran gangsters—complied with the request. Pete Gusenberg became suspicious after he turned his head ever so slightly to see five men pointing guns at his back. Then he reached for a handgun in a drawer nearby. Before he could get a shot off the machine guns began to chatter. Over 100 bullets belched out of the guns before the killers exited the premises. They left behind bloody carnage. There were only two survivors, a hysterical German Shepherd named Highball who was straining to escape from his leash in the back of the garage, and Frank Gusenberg, who was removed to an area hospital. Before he died of his wounds police and reporters asked him who pulled the trigger. "They were policemen," he said. Gusenberg took 25 slugs in his body.

A few minutes after the gunmen left the building in their detective squad car, the bodies were found by a neighborhood resident, Mrs. Jeanette Landsman, who called the police. Soon the neighborhood was swarming with curious spectators, some of whom heard the shooting, but thought it was nothing more than an automobile backfiring.

The police arrived on the scene within minutes. They had all they could do to keep matters under control. With reporters milling about the garage it was nearly impossible to conduct a thorough, exhaustive search for clues, but the police were able to lift fingerprints off the doorknob on the entrance way.

The press excoriated Russell and the police for "permitting" conditions to get out of hand. Of greater concern was the mockery of justice presented by the gangsters posing as police officers. "What bitter satire could there be on the enforcement of law in Chicago than that one band of murderers, weapons in hand, could get into the lair of another gang of equally desperate gunmen without opposition by disguising themselves as policemen?" the *Herald and Examiner* wanted to know.

In the face of an intense whipping administered by the press, the police conducted a surprisingly effective investigation. Within two weeks they had identified the principles involved in the slayings. Bringing them to justice was another matter, however.

John Stege was summoned from Miami, Florida, where he was vacationing near Al Capone. He took charge of the investigation to answer his many critics in the business community who demanded an explanation. "The Police Department is the only barrier between the decent people and the outlaws and as a whole they are the bravest and finest kind of men. I have the welfare of the lowliest patrolmen as much as heart as the highest and I think this unjust suspicion is harmful to the morale of the department because being a policeman is itself a handicap," he stated.

The first break in the case occurred when the Fire Department was summoned to a garage at 1723 Wood Street, where the smoldering ruins of a dismantled automobile were found. The car was being taken apart slowly by the hoods, until they got word of an alley-by-alley police search. The car was then burned with acetylene torches. Someone had tried to destroy the identification marks on the axles with hacksaws, but had fled in haste when the detective squad drew near. The Cadillac touring car had once belonged to County Commissioner Frank J. Wilson, who sold it to Kavanaugh Motors on Irving Park Road. By the time the gangsters made it look like a detective cruiser, the vehicles had changed hands six different times.

The garage was owned by Leo Joppet, who explained that he had rented it three days before the massacre to a man identified as Frank Rogers. He asked no questions because Rogers had paid cash in advance. Joppet accompanied the detectives to headquarters, where he picked out from the mug book three photos that resembled the mysterious Rogers and his associates.

Warrants were issued for the arrest of three men; Claude Maddox, Mike Farvia, and Sam Laverda, who belonged to an independent gang that frequented the Circus Cafe on North Avenue. The police located Farvia and Laverda, who carried a small notebook listing the addresses of various whiskey depots. The Circus gang performed various "services" for Al Capone from time to time, and one of its prominent members, Tony Accardo, eventually commanded the Chicago crime family in the 1950s.

While Stege pursued these angles, Officer Frank Morrell conducted a separate investigation in Thayer, Illinois, hometown of Byron Bolton, a gangster who worked for Alvin Karpis. A letter written by Bolton's parents was found in the Clark Street flat from which he maintained the vigil.

The trail led to Michigan, and to the positive identity of one of the triggermen: Fred "the Killer" Burke, former member of Egan's Rats and the man responsible for assassinating Frankie Uale of the New York chapter of the Unione Siciliane. Described as one of the most dangerous men alive, Burke was wanted in five states for kidnapping, extortion, bank robbing, and murder. The Chicago police issued a warrant for his arrest after ballistics expert Calvin Goddard testified at a corroner's inquest that bullets extracted from the seven dead men matched those found in Burke's home in St. Joseph, Michigan.

On February 28, Stege and detectives William Cusack and John Mangan surprised "Machine Gun" Jack McGurn at the Stevens Hotel, where he had been keeping company with his girlfriend Louise Rolfe. Taken to the "show-up" room, McGurn was identified by two eyewitnesses as having left the garage with the two uniformed gangsters following the massacre. The Capone trigger-man, who had battled the Moran men in the 20th Ward on behalf of Alderman Eller and his henchmen, was linked to Maddox through booze sales in the Cragin District on the Northwest Side.

McGurn was held without bail while Detective Chief John Egan and State's Attorney Walker Butler went after and located the distributor who secured the machine guns for the gangster: Frank V. Thompson, arms dealer to the underworld. Thompson was found in Kirkland, Illinois, and returned to Chicago in May. Facing his accusers he admitted that he had purchased nine "tommy guns" from North Side dealer Peter Von Frantzius several days before the hit. Why had Thompson gone into hiding if he was as innocent as he claimed, someone ventured to ask. "Maybe that was why I stayed away," he chuckled.

A clear picture had emerged. Jack McGurn masterminded, but had not participated in the massacre, despite the testimony of two witnesses. Since he was known to the Gusenbergs it was imperative that freelance gunmen be brought in to do the job. Maddox, a minor player in the booze and gambling rackets, assembled the death squad in order to make an impression on Capone, whose favor he sought. The two killers in police uniforms were Fred Burke and Fred Goetz, who were paid $2,000 a week plus expenses.[51]

The police suspected that Byron Bolton was the lookout, but he eluded capture until his arrest in 1930 for complicity in a kidnapping case. In January 1931 he made a full confession from his cell in the federal penitentiary at St. Paul, Minnesota. In addition to Burke and Goetz, Bolton identified Murray "the Camel" Humphreys and Gus Winkler as the other triggermen.

No one went to jail for the St. Valentine's Day Massacre. Burke was arrested in St. Louis and extradited to Michigan for the murder of a St. Joseph policeman. He died while serving a life sentence for this crime. Goetz and Winkler were killed in unrelated underworld shootouts. Murray Humphreys went to jail for income tax evasion in 1930, but returned to Chicago some time later to assume a position of leadership in the Capone mob.

Jack McGurn had the perfect "blonde alibi", Louise Rolfe, whom he claimed he was with from 9:00 PM until 3:00 PM on February 14, 1929. Since a wife could not testify against her husband in court, McGurn married Miss Rolfe and the case collapsed. On December 2, he walked out of court a free man. Seven years later, McGurn finally received his comeuppance. In a bowling alley on the Northwest Side, unknown assailants cut the gangster down, and left a comic valentine card on his vest. It was, after all, February 14, 1936.

Bugs Moran escaped the vengeance of the Capone gang only because he was incapacitated with a case of the flu. When reporters interviewed Moran in the wake of the tragedy he allegedly told them that "only Al Capone kills like that." A year later, Bugs was singing a different song. On October 21, 1930, the former boss of the North Side mob was arrested in Lake County on a charge of vagrancy. Brought before Judge John H. Lyle, he listed his current occupation as vice president of the Cleaner's and Dyers Union, which his gang had infiltrated during the mid-1920s when Weiss and O'Bannion were still alive. What about the massacre, a reporter asked. "I never accused Capone of that," he said. "I've been out of the racket for four years, and I've been living the life of a respectable businessman." The reporters knew better. Moran had been trying unsuccessfully to gain admittance to the Capone inner realm now that the North Side territory had been conquered and devoured by the Italians. Bugs would remain on the outside. He died of natural causes in 1957 after spending his last years blowing open safes, engineering minor holdups, and serving as a senior adviser to the "Bookie Gang"—a collection of West Side toughs that held up syndicate-run handbooks. It was nickel-and-dime stuff, and the well-entrenched Chicago mob paid Moran the supreme insult: they ignored him.

Aftermath

The massacre of seven gangsters closed out the period of open warfare in the streets of Chicago. Al Capone was in firm control of the rackets now that Moran was on the run and the Gennas were either dead or in exile. What Capone had not counted on was the public outcry resulting from the massacre. This was no longer just a local issue, but one that had come to the attention of the President and his top advisers. If the police could not get Capone, the government would. The day of reckoning for Scarface came on June 5, 1931, when U.S. Attorney George Johnson named Capone in an indictment, charging him with evasion of income taxes amounting to $215,000. Johnson, who had won a conviction against every gangster he had ever tried for tax fraud, was about to prove that the pen is mightier than the machine gun.

In the weeks following the gunplay on Clark Street, the City Council and various civic organizations debated the fate of the Police Department. Alderman John Massen proposed another reorganization plan on the floor of the City Council which received the endorsement of businessman and philanthropist Julius Rosenwald. "Establishment of a non-political police system is by far the most important thing confronting Chicago," Rosenwald said. "Until the police are taken out of politics we cannot expect the right sort of administration of the police affairs of our city."

Chief Russell agreed with Rosenwald, but did not mince words when he demanded an end to the unnecessary details assigned to private organizations. The first step of reform, he said, would be to put the men in the streets to fight crime. "Let the big companies that have details to guard their payrolls pay the check. Put those officers on raiding squads," Russell snapped. "Let the big stores and organizations who have policemen detailed to guard money collectors hire special police for this purpose and take our men away from them. I know that the manpower shortage in the department is a severe handicap. However, this is not an alibi. I will not accept it as an alibi."

Commissioner Russell endorsed a survey committee to study the situation and issue appropriate recommendations. He went so far as to appoint a blue-ribbon panel of civic leaders that included Henry Barrett Chamberlin of the Chicago Crime Commission, Walter Dill Scott, president of Northwestern University, Frederick C. Woodward, acting president of the University of Chicago, and Judge Andrew Bruce, president of the American Institute of Criminal Law and Criminology. This committee conducted the preliminary groundwork, and secured $30,000 in private contributions from various business groups to finance the actual survey work. Internal organization and the management of the police force was to the first topic on the agenda.

It was decided to go outside the city to locate the project coordinator. Following the precedent established in 1904 by the City Club, which recruited Alexander Piper to conduct an independent inquiry, the police committee announced on May 12, 1929, that Bruce Smith, an authority in police administration and a distinguished member of the Institute of Public Administration of New York, had agreed to accept the position. Unlike Piper, who had advocated the military approach in governing a big-city police department, Smith favored a comprehensive, scientific study that was more concerned with structure and management than spit and polish on inspection day.

Bruce Smith brought to the job a lifetime of experience. He had conducted similar surveys in 50 other cities at home and abroad, including a searching probe of the Royal Canadian Mounted Police. To his credit, Russell opened the books and allowed Smith and his committee free access to uniformed personnel as well as members of the detectives' bureau and administrative offices. For the next year, the Citizen's Police Committee delved into police affairs in ways not seen before or since.

Concurrent with an independent investigation conducted by Smith, plans were afoot to organize a scientific crime prevention laboratory through the auspices of Northwestern University. During the massacre investigation it became apparent to everyone that the police lacked the equipment, know-how, and resources to properly analyze spent shell casings found in the garage and at Burke's farm in Michigan. Major Calvin Goddard was brought in from New York. Working with the police, he was able to steer them on the right course through his knowledge of ballistics. He agreed to stay on and head up the laboratory, which was sponsored in part by the Chicago Association of Commerce. In the next few months Goddard quietly assembled one of the finest, most effective crime detection bureaus in the country. Major Herbert Yardley, a cryptographic expert who revealed the existence of a plot to poison President Woodrow Wilson, was hired to serve as the code and cipher consultant. "Codes used by gangsters and the underworld in general are of the crudest kind," he said. "Compared with the intricate and highly complicated coded messages used by the Allied Powers and the Entente during the war, they are child's play."

The city had mobilized to "get" Capone at all costs. The massacre had offended the sensibility of all good citizens and alarmed the civic boosters who looked forward to the coming of the World's Fair in 1932. More than anything else, The Century of Progress and the promise of millions of dollars in tourist revenue were the real reasons that the city decided at long last to curb the gangster scourge.

The Real Eliot Ness

Federal agents began a two-pronged attack against Capone. Following the government's decision to transfer responsibility for the enforcement of Prohibition laws from the Treasury Department to Justice, George Johnson laid the groundwork for the formation of a special squad to dig up evidence of Capone's flagrant violations of the Volstead Law, to be used by the prosecutors in the tax case.

With the blessing of Alexander Jamie, special agent for a private investigatory group known as the Secret Six, Johnson named 26-year-old Eliot Ness as head of the detail in 1929. Just four years earlier Ness was finishing his college classes at the University of Chicago. He was a grim-faced, no-nonsense investigator who rarely cracked a joke or made light of a situation. Getting Al Capone became a personal obsession for this government man, who was as green as the grass in Mr. Wrigley's ballpark. With only two years of field work in back of him as an insurance investigator, Ness was given the task of selecting a team of incorruptible agents to assist in the clean-up of Chicago Heights, Al Capone's other suburban bailiwick. Anthony San Filipo was the first boss of the booze traffic in Chicago Heights. He was a man of some culture and refinement, and had been educated at the finest university in Italy. San Filipo was also a power in Chicago Heights politics before Torrio-Capone gunners cut him down on April 24, 1924. Thereafter, the village was controlled by Lorenzo Juliano, a Capone stooge who supervised the alky-cooking plants and was rumored to be the man responsible for the bombs thrown at the residences of Senator Deneen and State's Attorney Swanson. Juliano's confederate and business partner was Oliver J. Ellis, who ran all the slot machines in the village. Ness and his 15-man squad first went after the breweries, where 3,500,000 gallons of illegal liquor were being manufactured each year. "We had to weigh our problems," Ness recalled, "and find a vulnerable point. We decided on the breweries because their product is bulky and because they have the toughest transport problem. We knew that regularity was necessary in their operation and it wasn't long before we learned of the special hauls on Friday in preparation for Saturday speakeasy business."[52]

State's Attorney Swanson directed the investigation against Ellis, while Ness and his raiders conducated a series of swashbuckling raids against the Chicago Heights breweries. These raids helped establish Ness's reputation as the greatest foe Capone ever encountered. In reality, this was an invention of Hollywood scriptwriters who borrowed an interesting press moniker—"The Untouchables"—for a highly entertaining television series 30 years later. The significance of the colorful nickname was not lost on the publicity-hungry Ness, who believed it was somehow tied to India's caste system. It is highly doubtful that one of Capone's men declared in a moment of pique that "these guys are untouchable." Once the press seized on it Eliot Ness did little to dispel the myth. There was much more at stake here than ridding Chicago of its vice: looking down the road, Ness had a future career to think of.

The Untouchables were selected from the Civil Service ranks. They were educated, hard-working, honest men for the most part. Some, like Al "Wallpaper" Wolff, were assigned to work undercover, seeking out illegal stills and saloons operating in defiance of the law. Wolff had served as a city inspector before receiving his appointment to the squad by Alexander Jamie. In deference to his years of experience and familiarity with Chicago, Ness allowed the only Jewish Untouchable greater freedom to roam the city at will to locate the booze. Many showy raids were conducted but more often than not, the proprietors of the beer warehouses had been tipped off. "Dry holes and no prisoners" could only mean one thing: the bootleggers had been tipped off, either by the police or one of the Untouchables. Ness often communicated his intentions to the police, in the hope that they could provide him with valuable inside information. Wolff warned his superior about this, but the plea often fell on deaf ears. "Be honest. Don't listen to a lot of people that tell you to do something wrong," Wolff would often say.

During their work in Chicago Heights, several Untouchables posed as corrupt Prohibition agents. For weeks they were on the payroll of the bootleggers for a fixed price of $1,000 a month. In nearby Calumet City, the mob actually paid the agents $100 each time they uncovered an independent still operating outside their jurisdiction. After Eliot Ness and his men conducted several highly successful raids against the suburban breweries, there came the usual offer of bribes, coupled by death threats.

Armed with enough evidence to convict Ellis and his cohorts, Swanson presented his findings to a grand jury which returned a series of indictments against the Chicago Heights gang. Documents seized at the brewery tied together city and suburban operations, and a distinct picture of the scope of Al Capone's control began to emerge. With Ellis out of the way, Ness and his cohorts refocused their efforts in Chicago, where a South Side brewery, another in Cicero, and one on Goose Island were broken down with heavily armored trucks. The raids were usually conducted without search warrants, because Ness feared the inevitable tip-off from City Hall. Still, there was no sure safeguard against corruption, even among the tightly knit Untouchables. One of their members committed suicide by means of carbon monoxide poisoning when his collaboration with the mob was revealed. The $2,500 a year salary the government paid each of the Untouchables paled in comparison with the larger payoffs being given to uniformed personnel and Prohibition agents who were not affiliated with this group.

The Untouchables were complemented by Treasury Department agents, city policemen, independent investigators, and the Secret Six in their war against Capone. They alone did not send Capone to jail, though their contributions over a three-year period were impressive. The 15 men were on call for Ness 24 hours a day, seven days a week. Sometimes they wouldn't see each other for weeks, with each man assigned to his own task. They shared the typical prejudices of the day, especially in regard to Al Wolff, who was described affectionately as a "different kind of Jew."

The diligent work of a battery of Internal Revenue agents armed with tax records listing 17 separate bank accounts for Al Capone finally sent the big man to jail in 1931. A year later, in April 1932, Ness was appointed chief investigator for the district of Chicago. Nothing more was heard from him until after Capone began serving his sentence in Atlanta.

Fired by J. Edgar Hoover, Ness shifted his base of operations back to Cleveland in 1934, where city officials gave him carte blanche to bust various gambling and extortion rings that had bled dry the city treasury and the resources of the local law enforcement agencies. Before he could begin his preliminary work, the first in a series of grisly mutilations occurred in northeast Ohio. A torso, minus arms, legs, and a head, was found floating in a pond. For the next six years Ness searched in vain for the "Torso Killer," who claimed responsibility for at least a dozen murders. His identity was never established, and the reputation of Eliot Ness as an anticrime crusader was permanently tarnished. After failing in an attempt to win the Cleveland mayoralty in 1947, Ness suffered a series of financial reversals. He retired to private life and died in 1957, a bitter, disappointed man whose best days had all occurred before his thirtieth birthday.

Had he lived just two more years he would have achieved what he had fought so hard for all his life: the glory and adoration bestowed upon him by John Q. Public, who first became aware of The Untouchables in the Desilu TV series.

Who Killed Jake Lingle?

The police bitterly resented the intrusions of the federal men and the independent crimefighting agencies such as the Secret Six who attempted to clean up the city. The underlying motive was to destroy the last vestiges of Thompsonism and make the city safe for the business boom that would surely accompany the World's Fair. The Secret Six was the brainchild of State's Attorney John Swanson, who answered to Charles Deneen. Vowing a "fight to the finish," Colonel Robert Isham Randolph, whose Association of Commerce sponsored the Secret Six with an outpouring of corporate cash, was forced to disband the covert group in 1932 when it was believed that he had pocketed $24,000 for himself.

When asked to list the accomplishments of the Six, Randolph said that his organization participated in the investigation of 25 different kidnappings in the northern Illinois district, and had helped put Capone away—a claim vigorously denied by government insiders.

The credibility of the Secret Six was completely destroyed when one of the "investigators" turned out to be Shirley Kub, an intimate of slain gangster Jack Zuta. Described as a "fat, grotesque, little woman" by the *Chicago Tribune*, Kub was married to a police stool pigeon and had served time in Bridewell Prison on a larceny charge. When Kub, Alexander Jamie, and Randolph began wiretapping the state's attorney's office, Swanson was outraged. According to Jamie, the Six had uncovered a "politico-criminal" cabal operating within Swanson's jurisdiction.

Disgusted business executives cut off funding, and the Secret Six faded into oblivion, another fable of corrupt Chicago politics. The residue of this latest scandal bore witness to the disarray of the county Republican Party. The Deneen faction, led by Swanson became a laughing stock. "Swanson was heavy, slow, and incapable of the type of swift and decisive action that would terrify criminals and thrill the public; he would add little strength to the leadership of his party," wrote Fletcher Dobyns in 1932.[53]

Prohibition and crime spelled the doom of the Republican Party in Cook County, and was the downfall of three police superintendents: Collins, Hughes, and Russell. The latest Chicago police chief was a tireless worker who was often on the job at four and five in the morning. William Russell cooperated with the civic groups in ways unheard of during earlier regimes, and had introduced a noteworthy innovation when two police-owned radio stations opened up on Warren Avenue and at Wabash and 48th. As the police squad cars cruised the city streets, WGN announcer Quin Ryan broadcast the first dispatches to specially equipped receivers in the "flivvers." The cost of this project was estimated to be $100,000, money that was hard to come by in the first months of Prohibition. To help finance the costly venture as well as the addition of a hundred new Fords to the auto patrol, Russell used revenue money earmarked for salary increases. This did not endear him to the rank-and-file but it was a necessary step to bring the department up to date. The days of the corner patrolman walking the beat were fast coming to an end.

The failure to suppress crime was not so much his fault, but rather the inflexible policy of the mayor in permitting vice coalitions to dictate policy in the police districts. Before the Secret Six was disbanded, Shirley Kub reported that James Breen and Daniel Serritella called Captain Willard Malone of the First District to the carpet when he proved to be too zealous in his persecution of downtown gambling. "Is Serritella the captain or am I?" Malone demanded. Breen, who had appointed Kub to the Secret Six, told the police captain to "go along with Serritella." Similar conditions were reported at the Chicago Avenue District, where Captain Richard Gill was "holding the reins too tight." Gill was transferred to the Hyde Park Station near the University of Chicago where he would do the vice operatives little harm.

Such was the political climate in June 1930. Mayor Thompson could ill afford more gangster scandal, for the administration was still reeling from the massacre fallout. Things remained generally quiet—for a while. There was an uneasy calm in gangland, as Al Capone allegedly made his peace with the remaining "independents." Those who bucked the system paid the price, like Alfred "Jake" Lingle, a $65-a-week crime reporter for the *Chicago Tribune*.

Lingle had a good friend. His name was Bill Russell, and they first became acquainted on the West Side in 1910, when the Irish cop was walking a beat and the aspiring reporter played semi-pro baseball. Sports was the common denominator that cemented their friendship in the early years. Sports and the volatile world of Chicago crime and politics sustained their relationship after both men attained prominence in two divergent fields.

Jake Lingle was a personable, easy-going man who was vitally interested in the world around him. He had a sixth sense for news and became a crack reporter within two to three years after joining the *Tribune*, although his critics maintained he could not construct a decent sentence. On the police beat it didn't matter if a reporter couldn't spell "cat." It was the contacts, and the inside information gleaned from snatches of conversation overhead in the corridors of Central that really counted.

Lingle had walked a beat with Russell. He learned the "police way" and respected the boys in blue all the same. With each successive promotion that Russell received, Lingle gloried in his friend's good fortune. In turn, the *Tribune* man was introduced to judges, police captains, aldermen and the colorful characters of Chicago night life. Sometimes they would meet on the golf links, always a good place to pick up inside information on the stock market, the movements of the underworld, and the latest police shakeup. Unbeknownst to his good pal William Russell, Jake Lingle was also breaking his bread with the Chicago underworld, notably Al Capone, who presented him with a diamond-studded belt buckle one year as a Christmas present. Lingle was also known to Mont Tennes and Bugs Moran. In January 1930 the reporter attempted to effect a reconciliation between the various racing wires operated by Tennes and a string of independents. It is doubtful, though, that Tennes had the muscle or the motivation to order Lingle's death. A more plausible theory advanced by City Hall observers held that Lingle alone had the power to reopen the Sheridan Wave Tournament Club, a Weiss-Moran gambling den that the police had closed down in the wake of the massacre. Joe Josephs and Julian "Potatoes" Kaufmann, acting as intermediaries, prevailed upon Lingle to intercede with Russell to get the police to "lay off." When this failed, former State Legislator John J. "Boss" McLaughlin, who had a financial stake in the club, called Lingle at the *Tribune*. With another reporter listening in on an extension Jake set McLaughlin straight. "Well," he said. "Russell can't let you run. That's final." McLaughlin cursed under his breath and said, "I'll catch up with you and it won't be long either!"

The murder of Alfred "Jake" Lingle was another syndicate masterpiece. On the afternoon of June 9, Lingle finished off a last cup of coffee at the Sherman House. He wandered about the lobby for about a half hour, conversing with hatcheck girls and the cigar stand clerk as was his usual custom. Lingle had a kind word for everyone, and was always there to lend a sympathetic ear. Whenever a cop died in Chicago, Jake was the first to phone in his order to the florist.

He exited the hotel and headed east down Randolph Street to catch the express train to Homewood and the Washington Park racetrack. As he walked, he scanned the pages of the morning paper. At the newsstand adjacent to the public library, Lingle purchased a copy of the *Racing Forum*. As he turned to enter the tunnel that led to the tracks under Michigan Avenue, three men in a parked roadster called to him. "Don't forget to play Hi Snyder in the third!" Lingle waved casually and replied, "Got 'em!"

In the tunnel two men followed closely behind. Eyewitnesses later testified that one of the men was dressed in a priest's garb. The walkway was crowded, and the shooting happened so fast that it was impossible to say with certainty just who killed Lingle. The killer darted down the tunnel, and into the anonymity of the crowd. For a very short time Jake Lingle, the cop-struck reporter known as the "unofficial chief of police," was a martyr. The *Tribune* offered a $25,000 reward for the apprehension of the killer and loftily declared in its editorial pages that those who sought to impugn the integrity of Lingle were guilty of passing "rumors [that] have been accepted by those wishing ill of the *Tribune* in its fight for decency and have been propagated by those who have neither the disposition nor the courage to make the fight themselves."

Visibly shaken by the news, Russell praised the character of Lingle: "His work brought him into contact with the highest and the lowest, and to my personal knowledge he was trusted by everyone who knew him. He led a clean and honorable life and was deserving of all the confidence placed in him."

Within a week an entirely different picture began to emerge. The $65-a-week reporter had an annual income of $60,000, and owned a home in Florida that resembled that of his good friend, Al Capone. A search of the financial records revealed that Lingle and Russell had maintained secret bank accounts together, and had played the stock market extensively in the boom and bust era of the late 1920s. In 1925 Russell deposited $4,315 into an account at the Lake Shore Bank. An additional $15,000 of mysterious origin was added several days later. Beginning in 1929, the money was used to purchase 800 shares of National Cash Register (NCR) stock. NCR stock took a beating in the 1929 crash, yet the account of Lingle and Russell showed a balance of $78,248.35 on June 26, 1930.[54]

There were other curious transactions reflected in the ledger. On December 13, 1929, Lingle made out a check to cash that was endorsed by Captain Dan Gilbert, who always managed to shield his shady dealings in the glow of some great issue, or crusade to rid the city of crime. John Swanson obtained the cancelled check and demanded an explanation. Gilbert was always happy to oblige. He said he ran into Lingle late one night at a downtown hotel. In need of cash, the reporter asked the captain for a loan to meet a pressing obligation. Said Gilbert, "I happened to have $500 with me," and as a friendly act gave it to him. Sometime later he repaid the loan with the check in question. I kept it for some time to meet an insurance premium." Gilbert escaped censure for this shady transaction, but Lieutenant Thomas McFarland, who advanced Lingle $300, was transferred from the prestigious homicide division of the detectives' bureau to the Burnside Station. Not satisfied with humiliating the man by sending him to the "sticks," the new chief of detectives, John Norton, ordered McFarland suspended after learning that he was late in reporting for inspection one morning. The reason for his tardiness was a gunshot wound that had given him trouble. McFarland was badly wounded in a shootout with the burglar Tony Larkin in November and had spent six months in the hospital recuperating.

Russell had erred badly in dealing with Jake Lingle on a personal basis following his accession to the highest office of the Police Department, and he paid dearly for it. A group of maverick aldermen led by the opportunistic Arthur Albert demanded the scalps of Russell and Stege. Albert wanted to know why certain police captains could afford summer homes and large automobiles, the question on everyone's lips after the financial records of Jake Lingle were made public. The City Council had clearly overreached in regard to Russell. There were many men in both the public and private sector that had speculated in the stock market during the heady days of the bull market. There is no evidence that Lingle actually influenced decision-making, as the newspapers implied. Jake was one of those individuals who had a "cop fixation." He lived and worked among them, and got to know their families. No doubt he boasted of his close personal ties to his friends in the newsroom. The motive for Lingle's murder may in fact have been his own inability to deliver on promises made to the syndicate.

Mayor Thompson met secretly with Samuel Ettelson, County Chairman Bernard Snow, and Eugene Pike, former city comptroller. It was Pike who had sponsored Russell in 1928, and it was Pike and Ettelson who decided it was time for a change. While his fate was being debated behind closed doors in City Hall, Russell drew up his own resignation notice. So that he would not end up in the street without benefit of income or future pension, he arranged a captaincy for himself at the Kensington Station, and one for Stege at Irving Park. These were their nominal Civil Service ranks before their assignments to headquarters.

Thompson did not act immediately on selecting a successor, and thus, according to Civil Service rules, John Alcock became acting commissioner by default. The reformers reeled. Here was a member of the old guard who no doubt wanted a return to the policy of noninterference. Alcock was brought before the City Council to answer some stiff questions about his qualifications, and his willingness to cooperate with the aldermen who were asking for a sweeping investigation of the department.

Alderman Taylor: Is the trouble caused by the collusion between crooks and police or by poor distribution?

Chief Alcock: I have no information as to collusion. That is one thing to be ascertained. Wherever I find it, I will hunt it down and the man is out. The main cause of the trouble is the Volstead Law. Prior to this we had our holdup men, safeblowers, and robbers but we put away 75 percent to 90 percent of these and kept supervision of them on parole. It was four or five years after this Prohibition law that they got the beer and moon business and started making money.

Alderman Albert: It is common gossip that the police would be punished if they interfered with gangsters?

Chief Alcock: I have heard of such instances.[55]

Vowing to cut waste by eliminating the "soft snaps," Alcock was given a vote of confidence by the aldermen. The threatened investigation was put on hold for the time being, as the usual post-scandal interdepartmental transfers were announced. The new chief of detectives was order to return 700 of the 900 detectives to uniform duty in the precincts. Under Hughes and Russell the size of the plainclothes detail had grown appreciably, a clear indication of political maneuvering at headquarters. The detectives' department was a plum, and it had been a rich source of graft and patronage even before Joe Kipley's time.

The old system of five districts under the direction of a deputy commissioner was abolished as Alcock made known his intention to centralize control. Five of the oldest men were returned to their Civil Service ranks of captain: Martin Mullen, James Mooney, Ira McDowell, John Hogan, and Thomas Wolfe. Chief Alcock answered Alderman Albert's charge that the "old men" were being protected. "One thing is now certain," Alcock said. "The captain will not now be able to pass the buck to a deputy commissioner. Each captain will be held strictly to account for his district and he must deliver the goods." Of course, it could also be said that the chief was bestowing even greater power to the captains, thus perpetuating the ancient feudal system that had existed since the Civil War.

The bold strokes impressed the City Council and temporarily placated the mayor, who was already looking ahead to the 1931 elections. Thompson's Waterloo was at hand. The Republican-dominated police were about to join the Tammany democracy—and they would learn to accept it, like a dose of castor oil in the morning.

Tammany on the Lake

Alcock had successfully forestalled a City Council probe, which no one really wanted. Given the opportunity to mold the kind of organization he wanted, and to reward faithful friends like Sergeant James Scanlan, who suddenly found himself elevated to first deputy commissioner, the new chief informed the Citizen's Police Committee that members of the department would no longer be willing to answer questions or supply information to Bruce Smith or anyone else. Forced to suspend the investigation, committee members began the arduous process of assembling the data. Frank Loesch promised a final report in six months.

> Tony, Tony, where's your pushcart at?
> Can you picture a World's Fair mayor
> With a name like that?
> What a job you're holding!
> And now you're crying for two,
> Better start thinking of one for me
> Instead of two for you![56]

And so began another Thompson campaign for mayor. After winning an impressive primary victory over Judge Lyle and Alderman Albert, Big Bill looked forward to his April showdown with Tony Cermak, a powerful four-term alderman who had served as president of the Cook County Board since 1922. Born in Prague, Bohemia, Cermak arrived in Chicago as a small boy. He worked side-by-side in the mines at Braidwood, Illinois. It was hard and dirty work but the few dollars he earned helped put food on the table. He attended miner's school in Braidwood only 90 days out of the year, but one of his teachers was George "Boss" Brennan, future kingmaker of the Democratic Party.

Brennan gave Cermak his start in the Lawndale section of the city, which included the Czech and Croation immigrant populations. Cermak the worker took care of the "little fellows" and fashioned a constituency along traditional Democratic lines: patronage, favors, and more patronage. While serving in the state legislature he cast a vote for Republican Party boss William Lorimer, who was censured by the U.S. Senate after receiving kickbacks from Edward Hines, one of Chicago's wealthiest builders.

By the mid–1920s Cermak was firmly entrenched as the leader of the county Democratic Party and the wet factions of the City Council. His unwavering opposition to the drys made him a hero of Chicago's large immigrant population. Although he never held a job that paid more than $12,000 a year, Cermak's estimated worth was $7,000,000, according to conservative estimates. During the 1931 mayoral campaign Cermak waged a dignified campaign free of the demogoguery and clownish antics of Thompson and his people. "You want a bohunk for mayor?" the mayor had asked. "An ally of King George?"

In principle they stood for the very same things: the open town, an end to Prohibition, and a "liberal" form of government. Their differences lay in organization and style. Thompson was elected in 1915 through the promotional genius of one man: Fred "the Poor Swede" Lundin. In later years a few of his henchmen, notably Robert Crowe and Samuel Ettelson, built ties to the criminal underworld. Thompson aldermen and city officials were among the most rapacious public figures in local history. Alderman Titus Haffa and Boss Morris Eller were convicted felons. Dan Serritella belonged to Capone, and another alderman who owned allegiance to Thompson and the gangs was later assassinated—Al Prignano, whose home ward took in the Weiss-Moran empire.

The political satraps of Thompson were powerless to deliver the key wards in the face of a superior organization, and a growing belief among black people that their interests were better served by a Democratic mayor. The most powerful black politician of the age, Alderman William Levi Dawson, switched parties when it became abundantly clear that Cermak and his cronies would turn the police loose on the South Side policy games unless his voting constituency fell into line. The Democratic machine of legend was in its embryonic stage.

The city reform element took the position that "even a yellow dog would be better than Thompson." The Lake Shore blue-bloods held their noses and voted for Cermak. When all the votes were counted the city had a new mayor. Pushcart Tony was swept into office by a majority of 194,267 votes. Commenting on the day's events in Chicago, Mauritz Hallgren of *The Nation* wrote: "Chicago is already beginning to ask itself whether the price it paid to get rid of Thompson may not in the end prove too high, for the man elected in his place is A. J. Cermak, Democratic boss of Illinois and sole proprietor of a complex political machine built entirely along the lines of the Tammany organization in New York."[57]

Cermak's first move as mayor of Chicago was to pay a social call on John Curry, head of Tammany Hall, and Mayor Frank Hague, the political boss of Jersey City. The subject of discussion was how to rid this great country of the social menace, Prohibition.

Volstead was the chief corrupting influence of the notorious 1920s. The dry law spawned the modern crime syndicate and gave birth to a period of unbridled corruption in the Police Department. No longer was a stigma attached to accepting bribes from underworld figures. Suddenly, police work became a very desirable occupation for young men seeking their rightful place in the world.

Local ward healers charged their constituents upwards of $1,500 for appointment to the force. Influence peddlers who "had it in right" would command much higher rates for promotions to the rank of sergeant, and with good reason. "Almost every cop was taking money," recalled a veteran reporter. "He had to take, in order to keep his job." How many cops were crooked in the 1920s? A good estimate would be 50 percent. Those officers attached to the vice, liquor, and gambling sections had the closest contact with the bootleggers, but it was the five deputy commissioners responsible for conditions in their respective districts who wielded the most power and were able to distribute graft among the captains if they so pleased.

With the end of Prohibition and a new political administration firmly entrenched in City Hall, the rules of the game began to change ever so slightly. In the 1930s it was the horse parlors, poolrooms, and traveling handbooks that channeled the graft. The gambling patrons in the Dawson Districts—the backbone of the "machine"—demanded freedom and noninterference. In many respects the 1930s were a throwback to the old Levee days and Hinky Dink Kenna. When all was said and done, nothing had really changed.

Notes

1. *The Fabulous Century: 1920–31* (New York: Time-Life Books, 1971), p. 154.

2. Alex Gottfried, *Boss Cermak of Chicago* (Chicago: University of Chicago Press, 1962), p. 118. Cermak's principal rival in the City Council during his alderman days was John H. Lyle, later a municipal judge and mayoral candidate. Lyle was an exponent of clean government. During his years on the bench he classified gangsters as vagrants in order to allow police to arrest them on sight.

3. *Chicago Tribune*, November 12, 1921.

4. Ibid. The largest percentage of liquor that flowed into the city in the early years of Prohibition originated in the distilleries of Kentucky, although break-ins at government warehouses in Ohio and Illinois were common. See also Kenneth Allsop, *The Bootleggers: The Story of Prohibition* (New York: Arlington House, 1961), pp. 34–36.

5. Frederic Thrasher, *The Gang* (Chicago: University of Chicago Press, 1927), p. 1. The author identified three sites of gang activity in Chicago: the North Side jungles, West Side wilderness, and South Side badlands. Each geographical region was populated by successive waves of immigrants whose tribal identities were manifest in their reactions to the tough urban environment.

6. Tim Murphy was assassinated on June 26, 1928, after he answered his doorbell at his South Side home. An automobile drove slowly past the house, occupied by a team of hired killers who sprayed a volley of bullets in the doorway where Murphy stood. The lavish funeral was typical of such affairs with the exception of the politicians, who succumbed to civic pressure and prudently stayed away; *Time Magazine*, July 9, 1928.

7. The police arrested only a handful of these labor gunsels. Not one was hanged, and only Moss Enright was convicted. In most cases the shooting victim refused to name his assailant, preferring to leave the act of vengeance to friends and union associates.

8. Enright eliminated rival labor slugger Vincent Altman in the Briggs House saloon on March 23, 1911. He was sentenced to life imprisonment, but won his release two years later after the state's key witness admitted perjury on his deathbed. A petition signed by 40,000 trade unionists convinced Governor Dunne to issue a formal pardon.

9. Moss Enright was serving as business agent for the Garbage Handler's Union at the time of his death.

10. *Chicago Daily News*, February 5, 1920.

11. *Report of the General Superintendent to the City Council (1919–20)*.

12. *Chicago Daily News*, January 22, 1920.

13. Ibid. It was estimated by Judge Olson that 60 percent of police activity was wasted effort, and the same could be said of the work performed at the municipal courts.

14. Wendt and Kogan, *Big Bill of Chicago*, (New York: Bobbs-Merrill, 1953), p. 75.

15. *Chicago Tribune*, November 25, 1918.

16. Ibid. Acting Chief of Police John H. Alcock, who had been in charge of the force in the eleven months following the death of Herman Schluetter, was returned to his Civil Service rank of first deputy. Reportedly, Alcock was offered the job on a full-time basis, but declined to accept.

17. William M. Tuttle, *Race Riot: Chicago in the Red Summer of 1919* (New York: Atheneum, 1978), p. 34. Garrity's strategy during the crisis was one of containment. He deployed the bulk of the 3,500-man force along the borderline of the so-called "black belt"—Wentworth Avenue. This left the rest of the city virtually without protection for a week.

18. Lindberg, *Chicago Ragtime*, p. 244. The 1919 riot was the culmination of nearly ten years of escalating racial tension on the South Side. In June 1919 the home of a white attorney named William Austin became the target of a bomb thrower. Austin had rented a building he owned on the near Northwest Side to a black family.

19. This was the consensus of the state's attorney, but not necessarily that of the all-white grand jury, which walked out of the courtroom in protest.

20. Tuttle, *Race Riot*, p. 254. See also *Summary of Chicago Riots Cases in Report*, submitted by A. Clement MacNeal, December 31, 1919.

21. *Chicago Tribune*, January 4, 1920.

22. Ibid., January 1, 1920.

23. Ibid., January 2, 1920. Garrity drafted his own revised ordinance without bothering to consult the city's legal department.

24. The intricate provisions of the controversial 1911–12 police ordinance would be

repealed by the Garrity plan. All departmental bureau would have been abolished and the records kept by the chief's office and the first deputy would be maintained by the secretary. The Garrity measure returned a degree of authority to the commissioner, which the City Council had usurped in 1912.

25. Ibid., November 9, 1920. *Chicago Daily News*, March 11, 1920. The Thompson administration won the floor fight with the help of Democrats who had opposed both the 1912 ordinance and the Guernsey bill.

26. Kobler, *Capone*, (New York: G. P. Putnam's Sons, 1971), pp. 38–51. Anson J. Smith, *Syndicate City* (Chicago: Henry Regnery, 1954), pp. 36–40.

27. *Chicago Herald & Examiner*, May 12, 1920.

28. Kobler, *Capone*, p. 52.

29. The theft of whiskey in transit was not an easy thing for the victim to report to the police or Prohibition authorities. This was especially true if the hijackers happened to be police. Such was the fate that befell Frederick Mann, manager of the Rainbo Gardens, who lost $30,000 of premium grade whiskey to four detectives from the Maxwell Street Station in 1920. Mann reported the incident to Captain William Russell, who assured him that the "merchandise" would be returned—no questions asked, *Chicago Daily News*, May 23, 1920.

30. Victoria Moresco was one of 18 children born to a poor Italian stonecutter. She married Colosimo in 1902 and each night read to him from the classics while Italian opera droned on in the background. Together they opened a brothel in the 22nd Street Levee, appropriately named "The Victoria." Nelli, *Italians in Chicago* (New York: Oxford University Press, 1971), pp. 149–51.

31. Testimony of the Chicago Crime Commission before the U.S. Senate Permanent Subcommittee on Investigations, Hearing on Organized Crime, March 4, 1983, Chicago. The Crime Commission reported 24 gangland slayings inside Cook County proper in 1919, and 23 a year later. Through 1983 the total number of mob-related hits stood at 1,081. According to Crime Commission statistics, the peak year for murder was 1926, when 75 gangland hits were reported.

32. *Chicago Herald & Examiner*, May 12, 1920.

33. Ibid.

34. The story was originally told to Jay Robert Nash by the playwright Charles MacArthur shortly before his death. Thirteen suspects were arrested by the police during the Colosimo investigation. Victoria's two vengeful brothers, Joseph and Jose, were detained for further questioning, but were not formally charged. Arturo Fabri, the Grand Rapids violinist who gave Dale Winter her start in show business, and "Crazy" Frank Razzino, a member of the Camorra, were other suspects. The description of the cafe diner given by Chef Caesarino closely matched Al Capone, a low-ranked mobster who had never been formally introduced to Colosimo. Capone allegedly tore open Big Jim's shirt and removed a wallet containing $250,000—his reward for bumping off Colosimo. The Roaring Twenties, at least from the standpoint of gangsters, Prohibition, and gunplay, began on May 11, 1920.

35. *Chicago Herald & Examiner*, May 15, 1920. A double brass band and a million flowers festooned the funeral cortege of Colosimo. The grieving widow was escorted by Colosimo's lawyer Rocco DeStefano, who promised to take "personal charge" of her dormant show business career.

36. Jack Lait, "How the Black Hand Came out of Little Italy," *Chicago Tribune*,

May 1918. The story seems to be a journalistic invention. The Black Hand terror spread from New Orleans and New York, and then across the country after 1890.

37. Smith, *Syndicate City*, (Chicago: Henry Regnery, 1954), pp. 83–89. New Orleans Police Chief D. F. Gastner assiduously listed 94 murders committed between 1886 and 1891 by Italian secret societies. Kidnapping was a favorite tactic of the early Black Hand. The city was home to a fraternity of assassins and kidnappers recruited from the *Garzoni di Mala Vitano*, or the Lads of the Bad Life. This particular criminal cabal was led by experienced banditi who had emigrated from Palermo, Sicily.

38. Thames Broadcasting, "The Making of the Mob," *Crime Inc.*, 1984.

39. *Chicago Tribune*, March 5, 1921.

40. The appointment of Charles Fitzmorris caught City Hall observers by surprise. The "Young David" of reform was handed the seemingly impossible task of curbing the escalating postwar crime rate. Fitzmorris proposed a radical departure from the usual Civil Service restrictions governing appointments and promotions as one solution. Civil Service hamstrung the superintendent while working to the advantage of the ward bosses.

41. Chicago *Tribune*, January 1, 1921.

42. This sequence of events was reconstructed from a description of the superintendent's typical workday, recounted in, *Chicago Police Problems*, (Champaign, University of Illinois Press, 1931), pp. 29–34.

43. Douglas Bukowski, "William Dever and Prohibition," *Chicago History* 7(2) (Summer 1978): 112. John Q. Schmidt, "William Dever: A Chicago Political Fable," in Paul Green and Melvin Holli, eds., *The Mayors: The Chicago Political Tradition* (Carbondale and Edwardsville: Southern Illinois University Press, 1987), pp. 82–97. Dever was an idealist who believed that an honest administration could cure the layers of graft and patronage that had accumulated over the years. To fight the scourge of crime he threw a great net out for the bootleggers, gamblers, and gunmen, which proved to be an abject failure. Crime rates actually became worse between 1923–27. The "scatteration" policy resulted in an escalating murder rate. In 1921 there were 190 murders; in 1922, 228; in 1923, 270; and in the first 11 months of 1924, 319. In some ways Thompson's "wide-open town" notions were more palatable, if not more realistic. During the Dever years Al Capone opened up Cicero after being driven out of Chicago. It is doubtful that Capone found conditions so intolerable for business that he was forced into exile in Cicero. Dever merely provided him with the impetus to expend his operations into virgin territory. It should be remembered that the crime syndicate began cultivating Stickney, South Chicago, and Burnham years earlier, when changing economic conditions and new modes of transportation made the distant suburbs that much more desirable.

44. *Chicago Tribune*, November 29, 1924. The "enforce all laws" doctrine was not readily adopted by policing agencies outside of Chicago. During Prohibition most big-city police departments focused their efforts on more traditional avenues of crime: robbery, rape, and fraud. Philadelphia was the only other city of note to come around to Dever's way of thinking, and it took a former military man, General Smedley B. Butler, to see it through.

45. According to Chicago crime aficionado Bill Reilly, a deal was cut at the popular North Side restaurant. In his memoirs, Clarence Darrow states: "After thorough consideration we concluded that the best chance was on a plea of guilty. Only a few knew what was to be done, the boys—and their parents, two or three relatives, and the attorneys in the case." Clarence Darrow, *The Story of My Life* (New York: Charles Scribner's 1932), pp. 236–37.

46. Thompson campaign literature appearing in the *Chicago Tribune*, April 1, 1927, proving that politics makes strange bedfellows. Twice during his mayoralty Thompson sued the paper for libel and lost. On election eve Colonel McCormick's editorial writers rejected a returned to "Thompsonism": "What he offered as public policies were grotesque vaporings and irrelevancies."

47. *Chicago Tribune*, January 11–12, 1960. Roger Touhy, arguably the most forthright Chicago gangster, was himself the son of a policeman. On a meager patrolman's pay the elder Touhy attempted to provide for seven children growing up on Robey Street. According to Touhy's recollections, he grew up with some of Chicago's most notorious gangsters, esteemed college professors, and a couple of mayors. Roger Touhy with Ray Brennan, *The Stolen Years* (Cleveland: Pennington Press, 1959), pp. 50–51.

48. *Chicago Tribune*, January 11, 1960. Gilbert was a close friend of Tommy Touhy, Roger's brother. Before he became the "millionaire cop" (see Chapter 11), of legend, "Tubbo" Gilbert saw quite a bit of Touhy on the West Side. The Touhys and Dan Gilbert became interested in the Teamster's Union about the same time. Tommy Touhy had been cut in on the lucrative union racket by Marcus "Studdy" Looney, an agent of Al Capone. Gilbert was questioned about the shooting attack on a union rival but was exonerated. Afterward he became a boss of the local branch while holding on to his job as top investigator for the state's attorney. Touhy, *The Stolen Years*, p. 90.

49. *Chicago Tribune*, January 27, 1928. The verbal sparring between the municipal court system and the police continued through much of the 1930s. Neither the courts nor the police were willing to accept the blame for the state of open lawlessness. The deficiencies of the court system came under sharp scrutiny by the Chicago Crime Commission, the only truly impartial referee in the city. In 1927, largely through the efforts of Frank Loesch and others, 37 bills were introduced into the same legislative session to improve administration of the criminal law and an intensive campaign was begun that aroused public awareness to the need for improvement in the administration of criminal justice.

50. *Chicago Tribune*, December 4, 1928.

51. Ibid., January 24, 1933; *New York Times*, March 27, 1931. The search for the triggerman focused on Burke after Major Calvin Goddard testified at a coroner's inquest that the bullets found in the bodies of the dead men bore markings identical to those fired from a gun in his St. Joseph, Michigan barn, and not from standard police issue. Goddard examined 70 spent bullets of .45-caliber automatic pistol type, many of them more or less fragmented, which had been recovered from the bodies of the victims and from the garage. Study of these exhibits showed that they had all been discharged from Thompson submachine guns. Every empty case showed the arc-shaped imprint on the rim left by the impact of the bolt of a Thompson gun, and not found on cases fired in any other type of weapon, including the police Colt revolver. Major Goddard, former director of the Bureau of Forensic Ballistics in New York, was invited to present his findings to all top officials of the Chicago Police Department and invited guests. A local millionaire named Bert A. Massey who served on the inquest, offered Goddard a $15,000 annual salary to move his laboratory to Chicago from New York in order to assist the police in firearms identification. Goddard proposed that a crime detection lab concern itself with all forms of physical evidence and not just firearms exhibits. In the summer of 1929 Goddard traveled abroad, studying scientific police laboratories and medical-legal institutes in 13 Western European countries. In April 1930 Goddard opened the Scientific Crime Detection Laboratory of Chicago in affiliation with Northwestern University. See Calvin Goddard,

"A History of Firearm Identification to 1930," an address by Colonel Goddard delivered to the student body of the Southern Police Institute, University of Louisville, May 11, 1953. See also Albert Hopkins, "Science Trails the Criminal," *Scientific American* (February 1932): 94–96. There is general agreement among scholars of the period that Burke, Gus Winkler, and Claude Maddox were present inside the Moran garage on February 14, 1929. According to John Kobler, who interviewed Alvin Karpis in 1969, George Ziegler and "Crane Neck" Nugent rounded out the assassination squad; Kobler, *Capone*, p. 254. Other prime suspects included John and Byron Bolton (who confessed to the deed in the St. Paul Penitentiary), Robert Conroy, a.k.a Robert Newberry, who was murdered in 1933. See also John H. Lyle, *The Dry and Lawless Years* (New York: Prentice Hall, 1960), pp. 222–27.

52. *New York Times*, June 18, 1931. By day the Untouchables completed their stake-outs, attended gangland funerals, and trailed the trucks carrying barrels of bootlegged beer. At night the Untouchables sprang into action, invading the nightclub domains of the gangs, often in disguise. Eliot Ness preferred men of Irish and Italian extraction, but he welcomed Al "Wallpaper" Wolff to the group, and often took him along on distillery raids in Wisconsin and Indiana. Wolff spoke three languages—German, Yiddish, and Polish—which made him particularly valuable to Ness; Oscar Fraley, *The Untouchables* (New York: Julian Messner Co., 1957).

53. Fletcher Dobyns, *The Underworld of American Politics* (self-published, 1932), p. 84. This is a strange political diatribe, very cynical for the times in which it was written, yet a remarkably candid viewpoint.

54. *Chicago Tribune*, June 29, 1930; John Boettiger, *Jake Lingle* (New York: E. P. Dutton, 1931).

55. *Chicago Tribune*, June 20, 1930. The usual citywide dragnet accompanied the change of administration from Russell to Alcock. The roundup of hundreds of gamblers and petty criminals convinced the City Council to delay its plans for a deeper probe of the police situation. The aldermen, alarmed by the sound of hundreds of prisoners' feet in the Bridewell, saw no further need to put the Police Department on trial at a time that such action could be "giving aid and comfort to organized gangsters."

56. Wendt and Kogan, *Big Bill of Chicago*, p. 329.

57. Mauritz Hallgren, "Chicago Goes Tammany," *The Nation*, April 22, 1931, p. 446. The election of Anton Cermak was not so much an affirmation of Democratic politics but a repudiation of Thompsonism, which had come to symbolize the ills of Chicago in 1930: municipal graft, gangster rule, and breadlines. The hanky-panky was given a wink and a nod when Thompson thundered into office for a third time in 1927. By the time the next election rolled around, such behavior by public officials was intolerable.

Frederick Ebersold, Chief of Police 1885–1888. Weak and indecisive, Ebersold commanded the police department during one of the most pivotal eras in Chicago history. Following Haymarket, he was denounced by the reformers for permitting open gambling. He died in 1900 receiving no callers and accepting no food.

John Bonfield, more than anyone, was responsible for the bloody Haymarket Riot. The "hero" of the industrialists was suspended in 1889. He died in obscurity nine years later.

William H. Ward commanded the front line of officers who faced the mob in Haymarket Square. The statue was supposed to depict Ward, but he did not pose for it.

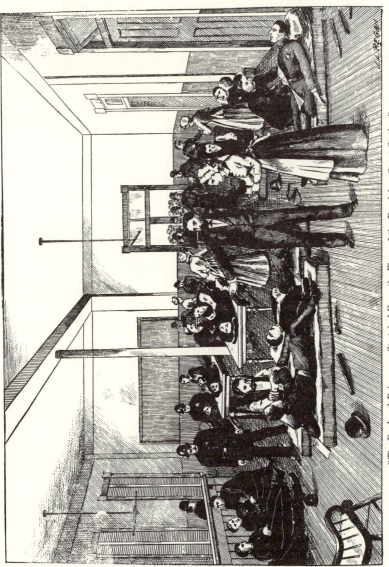

"The Dead and Dying were Stretched Upon the Floor of the Desplaines Street Station."

The squad room of the Des Plaines Street station following the Haymarket Riot.

Haymarket Monument as it looked at the time of its dedication. The foundation was constructed in December 1888 for a sum of $5,000, which was $1,500 more than what the contract originally called for. Railings, electric lights, and supports were an additional $1,000, running the final construction costs to nearly $10,000. The central cube which policeman Birmingham stands upon bore a shield and inscription giving the date of the riot. Worked around the shield were branches of oak leaves signifying ''strength.''

The Haymarket Monument as it looks today. The statue was moved inside of the Police Training Headquarters after student activists blew it off the pedestal on October 6, 1969, and again on October 6, 1970.

Height,	1 m| 58.9	Rem	Head, lgth	17.8	Rem	L. Foot,	25.1	Rem		Circle,	Or	Age, 29 years
Stoop,			" wdth	15.6		" Mid F	10.8		Color of Left Eye	Periph Z	H. Bl	
Outs. A,	1 m 65		Rgt Ear lgth,	57		" Lit. F	8.1			Lion Yel	Born in
Trunk,	87.6		Pecul.			" Fore A	43.4			Pecul.		Bohemia

Remarks incident to Measurement,

DESCRIPTIVE.

Incl. M	Profile { Ridge, Und	Married Yes	Beard Deep blue
Forehead Hght M. High	{ Base Hor Root m Broad	Teeth 1 lower	Complexion Fair
Width M. Broad	Nose DIMENSIONS	Weight 150	
Pecul.	Length, Projection M. broad Breadth,	Left side Out	Build Slender (stooped)
	Pecul. T'fo thin & pointed	Chin m short (heavy)	Hair Dk Chest

Measured at CHICAGO, ILL. July 18 1888 by Geo Bengley

Remeasured, When and Where,

JOHN HRONEK'S PORTRAIT AND DESCRIPTION—I.
Showing the New Method of Recording Criminals for Identification.

Bohemian-born John Hronek was arrested on July 17, 1888 for conspiring to assassinate John Bonfield, Judge Joseph Gary, and State's Attorney Julius Grinnell. He was convicted and sent to prison for 12 years. The above "rogues gallery" photo and captioned Bertillon measurements were eclipsed by fingerprinting techniques in 1905.

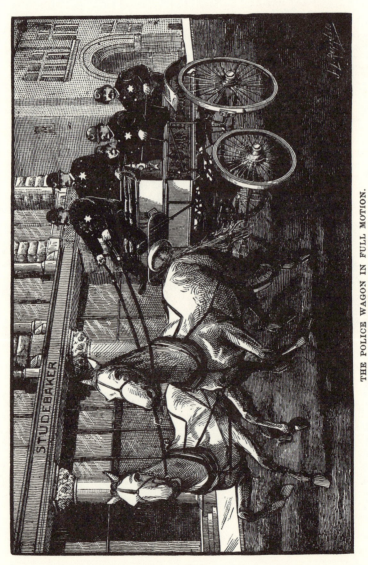

THE POLICE WAGON IN FULL MOTION.

From an instantaneous photograph, taken in front of Studebaker's Carriage Repository, on Michigan Ave., by the Police Photographer.

The Police Patrol Service was an important innovation in the 1880s. For the first time a horse-drawn wagon could respond to an emergency from a remote location.

Dr. Patrick Cronin, Irish nationalist leader, was murdered on the third anniversary of Haymarket, May 4, 1889. Cronin was a leader in the local Clan Na Gael, successor of the radical Fenians. He was murdered by fellow Clansmen who accused him of treachery and double dealing.

HERMANN SCHUETTLER.   MICHAEL HOFFMANN.   MICHAEL WHALEN.

CHAS. REHM.   JOHN STIFT.   JACOB LOEWENSTEIN.

Michael Schaak's cadre of hand-picked detectives. Whalen was implicated by association in the Cronin murder cover-up. Loewenstein was discredited in 1889 after being accused by the *Times* of running a fencing ring. Only Herman Schluetter went on to distinguish himself as Chief of Police, 1917–1918.

THE EAST CHICAGO AVENUE STATION.
From a Photograph.

The East Chicago Avenue Police Station was a seedbed of radical Clan Na Gael activity. "Who is telling the Cronin suspects of every move made by the police?" asked Chief Hubbard indignantly on June 22, 1889.

Joseph Kipley, Chief of Police, 1897–1901. The "Clean Up Chicago" forces that elected Mayor Harrison the second time around demanded and received Kipley's ouster in 1901. His successor, Francis O'Neill, maintained a bedside vigil before Kipley died.

One of Chicago's most capable police superintendents, scholarly Francis O'Neill, taught school, worked in the shipyards, and was a rail section hand before settling in the United States to begin a career in law enforcement.

Taking the Civil Service exam for patrolmen, © 1905. Civil Service created more problems than it was intended to solve. Courtesy of the Chicago Historical Society.

George Shippy, Chief of Police 1907–1909. Articulate and highly read, Shippy's written reports to Mayor Roche in 1887 earned him a quick promotion to Sergeant. For a time Shippy commanded the city's only all-black fire station at 22nd and Wentworth. When Hyde Park was annexed to Chicago in 1889, the local police refused to vacate their office and make way for the Chicago contingency. Shippy, then a policeman, led the ''attack'' on the station, personally battering down the front door. When the symptoms of paresis forced him to take a medical leave, Mayor Busse granted him a paid furlough.

Charles C. Healey, Chief of Police, 1915–1917. Courtesy of the Chicago Police Department.

Charles C. Fitzmorris, Superintendent of Police, 1920–1923. Courtesy of the Chicago Police Department.

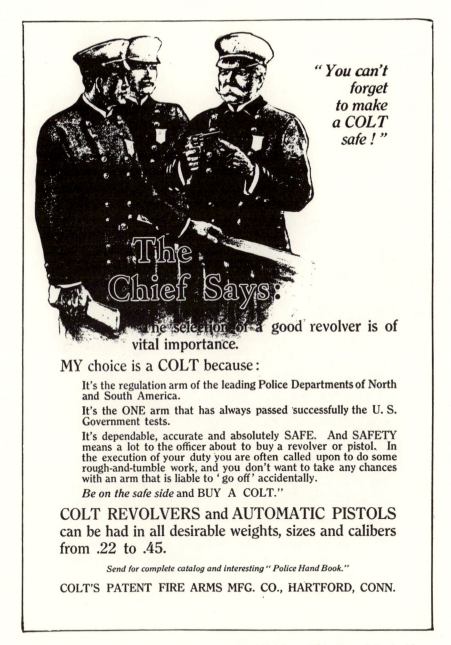

Advertisement in *Police 1313*, a departmental publication, 1921. One of the legitimate complaints of the rank-in-file was the city's requirement that the men purchase their own equipment. Manufacturers enjoyed a virtual monopoly.

Left to right: Deputy Superintendent Matthew Zimmer, Chief of Detectives William H. Schoemaker, and Captain of Detectives John Stege. These three comprised Morgan Collins' "front line" against the prohibition gangs of the 1920s.

Central Police Headquarters at 1121 S. State. Constructed from 1925 to 1928 when the Detective Bureau took occupancy. Central was built at a cost of $3,010,000.

James Allman, Chief of Police, 1931–1945. Courtesy of the Chicago Police Department.

Timothy O'Connor, Chief of Police, 1950–1960. Courtesy of Chicago Police Department.

Orlando W. Wilson, Chief of Police, 1960–1967. Courtesy of Chicago Police Department.

Close Up on the Chicago Police: Tommy O'Connor Breaks Out

Jimmy Cherin, the "Peacock of the Underworld," was sitting in the back seat of a stolen automobile laughing and joking with his old pal Tommy O'Connor. Jimmy was a tough bird, but all the coppers liked him. His father Dominick was a municipal court bailiff and well known to the police as a square-shooter. Arrested time and again, the only punishment Jimmy Cherin ever received was a short stretch in the city Bridewell. Dominick Cherin saw to it that his kid avoided serious trouble. And for his part, Jimmy said he was willing to go straight. He had a wife and a new baby girl to think about.

It was January 21, 1919, and the Model T rambled down the deserted country road. Louis J. Miller was behind the wheel when the little rat in the back seat suddenly pulled out an army service revolver and pumped three bullets into Jimmy's brain. What was left of Jimmy was dumped in a ditch in Stickney, south of Chicago. "Terrible" Tommy O'Connor told the shaken Miller to keep driving or suffer the consequences. Jimmy Cherin had gotten his come-uppance. He had violated the code of gangland by refusing to do a favor for a friend, and now he was dead.

O'Connor was one of four hoods accused of robbing the Illinois Central Railroad depot at Randolph Street on February 1, 1918. Policeman Dennis Tierney was killed during the affray. Harry Emerson, George Raymond, and James Howard were the other gunmen. Howard and O'Connor escaped. Raymond was killed in a shootout with Lieutenant John Norton, and Emerson was forced to surrender. While awaiting arraignment in court, Emerson volunteered the information that O'Connor had pulled the trigger, and offered to repeat the story in court in return for lenient treatment. O'Connor got wind of this, and decided that Emerson must die before he got to trial. Tommy offered $200 to his best pal Cherin to take to "Big Joe" Moran as partial downpayment on a hit. Cherin, mindful of his promises to foreswear crime, refused. Jimmy was killed, and O'Connor was arrested on November 12 on robbery charges (the police had no clues at this point to link Tommy to the Cherin slaying). He went to trial the following April. Despite a positive identification by Emerson, O'Connor was acquitted.

Meanwhile, the Cherin family was beset by personal tragedy. Jimmy's widowed wife turned on the gas five months after her husband's death, taking her life and that of her infant daughter. Old Dominick refused to give up. He swore a vendetta against his son's killer. Cherin had O'Connor indicted for murder a second time, but Tommy outsmarted him. He had the state's star witness, Lou Miller, kidnapped from a Montrose Avenue saloon and spirited away to Madison, Wisconsin and then California. The case against O'Connor was not prosecuted. But on January 8, 1921, the state's attorney's police, acting on a tip from *Tribune* reporters, grabbed Miller at his sister's home. Clad only in his underwear, and clinging desperately to a second-floor ledge, Lou Miller was afraid. He was afraid of the police, but most of all the robber was terrified of what O'Connor might do to him if he turned state's evidence. Despite the obvious reluctance of Miller to blow the whistle on his "pal," the police issued a warrant for O'Connor, but the gunman had skipped out on $45,000 bail. "Terrible" Tommy was again a wanted man—so what else was new?

On March 23, 1921, Detective Sergeant Patrick (Paddy) O'Neill, one of the gamest men on the force, received a hot tip that O'Connor was hiding out at the home of his brother-in-law William Foley, at 6415 South Washtenaw Avenue. Five detectives circled the frame house. Realizing that he was cornered Tommy O'Connor burst through the rear screen door, with his guns blazing. "Well, I'll get you anyway! he yelled at the cops. O'Neill, standing in the center of the yard and caught in the crossfire, was cut down in his tracks. It was impossible to determine whether the shots came from O'Connor's gun, or those of Detectives Tom McShane, Joseph Ronan, or William Fenn who stood on opposite sides of their fallen comrade. "Joe! Joe!" O'Neill cried out, but he would lie there in his own blood for a full 15 minutes before an ambulance arrived. He later died of gunshot wounds at St. Bernard's Hospital.

The remaining detectives regrouped in front of the house. Quick thinking was needed here, but these men were completely befuddled. O'Connor buttoned up his coat and leaped over the rear fence while O'Neill twisted in helpless agony on the ground. At 63rd and Western, O'Connor boarded a Checker cab. He alighted from the auto a mile away, and comandeered a vehicle driven by W. R. Condon, who took him out of the city and down a familiar path into suburban Stickney, where Jimmy Cherin once kept him adequately supplied with food, money, and clothes all the other times O'Connor had taken it on the lam.

For days the search for Tommy extended through the city and suburbs. There were daily reports of O'Connor sightings. At the Crystal Palace dance hall on the far South Side a squad of blue-coats burst in when it was reported that Tommy was "toddling" with some dames. "Throw 'em up!" yelled the sergeant in charge of the flivver squad. The orchestra and dancers abruptly stopped in the middle of a shimmy. The patrons were lined up against the wall and searched. It was reported that O'Connor was dressed in women's clothing. Not true. "Beg your pardon, folks, on with the dance," Officer O'Leary said.

The Foleys and Mr. and Mrs. O'Connor were arrested as accessories to murder, but this was small consolation for Chief Charles Fitzmorris and Deputy John Alcock, who bristled at each new example of police inefficiency. Five against one and the stinking little bird had flown the coop! Lieutenants Schoemaker and Norton, the most seasoned detectives on the force, combed the hinterland with no luck. Fitzmorris filed charges against the five detectives with the Civil Service Commission. "This case was bungled and mismanaged!" he snapped.

O'Connor and his new pal Jimmy Gallagher were arrested in Minneapolis on July 25 after they unsuccessfully tried to rob a Pullman porter on board a Chicago-Great Western passenger train bound for Omaha. A switch foreman named W. L. Woods accomplished what 50 of Chicago's finest had failed to do for three months: he captured Tommy O'Connor and brought him to justice. Taking no chances, Chief Fitzmorris dispatched Detective Chief Michael Hughes to Minnesota to escort O'Connor back to Chicago to stand trial. "We know at least three of O'Connor's toughest pals have left for St. Paul with the intention of rescuing him," Fitzmorris warned. Hughes snatched Tommy away from the Minneapolis police, who planned to file separate charges against him for an earlier payroll robbery for which he was believed to have been responsible. County Attorney Floyd Olson charged Hughes with kidnapping. His men chased the Chicago police to the state line in a vain attempt to steal O'Connor back.

On the way back to the city Tommy told his side of the story. "It wasn't my revolver that killed him [O'Neill], he said "O'Neill was shot down by his own pals. A mistake of course, but they shot him. And after that mistake they ran away and put the blame on me. Do you wonder why I ran away? What chance had I with every policeman in the city out to get me dead or alive? Me with the con—only 138 pounds, and I never shot to kill in my life."

Tommy O'Connor was no choir boy. He was a tough little Irishman from Maxwell Street who committed a string of burglaries between 1907 and 1920. A murderer? Perhaps. A thief? Without a doubt. But a cop killer? It seems unlikely that he shot O'Neill. Whether he did or not was no longer the issue to Hughes and Fitzmorris. Get the red necktie ready boys! Tommy's coming home!

With the greatest manhunt in Chicago police history at an end, Assistant State's Attorney Lloyd Heth drew up the particulars of the case against O'Connor. Feelings ran high; it would have taken an act of God to help "Terrible" Tommy beat the rap this time.

On September 24, 1921, O'Connor was found guilty of first-degree murder. By a unanimous vote the jury decided that Tommy should die by the rope. There was an anguished cry from O'Connor's father, sitting with his other son "Darling" Dave, a La Salle Street investment broker who lost his license for immoral conduct in 1919. "It's the wrongest verdict in the world," he cried. "We couldn't get justice! We couldn't get justice!"

A motion for a new trial was denied by Judge Kickham Scanlan on October 15. Date of execution was set for December 15 between dawn and dusk. Outside his jail cell in back of the Criminal Courts Building, O'Connor could hear the carpenters building the scaffold. His day was at hand . . . or was it?

"Tommy O'Connor will never hang!" was the word out on the streets. On Saturday, December 19, a man drove to the Illinois Street side of the jail and loitered outside. He got out of his car and was observed walking up and down the sidewalk for three hours. The next morning the guards pulled the lever that unlocked the cell blocks. The inmates shuffled out of their cells and filed into the prison yard for their Sunday exercise. Before another night would pass, the guards would transfer O'Connor to "death row" cell 427 in anticipation of his impending execution, now just three days away. O'Connor laughed and joked with his cellmates, James LaPorte, Charles McDermott, Edward Darrow, and Clarence Sponagel—as dangerous a group as ever lived.

LaPorte and O'Connor inched closer to guard David Straus. The latter asked for a hospital pass, and the obliging Straus opened the gate that separated them. In that brief instant, as Straus's attention was diverted, LaPorte collared him by the neck. O'Connor whipped out a pistol that someone had smuggled into the jail and stuck it in his ribs. Darrow, standing inside the gate, seized the keys from Straus.

Meanwhile, O'Connor held off the other prisoners with his gun. If he was going to make a run for it, he didn't want a lot of jailbirds getting in the way. The inmates were ordered back into their cellblocks. O'Connor and his four friends ran down the stairs, where they seized guards Charles Moore, Thomas Jefferson, and Thomas Wetta. Before the startled eyes of the inmates on the fourth floor, the O'Connor gang bound and gagged the guards and tossed them into the cell block. Dashing down the stairs, the fleeing prisoners reached a small shed leading to the outer alley and freedom. Amidst the pandemonium of the jailbreak and the plaintive cry of guard Wetta yelling, "Prisoners escaping!" O'Connor maintained his wits. The convicts scaled the shed and jumped nine feet down into the alley. Sponagel, a heavy man with small feet, crashed to the ground and broke both his ankles. LaPorte, Darrow, McDermott fled down the alley in separate directions. Within a half hour they were picked up by the police. Tommy O'Connor—"Lucky" Tommy, as it was proven time and again—escaped. He comandeered a flivver driven by John Jensen, a city light inspector, and instructed the man to "drive like hell." Jail Clerk Austin Jacobson grabbed a piece of O'Connor's coattail. Tommy wheeled around and pointed a gun menacingly at Jacobson, who prudently backed away. The auto sped around the corner, but in his haste to placate O'Connor, Jensen inadvertently killed his engine. O'Connor abducted a second motorist a few blocks away, and drove into the residential North Side. The trail was fast disappearing.

At Sedgwick and Clark, the car drive by Law Student Henry Busch careened into a curbstone. The streets were wet and slippery, and the chauffeur was understandably edgy. O'Connor found a third driver seconds later. Paul Sorci took the gunman to Larrabee and Hobbie Streets before his car skidded across the pavement, crashing noisily into a store front. Mr. Sorci was the last man to see O'Connor in Chicago.

Chief Fitzmorris, a man of calm demeanor who could usually be counted on to think a problem through, exploded in rage. "It's ridiculous to believe that he got away by himself, he said. "It would be impossible for a criminal to escape like that unaided. O'Connor did not escape. He was let out."

"Stone walls do not a prison make," he continued. "That might refer to our county jail. Conditions there are absolutely appalling. If the people knew how bad conditions were they would not go to sleep at nights, or they would wake up screaming."

When questioned by police, David O'Connor expressed thanks to the almighty for freeing his son. "We knew that the power of God would save Tommy, he shouted, "and show the police and all the people that were against him that he was innocent. We're going to have a merry Christmas at our home now!"

The nickel-plated revolver used by Tommy O'Connor in his escape was smuggled into the jail concealed in a pork chop sandwich. It was intended for someone else, but baker William Fogarty decided to give it to O'Connor instead. Fogarty was a soft-hearted sentimentalist who had witnessed Carl Wanderer's trek to the gallows on March 19. Wanderer was a former choir boy who had been convicted of murdering his pregnant wife, Ruth Johnson. Fogarty had been moved to tears when he listened to Wanderer sing his rendition of "Old Pal, Why Don't You Answer Me?" So too were Ben Hecht and Charles MacArthur, who covered the case for the *Herald* and the *Daily News*. Determined not to see an innocent man die, Fogarty passed the gun to McDermott who in turn gave it to O'Connor.

On December 17 the body of a man was found underneath a bridge three miles north of Palmyra, Wisconsin, in rural Jefferson County. The sheriff of the small Wisconsin town reported to Assistant State's Attorney Charles Wharton that the deceased had been shot by a .32-caliber handgun. The police believed that O'Connor in his flight, found it expedient to murder the driver of the car he had comandeered north of the state line. The body was stripped of its clothes and abandoned.

Detective Chief Hughes received the daily reports with grim resignation. O'Connor had taunted the police and exposed a weak flank at an ill-chosen time. "It is a disgrace," Hughes said, "My men risk their lives to take this gunman and then just before his hanging he is allowed to escape." Hughes dispatched a carload of five detective sergeants to Hartford, Wisconsin, after receiving a report that a "traveling man" resembling Tommy was holed up in the Kasper Hotel. Then a note arrived from Milwaukee, allegedly written by O'Connor: "Chief: Don't send anybody after me. I am innocent. Much obliged to Straus. I am gone, but my friends will reward him. Good luck to you all. I will be posted by friends and will shoot the first man who comes near me."

The team of sergeants drove through the snow-packed Wisconsin backroads

Figure 12

WHERE DOES O'CONNOR'S TRAIL LEAD?

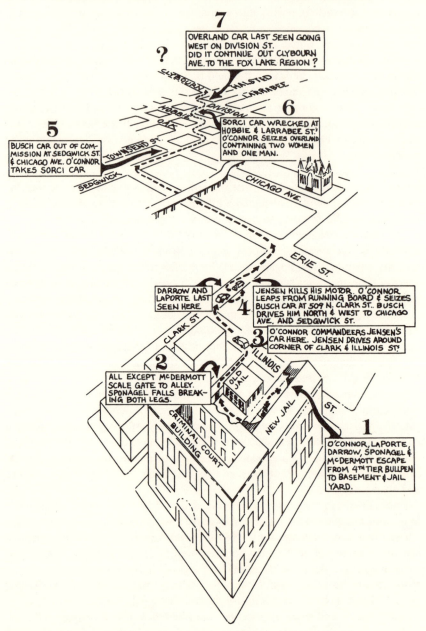

7 OVERLAND CAR LAST SEEN GOING WEST ON DIVISION ST. DID IT CONTINUE OUT CLYBOURN AVE. TO THE FOX LAKE REGION?

?

6 SORCI CAR WRECKED AT HOBBIE & LARRABEE ST. O'CONNOR SEIZES OVERLAND CONTAINING TWO WOMEN AND ONE MAN.

5 BUSCH CAR OUT OF COMMISSION AT SEDGWICK ST. & CHICAGO AVE. O'CONNOR TAKES SORCI CAR

4 JENSEN KILLS HIS MOTOR. O'CONNOR LEAPS FROM RUNNING BOARD & SEIZES BUSCH CAR AT 509 N. CLARK ST.. BUSCH DRIVES HIM NORTH & WEST TO CHICAGO AVE. AND SEDGWICK ST.

DARROW AND LAPORTE LAST SEEN HERE.

3 O'CONNOR COMMANDEERS JENSEN'S CAR HERE. JENSEN DRIVES AROUND CORNER OF CLARK & ILLINOIS ST.

2 ALL EXCEPT McDERMOTT SCALE GATE TO ALLEY. SPONAGEL FALLS BREAKING BOTH LEGS.

1 O'CONNOR, LAPORTE, DARROW, SPONAGEL & McDERMOTT ESCAPE FROM 4TH TIER BULLPEN TO BASEMENT & JAIL YARD.

Cutaway diagram showing Tommy O'Connor's escape route from the Cook County Jail on December 19, 1921. (Deckert)

at breakneck speed. Three miles east of Menominee Falls the flivver skidded off the highway and tumbled into a ditch. Sergeant Jack Boschulte suffered a crushed pelvis and was placed in intensive care at a Milwaukee hospital. The two men registered at the Hartford hotel had no connections with O'Connor, as it turned out. "Terrible" Tommy claimed yet another victim from the ranks of the Chicago police.

Back in Chicago the day of the hanging passed quietly. Attorney Lloyd Heth filed motions in the criminal court to ensure that no possible legal entanglements would hinder the hangman in the likely event of O'Connor's recapture. But that day would never come. The wooden gallows began to sport cobwebs, and with each passing year some newspaper wag would visit the forlorn sight and note the anniversary the next day with some pithy comment: "Listen, Terrible Tommy, if you're still out there, you old rascal, it's time to give yourself up. Enough is enough!" They were still visiting the rotting gallows when Thomas Powers filed that report in 1974.

But where did Tommy O'Connor disappear to? The Chicago police believed that he was on his way to St. Paul, and then the Canadian border. On May 28, 1924, the Minneapolis police arrested a man named Tommy O'Connor who looked like the fugitive, and in fact knew him in Chicago. The man under arrest admitted that he had visited his namesake in the jail just a few days before the great escape. Knowing that it was only a matter of time before the Minnesota authorities fingered him as the killer, the man changed his name to Jack Ryan, and then got married—only to have his father-in-law turn him in. The second Tommy O'Connor was quietly released.

Two years later, in April 1926, a man answering the description of Tommy O'Connor was arrested in Grant's Pass, Oregon. The man gave the name of Tom O'Brien and was detained until William Schoemaker was able to send a photograph of the rightful O'Connor. It was yet another mirage.

A more plausible theory was advanced that O'Connor left the country to return to Ireland, where he embraced the cause of the Irish nationalism. Whatever the case, it was a police fiasco of the greatest magnitude that had some far-reaching consequences. O'Connor's mad dash through the northwest suburbs of Chicago illustrated the critical need for a county highway patrol to safeguard the lives of motorists and rural residents outside the jurisdiction of the Chicago Police Department. Such a police force would have impeded the movements of O'Connor and other fugitives making their way to freedom. In 1922, the Cook County sheriff's police were organized to do battle with desperados like O'Connor, and the beer barons who were only just beginning to realize the potential of the hinterland as a base of operations.

Those wooden gallows remained in the basement of the jail until 1977, when they were at last torn down.

10

Pawns of the Machine: The Cermak-Kelly-Nash Years, 1933–47

Dear Mr. Mayor:

Our morale is bad in places. Leadership can raise the morale. A raise in pay can and will improve the standards of the men originally selected if the selection is based on merit and merit alone. We are slovenly in some respects. Our quarters are not clean. We don't always have impartial enforcement of discipline. We don't always have promotion based on merit. We have some officials who don't back up the men when they are right, are quick to pass the buck and leave the men grumbling about holding the bag. I could couch these words in more flowery rhetoric but these are expressions our men use and know so well. Visit a police station and hear them.

Some of our previous chiefs have been content to sit as close as they could to the mayor in a smug complacency, hoping against hope the publicity wouldn't be too bad nor the grand jury too angry. If the day passed without them doing any good or too much harm without a blast from the press, they were contented.

Anonymous letter to *The Police Digest*,
April 1947

Tony Cermak served notice on Chicago's black population that the old rules no longer applied. To build a Democratic power base in the 2nd and 3rd Wards the mayor replaced three powerful South Side captains whose benign tolerance of policy gambling was in accord with the political strategy of the Thompsonites.

Until black voters understood the changing political realities, Cermak would send in the bloodhounds to close down every illegal bookie operation they could find. "Soon after I assumed office I had a survey made of the city," he said. "As a consequence I know what the situation is. It is not good. On the near

South Side, for instance, I found that policy games were operating and taking a huge toll from the victims. As captains who were then commanding the districts had failed to take any action I assigned new commanding officers."[1] The survey, of course, encompassed only the Republican wards.

Without bothering to consult Acting Commissioner Alcock on the matter, Cermak transferred John Stege to the South Wabash Station on September 17, 1931. The next day he dispatched a raiding squad to the 5700 block of Prairie Avenue, where a number of big-time policy games were "pulled" even though the police had entered the premises without search warrants. Municipal Judge Matthew Hartigan dismissed the prisoners the next day but Cermak vowed to continue the raids.

Alcock, who was occupying a chair in City Hall only until the new county party boss Pat Nash could come up with a suitable replacement, remained silent about the numerous personnel shifts Cermak made in the first 90 days of his regime. The acting chief was forced to bite the bullet when a special vice and gambling detail was organized under Captain Martin Mullen to go after the big-time gamblers on the South Side. Even Al Capone was not immune. A second-floor gambling den at his Vanity Fair night club on Broadway and Grace was raided one night by the axe-wielding Mullen, who was accompanied by a flying squad of detectives. The resort was owned by a former Moran-disciple, Ted Newberry, who had changed sides shortly after the massacre. Tony Cermak was sending a loud message to the criminal underworld that it would not be allowed to flourish unless the mayor said so. It was a departure from long-standing tradition, and Al Capone, now facing a wave of federal income tax indictments, did not like it one bit.

Cermak invited the public to write him letters advising him of the existence of gambling dens, but added: "There will be no gambling with cards or wheels. We're not going to make Chicago a hick town, because Chicagoans don't want that. We are going to drive out hoodlum joints of every description."

The mayor's Prohibition policy raised the hackles of the syndicate, which had become accustomed to the old way of doing business. Cermak and the Tammany Democrats targeted repeal as the number one priority on their agenda. In 1932 there were hopeful signs that Volstead was on its way out. So that legislators would not be dissuaded from voting for repeal due to adverse publicity attached to crime syndicate activity, Cermak ordered a crack down on the "beer flats" that operated in defiance of the law.

Legitimate dealers who sold legal near-beer were more often than not forced to buy the real stuff from the syndicate at $55 a barrel. Near-beer could be purchased for $25 a barrel, and was distributed to coffee shops, drug stores, and restaurants. Cermak proposed a stiff $250 licensing fee to keep the operators in line and out of the clutches of the syndicate. "I am convinced that if we put a licence fee on the sale of malt beverages we could keep those places under control and trim the wings of the racketeers," he said.

It was the second-floor beer flat, accessible only by a rear stairway and virtually indistinguishable to pedestrians on the street, that the mayor ordered closed by the police. In his weekly radio address Cermak condemned these places as the worst breeding ground for crime, because they provided a safe haven for syndicate thugs, bank robbers, and confidence men to meet and discuss criminal operations. When Policeman Albert G. Magoon was shot and killed at one of these beer flats on Halsted Street in December 1932, Cermak declared war on these hoodlum hangouts, and may in fact have signed his own death warrant. "You are going to help me carry out this job," he told his new commissioner. "If I can't carry it out, I'll resign and I think you should too."

James Allman weathered this storm, and many others during his long 45-year career in the Chicago Police Department. Born in Ireland, but reared on the South Side of Chicago, the thin, reed-faced Allman joined the department on November 21, 1900. He was a tireless workaholic who sacrificed his private life in his determination to advance through the ranks. Like Garrity before him, Jim Allman was happiest shooting the breeze with the boys in the neighborhood firehouse. But unlike Chicago's first Prohibition chief, Allman had a pretty good idea of how to reform a Police Department. During the "whoopie years" the reform block of the City Council touted Allman for police chief on several occasions but were turned away by the Thompsonites. His reputation as the department "clean-up man" sent in to organize a corrupt precinct station was an enviable one.

As the World's Fair mayor, Cermak needed a police chief untainted by the shifting winds of patronage politics—a new face to present to the press and out-of-town dignitaries expected to attend Chicago during the celebration. After pondering the matter at length, the mayor's advisory committee, headed up by crusty old Sewell Avery of Montgomery Ward, recommended Allman to the City Council on October 1, 1931. He was approved unanimously. "A hard-boiled egg," remarked one. "As clean as a whistle," said Avery. Allman didn't even smoke cigarettes. Henry Barrett Chamberlin and Frank Loesch, relics of the long-forgotten prewar reform era, endorsed the new chief wholeheartedly: "During the 12 years that the Chicago Crime Commission has been observing the Police Department there has not come to the notice a single adverse word as to Captain Allman's integrity, ability, efficiency, or independence."[2] Allman traded his blue uniform for civilian garb, and embarked on his new assignment with enthusiasm. His term of office remains a department record for longevity.

Commenting on the impending reorganization of the Police Department, the *Tribune* noted with concern that the good citizens of London were paying $5.69 per inhabitant as their cost of protection. By contrast, Chicagoans doled out an average of $6.91 per head, and were receiving much less in return. Because of both political and organizational reasons, the department was returning far less than the public was paying. Inefficiency resulted from poorly defined job descriptions, and a decentralization of power through the ranks. These problems were adequately addressed by the Citizen's Police Committee but were benignly neglected by John Alcock.

In its final report, entitled *Chicago's Police Problems*, the committee argued for additional appropriations to bolster the force to 14,700 men after the perfunctory reorganization. To these ends committee members recommended abolition of the five deputy commissionerships, and the creation of a single inspectorship to oversee the operation of the various uniformed departments.[3] The inspector would have direct accountability to the commissioner, thus returning a degree of control to headquarters. The chief inspector would be given the responsibility to formulate and enforce the policies of the chief. Under his immediate control were the six divisional inspectors.

Allman carefully considered the survey, which had cost the city nearly $32,000 and so far had collected dust on the shelf. At the chief's insistence, Bruce Smith of the National Institute of Public Administration of New York was brought back to Chicago as a civilian adviser during the reorganization.

There was immediate opposition to Allman's suggestion that Smith be appointed a salaried deputy chief. Michael F. Ryan, the policeman's lobbyist in Springfield and attorney for the Annuity and Benefit Fund Association, announced he would file an injunction on behalf of the Civil Service Protective Association to prevent Smith from collecting a salary. He was an outsider and not part of the grossly inefficient Civil Service infrastructure. Therefore Bruce Smith was objectionable to the rank-and-file just as Alexander Piper had been a quarter-century earlier. Resistance to outside forces of reform continued to hamstring the efforts of good and capable men like Francis O'Neill in 1904 and James Allman in 1931.

Bruce Smith did return to Chicago, and working in tandem with Elmer Stevens, chairman of the advisory committee, formulated an ambitious plan of reorganization that was announced in October 23, 1931. It took effect ten months later, on August 1, 1932.

The plan, which called for six divisional inspectors reporting to a chief inspector who would oversee the 40 police districts, was submitted to Mayor Cermak for his approval. Contingent on his acceptance of the ambitious plan was the proposal to extend the traffic division across the city, and to eliminate a number of unproductive desk jobs. The city could not afford to double the size of the force as Smith had originally recommended, but under Allman's plan the "soft snaps" would be eliminated and existing personnel would be returned to uniformed patrol.

Allman moved his offices from City Hall to the new headquarters building at 11th and State, taking with him various headquarters units that were brought under the control of the appropriate bureau and division chiefs.

The plan was reminiscent of the 1890 reorganization that created five inspectorships for the first time. Then in 1911–12, the Civil Service reformers decided the inspectors had to go because they were too closely tied in with the bosses of the Levee vice districts. In 1931 the Chicago Police Department was returning to a system that had been assailed as inefficient and laden with graft. It was an interesting development, and its success was tied to the caliber of men that

Allman appointed. The police inspectors of former years were corrupted by Levee bosses and powerful gamblers. The situation in 1931 was not entirely different, except that the controlled vice districts had all but disappeared. Vice had scattered into the county and small pockets across the city. The creation of a highway patrol in 1922 shifted the concentration of graft away from the Chicago police and out into northwest Cook County—the city's "Bohemia" district, with 500 roadhouses and casinos.

The seven men that Allman and Cermak decided on were for the most part political lackeys not likely to offend the Democratic Party bosses. The list was drawn up in November. It contained the names of Captain John Ptacek, a grizzled old veteran of many political battles dating back to 1900 and a close friend of Cermak's; Captain Richard Gill, who cleaned up the South Side badlands, but was given this assignment only because his brother was Municipal Court Judge Joseph Gill, a prominent party leader; Captain John Horan, whose brother Al was a bailiff of the municipal court and one of the leaders of the emerging West Side bloc; Matt Zimmer, who was Morgan Collins's deputy commissioner, and a good Democrat; and the redoubtable Dan Gilbert, whose star was inexorably tied to Thomas J. Courtney, the City Council sergeant-at-arms who would succeed John Swanson as state's attorney in December 1932. By virtue of his connections to City Hall, and his uncanny ability to hoodwink the press, Gilbert had become the second most powerful policeman in the city. In a few years he would earn another sobriquet: the "millionaire cop."

If the selection of inspectors was a disappointing affirmation of political cronyism, Chicagoans were consoled by an improving crime picture. The city murder rate, which had pushed Chicago to national notoriety, continued to drop. In 1931 Allman reported to the City Council that the city ranked twenty-fifth among 86 municipalities surveyed. In the category of murders per 100,000 population, Chicago still ranked behind New York on a percentage basis; 9.84 to 6.89 percent. In 1932 the all-important murder rate continued its downward trend, with the rate per 100,000 dropping to 8.9 percent. In a corresponding period, 65 U.S. cities showed a rise of 3.5 percent.[4]

Mayor Cermak's campaign pledge to end the rule of the gangsters had taken effect. Al Capone was on his way to jail. Prohibition was coming to its deserved, ignominious end, and the police under James Allman had entered a period of stability and retrenchment. The emphasis, as the chief explained, was on "constant redistribution of its manpower in accordance with demonstrated need; and upon personnel management with particular reference to training and discipline." That the police were part and parcel of a new machine, there was no denying. But at least in the early years of the Depression, the belt-tightening had some positive effects.

The Martyred Mayor

Mayor Cermak continued his war against the Capone beer flats right up to the moment of repeal. At the same time, he left other gangs alone. Out in the

Northwest Corridor Roger Touhy was reportedly "encouraged" to go to war against the Capone mob, now under the direction of Frank Nitti. According to Judge Lyle, Cermak told Touhy that "you can have the entire Police Department."

Meanwhile, the small fries were undercutting the price of bootleg liquor to $10 for a five-gallon can. Nitti's people were trying hard to hold the line at $15. Syndicate beer peddled in the Loop held at $55 a barrel, but at "Little Bohemia" along the Dempster Street strip in Morton Grove, Touhy dropped his prices to $30—$35. In retaliation Capone lieutenants planned the assassination of Touhy's business associate Matt Kolb, who was gunned down—allegedly by the big man himself—at the Club Morton on October 17, 1931.

The Touhy mob supposedly extracted their revenge by kidnapping John "Jake the Barber" Factor outside the Dells Roadhouse on July 1, 1933. Factor was a smooth confidence man and international swindler who was a intimate of Murray Humphreys and other Capone gunmen. Facing extradition back to England, Factor went to his friends in the Chicago mob with a wild plan to fake a kidnapping that might buy him enough time to work himself out of his dilemma with the immigration officials.

Kidnapping was a hot racket in the wake of the Lindbergh abduction, but this was one that even the Capone torpedoes were reluctant to touch. Nevertheless, it was too good to pass up, especially if Roger Touhy could somehow take the fall. The Dells was a Capone place, opened by Dell Jones in the 1920s but later run by a mobster named Sam Hare. The second floor was a casino lined with slot machines and roulette wheels, placed there by the syndicate and protected by Sheriff William Meyering.

Factor was "kidnapped" outside the Dells on July 1, 1933. He was held in the basement of a house in nearby Glenview for a period of twelve days, before being released. Murray Humphreys negotiated with the "kidnappers." Factor returned to his wife without so much as a scratch, and was more than eager to finger his abductors.

Waving the banner of reform, Tom Courtney became the new state's attorney. He appointed his friend and adviser "Tubbo" Gilbert to serve as chief investigator. Gilbert's high marks in the Police Department and his flair for the dramatic made him a natural to help further the aims of this politically ambitious politician, cut from the same cloth as Robert Emmett Crowe. Courtney had high hopes and perhaps fancied himself to be presidential timber some day. What the public did not know about Courtney was that he operated his own little tavern and bookmaking parlor at 43rd and Halsted, and would stop at nothing to crack the Factor kidnapping case.

Gilbert, whose influence extended into the corrupt Teamster's Union, bitterly resented Roger Touhy, who had aided labor officials attempting to fend off infiltration by Capone mobsters. An article in a 1943 issue of *Police Digest* stated:

It is worth mentioning that in the realm of labor difficulties, Capt. Gilbert proved to be especially valuable because of knowledge gained from experience as a former labor union official. His usefulness in this field has been widened to include the responsibility of mediating where possible in labor conflicts to prevent flare-ups.

Gilbert located and bribed a Baltimore convict named Ike Costner to come to Chicago and give evidence against Touhy and his gang. Costner was promised a reduced sentence in return for his perjured testimony, which had the effect of sending Touhy to prison for 25 years in the second of two sensational trials in 1934. In 1959, Judge John Barnes freed Roger Touhy from Stateville Prison, citing the perjured testimony of Factor and Costner, and the well-known enmity that "Tubbo" Gilbert harbored for the north suburban bootlegger.[5]

Courtney and Gilbert were the men of the hour in Chicago. They were young, handsome men who had earned their stripes by putting away a vicious depraved kidnapper and rum-runner. The *New York Times* even sat up and took notice:

For some months State's Attorney Courtney has been represented in the working force of the Police Department by one of the ablest officers, Captain Gilbert. The arrangement made by agreement between the mayor and the State's Attorney provides a liaison which enables Mr. Courtney to keep informed on crime and its tendencies as discovered by the police and to cooperate promptly and efficiently in detection and suppression.

So much for Roger Touhy, the Robin Hood of Chicago gangdom, who swore up and down that he never killed a man or busted an honest labor union. Perhaps that is where he went wrong.

The indignity the outfit suffered at the hands of Mayor Cermak was another matter. After the murder of Patrolman Magoon in the North Side beer flat, Cermak put out the word on the streets: shoot first, ask questions later. By the end of 1932 Allman's blue-coats had sent 37 men to the morgue. Another 26 hoodlums were gunned down by licenced private detectives. So zealous were some of the citizen cops that the mayor was forced to permanently muzzle the Secret Six in January 1933. "I'm tired of seeing Mrs. [Shirley] Kub intruding on police investigations," Cermak said. "It's time that it is stopped. I never want to see a Chicago policeman talking to her and I don't want to see her around City Hall." Shirley was out, and the four uniformed policemen were withdrawn from the agency's service.

Cermak kept the police on Frank Nitti's trail. A first cousin of Al Capone and heir to the criminal throne, Nitti had served his time in Leavenworth for income tax evasion. With time off for good behavior, he returned to Chicago to assume control of the remnants of the South Side mob. Frank Nitti was a bland, moon-faced character who lacked Capone's charisma, but none of his ruthlessness. He was educated in Italy and trained as a watchmaker. It was said that Nitti was well-versed in chemistry, but these talents did not save him from the government tax lawyers. "I have never been guilty of a crime of moral turpitude," Nitti said. "I paid no income tax simply because lawyers could not tell me whether I owed anything or not. But if I owe a debt to society I am ready to pay for it."

Cermak sanctioned wiretaps against Nitti, relied on the information of stool pigeons, and used whatever means, legal or otherwise, to make sure the Chicago mob did not thwart the progress of Prohibition repeal. Perhaps the mayor had deeper, more personal reasons for wanting to subdue the Italian gangsters. His people—the Croats, Slavs, and Bohemians of Lawndale—were forced to buy Capone beer at inflated prices. The elimination of rival bootleg gangs reduced the quality of the brew. Ethnic pride and a desire to clear the decks for the entry of his voting constituency into the liquor trade in the post-Prohibition era may have guided his police policies in the early years. Certainly the mob had not experienced anything like this since the Dever administration.

Events reached a head on December 19, 1932, when the mayor's private elite squad was dispatched to Nitti's downtown headquarters at LaSalle and Wacker, near the Chicago River. Acting under the mayor's orders to break up "all meetings of gangsters," the detective squad burst into the private offices where they found Nitti, Louis "Little New York" Campagna, Johnny Pope, Louis Massessa, Charles McGee, Marty Sanders, and Joe Parrillo huddled in private conference. Detective Harry Miller of the mayor's squad and Chris Callahan of the detective bureau herded the six hoods into an inner office, leaving Nitti alone with Sergeant Harry Lang, an honest, but trigger-happy policeman.

Nitti stared stupidly at Lang, both men unsure of their next move. Then Nitti reached for a memorandum lying on the desk. He stuffed it in his mouth and began chewing. Lang ordered him to spit out the paper, at which point the gangland boss reached for a.33-caliber pistol in his desk. Lang fired first, dropping Nitti to the floor. There were three more shots fired. Nitti took two slugs, and Lang took one before the gunfight ended.

The six gangsters were arrested and taken to the Bridewell where "Tubbo" Gilbert was on hand to take their statements. Nitti was listed as being in critical condition, but was saved from death only because he had neglected to take his lunch. This was common practice in the underworld, according to Edward Denemark, superintendent of the Bridewell. When a gangster was on his way to a "job," he would go without food. In the event of a gunshot wound, the victim was thus ready for immediate surgery.

The arrested men told Gilbert that they had stopped by the office to get their bets down for the afternoon race. This was hotly disputed by Lang and Miller, who found a detailed map of the 42nd Ward speakeasys and nightclubs. Ledgers bearing the name of the Quality Flour House, a wholesale business once owned by deceased gangster Joe Aiello, were seized in the raid.

The half-chewed note was sent to the cipher lab of the Northwestern Crime School for analysis. The torn scrap of paper was cryptic and shed no new light on the inner workings of the Chicago mob.

> Bob Rommodo. Sat. 6:20 P.M.
> Ask J.P. if the party
> over worked for Smithy

"If I am here tell Lewis
to ask for Minie Kunon—in
Pine
Tel y—
Potatoes—
Warm
Ask ich for him
and I—

Mayor Cermak was overjoyed by his men's actions. He vowed their work would continue and as a reward for good effort he promoted Lang and Miller to head up the special "hoodlum squad" created two weeks prior to the shooting. "The Chicago police can fight," he said. "My orders are to stop the notorious activities of organized crime. The police intend to carry out those orders. If necessary, every place where hoodlums congregate will have its license revoked."

Privately, Cermak was apprehensive about his personal safety. The mayor believed that Louis Campagna, who would figure prominently with Willie Bioff when the syndicate muscled in on the big Hollywood studios later in the decade, was on a permanent retainer to kill him. It was this story that Sergeant Lang told the grand jury when indictments for assault were returned. Judge Thomas Lynch granted a new trial to Lang after he was found guilty of the charge. The sergeant had vowed to "blow the lid off the Democratic Party if he served so much as a day in jail."

The trial was never held. Another favorite gangland story that has made the rounds over the years involves the bodyguard Miller, who went before Nitti several months later, and begged the gang chieftain on his knees to spare the life of Cermak.

Anton Cermak traveled to Miami, Florida in February 1933 on a working vacation. He was to meet with the new Democratic President in an effort to mend some political fences that were badly damaged during the recent election, when Cermak backed Governor Al Smith for the nation's highest office. Prior to the trip, the mayor beefed up his security forces and moved from the Congress Hotel to the Morrison after hearing about the assassination of Ted Newberry, who in recent months had tried to muscle in on Nitti.

Cermak was in attendance at Bayfront Park the night of February 15 for a large torchlight rally for Franklin Roosevelt. It was a festive, warm evening and the searchlights panned the audience, estimated at 10,000. As the president-elect's motorcade slowly entered the park, people pushed forward for a closer look. Roosevelt gave a short extemporaneous speech, then settled into the open automobile. Seeing Cermak in the line of dignitaries, the president motioned him over. The two men shook hands and spoke for only a second. Then the shots rang out. A fatal bullet bit the mayor under his right arm, but Roosevelt escaped unhurt.

A diminutive Italian immigrant who had been in the country since 1923 was seized by police and taken into custody. The assassin was identified as Guiseppe Zangara, a 32-year-old bricklayer who had been out of work for three years. He was neither a Communist, a Fascist, or an anarchist. In fact, Zangara was a registered Republican since taking out his citizenship papers on September 11, 1929. His motives for shooting the mayor were peculiar. He claimed that Roosevelt was the real target, but yet he waited until Cermak had backed away from the car. By doing so Zangara gave up a chance to shoot the President at point-blank range.

"Did you plan this shooting?" he was asked. "It came into my mind when my stomach began to hurt," he said. Zangara decided to kill a "king" or "ruler." That is all he would say about the matter. He did not seem to have any qualms about the electric chair.

Mayor Cermak lingered until March 6. Two weeks later Zangara was put to death and the secret died with him. It seems certain, however, that the Cermak shooting was neither an accident nor the work of a crazed lunatic. Zangara had lived in Florida for two years prior to his execution. He spent a lot of time at the dog tracks and, according to Ovid Demaris in his book *Captive City*, had worked briefly on the docks of a syndicate pier where he received bootleg whiskey shipped in from the Caribbean.[6] Threatened with his life, he agreed to shoot Cermak. This followed an earlier unsuccessful plot to have Campagna, a Chicago insider, attend to the matter. With Cermak out of the way the syndicate had achieved its purpose. On shakey ground after the 1929 massacre, the Capone gang consolidated its interests by eliminating individuals who sought to threaten its livelihood. Anton Cermak never got to be the World's Fair mayor, but Murray Humphreys, Jimmy Mondi, and Ralph Capone ran the roller coaster, the Italian Village, and the roulette wheel concessions on the fairgrounds. Everyone made money on the deal.

Fine-Tuning the Machine: Edward Kelly and the Police

The political organization A. J. Cermak left behind was a formidable one. Republicans in the City Council were a dying breed. All that was left to do was to select the king. This task was left to the county's best kingmaker, Patrick Nash, who, like all big-city bosses, worked quietly behind the scenes. As 28th Ward alderman, Nash profited from his close ties to Edward Kelly, chief engineer of the Sanitary District. During his tenure of office millions of dollars in city contracts had been awarded to Nash's own sewer contracting firms. They became good friends and it came as no surprise to City Hall watchers when Nash submited the name of Kelly as his choice to fill the unexpired term of Cermak. Behind the scenes there was considerable wrangling between Tom Courtney and Nash, who harbored a strong desire to become mayor himself. Courtney backed Corporation Counsel William Sexton. They compromised on Ed Kelly, which in hindsight was the worst possible choice the eager young prosecutor could have made. Then, in an unprecedented testimony to the Democrats' awesome state-wide power, the legislature passed a measure that allowed the City Council to *elect* its own successor. Governor Henry Horner, an otherwise capable executive, forced the bill through the General Assembly to repay old political debts to the Brennan-Cermak team. It was Horner who delivered the eulogy at A. J.'s funeral. But it would be Kelly, a horse of a different color, who would preside over Governor Horner's own political dirge seven years later.

Ed Kelly, an Irishman from the 11th Ward, generally earned high marks during his first two years in office. He made deep cuts in City Council spending, amounting to $80,000,000. The floating debt that had plagued the city since the onset of the Depression was reduced substantially. The first six months of 1935 witnessed a remarkable 20 percent reduction in reported crime, with murder down 40 percent from the previous year. The fact that Chicago was becoming a safe place to live was reflected in lower insurance premiums. "He is a good model for mayors and even officials of loftier title," the *New York Times* commented in 1935.[7]

A well-oiled political machine has this soothing effect on a city. The deeper problems are masked by efficient municipal service and great civic undertakings. The price is obedience, and the Democratic ward bosses expected no less. Politics, gambling, and vice again became indigenous to the ward as it had been when Mike McDonald ruled the roost nearly 50 years earlier. A new generation of boodling aldermen dispensed the patronage and controlled the actions of the police and the courts in interesting new ways.

Tom Courtney and Dan Gilbert ran the state's attorney's office with savvy and flair. As the rift between the mayor and Courtney widened, Prosecutor Tom found new ways to embarrass his rival, while enhancing his own reputation as a tough, no-nonsense lawman. On January 1, 1936, just 24 hours after 176 police veterans were forced to retire upon reaching the age of 63, Courtney hired two of the most famous names in the department—Captain William Schoemaker and his Lieutenant John Norton—to serve as investigators.

Shoes was 67, and Norton, a man to whom he was barely civil, had passed his seventy-third birthday. Norton had put in 45 years on the force. Schoemaker had fought the Capone gang for the better part of two decades, and was instrumental in helping the "G-men" nail John Dillinger outside the Biograph Theatre in July 1934. Courtney recognized the inherent public relations value in such a move. The collective wisdom of these two old war horses was invaluable, of course. But their exploits were so well publicized over the years that they had become sentimental favorites of many Chicagoans. Speaking for Courtney, as he usually did when there was happy news to tell, Dan Gilbert predicted great things for the rookie investigators: "They will spread fear in the underworld and keep the lid on."

The retirement of Norton and Schoemaker led to considerable consternation among the machine aldermen, who sought new ways to circumvent the Civil

Service laws governing age requirements. Alderman Jacob Arvey had the support
of Mayor Kelly when he proposed that the City Council create jobs for them as
"investigators" for the city police.

The office of the state's attorney took on greater significance in the 1930s, as
Courtney waged a vigorous war against automobile thieves, labor racketeers,
and several arson rings operating in the city at this time. However, the mayor
and his army of ward hacks and committeemen left the big-time gamblers alone.

In 1934 the *Chicago Daily News* estimated that 7,500 illegal gambling dens
operated within the city limits.[8] Just about every slot machine sold in the United
States was manufactured by the Mills Amusement Company, or a sister firm in
Cicero—Taylor Manufacturing, whose president was none other than Claude
Maddox of the old Circus Gang. Eddie Vogel distributed the machines to
hundreds of taverns on the North and Northwest Sides following Prohibition
repeal. Collection agents would appear on a weekly basis with their key and
empty out the contents. The tavern owner received 40 percent of the take, with
40 percent returned to Vogel, top agent of the Capone interests. During Prohibition the slots were controlled by Mike Heitler and Oliver Ellis in Chicago
Heights. The districts these men controlled were outlined to correspond to the
jurisdiction of the deputy sheriffs on the outskirts of the county.

Chicago was the home base of the Continental Press Service, a scion of the
old General News Bureau founded by Mont Tennes at the turn of the century.
Headquartered in the same building where Tennes once distributed race results
to his off-track parlors and handbooks, Continental serviced 200 outlets in Chicago. The United Press and Associated Press paid a fee of $70–$80 a month to
Hymie "Loudmouth" Levin and other syndicate men who had successfully
muscled Tennes, and then Moe Annenberg, out of the racket through strong-
arm techniques. The most lucrative return was from the South Side policy wheels,
played by thousands of poor blacks on a daily basis. With such interesting and
mysterious names as the Erie-Buffalo Wheel, the Standard Golden Gate, and
the Rome-Silver Wheel, the estimated take from just one of these games was
$278,000 in 1949. Just as in the days of old, local control of ward gambling
was vested in the alderman, who split it with the syndicate henchmen. The party
organization pocketed its share of the proceeds to defray the costs of future
election campaigns. The ward office in the 1930s was a money-making machine.

A Tavern by Any Other Name: The Shooting at Paddy's Place

When Fort Dearborn towered above a sea of grass, the frontiersmen who
didn't care a hoot about temperance opened the first tavern. It was, by popular
definition, a place where food, liquor, and lodgings could be found. As the city
grew, the word "tavern" came to denote a place of open licentiousness and vile
habits to the prim nativists who demanded no less than sobriety and clean living.

The liquor distributors who had a financial stake in the taverns suddenly hit
on the idea of painting gaudy new signs outside the drinking emporiums pro-

claiming the advent of the saloon. At the time, according to dictionaries, a saloon was a "spacious and elegant apartment for reception of company for works of art; a large room or parlor."

By the time the Anti-Saloon League was founded, the word had fallen into disfavor until the dictionary was revised to describe these establishments simply as places where "intoxicating liquors are sold and drunk; a grog shop." With the return of legal liquor in 1933 the much maligned saloon became at long last the *tavern*.

Running a public house became a lifelong avocation for generations of political families in Chicago. The liquor business brought together the elements of city government, entertainment, sports, and law enforcement in a congenial atmosphere. The saloon or tavern functioned as a ward headquarters, a counting house, and a command post at election time. In 1933 the living, breathing heart of the Democratic machine was Mathias "Paddy" Bauler's two-story saloon at North Avenue and Sedgwick in the 43rd Ward.

Paddy Bauler remained a power in Chicago politics for five decades, spanning the era of Bathhouse John Coughlan to Richard J. Daley. He was the son of Herman Bauler, Sr., who arrived in Chicago about 1870 with his 13 hungry children.

Paddy was the third Bauler son to warm a chair in the City Council. Herman Jr. directed the redistricting program in 1920 and was succeeded by his brother John upon his death. John Bauler served four terms as alderman until relinquishing his seat in 1933 to his paunchy, jovial brother Mathias. As a young man Mathias regaled the hangers-on in his father's saloon with racy stories and sentimental Irish ballads. He took the nickname "Paddy" when he had some designs on a career of pugilism; Mathias Bauler was too effete a name when the top prizefighters were called "Iron Mike" and "Irish Red."

Bauler entered into ward politics after his eighteenth birthday. He was a minor player through the 1920s, someone who couldn't be taken seriously. Wise-cracking Paddy with his salty tongue and uncouth manner was a Democratic court jester. But the boys in the back room raised their eyebrows when Paddy was invited to accompany Mayor Cermak on a vacation to Europe along with County Commissioner Charley Weber. The next year he was elected alderman on his second attempt.

Suddenly the corner saloon on North Avenue became a focal point of Democratic decision-making. Cermak liked the clownish antics of Paddy, who was known to quaff a half-gallon of beer in one swallow. Alderman Bauler, a roistering, jug-handled entertainer, retained a small orchestra and presided over a nightly gathering of gamblers, payrollers, and favored police in a building that was once the home of the Immigrant State Bank.

The alderman was in rare form the night of December 19, 1933. His annual Christmas basket benefit returned a tidy profit to the organization, and the food dispensed to the unfortunates living in the 43rd Ward would earn the alderman the gratitude and votes so necessary to sustain his job. Among the happy celebrants present that night was Sheriff William Meyering, a World War I hero who once boasted: "I am no reformer. I do not intend to become one." With him were Lieutenant Thomas Rowan of the city police, and three uniformed officers.

Within the brightly lit cabaret the ward revelers toasted each other one last time as the 1:00 AM closing came and went. At four, a half-drunk Chicago policeman named John J. Ahearn pounded on the locked door of Bauler's saloon, demanding entrance. "Go away!" the alderman yelled, but Ahearn was persistent. Officer Edward Hayes and his girlfriend returned to the automobile. Their backs were turned when the shots rang out. Bauler, who was never one to stand by when someone called him a name, brandished a revolver and used it against Ahearn. The shots were not fatal. Ahearn fell backwards. He pointed his gun wildly, and an errant shot struck Assistant Sheriff Frank Wright, who stood beside his boss, William Meyering.

From his hospital bed Ahearn identified Bauler as his assailant. Attorney John K. Murphy, representing the alderman, issued a terse angry statement. "It is not necessary for Alderman Bauler to make any statement," he said. "He was in the right. Two hoodlum policemen came to his place of business and tried to make a foreign entrance. He was emerging from his palce with a large amount of money, the receipts of the Christmas basket party, when he was attacked by the policeman. He carried a revolver to protect his money and he defended himself as he was justified in doing."

Making light of the matter, Mayor Kelly remarked that Bauler "was a real straight-shooter." Commissioner Allman closed down the saloon and assault charges were filed after eyewitnesses testified that it was Bauler who instigated the ruckus. Ahearn had been cruising the North Side, dropping in on the political bars in search of the Christmas spirit. The shooting was a rather minor one in the history of the department, but it illustrates the symbiotic ties the police had to the taverns of Chicago. Liquor, politics, and police—it was a familiar equation. Officer Ahearn owned his own little place on Western Avenue. Since he was not one of the boys attached to the nearby Hudson Avenue Station, he was not wanted in Paddy's place. The charges against the alderman were eventually dropped, and Paddy's licence was quietly restored. He remained the alderman of the 43rd Ward for the next 33 years, in which time he cultivated deeper ties to those noted syndicate statesmen, Ross Prio and Murray Humphreys. "What's it all mean?" Bauler said years later, when asked to expand on his interpretation of life's meaning.[9] "Nuttin'. All you get out of it, all you get out of life is a few laughs."

Police Jobs for Sale

North of the Chicago River and east of Paddy's Place stood one of the largest wide-open gambling dens in Chicago. The second-floor establishment at 750 Clark was in the jurisdiction of the East Chicago Avenue Police Station, commanded by Captain Andrew Barry, who in turn received his mandates from the 42nd Ward committeeman John "Botchie" Connors. Each Saturday night Connors, a big spoke in the gambling-graft wheel of the Kelly machine, dropped by the station to give Barry his orders for the week. The denizens of the Gold Coast underworld demanded and received protection. Captain Barry understood the realities of the split. It was understood that 20 percent of the gambling proceeds were to go to the 42nd Ward Democratic organization. Thirty percent went to the county war chest, and the remaining 50 percent was earmarked for the syndicate members who enjoyed influence in what was once Bugs Moran's lair.

In the 1920s Connors was known as the "Duke de Keno." He owned the C and O restaurant, where the Moran gang regularly met to plot strategy. A decade later Connors directed ward operations from his office in the Ohio-Michigan Pleasure Club. No one operated in this ward without his consent. On September 16, 1926, Captain Daniel Murphy of the Chicago Avenue Station tossed Connors out the door when the gambler suggested that the policeman might be looking for new work soon. Murphy slammed Botchie into a parked car near the curb and told him to peddle his graft elsewhere. It was an indignity Connors would never forget. Captain Murphy became a lawyer, and future police captains assigned to this ward quickly fell into line. Brothels, gambling dens, all-night taverns, and clip joints inhabited the 42nd Ward as they had in the 1920s when Moran held sway. The *Daily News* estimated that the monthly payout from the 7,500 gambling dens was $1,000,000 to the politically autonomous ward organizations—such as the one astutely run by Botchie Connors in the 42nd.

The joints operating outside the control of the syndicate-machine quickly fell into line through coercion, blackmail, and strong-arm techniques. George Kries, former bootlegger and one-time associate of Bugs Moran served as Botchie's bagman. Unless the tribute was paid—and that meant a commission on every barrel of beer sold in the ward—the proprietor risked a raid from Captain Barry's blue-coats. In a workman-like manner that belied the true skullduggery of the illicit operations, the Connors bagmen placed the stacks of bills into strongboxes, which were picked up each night by armed guards sent from the Brinks Express Company to carry the loot to the downtown banks.

Even the big-name clubs like the Chez Paree were not immune from this kind of intimidation. On opening night Jake "the Barber" Factor dropped $40,000 in the gambling room, which raised the eyebrows of Kries. Joey Jacobson, who made the Chez Paree a legendary night spot in the 1930s, was forced to ante up. Lamented one unhappy barkeep, "If they don't get into your bankroll one way, they'll get to it some other way."

The situation was much the same across the city and out into the county. As Mayor Kelly consolidated his power and began winning elections in a big way, his sole concern became the livelihood of the machine that he inherited from his predecessor. To offend the saloon owners and gambling bosses who comprised the flotsam and jetsam of the liquor-fueled organization would be folly. The people, if polled individually, would probably say, "So what?" Dice, cards, and booze hurt no one, and in the hard times of the Depression this cottage industry provided jobs.

"To be a real mayor you've got to have control of the party," Ed Kelly once explained. "You've got to be a potent political figure. You've got to be boss."

But how much of a boss was he really? Is it safe to say that Botchie Connors, Paddy Bauler, Charley Weber, and dozens of other like-minded politicos were the *real* bosses of Chicago? In many ways Ed Kelly was as hamstrung as Commissioner Allman. In the case of the police chief, he knew his limitations. Perhaps the same could not be said of Ed Kelly, whose control over appointments was mostly illusory. Commenting on the method of police promotions in Chicago, Michael Flynn, Cook County clerk and boss of the 13th Ward, told the October 1943 grand jury that "everybody knows how promotions are made in the Police Department. Most captains are appointed by the mayor on recommendations of the ward committee man. Every ward committee man knows that Civil Service examinations for promotions are mostly a sham."[10]

The point is best illustrated in the case of three West Side men named James Walsh, John McAuliffe, and David Levine who paid $750 each to Jim Galvin, brother of slain Teamster's Union boss Mike Galvin, in order to secure a place on the "eligibility list" of new patrolmen. The money was given to Jerry Flanagan, a saloon owner who passed it on to Galvin, a man said to "have an in with the Civil Service Commission." The three men were provided with a list of examination questions before the actual test was scheduled to take place. Walsh was called in for the physical exam, but was rejected. He relayed his protest to Galvin, who told him "not to worry." Walsh was directed to the Civil Service offices along with McAuliffe, who showed their cancelled cashier checks. They were both told that their names would be added to the list. A letter signed by George Goetschel promised that the "misunderstanding" had been cleared up:

Dear Sir:

This is to advise you that things have been taken care of downtown and your name is now on the list which will come out the latter part of June or the first part of July. For your own benefit it will be wise for you to refrain from taking an active part in the coming primary; conditions being as they are we suggest that you remain inactive.

Naturally, this matter is strictly confidential and should not be discussed with anyone and we trust we for your own interests, you will not reveal the contents of this letter to any other person.

Very truly yours,
George Goetschel[11]

Shortly after the letter was made public a grand jury voted against Attorney Patrick Lynn on January 17, 1939. Lynn was a former assistant corporation counsel until he forfeited bond in 1938 and became a fugitive following the disclosure of the jobs-for-money scheme. He was then rearrested and charged with running a confidence game. But while many politicians and fixers like Pat Lynn were known to take fees and emoluments from prospective police officers, only one man actually served time—Alderman Frank Konkowski of the 26th Ward. The rest were too smart or too powerful to get caught for a practice that was nearly as old as the city itself.

Critics maintained that the sudden interest in police graft on the part of the state's attorney in an election year was politically motivated. The indictments were handed down in the wake of Tom Courtney's announcement that he would challenge Kelly for the mayoral nomination in 1939. "The state's attorney's office," he said in an opening salvo against the Kelly juggernaut, "is a position in which a man if he were corrupt and dishonest could make a lot of money. I can answer for myself, however, and tell the public sincerely that I have never used my public office as a means of gaining corrupt and dishonest revenue for myself." No mention was made of Dan Gilbert's indictment in November 1936 on charges of aiding and abetting Teamster's Union officials in helping fix retail milk prices in Chicago. It was a particularly odious scandal involving Dr. Herman Bundesen, president of the Chicago Board of Health, and officials of Local 753 of the Milk Driver's Union. These men conspired to restrict the city's milk supply in order to squeeze out the little guys. Charging politics, Courtney refused to allow Gilbert to resign under fire: "If many people feel that politics enters into this, I don't disagree much with that conclusion." Gilbert remained on the payroll.

During the months preceding the Democratic primary of 1939, Courtney renewed his long-dormant attack on the gambling dens. A sensational raid was staged on the South Side domain of Bill Johnson on December 23, 1938. Two hundred patrons were rounded up in a sweep. Courtney reminded the public about his unceasing crusade against Kelly-run gambling syndicates:

Large gambling places catering to hundreds of patrons every afternoon and evening, where roulette, dice games, blackjack and extensive race horse betting are conducted by professional operators is not conducive to good government and breeds crime. On Thursday, July 29, 1937, by telephone I informed you that an investigation by this office revealed that wide-open gambling was rampant in Chicago. Since that time a constant recheck by my investigators indicates that conditions have not improved; in fact, are worse.

Courtney named Frank Nitti, William (Billy) Skidmore, Louis Campagna, Charles Fischetti, Danny Stanton, and Eddie Vogel as the ruling pantheon of the syndicate.

In the nether world of Chicago politics and crime it is not always easy to distinguish between the white and black hats. Tom Courtney's actions in regard to the crooked labor unions infiltrated by the Capone heirs is an interesting case.

Relying on Gilbert's ties to the Teamster's, the state's attorney took credit for foiling an attempt on the part of Murray Humphreys to force every truck owner to join the Trucking Transportation Exchange known as TNT in 1932. This attempt to muscle in on the Teamster's Union was typical of the kind of labor racketeering going on in the 1930s. Yet he was strangely mute when Dan Gilbert was under fire for the milk swindle.

The Gilbert-Courtney-Teamster's alliance was a shadowy one. The state's attorney appears to have selectively harassed the local leaders to the point that they considered the ways and means of doing away with him. Early in the morning of March 24, 1935, Courtney, Alderman Harry Perry, and two Chicago police detectives were driving home on the South Side from a political rally in the Sherman House when another car pulled up alongside. Eight shots rang out in the night. The state's attorney's car swerved out of control, but none of the occupants was injured from the gun shots. The unknown assailants sped away. "When rats are cornered they will fight the only way they know how to fight," Kelly snapped. "These gunmen who have been trying to convert honest labor unions into rackets of the most vicious sort are cornered now and they will be stamped out by fearless, rigorous prosecution that cannot be stopped by even terrorism." Courtney had charged that the Chicago Teamster's Union, formerly dominated by slain gangsters George "Red" Barker and William "Three Finger" White, was still firmly in the control of the mob. It was the same union in which Gilbert was vitally interested.

In the mayoral primary of 1939 Courtney attacked the Kelly spoils system, the downtown alliance among the gangsters, the gamblers, the union racketeers, and the mayor's ward stooges. Kelly was renominated by an astounding 2–1 margin. It was the largest primary victory recorded up to that time. The prosecutor failed to sway the New Dealers who were in Kelly's corner to cast their lot with him. The governor, who was about to be deposed by the mayor, remained noncommital. It is undisputed that Courtney was not the kind of reformer to cleanse the city stem to stern; he had his own agenda after all. But at least during the campaign he presented an accurate assessment of Chicago's true conditions.

The State's Attorney's War II

Chief of Detectives John L. Sullivan remarked that he was the happiest man in the world when he reported to Commissioner Allman on January 1, 1940, that not a single police officer was killed in the line of duty in 1940. It was the first time since 1897 that the department was free of murder in its ranks. At the same time, 11 criminals were killed, eight by police bullets, and three by civilians. The statistics reflected Allman's commitment to upgrading the crime-fighting techniques in his department.

The Scientific Crime Detection Laboratory, organized in the wake of the St. Valentine's Day Massacre, had emerged as one of the most sophisticated research law-enforcement agencies in the country under the direction of Professor Fred

Inbau. Through the efforts of Allman and Jake Arvey, chairman of the City Council finance committee, the crime lab was purchased from the university for $25,000 on July 13, 1938. Allman ordered his men to attend regular classes and to make use of the laboratory facilities to analyze forensic evidence taken from the scene of a crime. Within a year's time, 98 criminal cases had been turned over to lab investigators. By the early 1950s the unit was supplemented by the addition of two mobile cruisers and document, chemistry, microscopy, and spectographic divisions.

That same year a Sex-Homicide Offense Bureau was established by Allman following a series of particularly brutal sex crimes. Supervised by Captain John L. Sullivan, index card files were created for each known offender and classified by Emmett Evans, who inherited the identification bureau from his father Michael Evans. Evans had introduced the fingerprinting technique to Chicago years earlier. At the time, there was very little attention given to the modus operandi of violent sex offenders by the big-city policy. Individuals committing these kind of crimes were invariably "morons," in the lexicon of the day. Frequently, they would be turned over to the "alienists" (psychiatrists) who determined their fitness to stand trial, and that was the end of it. In the late 1930s Lieutenant Otto Erlanson, one of the original members of the first Homicide Bureau created in the 1920s began to solicit the opinions of leading members of the psychiatry profession. He concluded that there was a pattern to the crimes committed by repeated sex offenders. Certain clues, trademarks, and other identifying imprints left behind were assiduously recorded by the police for the first time and catalogued in the Sex-Homicide Bureau. Police work was becoming increasingly more sophisticated as the years wore on. It was not enough merely to arrest a suspect and brow beat a confession out of him—although this was still the preferred tactic of many officers in vice and homicide. The Allman years witnessed a remarkable expansion into uncharted areas of technology, and the advancement of college-educated men into positions of authority. In November 1939, a general order issued by the commissioner created a special robbery detail that was given wide latitude to investigate cases outside the jurisdiction of the detective's department. The intention on the part of Allman was to follow the course of an arrest through arraignment and trial. Lieutenant Kryan Phelan was placed in charge of the robbery detail as recognition of his membership in the Illinois Bar. It was not enough to be street-smart, and politically wise; the robbery detail required the man in charge to be able to prepare cases for court and to have an understanding of Illinois criminal law.

Mayor Kelly answered the critics of the "machine" by saying that he maintained a policy of noninterference in police matters. This was probably true to the extent that he did not question his subordinate's judgment in the handling of criminal investigations or the deployment of personnel in the departments. Allman was a clear-thinking pragmatist, but he was completely hamstrung by the corrupt aldermen and ward committee men who forced his hand on appointments, gambling suppression, and internal promotions. The accomplishments of the chief in ridding Chicago of its gunplay in the streets was largely overshadowed by a major gambling scandal that pitted Tom Courtney against the mayor, with Jim Allman caught in the middle. The underlying motive was politics—as usual.

Once they were friends. But like Thompson and Crowe 15 years earlier, Courtney and Kelly split into two warring camps after the machine dumped Edmund Jarecki as its choice for judge of the circuit court in 1938. The state's attorney organized a "disenfranchised" coalition of former party stalwarts cast into oblivion by Kelly and Nash. Judge Jarecki won a surprising upset victory in the primary, which encouraged Courtney to burn his bridges with Ed Kelly and run for mayor. The axe-wielding raids against gambling strongholds in the Chicago wards made headlines, but did little to influence a favorable outcome for Courtney and his ally, Governor Horner.[12]

Tom Courtney was reelected state's attorney in 1940. He bided his time, collecting hard evidence of the gambling profits reaped by the machine, and the levels of protection provided by the Kelly-Allman police.

The first big break occurred in October 1941 when *Chicago Tribune* reporters came into possession of secret records of the Nitti-Jake Guzik gambling syndicate. These records listed payouts to politicians, police, and other corrupt public officials totalling $300,000 a year. Colonel McCormick published photostat copies of secret syndicate ledgers on page one of his morning editions on October 28, and then turned over all other records to Tom Courtney for further investigation.

The bookkeeping records were for the month of July 1941. Every suburb north, south, and west of Chicago listed its income and "kickout"—graft money paid by operatives to the county police. A total of $26,280 was paid to officers reporting to Chief Lester Laird of the county patrol, and his boss Sheriff Thomas "Blind Tom" O'Brien. It was an abundance of graft that confirmed the existence of a multimillion dollar slot machine industry. The syndicate purchased its machines from Mills, the Monarch Coin Company, and Bally manufacturing under a separate "equipment account." Understandably, none of the slot machine companies ever repossessed a piece of equipment because of delays in payment. Eddie Vogel, who dictated acquisition of new equipment through his henchman Fred Evans, enjoyed an "A–1" credit rating despite a history of delinquent bill-paying.

Payments were made to Cook County officials in cash. The amount of graft was figured on an annual basis, with an up-front understanding that three months out of the year would be reserved for raiding activities. During this time the "slots" would be closed down. Two names figured prominently in the list of payees: "Skid" (Billy Skidmore) and "Tub" (allegedly Dan "Tubbo" Gilbert), who received $2,500 and $4,600 respectively in July 1941.[13]

Thomas O'Brien, who gave up his congressional seat to become sheriff in 1938, was a confidant of Capone-mobster Murray Humphreys. It was widely known that Sheriff O'Brien received a cut of the take from county gambling operations, yet professed to being wholly ignorant of conditions. He had been warned about the existence of slot machines outside the city in March 1939, when Attorney General John Cassidy ordered him to clean up. "He has a tough job," a sheriff's aide explained. "When policemen with axes can't shut down large handbook resorts in Chicago, it's easy to see how difficult it is to get rid of small gambling devices such as slot machines, which can be concealed at will."

With a force of 100 men it was hard to strike at the root of the problem, Chief Laird added. Yet he had no problem locating William Skidmore; the fixer and the county cop were observed having dinner together in a suburban eatery. The publication of photos led to Laird's dismissal in August 1940. O'Brien meanwhile, returned to Congress in 1942 where he remained a fixture for the next twenty-two years.

Guilt by association was the theme of Commissioner Allman's stern rebuke to 50 district captains the day after the revelations were made public. Reports had crossed his desk that certain captains had permitted the city to "open up." In an uncharacteristic show of temper, Allman said:

I don't know who you think you are taking orders from, but I want you to know I'm still boss of this department. You weren't taking orders from me when you allowed gambling to be resumed. In the past few months I had occasion to suspend a few captains for 30 days because they didn't follow my orders. Get back to your districts and see that you do what you have been told to do. You'll take orders from no one but me.

As it turned out, the lid was clamped down only for a short period of time. Allman gave assurances to the grand jury that he would permit no more gambling in the city, and accepted their recommendation to eliminate the morals squad, long a source of bribery and coverup. Captain Martin McCormick was interviewed by the grand jury, at which time it was revealed that Courtney's office had been conducting a secret citywide investigation into gambling and graft.

Courtney and his first assistant Wilbert Crowley disclosed that a tolerance of gambling and lax police work were making the chief's assurances a farce. His statements to the grand jury enflamed the already strained relations with the mayor's office. This antagonism filtered down through the ranks to the lowliest detective, who refused to cooperate with the state's attorney.

The sniping continued even after World War II broke out, and Allman was forced to deploy his thinning ranks across the city to guard sensitive federal installations and to assist the shore patrol and military police.

The captains stirred uneasily in the spring of 1943. The empire of cards, dice, and slots threatened to collapse around them when Danny Stanton, former labor organizer and South Side gambling boss for the Nitti-Guzik syndicate, was shot and killed in a tavern on May 5. In his heydey Stanton controlled 34 handbooks, but had earned the enmity of Martin "Sonny Boy" Quirk, who tried to have him killed in 1931. Quirk was an outsider, who wanted "in" very badly. At stake was control of the handbooks and the 200 former convicts who worked for Stanton. After Quirk got rid of Stanton, he temporarily sat atop the throne, but he had neglected to win the hearts and minds of his former employees such as James Fawcett, the bodyguard, and John Williams, a tavern owner and gambling house proprietor. These men fatally shot Quirk on September 18, sparking a gambling war that provided Courtney with enough new material to present to the grand jury in a renewal of his attack on the Kelly machine.

This latest investigation focused on Williams, whose tavern was situated in the 13th Ward, the bailiwick of Democratic committee man and County Clerk Michael Flynn. Flynn shook the system to its roots when he told the October grand jury that only the candidates approved by the ward bosses and precinct captains made it into the Police Department in the first place. Such was the case of John Williams, who was ranked ninety-fourth on the Civil Service eligibility list for patrolmen.

The ward encompassed the Chicago Lawn police district, commanded by the jowlly Captain Frank Malone, whose career dated back to 1906. Reporting to Malone was Captain Andrew Barry who earned his stripes serving Botchie Connors ten years earlier. When the state's attorney's men solicited the help of the police, Barry's men could only ask, "What gambling?" This was the gist of the story told to the grand jurors in October. When asked what recommendations he might make if the Chicago Lawn police were incompetent or had neglected their duty, Barry said in a matter-of-fact tone, "No recommendation."

The grand jury, one of the most ambitious in Cook County history, hammered away at Mayor Kelly and Allman. The commissioner was called before the 23 citizens to make a good accounting of himself and explain, among other things, why Captain Frank Demski had been transferred out of Chicago Lawn after he had refused to take direct orders from Michael Flynn.

Q: Why didn't you act against Captain Frank Malone of the Chicago Lawn Station after you learned what this grand jury unearthed about the gambling resort at 3227 West 63rd Street, where a gang murder plot [to plan the death of Quirk] was hatched?

A: I didn't want to do anything that might embarrass this grand jury while the investigation was still going on. But now that I know the grand jury's attitude, action will be taken.

Q: Why was Captain Demski transferred from that district after he refused the request of County Clerk Mike Flynn that he let the gamblers alone?

A: I didn't know anything about that incident. I transferred Demski after he was sued for false arrest as a result of the complaint of a man arrested in a raid on a tavern.

Q: Did you try to find out what was back of the complaints against Demski?

A: No.[14]

Allman showed remarkable composure during the four-hour grilling. The jurors were reasonably satisfied that the chief was a man of personal integrity who had not profited from the graft "kickouts." The system on trial here was one that permitted police captains to become fat, lazy, and rich under the rule of the gamblers. After numerous personnel shake-ups, years of "piperizing" by

Bruce Smith and other like-minded reformers, the creation of inspector divisions, the elimination of the morals squad, and other cosmetic moves, nothing had changed since the days of Mike McDonald. It was a startling conclusion, but not so surprising given the unwillingness to create an internal affairs division to police the police. "What the grand jury told me was enlightening," Boss Kelly said. "But 'piperizing' [police spying on police] would break down the police morale." It was an interesting statement, given the fact that Chicago had never seriously tested the concept.

Meanwhile, John Williams had gone into hiding, but his apprehension became of secondary importance when it was learned that the gambler's mother was listed in the Civil Service records as a temporary policewoman. With whom was she employed? Sergeant John Healy, in charge of the crime prevention bureau and responsible for the assignment of policewomen, charged that Mrs. Williams belonged to Courtney's staff. Originally appointed by Mayor Cermak, Ann Williams was also the committee woman of the 13th Ward, working hand-in-hand with Mike Flynn. "We haven't seen her around here in two and a half years," Courtney answered. "When she has been here it was only when we asked the Police Department for a policewoman to guard a woman witness or prisoner. And it was seldom that she came here in response to such requests."

It was a month of record-breaking action on the part of the state's attorney and the grand jury. The "big fish" were being fried right in front of the disbelieving eyes of Virgil Peterson of the Chicago Crime Commission. On October 20, Theodore Svoboda, chief of police in Cicero since the days of Eddie Tancl and Al Capone in 1924, was forced to step down amidst widespread allegations of open gambling in his suburb.

Captain Hugh McCarthy, a 37-year veteran of the Chicago Police Department who retired in 1942 to take over the reins of the county highway police was removed after refusing to cooperate with the grand jury. In his early days in the department McCarthy won the Lambert Tree Award for bravery in the line of duty. It was the "Medal of Honor" for Chicago policemen, and the mark of a distinguished officer. Included in his record were 24 citations for meritorious service. Yet in his waning years he decided to go to work for "Blind Tom" O'Brien and the graft-ridden county police. Thus ended a tarnished career.

The grand jury investigation into Cook County gambling and police protection temporarily slammed down the lid. Veteran police observers said at the time that handbook betting in the city and county was tighter than it had been in years. Over 700 syndicate handbooks were closed, resulting in a loss of revenue to the syndicate of over $50,000,000—if the lid stayed on. "It demonstrates what can be done when the police and other law-enforcing officials make a determined effort to enforce the gambling laws," said Peterson.

For the Good of the Service

At 1:00 AM in the morning on October 26, a weary and exhausted grand juror emerged for a breath of fresh air. Turning to reporter Jim Doherty, who covered the crime beat in the 1930s and 1940s, the man sighed: "That Summerdale Police Station certainly is on fire."

Inside the cramped and narrow courtroom Policeman Harry Stollary, who served as secretary to Captain Thomas Connelly, told the grand jury that the gambling reports submitted by the detectives were hastily prepared fakes, drawn up for the investigation when the originals, covering fifteen months, turned up missing. None of the documents listed any gambling resorts in the North Side District, which encompassed the 48th Ward, yet Courtney's raiders located at least 50 resorts.

The problems were not confined just to Summerdale or the 13th Ward. They were citywide, and Mayor Kelly seemed all too willing to shift the blame to Commissioner Allman. All the evidence pointed to one undeniable fact. Kelly had systematically undermined the Civil Service Commission, and had usurped the discretionary powers of the commissioner to select his own men by awarding promotions to policemen who were special pets of the administration.

Q: Why is it the policemen don't know who to look for in the Quirk murder case?

Kelly: I suggest you ask Allman.

Q: Why is it the Fischettis, Guziks, and their ilk are not arrested but instead seem to have enjoyed immunity?

Kelly: I don't know.

Q: Why is that during the 27 days we have been investigating police laxity and seeking information about the gambling syndicate we have had no help from the police department or from anyone connected with your administration so that we have been able to get only what we could by our own efforts and the work of the state's attorney?

Kelly: I'm sure I don't know. Maybe Allman isn't as efficient as I thought he was. But anyway he is honest and conscientious and can't be corrupted.[15]

In the same breath Mayor Kelly threw his beleagured chief a carrot by promising not to replace him in his term. The onus of responsibility had been effectively shifted to the chief. Stung by three grand jury appearances, Allman blamed the captains and vowed to make changes. In the next two weeks he suspended six police captains and one lieutenant, stopping short of firing them outright. This chore he would dump in the laps of the Civil Service Commission. It would have been a hard blow to fire men with whom he had come through the ranks— men who were suppose to be his most trusted advisors. The suspended men were decorated veterans, with many years of experience behind them. How could "Chicago's finest"—a sobriquet applied by Edmund Cikanek of the *Daily News*—possibly succumb to the gambler's graft? A roll-call of the accused included:

Captain Walter Healy, Hyde Park. A member of the Police Department since 1915. Promoted to sergeant on February 6, 1923; to lieutenant on February 6, 1931. Appointed captain on November 6, 1940. Transferred from Chicago Lawn to Hyde Park in 1941. Record includes two extra compensations for meritorious service and ten creditable mentions. No prior suspensions. Captain Michael Naughton of the commissioner's office uncovered a large gambling den on West 55th Street that advertised: "This club is open all night. Poker games start 2:30 every afternoon, limit 50 cents. Our limit on horses is $1,000 to any wager."

Captain Tom Connelly, Summerdale. Appointed a patrolman in 1922. Promoted to sergeant in 1934; lieutenant in 1936; captain two years after that. For a short time he served as Mayor Kelly's bodyguard. Awarded a citation for bravery in 1938 after saving a fellow policeman's life in a shootout. His record included six extra compensations and 15 creditable mentions up to 1942. Appointed captain of Summerdale that same year. Connelly and five of his detectives were suspended after state's attorney investigators uncovered 50 protected gambling dens in the 48th Ward. The five detectives complained that they were being singled out unfairly because they were not the "money men" (collectors) in this graft-ridden district, which would explode with revelations of another kind in 1960.

Captain Frank Malone, Chicago Lawn. One of the police veterans. Joined the department in 1906. Promoted to sergeant in November 1913, to lieutenant in 1924, and to captain 12 years later. Received one creditable mention, but was suspended by Allman from July 23 to August 19, 1941, after failing to raid a handbook operating in Malone's district. In the 1943 grand jury probe, Malone, gambler John Williams, and Detective George Gore were charged with aiding and abetting the operation of a gambling house. Martin "Sonny Boy" Quirk was slain on September 18, 1943, in Malone's district.

Acting Captain William Drury, Town Hall. One of Chicago's best-known policemen to emerge from the "dry era." Appointed a patrolman on May 10, 1924. Transferred to the detectives' department a year later, and was teamed with John Howe. Became known as one of the "watchdogs of the Loop." Promoted to sergeant on April 21, 1933, and to lieutenant on May 10, 1938. Tough and uncompromising, Drury was considered to be one of the best amateur boxers in the department. Awarded the Lambert Tree award for capturing a bandit who attempted to hold him up in his car on October 8, 1927. Drury told the grand jury that he knew nothing about gambling in his district, and had never met a gambler in his life. The state's attorney's men located eight gambling dens in his district operated by Democratic precinct captains.

Captain John Cartan, Des Plaines Street. Appointed a patrolman on December 10, 1910. He worked as a railroad clerk for ten years before joining the force. Promoted to sergeant and assigned to plainclothes duty in the detective bureau, 1913. Appointed lieutenant in 1931. Two years later Cartan was placed in charge of criminal correspondence when the detective bureau was partitioned into four areas in 1933. Transferred to Des Plaines Street in 1941, Cartan's suspension came as a surprise. His name had not been mentioned in connection with the investigation. At the time of the grand jury hearings, the Des Plaines Street district encompassed the flop-house, skid-row section of Chicago. Bums, heroin junkies, panhandlers, and transients of all kinds populated the district, which had badly deteriorated in prestige since the time of the Haymarket Riot in 1886.

On June 16, 1944, the Civil Service Commission struck the single greatest blow against police corruption in the long bleak history of the department when it announced that Healy, Connelly, Drury, Cartan, and three other captains—Louis Klatzco, Thomas Harrison, and Eugene Barry—were fired for failing to suppress gambling in their districts. Frank Malone and Patrick Crotty of the Kensington District were found guilty, but the evidence against them did not warrant outright dismissal, the Civil Service Commission argued. "There will be a fight to the finish to vindicate Harrison," promised his attorney Walter Tinsley.

For the next two years the expelled police captains drifted into limbo. But as is so often the case, a new regime breathes fresh air. On the night of September 17, 1946, newly installed Commissioner John C. Prendergast quietly restored Captains Harrison, Drury, Barry, Connelly, Healy, Cartan, and Klatzco to active duty. After two years of legal wrangling in the appellate court, a decision was handed down in their favor. The men were reinstated to duty and the Civil Service Commission struck a deal whereby they promised not to appeal the matter to the Supreme Court in return for a guarantee that the captains would agree to waive 12 months of the 27 months of back pay due them from the appellate court ruling. In the case of Harrison at least, it was a small price to pay for the greater glory of serving Botchie Connors at East Chicago Avenue.

The Twilight Years of Mayor Kelly and Chief Allman

In the political parlance of the 1940s and 1950s a man with an influential political backer was a man with "stick." To the aspiring applicant filling out the Civil Service forms, the "stickman" might be the ward committee man or precinct worker who could finagle a deal with the commissioners to add his name to the eligibility list. Pernicious political interference by the Kelly machine prevented capable individuals from advancing through the ranks if their "stick" was an exceedingly short one. The "fix," so well known to the uniformed patrolmen, came through the dreaded efficiency ratings prepared by the captains and other high-ranking officials. "I've quit taking the sergeant's examination," complained one applicant. "What's the use? Those efficiency ratings kill me." The ratings were submitted to the commissioner's office each morning by the captains. Informed City Hall observers knew that political considerations, and not skill as a police officer, determined the ratings.

The absence of merit selection for the choice assignments in the state's attorney's office and the detectives' bureau demoralized the force and diminished the effectiveness of the crimefighting organization. The paralysis extended from the uniformed patrol to the Scientific Crime Laboratory, which by the end of the Kelly administration was undermined by Chicago politics. At the end of 1945 the city was in the throes of a dangerous crime wave. The serious crimes of murder, rape, burglary, and auto theft were up. The average increase for reported offenses was 9.56 percent. Wartime reductions in staff impaired the ability of the police to keep the statistics at acceptable levels. By 1945, the department was clearly out of the hands of Allman, who counted the days to his retirement. Embarrassed by the 1943 grand jury indictments, Chicago's longest-reigning commissioner forestalled his retirement until December 8, 1945, when, in a tearful announcement to the press, he said it was time "to loaf." "I am the first police commissioner to leave the office voluntarily," he said with a measure of pride. At 70, Chief Allman was a shadow of his former self. In the 1930s he did a capable job of modernizing the force despite the obvious political constraints imposed upon him by the mayor. Unfortunately, his record was tarnished by revelations that his captains were less than circumspect in their dealings.

Captain John Prendergast, chief of the uniformed police, succeeded Allman. The 38-year veteran decided to become a policeman the day his father Luke, a member of the force, was shot and killed by a burglar. At the age of 15 Prendergast took a job heating rivets to help support his widowed mother. He joined the department in 1907, hitching his star to Morgan Collins, who named him secretary—a sure stepping stone to greater glory—in 1924. His career reflected the usual political drag that invariably accompanies an appointment of this nature. Prendergast was one of the oldest men in the department, a firm believer in the status quo who somberly reflected on the changing nature of police work. Given the chance, the new commissioner would have turned the clock back 50 years by eliminating the patrol cars. "In those days the policemen knew everybody in his neighborhood and everybody knew him. Today we've got 400 beat men left in the department of 7,000. I wish I had 10,000 patrolmen so I could put it back on that basis again."

Prendergast was in office barely a week when he was called on to solve Chicago's most sensational kidnap-murder since the Loeb-Leopold case in 1924. For the second time, the police dropped the ball and drew more unwanted publicity to the ineptitude of the detectives' bureau. On January 7, 1946, James E. Degnan looked in on his 6-year-old daughter who was asleep in the rear of the family home on 5943 Kenmore Avenue, in the fashionable Rogers Park section of Chicago. The child was gone. The kidnapper had fled through an open window, leaving behind a ransom note for $20,000. Arriving on the scene minutes later, detectives from the Summerdale Station concluded that it was indeed a kidnapping, and that the FBI should be called in. Before the experts could be summoned, a swarm of Chicago detectives moved through the house, trampling valuable evidence underfoot. A professional acting out of malice against Thomas Degnan, declared one of the investigators. "A professional would have known how much money Degnan had and if he was able to pay $20,000. Also, no experienced snatcher would take a child as old as six years old. Such a child is too difficult to manage," Tubbo Gilbert said. Charles Wilson of the crime lab examined the ransom note and said there was positively no link to the "lipstick killer" who, just a month earlier, had scrawled a message on the wall of a North Side hotel room that read: "For heaven's sake catch me before I kill more. I can't control myself."

The murder of 33-year-old Frances Brown, a former Navy WAVE at the Pine

Crest Hotel in December 1945 was a shocking one, but it did not stir the feelings of the community the way the Degnan kidnapping did. Detective John Sullivan, a distant relative of the bare-knuckle fighter of the 1880s, dismissed the Brown murder as a crime of passion carried out by a jealous rival. "I am positive a woman did this murder," Sullivan told *Herald-American* reporters. "Only a woman would have used the words 'for heaven's sake'."[16]

The police reasoning was defective, as it turned out. The investigation of the Brown murder and Degnan abduction ground to a halt amidst a great public outcry that forced the beleaguered mayor to go on the radio to assure the public that the police had matters well in hand. The reverse was true, as neighborhood residents soon found out. The torso of the child was found at Ardmore and Kenmore, the bones in a furnace on Winthrop Avenue, and a leg across the street from the Degnan house. The killer had remained in the neighborhood in defiance of the police dragnet.

Two middle-aged janitors named Desere Smet and Hector Verburgh who happened to work on the same block were taken to the "blue room" and given the notorious third degree by police detectives. Afterward, they were given polygraph tests that were inconclusive, according to Charles Wilson of the once vaunted crime lab. The two janitors filed lawsuits against the city totalling $25,000 for injuries sustained during the third degree—still an integral part of police work, even in these enlightened times. The interrogation of the two Degnan suspects was reminiscent of the case of *People v. Cope* in 1931, when Chicago detectives wrung a confession out of a suspected car thief by chaining his ankles together and stringing him up by the heels from the parallel bars in the police gymnasium. When Cope still refused to confess to this and other crimes, he was beaten with a truncheon in the back.

The real killer had already been identified by police during the Frances Brown investigation, but was freed on the grounds of insufficient evidence. He was William Heirens, a brilliant but twisted college student from the University of Chicago. The gun that was taken at the time of the first arrest had not been sent to the crime lab for analysis; neither did the police bother to search his room. Heirens was a seasoned criminal by his early teens, responsible for hundreds of North Side burglaries. Yet the police seemed to overlook these details until they conducted a cursory search of his room several months later. On August 5, 1946, the killer reconstructed his crime before the state's attorney's police and Chicago detectives. Chief Prendergast admitted that his department had failed the city in this case. The professional standards of crime detection were absent and it took two murders to draw attention to these gross deficiencies.

Kelly dealt with this problem by turning to his ward committee men for help. At a meeting of the Democratic organization in the Morrison Hotel, he dropped 4,000 "vigilante" jobs into the laps of his precinct workers to tide the city over during the crisis while he went before the City Council to solicit additional funding from the aldermen to hire 1,000 new men. The newly created patrolmen positions were eventually given over to the committee men to distribute as they saw fit. The training of these men was left to Chief Prendergast, who adhered to the usual attitude toward rookies—that they would "have to learn the hard way" without schooling. He later modified his statements and promised to thoroughly indoctrinate the new men with hands-on training in the crime lab, taught by FBI agents flown in especially for the purpose.

Mayor Kelly's response to the postwar crime threat angered the Chicago Crime Commission and offended the voting public. In the words of John Q. Public, who had pulled the Democratic lever without question for 14 years, it was time for a change. The party cadre now led by Boss Arvey acted with something approaching political genius. Aware that the name of Kelly no longer translated into automatic votes as Chicagoans stared unhappily at dirty streets, a deteriorating board of education, and most of all a Police Department seemingly unable to safeguard lives and property, Jake Arvey decided to shelve the mayor and select a squeaky-clean candidate who would preserve the machine so carefully assembled by Tony Cermak.

Arvey looked to South Side Bridgeport, the spawning ground of many Chicago mayors, to find a worthy successor. He was Martin Henry Kennelly, a moving van executive who shot a good game of golf—in season—and was so personable with his neighbors that he was a cinch to charm the voters and cull enough votes to win in April 1947. Never mind that Kennelly had little experience in public affairs, and would ruefully ask his aides what a crime syndicate was. The slate-making committee got together and surveyed the list. The offer to Kennelly was conditional. He was to be a compromise candidate, put up by the Courtney-Jarecki faction with the approval of Jacob Arvey. At first he demurred, but later accepted the nomination with the understanding that he would be unfettered in his dealings as mayor.

The slate-makers promised many things, most important of all that he would be his own man. More deceptive words were never spoken, despite Arvey's post-election comments: "He accepted only when the unanimous urging of the nominating committee convinced him that he was uniquely equipped to return this service to the community in which he had prospered. Mr. Kennelly was asked for no commitment to the party organization and he gave none." In the spring election Kennelly swamped the latest Republican sacrificial lamb by a margin of 273,000 votes. The Republican *Tribune* was cheered by the large vote count of their candidate Russell W. Root, who exceeded the totals of three prior candidates that had attempted to unseat Kelly. Yet "Fartin'" Martin, as City Hall regulars liked to call him, won more votes than Kelly in his record-breaking reelection bid in 1939. The Chicago machine endured.

Edward J. Kelly's political epitaph had been written. He was very much the big-city political boss in the fine tradition of Frank Hague, Tom Pendergast, and James Michael Curley. Kelly became mayor just as Chicago was changing its colors from the whoopie decade to the era of social welfare. The gangland guns were stilled after repeal as the remnants of the Capone organization retrenched and carved out new pieces of the pie for themselves. Kelly's philosophy was guided by his personal belief that "politics was for the people," yet he ran the administration according to the wishes of his ward bosses. While personally opposed to commercialization vice on a large scale, the mayor permitted Botchie Connors and others to dictate policy to district police captains, which ultimately led to corrupt arrangements between the underworld and the city's principal law enforcement agency.

Kelly was the son of a fireman. He worked hard to build a superior Fire Department, but failed to forge a strong, honest police force. Morale was low. The rewards were few, and the system was inherently rotten.

Notes

1. *Chicago Tribune*, September 17, 1931. Mayor Cermak took personal charge of the administrative arm of the police. He sought to reduce the dead weight by returning a maximum number of men to uniformed duty in the streets, and to make effective use of the undercover men at his disposal. It was common for Cermak to drop by unexpectedly at various precinct stations to conduct surprise inspections. The intention was to make Chicago crime-free on the eve of the 1933 World's Fair. Gottfried, *Boss Cermak*, (Seattle: University of Washington Press, 1962), pp. 280–81.

2. Allman received generally high marks from the Chicago Crime Commission and the Secret Six, its investigating arm. Bruce Smith described Allman as a "fine, enlightened and vigorous commissioner who is giving us a remarkable administration."*Chicago Tribune*, October 3, 1931.

3. *Chicago Police Problems*, (Champaign: University of Illinois Press, 1931), pp. 17–19. Nineteen separate bureaus, divisions, and department heads were accountable to the commissioner prior to reorganization. The chief was burdened with the task of detailed supervision greater than that of any one subordinate. The 1920 Garrity plan succeeded in returning control of the bureaucracy to the commissioner—in theory—but it soon proved impossible to exercise effective control over the department. Central supervision was further hampered by the commissioner's office being located in City Hall, a mile away from police headquarters. Allman moved his office from City Hall to 11th and State to symbolize his commitment to reform.

4. *Report of the General Superintendent to the City Council (1932)*, p. 8. The structural reorganization went into effect on August 1, 1932. The number of units directly responsible to the commissioner was reduced from 49 to 8. The improved discipline and economies of manpower was reflected in a smoother functioning Police Department—for the time being.

5. Touhy and Brennan, *The Stolen Years*, (Cleveland: Pennington Press, 1959), pp. 264–70. "The relationship between the State's Attorney's office under Courtney and Gilbert was such that during the entire period that Courtney was in office no syndicate man ever was convicted of a major crime," said Judge Barnes in 1959. The court expressed the belief that Touhy was at home, as he claimed, when Jake "the Barber" Factor was abducted on June 20, 1933.

6. Ovid Demaris, *Captive City* (New York: Lyle Stuart, 1969), pp. 120–21. After the Nitti shooting the mayor expanded his complement of police bodyguards. He moved from the less secure Morrison Hotel to a private suite at the Congress. Fearing syndicate reprisals, Cermak purchased a bulletproof vest, which he was not wearing the night he

was shot. After Cermak's death Officers Lang and Miller were questioned about an alleged $15,000 offer to kill Nitti. They denied it. Lang, as the man who fired the shot at Nitti, was convicted of assault with intent to murder. A new trial was granted and the charges were later dropped but both men were discharged from the force.

7. *New York Times*, November 29, 1935. Kelly made great strides toward improving the city's financial picture by cutting the budget and winning important concessions from the Democratic-controlled legislature. See Roger Biles, "Edward J. Kelly: New Deal, Machine Builder," *The Mayors* (Carbondale: Southern Illinois University Press, 1987), pp. 111–25.

8. *Chicago Daily News*, October 29, 1934.

9. Demaris, *Captive City*, p. 187.

10. *Chicago Daily News*, October 20, 1943.

11. *Chicago Herald & Examiner*, October 29, 1931 and January 17, 1939. Appointments and promotions were available to anyone possessing the ability to pay. In October 1931 the state's attorney revealed the existence of a job-vending ring that collected $100,000 from 100 Police and Fire Department applicants over a five-year period. Attorney Wilbur McGinniss, a former stenographer for the Civil Service Board, was indicted by a grand jury and held as a voluntary prisoner after confessing to selling preferred spots on the Civil Service exam list. McGinniss charged fees ranging from $250 to $1,000 for patrolman positions. Those who desired promotion to sergeant or a corresponding rank paid $1,500 to $4,000. Members of the force who received their appointments in this way were granted immunity from prosecution in return for their testimony.

12. Robert B. Howard, *Mostly Good and Competent Men: Illinois Governors, 1818– 1988* (Illinois Issues, Sangamon State University, and the Illinois Historical Society, 1988), pp. 257–58. In 1936 Governor Horner was reelected by forging a coalition of down-staters and Cook County Republicans anxious to undermine Kelly-Nash bossism. Poor health prevented him from seeking a third term in 1940. Thomas Courtney was the minority leader in the state senate before he was elected state's attorney in 1932. An early proponent of tough handgun legislation, Courtney hoped that his anticrime stance would discredit Kelly's administration. The Jarecki-Horner alliance was a case of the political have-nots seeking control of the machine patronage. Only Jarecki remained unscathed by the Kelly juggernaut. In 1940 the judge took advantage of an Illinois statute in order to ensure a clean and honest election: he deputized the Chicago police force to stand guard at the polls. See Douglas Bukowski, "Judge Edmund K. Jarecki: A Rather Regular Independent," *Chicago History* 8(4) (Winter 1979–80): 206–18.

13. *Chicago Tribune*, October 27, 1941; and Roger Biles, *Big City Boss in Depression and War: Mayor Edward J. Kelly of Chicago* (DeKalb: Northern Illinois University Press, 1984), pp. 103–13. Slot machine gambling in Cook County went big business in 1928 when Willie Heeney, described as a "practical slot machine operator," became the general manager of the syndicate operations, and organized it on a sound business basis. He systematized procedures such that the transfer of machines from one dive to another was provided for in printed form. The City Hall wheel horse was Dr. William H. Reid, a close friend of Thompson's and a veteran of the Lorimer-Lundin cabal. The city was divided evenly among the gangsters. On the Northwest Side, Marty Guilfoyle represented the Capone interests. The South Side was controlled by Edward "Spike" O'Donnell, James "High Pockets" O'Brien, and Danny McFall, who were the outside men for a clique of politicians and police captains providing the protection. Estimates of the amounts rumored to have been paid by the gambling ring ran as high as several thousand dollars

a day. Six police captains who enjoyed the protection of City Hall while collecting gambling payoffs from gangsters were named in a blanket indictment handed down by the April 1929 grand jury. Named in conjunction with the pay-off ring were Captain Hugh McCarthy of Town Hall, who would become the central figure of the 1943 payoff probe; Patrick J. Collins, in command of the South Chicago Station and a brother of Michael Collins, leader of the Irish Free State; Richard P. Gill of the Wabash Avenue Station; Michael Tobin, commander of Hyde Park; Dennis Malloy of Sheffield; and Michael Delaney of Stanton Avenue. It was believed that the 1928 bombing attacks against the homes of "Doc" Reid, Charles Fitzmorris, and Captain Luke Garrick were the result of a disagreement over the splits of the gambling graft. See the *Chicago Daily News*, May 13–15, 1929. After Roger Touhy went to jail in 1934, Frank Nitti and Jake Guzik swallowed up his northwest suburban domains. Eddie Vogel, who had no financial stake in citywide gambling was the slot machine and juke box boss of Cook County throughout the 1930s and 1940s. Vogel was ranked fourth in the syndicate hierarchy behind Guzik, Nitti, and Murray Humphreys.

14. *Chicago Tribune*, October 28, 1943. Prior to 1942 the responsibility for enforcement of antigambling laws was entrusted to the Morals Squad, commanded by Captain Martin McCormick. It was later revealed that McCormick and three subordinates—Sergeant Thomas Lee, Patrolman James Kehoe, and Fred Trauth—were filing false reports showing that hundreds of gambling dens were closed by the police. The state's attorney's police raided these same establishments and reported that ten of eleven addresses were still open. Sergeant Lee reported one arrest during five months of work in 1941. McCormick was subsequently suspended by the Civil Service Board only after considerable pressure had been brought to bear by the Chicago Crime Commission. See Virgil Peterson, *Barbarians In Our Midst* (Boston: Little Brown & Co., 1952), pp. 196–97.

15. *Chicago Tribune*, October 28, 1943. Kelly's appearance before the grand jury was a fait accompli for Tom Courtney and the beginning of the end for the mayor. With the death of party sachem Pat Nash, Kelly's ability to control the renegades in his organization was diminished. Sensing his vulnerabilities, Courtney hammered away at Kelly, demanding to know why he had failed to live up to his 1941 promise to drive the gamblers out of Chicago. The mayor offered the excuse that he had endeavored to do so, but henceforth would pay more attention to the Police Department.

16. *Chicago Herald & Examiner*, December 12, 1945. Frances Brown was Heirens's second victim. On June 3 he strangled 43-year-old Josephine Alice Ross in the same North Side neighborhood. Like Brown, she was repeatedly stabbed. The police found Miss Brown, the Navy WAVE, gored through the throat with a bread knife. Sullivan's hypothesis that the killer was a woman was preposterous, in retrospect. For a good account of the Heirens-Degnan case, see Edward Radin, "The Other Man," *The Chicago Crime Book* (New York: Pyramid Books, 1969), pp. 263–84.

Close Up on the Chicago Police:
Confessions of a Vice Cop

Art Manger liked to recall the old days: swindlers, stool pigeons, perverts, and prostitutes of every shape and color. Sawed-off shotguns, straight razors, and secret passageways. Strip joints, gambling casinos, and opium dens. They were a part of Manger's daily life as Chicago's toughest vice cop of the 1930s and 1940s.

55th and South Park Avenue . . . a big tough whore rolling her tricks. I ran into the building and kicked down the doors but found no one inside. "Turn on the water faucets boys!" I said. It was 10° below outside. There was a bullet hole in my car when I returned. Police paid to have it fixed. A week later I spotted her at 57th and Prarie. She picked me up and led me down an alley into a basement room. I paid her, got undressed, then made a call to the boys downtown. She leaned up against the wall and flashed a straight razor. Guess she didn't appreciate chipping six inches of ice off the pipes. "I'm not gonna cut you up you sonnuvabitch! I'm gonna cut yer head off!" "C'mon and find out," I said.

Jobs were hard to come by in the 1930s. You had to know someone or, in the case of Manger, have a friend in high places. Art's "stick" was Cook County Sheriff William Meyering, the Democrat who lived down the street. A phone call to the sheriff landed Manger in the Cook County jail—where he got a job as a prison guard, and later as private chauffeur to the sheriff.

I witnessed seven executions. Four were singles and the fifth time there were three being executed the same night. The reporter who was present said that at the beginning that

Note: All quotes in this section are taken from the author's interview with Art Manger in July 1988 for *Inside Chicago* magzine.

these executions did not phase him. By the time the third was strapped in the chair and the smoke was seeping through the glass partition . . . we were seated on plank seats a few feet away. . . . [W]e heard a thump and found that the reporter had fainted.

After four years with the righteous, Bible-thumping sheriff, Manger was ready for stronger stuff. He was sworn in as a Chicago police officer in 1935, and walked a beat out of the Burnside Station at 91st and Cottage Grove on the South Side. Two years later he was handpicked by a reform group called the Committee of Fifteen to go undercover to clean up prostitution and other vice rackets in the old Levee section, near 22nd and State Streets—once the most notorious red-light district in the country. The Committee, a do-good coalition of clerical leaders and prominent businessmen, believed that a handful of honest cops working in two five-man squads could clean up a cesspool of vice. The smart boys, many of them dirty themselves, chuckled at the thought.

Racketeering during those Depression years stretched from North Clark Street to Calumet City. Capone's empire of whores, dope peddlers, and backroom bookies had been divided up among the mob boys after Big Al went to jail on a tax rap in 1931. Murray "the Camel" Humphreys ran the syndicate punishment squad. His mug appeared in the papers every time the cops fished another body out of the drainage canal. The Camel never took much interest in the gambling end of the business. He had Ed Vogel and "Loud Mouth" Levin tend to the slots and the handbooks. Then there were the usual problems at the "Hall." While Mayor Kelly vowed in 1937 to get to the root and branch of this business and drive out the despoiler of the fair name of Chicago, his army of precinct captains and ward healers collected a monthly swag of $1 million from some 7,500 gambling dives.

Against these odds, Manger, Captain John Howe, the "cultured policeman" who did his detective work in tie and tails at symphony concerts, operas, and society balls, and other handpicked members set out on their mission to close the Levee scarlet patch. Warrants? You had to work *around* them, and you had to be a boy scout or half-balmy to think that a vice cop wouldn't kick in a door— or someone's face—if necessary.

500 N. Clark . . . a bawdy theatre known as the Playhouse. From the back of the darkened auditorium I sipped a shot of bourbon while I watched a man dressed in a gorilla costume push a naked young girl over the back of a chair. Scum. The next night the same act was shown again but we put a stop to it just as the gorilla man moved into position. The costume was permanently confiscated and the "Beauty and the Beast" was taken off the marquee forever.

Depression Chicago: Mayor Kelly kissed the babies, cut the ribbons, and put the old town on a firm financial basis. The Century of Progress was testament to the city's past greatness, and seemingly unlimited future. On the North Side the Green Mill pulsated to Dixieland jazz and the torchy ballads of Ruth Etting. It was the other Chicago, the one of transvestities, pimps, and bookies, that

Manger knew best. Soon he became revered by colleagues and feared by criminals. These were the days before Miranda, when the tools of a cop's trade consisted of a .38, a sledgehammer, and a "Chicago Bar," a heavy crowbar with a cane hook end. Manger described with an approving smile how he worked over offenders and smashed up slot machines and canopy beds at brothels.

I was in the front room of Jake "Greasy Thumb" Guzik's gin joint at 600 South Wabash, placing side bets with the bartender. Guzik, heir to the Capone dynasty, earned his nickname during the days he worked as a waiter, when he kept sticking his fat thumb in his customer's soup. Everyone knew that Guzik never packed a heater and this helped us in the set-up. Guzik was in the back with a blonde floozy—one of his many cash commodities—who walked the streets of the Levee. I motioned to the boys outside. They burst through the front door, pistols held high. I splintered Guzik's door with my Chicago Bar and casually approached him, his jowls quivering and eyes opening wide over large bags. "The chief wants to see you downtown," I said.

These were the hard-scrabble days. Sometimes a man had to compromise his principles to put food on the table or avoid joining the army of homeless who built their cardboard shanties on "Prosperity Road" and "East Street." This was the main intersection of broken dreams known as "Hooverville." Here Manger frequently encountered the broken and weary victims of the Depression.

Zebra Lounge. A half-block east of Cottage Grove on 63rd Street. Prostitution going on here. Parked the squad car two doors away and went inside. A young blond guy about 25 approached me with an offer of a beer. "You want to meet a nice girl?" he asked. "Sure, anytime," I said. We hailed a checker and drove to 50th and Drexel to an apartment basement. A pretty young thing in a housedress was rocking a baby to sleep. "Twenty bucks and she's all yours," the man said. "The baby or the girl?" I asked. "Don't be a wise guy . . . what do you think?" The woman turned out to be his wife. My men broke through the door. When I told 'em what happened, they busted the guy in the jaw. The baby was sent to a good home and the parents were locked up. Hope they never let him out either.

There was a flip side to the Depression that Manger knew well. Chicago bustled in the 1930s, and Manger was welcomed into the private homes and tennis courts of the Newport set. He got to know the Bon-Ton babes as they stepped off the Twentieth-Century Limited at Union Station. For a time he squired "Tucky" Astor around town. This tough cop from Chicago's South Side loved her. There was a far-away look in his eyes as he recalled mint juleps and the blooming crocuses of summer on the island. The job had its benefits. "My world was a little different from theirs," Manger said, his voice dropping off.

He liked to bust the well-to-do as much as the down-and-out. On July 20, 1941, Manger arrested more than 700 people in a classy gambling operation on the 3100 block of Ashland Avenue. It took 32 paddy waggons to cart away the men in tuxedos and their women, resplendent in evening gowns. The commotion held up traffic for four hours. The newspapers had a field day with this one. The gambling joint was owned by the State Representative Charley Weber— big-time trouble.

"Got a case for you, Manger," Captain Naughton told me one day. "Two society dames are arranging dates for the sailor boys. Some of 'em aren't old enough to shave. Go check it out." In a swank apartment next to the Drake, Carl Stockholm, the famous six-day bike rider and owner of a chain of West Side dry-cleaning stores had the Navy boys up for tea. They were joined by three society girls who had the addresses and names of the right places to go in Chicago. Waiting outside in an unmarked car, my boys followed them. First stop was the Club Elisha at 55th and State, and then the Cocktails For Two by the 47th Street Elevated. The owners of these dives squawked when we told them they were out of business. The wagon man came and took 'em all away. Turns out the society dame who supplied the girls was Edith Loyal Davis, Nancy Reagan's mother. She was working as an undercover cop. The whole thing had been a set-up.

Manger killed a man once, a long time ago. It happened after he was transferred back to the Burnside District. A gang of stick-up men were knocking off a South Side store. In the exchange of shots that followed Art took a bullet in his foot but managed to nail the crook: "His pals didn't think much of him, I suppose. Later that night I heard about a stiff being dumped on the stairs of County Hospital. The car just drove away."

It was pretty routine stuff, compared with those few years he spent in the Levee. But then, one tough-guy cop who refused to share in the spoils could not be expected to last long in vice. Manger missed the dirty work. "Nothing was like those lively days in vice," he recalled. After 30 years on the Chicago Police Department, Art Manger called it quits. "I wanted to be home with my wife," he said. "It was great spending more time with such a wonderful fine woman after spending so much time with those sluts and other trash."

His wife Lillian died in 1968. Art lived alone in his modest little South Side bungalow for the next 21 years, comforted by yellowing newspaper clips, a few good memories, and a bottle of Old Bushmills under the sink. He died in 1989.

11

A System at Fault, 1947–60

Anyways, we were running around [in the store] when we were getting this stuff. I happened to think, "Who was listening to the radio calls in the squad car?" I said I would. So I went to the car and I was sitting there. They were coming out with bacon and hams and everything you could think of in the store. Real expensive foods! They kept filling the back seat of the squad car. So that's how rotten these cops were. They did just anything to get a dollar.

Richard Morrison, cat burglar, 1960

In my younger years I had been chief of police in Wichita, Kansas, and had there instituted many new and progressive ideas. But this was Chicago, our second largest city and by reports one of the wickedest. Would the ideas that worked in Wichita work in Chicago? I felt I owed it to the whole police profession to demonstrate that they would.

Orlando W. Wilson

Honky Tonk, USA: The East Chicago Avenue District—A Second Look

When Mike Schaak made the rounds of the neighborhood, he confronted the usual array of saloons, gambling dens, and bagnios. The bulldozing "burgomaster" of yesteryear allowed the gamblers just enough rope to turn a profit. Inspector Schaak knew every "low dive" in the vice-ridden district. Behind the scenes lurked the sinister Clan Na Gael, with its tentacles in the city government, the police, neighborhood saloons, and billiard parlors. Schaak was inclined to look the other way. When confronted with the evidence of job malfeasance, Mike Schaak would defiantly look his accuser in the eye and say: "Resign? I? No indeed! I'd rather have my tongue pulled out by the roots then resign." That was 1889.

Sixty years later Captain Thomas Harrison ran the district in much the same way as Schaak and a dozen other high-handed captains in the intervening years. Gone were the Clan-Na-Gael, for the Irish North Side had given way to a diverse ethnic culture. The seamy bars remained. So too did vice, numbers, and payoffs.

This was Honky Tonk, USA, the miserable mile, Hell's Half-Acre, and the old Levee all rolled into one. Between the final downfall of the Bugs Moran gang and the arrival of Martin Kennelly, the neighborhood had taken on new significance. For the thirsty, fun-seeking conventioneers, the Rush Street strip provided the sizzle and pop. A few blocks away on Clark Street there stood a row of neon cabarets and rialtos—the grand white way of sin. In any dimly lit dive, a patron would be accosted by a scantily clad B-girl cooing the old shop-worn cliche, "H'lo dearie, how's about buyin' me a drink?" Any John or Jack who knew the score could expect to be invited into the back room. The girls who worked at the Talk of The Town Cocktail Lounge at 1159 Clark kept score by breaking off one piece of swizzle stick for every drink their "John" ordered. The little pieces of wood were discreetly slipped into a bodice or garter belt to be tallied at the end of the evening. The B-girl received 25 cents for each 75-cent drink she hustled. Every cabby worth his salt knew the sure way to earn a few extra bucks before payday: for each vacationing Shriner delivered safely into the arms of a Clark Street "pros" he could expect a $45 tip.[1]

In the pool halls and corner "pharmacies," drug addicts could easily purchase a "stick of tea," or "the white stuff" without interference. Bleary-eyed revelers from the B-girl joints would rub shoulders with the junkies, male prostitutes, fences, gamblers, and syndicate bouncers who populated the district. "Girls! Girls! Girls!" the marquee read. From nine until four the joints remained open. The night air was ablaze in neon, while the melodic strains of Patty Andrews's "I Can Dream, Can't I?" played from just about every juke box in the district. It was number one in 1949.

Then as the light of dawn chased home the last remnants of the rough trade, the streets were reclaimed by the respectable elements, who peeped nervously out at the passing traffic from behind drawn shades come sunset. It was the symbiosis of the street culture.

Honky Tonk, USA was still run by the dependable "Botchie" Connors, who could always be counted on to deliver the ward to the machine at election time. The "Roaring 42" observed only one rule: "You gotta get the okay from on high if you wanna open in this district." The okay meant the blessing of the rotund, thick-lipped Senator Connors, his ferret-faced lieutenant Eddie Sturch, and, if the moon was right, Captain Thomas Harrison. "Tommy's a good guy, maybe a little tough with his fists," said one. "But why blame him when the joints are runnin' wide open or when they shut down? Any shmoe knows there are lots of guys bigger than a police captain and they give the word who runs and who don't run."[2]

Harrison had served the East Chicago District since 1936—in between his suspension and various political transfers. Tommy's supporters would claim that even if there were a uniformed patrol on every block from Grand Avenue to Division, it would still not be sufficient to close down strip row. Harrison received his orders from on high. When the heat was on, as it was in 1949 when a grand jury was summoned to investigate the conditions, the word went out on the streets and the dives temporarily closed up. Captain Harrison, meanwhile, took a much-needed vacation in Florida. His brother-in-law, Patrolman Walter Binder, filled in at the hearings, describing the precinct as "lily white."

Those who surveyed the human wreckage passing through the East Chicago Avenue court every morning would have disagreed. Homeless drunks arrested on vagrancy charges, an out-of-town businessman who was jackrolled at the French Casino—the worst of the Clark Street dives—and the young prostitute charged with soliciting would have their five minutes in court. Those with clout would be rescued by the bondsman, a political tapeworm as old as the city itself. The true conditions of Chicago Avenue belied the rich lifestyle enjoyed by Tommy Harrison, one of Chicago's "millionaire cops." While taking home the usual captain's pay of $5,200 a year, Harrison somehow managed to afford a deluxe country-style house in Sauganash, an upscale residential development in a wooded glen far removed from seamy Clark Street. How was it possible that a one-time bricklayer who became a police captain could be worth an estimated $100,000 in the lean post-Depression years? It turned out that Harrison had several generous benefactors who had taken a personal interest in his well-being.

Jack Lynch, a partner of Mont Tennes and Moe Annenberg in the Nationwide News Service, was one. The aging gambler made the acquaintance of Harrison in 1931 when Harrison was only a lowly sergeant. On August 20 of that year, Jack Lynch's car was forced off a country road in Walworth County, Wisconsin, just outside Lake Geneva. Three armed gunmen dragged the frightened gambler from his car and held him captive until a $125,000 ransom was paid. Harrison was assigned to the case, but could do little to secure Lynch's release, or apprehend the kidnap gang, reportedly headed by George "Red" Barker and Alvin "Creepy" Karpis. Through the intervention of Al Capone, who masterminded the abduction in order to squeeze Tennes, Jack Lynch was returned with only minor injuries.[3]

Fearing for his personal safety, Lynch asked for and received an assurance from Harrison that he would act as his personal bodyguard during his off-hours. Harrison agreed and went to work as Lynch's strong arm against the rival bad guys. It was more than a simple business arrangement. Lynch was very much impressed with his young charge. Over drinks at the Drake Hotel one night, he slipped the earnest young sergeant an envelope containing $30,000—security for his wife and infant daughter, it was explained. It was the second "gratuity"

Harrison had received. A year earlier he was given a $2,500 check "without asking for it." "Lynch asked me what security I had for my wife and daughter," Harrison told a Senate hearing in 1950. "He wanted to know why I couldn't go into business and make some money. I told him a policeman wasn't allowed to go into business."

Lynch was estimated to be worth $10 million. Living in semi-retirement after 50 years as one of Chicago's reigning gambling princes, he divided his time between Hialeah Racetrack in Florida and Sportsman's Park, Chicago, with Harrison as his friend and bodyguard. This arrangement continued until 1937, by which time Harrison had been placed in command of East Chicago. At the same time that he was protecting Lynch from Capone triggermen, Harrison was also safeguarding several construction companies owned by Democratic Party boss Pat Nash. "He watched the payroll while sitting with a gun over his knee," explained Senator Estes Kefauver in 1950.[4]

The gifts he received from Nash, coupled with the $30,000 emolument from Lynch, was parlayed into a number of lucrative stock investments between 1933 and 1948. Many of the stocks doubled in value, returning annual dividend payments to Harrison of $5,000 to $6,000. In 1946 he dabbled in wheat futures using $1,200 of William Ronan, a millionaire flour broker. By 1951, the year that the Civil Service Commission fired him for accepting illicit "gifts," Harrison was a wealthy speculator. His dismissal occurred under the regime of a new commissioner. While Chief Prendergast was in office, Harrison was "protected." A 44-year veteran, Prendergast was reluctant to turn against rank-and-file men. His curt answer to those who would accuse his captains of corrupt practices was always the same: "Back up the charges and I'll do something about them!"

Mayor Kennelly fell into lockstep behind his commissioner. During the May 1949 grand jury probe into the goings-on at Chicago Avenue, Kennelly praised Captain Harrison for his courage in closing down the French Casino after complaints were received from men who had been mugged on the premises.

"Prior to my administration," he explained, "we didn't have any top command of the Police Department after eleven o'clock. That's all been changed. The Police Department is on the job and doing a good job every one of the 24 hours in the day, fighting it out with criminals who come here from all over the country." Here was a mayor who was an old-fashioned civic booster, an optimistic, white-haired politician who pushed aside grim reminders of inefficiency, preferring to bask in the warm glow of a few meager accomplishments. Kennelly pointed with pride to the introduction of the first three-wheel tricycles which replaced the Loop horse patrols in December 1947. The addition of motorized bikes to better regulate traffic flow was a recommendation of Franklin Kreml, director of the Northwestern University Traffic Institute. Kreml was hired by Kennelly to provide solutions to the daily traffic snarls, and to reequip the force. According to the mayor, his new safety plan saved 100 lives a year. "It adds to the strength of the crimefighting forces in the city. Its primary duty is traffic control but it has an excellent record of arrests in the various categories of crime,'' Kennelly said of his radio-equipped traffic patrol.[5]

Regarding the Chicago Crime Commission's persistent charge that the police and politicians were extorting a million dollars a year in graft payments from Clark Street burlesque houses, the mayor was indignant. ''We don't do anything half-heartedly or halfway,'' he said, reminding them that it was war to the finish.

On June 22, 1951, just six short months after the Civil Service fired Captain Harrison, a court order restored him to active duty. The edict was handed down by John Sbarbaro, gangland's favorite undertaker who now sat on the bench of the superior court and was in a good position to reward his cronies. ''Harrison was called one of Chicago's most capable police officers since joining the force,'' Sbarbaro said. He ordered that the city file an immediate appeal or restore him to full pay. The Civil Service Commission, which had voted 2–1 to oust Harrison in the first place, threw up its hands and dropped the case. The captain was reassigned to duty and placed in command of the Monroe Street District, where he was credited with ridding the area of its winos and derelicts. In 1958 Harrison joined the sheriff's police at the insistence of another old pal who had just stepped into office, Democrat Frank Sain, whose failure to arrest the gamblers prompted Ben Adamowski to remark that he (Sain) ''Can't find an elephant in a telephone booth.''

Tommy Harrison took pride in the fact that he had never filed charges against any policeman with the board. He said that he preferred his own disciplinary methods. He took care of the boys, and the boys took care of him. After he left Chicago Avenue in 1951, Commissioner Timothy O'Connor placed Captain John T. Warren in charge. The new captain was a highly decorated veteran who proved to be far less cooperative than his predecessor. He closed down several of the notorious B-girl dives in the district, which did not endear him to Connors or his handpicked alderman, Dorsey Crowe, a living relic of the Prohibition wars who had sustained his power base through four decades. When Warren passed away from a sudden heart attack in 1953, Crowe succeeded in blocking a City Council resolution that would have paid tribute to his 3-year career and accomplishments. The ''42'' politicians rewarded their friends and punished their enemies.

By the late 1980s there was little left to suggest that Clark Street north of the river was once a flourishing ''tenderloin'' that rivaled the First Ward Levee for sheer licence. Neighborhood gentrification and slum clearance flattened entire blocks, taking with it the Talk of the Town, the French Casino, and the Gaiety. What stands today is a collage of wine-sipping pubs, commercial offices, condominiums, and a solitary peep show with the tasteless name of ''Puss In Boots.''[6]

To the east, however, the Rush Street nightclub district is not so different now than it was in the early 1950s. The pervasive Chicago crime syndicate refused to let go. The strip clubs coexisted with some of the city's toniest nightclubs and jazz bistros for years. In 1973, Captain Clarence Braasch, borrowing a page from Harrison, winked at the syndicate thugs who jealously guarded their turf. Unlike Harrison, the smooth, urbane Braasch, a cop considered to be a "breed apart," systematized the collections. He organized his own personal vice club to collect payouts from owners of the tawdry little saloons and clubs. The siren song of prostitution, gambling, and drug dealing was not confined to one wide-open administration, or a single captain eager to play ball; it cut across all generations.

Bill Drury's Problems

The "watchdog of the Loop" fought long and hard to vindicate himself following the 1943 exposures of wide-open gambling in the Town Hall District. Until the allegations were made by the grand jury, Bill Drury was somewhat of a "white knight" to the reformers. He was widely known to the society swells for his standing guard in formal clothes of jewels, furs, and works of art at fancy weddings and other fashionable events. During the Century of Progress, Drury resurrected his role of police dandy by heading up a detail of nattily dressed World's Fair policemen who safeguarded the property of tourists.

In 1930 Drury and his partner Johnny Howe were mysteriously transferred from the downtown plainclothes detail and reassigned to uniform duty through the intervention of Jake Guzik and Hymie Levin, two Capone hoods they had arrested. From that point on Drury enjoyed the reputation as a resolute foe of the syndicate before the luster of his star was permanently tarnished in 1943. Following his court victory in 1946 Drury was restored to active duty and given a choice assignment. There were 20 unsolved murders on the books, and Chief Prendergast told Drury and Captain Thomas Connelly to solve them. It was a chance to repair two frayed careers. They decided to focus their efforts on the sensational gangland slaying of James M. Ragen, former Colt, brother of the county commissioner of days gone by, and the owner of the Continental Press, nationwide distributor of racetrack information.

Ragen had purchased the old Nationwide News Service from Moe Annenberg on November 15, 1939. The aging press czar and one-time Hearst newspaper slugger was anxious to extricate himself from the troublesome racing wire, which had spelled nothing but disaster since Annenberg bought it from Mont Tennes in 1927.[7]

Ragen jealously fended off hostile takeover attempts by Jake Guzik and Tony Accardo for nearly seven years. When the syndicate goons failed to buy Ragen out, they organized Trans-American, a competitive service fronted by Dan Serritella. Still Ragen would not budge. It was then decided to shove aside the 64-year-old gambling boss through more persuasive means. At stake was an estimated $2 million in gambling revenue. Sensing that his number was up, Ragen appeared before State's Attorney William Touhy on May 2, 1946, asking for protection. Six weeks later he was dead.

Ragen was motoring south on State Street on June 24 when a truck loaded down with orange crates pulled up next to his sedan near Pershing Road. The car in front of Ragen stopped abruptly, blocking any possible path of escape. Shotgun muzzles poked out from under the tarpaulin-covered truck, shooting Ragen in the chest and shoulders. He lingered until August 14, before succumbing to kidney failure complicated by the gunshot wounds. Ragen revealed the existence of an affidavit claiming that Guzik, Accardo, Murray Humphreys, and others had conspired to take control of the news service. As it turned out, the affidavit disappeared. At this point Drury and Connelly stepped in.

It was shown that the shotgun used to kill Ragen had also been turned on Danny Stanton two years earlier. Ironically, this tipped the 1943 grand jury investigation *against* Drury and the West Side police who had protected syndicate gambling. Then, to the astonishment of the syndicate and the police superiors, Drury arrested Guzik for the second time in 16 years, subjecting him to the humiliation of a polygraph test. "They won't like it!" Chief Prendergast cautioned. Guzik, who had been through all this before, was more to the point: "If I took a test, 20 of Chicago's biggest men would jump out the windows." Guzik was freed.[8]

Drury and Connelly found three witnesses—a laundry sorter, a church deacon, and a newsboy—who put the finger on three syndicate gamblers: Lenny Patrick, William Block, and Dave Yaras. Brought before a grand jury, their memory suddenly proved to be faulty. John White, the laundry man, told the grand jurors that Drury had threatened to expose his parole violation. Lie detector tests showed that the three black men had committed perjury when they said they could identify Block. Their testimony had been coerced by the detectives. But then State's Attorney William J. Touhy had allegedly applied the third degree against the witnesses so that they would *not* put the finger on Jake Guzik's men. This was the story leaking out of the courtrooms, and one that Drury swore to be true.

The two detectives, with more than 48 years of service between them, were presented with immunity waivers on the eve of their grand jury appearance. They refused to sign unless instructed to do so by Chief Prendergast, who at first stood behind his boys. On April 2, 1947, the commissioner reversed himself and ordered their immediate suspensions. Charges were filed with the Civil Service Commission through the state's attorney's office in what smelled like a cover-up. Speaking before the board in October, Drury pinned the blame on Touhy and his First Assistant Wilbert Crowley, who had been seen nightclubbing with Guzik's attorney George Bieber. This was the same lawyer who presented the writ of habeus corpus that freed Guzik shortly after Connelly and Drury had taken him into custody. Drury said that Touhy and Crowley had "bulldozed" him, but the Civil Service Commission ignored the charge and dismissed both men on October 16. While the suspension hearing was pending before the board, Touhy ordered the conspiracy charges against Bill Drury dismissed after syndicate gunmen silenced a dangerous witness, John White.

Drury sought exoneration in court. He found a sympathetic listener in Judge

John Sbarbaro, who overturned the decision of the Civil Service Board. Then, in an unusual twist, Sbarbaro was reversed by the appellate court after the city filed an appeal. The cost to the taxpayer for these actions was $30,000. The dismissal of Drury marked the first time in the history of U.S. law enforcement that a police officer had been discharged on the grounds of refusing to testify regarding his own personal conduct during a murder investigation.

Drury's career drifted into permanent limbo following this second disgrace. He went to work as a crime reporter for the *Chicago Herald-American*, commenting on his battle with Guzik and the stooges in the state's attorney's office. He was dropped by the paper after the Illinois Supreme Court refused to rehear the case. In 1949 he accepted an invitation from the *Miami Daily News* to write a series of penetrating articles about Chicago mob influence in South Florida. When the project was wrapped up Drury returned to Chicago to open a private detective agency to help him finance future legal battles. He took out advertisements in the local media stating that his service was available to any group desiring to smash the syndicate at all costs. It seemed that Bill Drury's personal demons were now getting the best of him. He had fought a good fight, but had lost. At the age of 48, he was not yet convinced that he was washed up in local law enforcement, although "Pontiff Prendergast" had effectively cast him into the shadow. Instead, he set out to prove that his handling of the Ragen inestigation was unassailable, hoping that with new evidence he might recieve a third chance to clear his name. These were depressing times, a far cry from those cheeky days of the late 1930s when he sipped champagne in the foyer of the Opera House with the Insulls, Palmers, and McCormicks.

Drury had become a "canary" who was chirping a pretty tune to reporters and anyone else who might be listening. He was supplying choice items to Jack Lait and Lee Mortimer, two expatriates who had returned to the midwest to write *Chicago Confidential*, a breezy "expose" of the nether world, told in tongue-and-cheek style. Mortimer was assaulted by syndicate goons in Fort Lee, New Jersey as a warning, perhaps, that he should be more circumspect in his dealings with Drury.[9]

Without visible means of support Drury motored around town in a freshly minted Cadillac. The car puzzled his attorney, Luis Kutner, who could only wonder where the money was coming from. At the same time Drury approached Senator Estes Kefauver (D-Tenn.) for a salaried position on the organized crime task force on its way to Chicago to conduct hearings in October 1950. Officials in Washington welcomed Drury's help, but in the process the mercurial captain became a moving target.

While Drury collected material for Kefauver, he sent a confidential letter to John E. Babb, the Republican nominee for sheriff who was pitted against Dan "Tubbo" Gilbert in the fall election.

September 13, 1950

Mr. John E. Babb
c/o Republican Central Committee Hdqts.
139 N. Clark Street
Chicago, Illinois

Dear John:

Just a few lines to offer my congratulations to you on the wise choice of the Republican Central Committee in choosing you to oppose the menace to the safety of every citizen of Cook County, namely "Tubbo" Gilbert.

I served as sergeant of police from 1932–1937 under Gilbert and have first-hand evidence and knowledge of how crooked and corrupt Gilbert conducted his office as chief investigator and how after I arrested gunmen of the ilk of Charles Fischetti, Little New York Campagna, Machine Gun Jack McGurn, Murray Humphreys, Tony Capezio (sic), Three Finger Jack White, Gus Winkler, and other top-flight members of the National Crime Syndicate, he either speedily released them, or if the newspapers played them up too big, fixed their court cases. When I arrested Frank Nitti in 1933 while he was the boss of the Chicago branch of the Crime Syndicate, he said, "Dan will get me on the street in an hour," and he did just that.

In addition to my detective agency I also specialize in public relations work and would be happy to assist you in the coming campaign. I believe, because of my 26 years of experience in arresting gangsters, the trail of which always lead directly to the door of your opponent "Tubbo" Gilbert, I could be of great assistance and insure your victory in November.

Cordially,
William J. Drury[10]

Gilbert took to the airwaves to deny the damaging allegations. "We arrested and convicted Charles Fischetti (Al Capone's cousin), and Gus Winkler," Gilbert retorted, but the facts suggested otherwise. Drury had arrested everyone he mentioned in the letter, with the exception of White and McGurn. Interestingly, neither mobster served any time. Fischetti's conviction was reversed by the Supreme Court, and Winkler was murdered in front of a beer depot belonging to 45th Ward committee man Charley Weber.

Dan Gilbert never recovered from these serious charges. His 18-year career as the principal investigator for the state's attorney's office coincided with the reemergence of the Chicago Cosa Nostra, following Al Capone's tax conviction in 1931. Gilbert was easily defeated in the general election by "Two Gun" Babb, who sported a pair of pearl-handled revolvers and a trench coat.

"I'm awfully hot," Drury told Lou Kutner, who immediately requested bodyguards for his client from Kefauver staff members. The protection was authorized by the committee's chief counsel Rudolph Halley, but it came too late.

On September 25, 1950, hours before his first scheduled appearance before the Kefauver Rackets Committee, four shotgun blasts from unknown gunmen ended the stormy career of William Drury. His wife was cooking dinner in the kitchen of their Addison Street home at the time. Drury was backing his Cadillac into the garage when the killers emerged from the shadows. Mrs. Drury would later say that she thought she had heard an automobile backfire, and then she returned to her cooking. An hour later, when her husband did not appear at the door, she had second thoughts. The concerned wife pulled a flashlight out of the drawer and walked to the alley to see if everything was all right.[11]

At the same time the dry-eyed widow related her story to Damen Avenue homicide detectives, Marvin J. Bas, a Chicago attorney mixed up in the mire of 42nd Ward politics, was shot to death on a quiet residential street on the city's near West Side. Bas, who was assisting John Babb in his campaign efforts, had been working on a dossier on syndicate gambling for the Kefauver Committee. Drury had been assembling data for nearly a month. Attorney Kutner said that the lawyer and the former policeman, both critical to the success of the hearings, were planning to reveal sensitive new information about the Ragen assassination. Startling facts taken from a convict at Stateville Penitentiary would show that the 1946 investigation and subsequent indictments were essentially correct.

The cold-blooded slayings of Drury and Bas on the same day was the most brazen act of defiance perpetrated by organized crime to circumvent the judicial process. "The assassins might escape from a politics-ridden police force but they will not escape from every agency we can mobilize," said Babb. "I will urge the immediate mobilization of the FBI, the Department of Justice, and any other agency that can help."

The sad truth was that not even the FBI could crack this one. Drury and Bas were to become the third and fourth unsolved gangland slayings of 1950. There were many theories advanced by the media, however. *Chicago Sun-Times* columnist Irv Kupcinet broke a story ten months after the slaying in which he claimed that the killers were the same heavy-handed triggermen who had assassinated South Side policy king Theodore Roe. According to unnamed underworld "spokesmen," Marshall Caifano, Dominic Brancato, Sam "Teetz" Battaglia, and Dominic Bello plotted Drury's death in accordance with instructions sent down from on high. It can be deduced that the cadre of gangsters included Jake Guzik and Accardo.[12]

Washington columnist Drew Pearson had been in communication with Roe shortly before Roe's death in August 1951. Roe had refused to bend a knee to the Caifano brothers and, perhaps sensing his own imminent demise, was anxious to square accounts. Pearson tried to call Commissioner Tim O'Connor with the information, but the newly installed chief refused to take his call.

For Bill Drury, the discredited cop, there was no tea and sympathy. He had made his bones with the syndicate and paid the price for it. Unfortunately, many unanswered questions went to the grave with him. These were questions that begged an answer, but nobody was talking. Such was the state of affairs when Senator Kefauver came to town.

"Our Job Is to Get the Facts of Crime—Not to Make Arrests"

Carey Estes Kefauver, it was said, had everything it took to be president except an agenda. As a Southern congressman he was somewhat of an anomaly: a moderate on the race issue who had the temerity to support anti-poll tax legislation and anti-lynching laws. Kefauver was an exponent of President Truman's Fair Deal, but outside of Tennessee, the soft-spoken senator was hardly a national figure. In 1945 he found what he believed to be the issue that might catupult him into the limelight: domestic crime, perhaps the biggest concern to the voting public in postwar America. As the chairman of the House Judiciary Subcommittee, Congressman Kefauver exposed the links between the criminal underworld and certain judges on the federal bench. "One judge was receiving money for the dispensation of justice," Kefauver said. To Chicagoans such news would be hardly cause for alarm. It was the price of doing business. For a boy from Madisonville, Tennessee, it was no doubt an earth-shattering revelation.

In exposing Pennsylvania District Judge Albert Johnston as a crook, Kefauver inadvertently laid the groundwork for his comprehensive 1950 investigation of the national crime syndicate—whose existence was a piece of fiction, according to FBI Director J. Edgar Hoover.

On January 5, 1950, the freshman senator from Tennessee introduced a resolution to the Eighty-first Congress calling for a nationwide crime probe. It was referred to the Judiciary Committee, then chaired by Senator Pat McCarran of Nevada, who was not eager to offend the syndicate gamblers in Las Vegas. McCarran and other like-minded congressmen attempted to forestall the vote, but Kefauver was resolute. Opposition was cloaked in the usual argument that the government would be usurping the power of local law enforcement agencies. The press came down hard on McCarran, which loosened up the committee logjam. The vote was taken on May 2, with the deciding vote cast by Vice President Alben Barkley.

The 52,000-mile odyssey took the Committee deep into the heart of syndicate America. The disclosures of this largely fact-finding mission ruined several political careers, including that of Illinois Senator Scott Lucas, who blamed Kefauver for his reelection defeat.

In Chicago, the arrival of Kefauver scared not only the mobsters, but John Prendergast as well. The 67-year-old chief decided it was time to take that long anticipated "vacation," rumored since the grand jury hearings of 1949. Before he could be summoned before the committee to explain what he knew about protected gambling in Cook County, Prendergast tendered his resignation to the mayor. This followed the issuance of subpoenas for six of his top captains, including Tommy Harrison whose public disclosures of the $30,000 "loan" from Lynch proved to be the *pièce de résistance* of the entire proceedings. Prendergast did not wish to become the scapegoat who would go before the Kefauver crime investigating committee and the captains. This, coupled with the incessant demands of the Chicago Crime Commission for his resignation and the still-simmering Drury case, convinced Prendergast that now was as good a time as any. "What does he have to look forward to?" said one City Hall observer. "A lot of heat which he would have to take alone. He would have been asked to hurt a lot of long-time friends in the Police Department." And no one in his right mind would do that if he had come up through the ranks the hard way and taken the jolts like Prendergast.

"After 44 years Prendergast goes out with an unblemished record and with the respect of most people," commented Mayor Kennelly. But that wasn't quite true. During Prohibition Prendergast was indicted on Prohibition charges while serving as a captain on the South Side. He was granted a year's leave of absence while the storm passed. When he returned to duty the indictment was dropped and he resumed his career without further incident. Almost by default, Deputy Chief Tim O'Connor, 49, became Chicago's sixth commissioner of police. (Prior to 1929 the title of "general superintendent" designated the department head.) A graduate of the FBI Academy, O'Connor's principal claim to fame was his "revitalization" of the Crime Laboratory, which had declined badly in prestige and effectiveness following its integration into the department in 1938. O'Connor replaced the capable civilian heads of the bureau who had moved on because of long hours and inadequate pay. The failure of the police to solve puzzling murders in the mid–1940s was a consequence of this short-sighted budget-cutting policy. O'Connor was praised by Austin Wyman of the Chicago Crime Commission as a man of "complete integrity." Plodding, methodical, and lacking a college education, Commissioner Tim presided over the department throughout the scandal-ridden 1950s. He was a man of honesty, and he initiated a few cosmetic reforms during his tenure of office, but the clanking machine of spoils, patronage, and gambling rolled on its merry way, impervious to the muted cry of the Chicago Crime Commission, a voice in the dark during some quietly troubling times.

The names of the players had changed, but Senator Kefauver opened the Chicago hearings on October 17, 1950, according to plan. When asked what steps might be taken to clear up the Drury mystery, Kefauver demurred: "It is not our function to investigate the slaying. Our job is to get at the facts of crime, not to make arrests." Kefauver focused on the links between Chicago gambling and the national crime syndicate, particularly the Continental Press, of which Drury had intimate knowledge. The committee learned that Chicago is the living, breathing heart of the race wire service, and that syndicate-run companies like Continental routinely supplied information to the Associated Press and UPI for a nominal monthly fee. Policy, punchboards, and slots spelled big business— and big muscle in "Clout" City. This much was readily apparent to Kefauver, who subpoened members of the "West Side Bloc," the notorious bipartisan coalition against reform that supported every wide-open town politician from Bill Thompson to Ed Kelly. This coterie of corrupt West Side aldermen and state legislators had become a potent voting bloc that thwarted every worthwhile piece of anti-crime legislation to come up for a vote in the General Assembly.

The bloc was a byproduct of the 1920s, when the syndicate realized that the best way to achieve favorable results was not with the gun, but with the ballot.

Roland Libonati and James Adduci were typical of the new breed of syndicate-backed politicians who came to power at the same time that the Tommy guns were silenced on the streets of Chicago. Both men represented syndicate enclaves on the West Side and had switched allegiance from the Republicans to the Democrats to suit their purpose. The Chicago mob is essentially apolitical. Whatever party happens to be in power is good enough for the local mafiosi, as long as the goods are delivered. In 1949 Libonati, now a Democrat, forced through a piece of legislation that authorized harness racing at Sportsman's Park. Libonati and nine of his colleagues had engaged in an early version of insider trading by purchasing racing stock for the ridiculously low price of ten cents a share before the bill cleared the assembly. Representative Adduci of the 2nd District told Kefauver that in addition to his $3,000 annual salary, he earned an additional $7,000 selling stationery to the state auditor. Adduci was elected in 1934, three years after he had been arrested for the murder of Mike "de Pike" Heitler, and a year after he and Willie Bioff tried to "muscle" the poultry handler's union.

The West Side bloc, of course, threw its full support behind Dan "Tubbo" Gilbert for sheriff. For his part, Mayor Kennelly distanced himself from the man the media had dubbed "the world's richest policeman." The mayor probably burned his political bridges by refusing to appear at the slate-maker's meeting at the Morrison Hotel on December 19, 1949. At a large West Side testimonial dinner thrown by ranking members of the bloc, Mayor Kennelly was asked to say a few words on behalf of their man Dan. The mayor stood up, and effectively threw a wet blanket on the proceedings by calling Gilbert "Two Ball Dan," a nickname he gave him during a recent round of golf. If the captain were to knock a ball into the rough, Kennelly said, you could bet he would drop a second ball in a more favorable position and play it from there if nobody was looking. The West Siders were aghast.[13]

Concerning Dan Gilbert, the Democratic Kefauver Committee kept his testimony secret in deference to the county ticket. The newspapers got hold of it, which spelled defeat in the general election. A report filed by Kefauver had this to say about Gilbert:

A reason for lack of conscientious enforcement of gambling laws was disclosed by the testimony of Police Captain Dan Gilbert, known as the world's richest cop and for many years chief investigator for the office of State's Attorney for Cook County. Gilbert, Democratic candidate for sheriff of Cook County, testified before the committee that he placed bets himself with a well-known Chicago betting commissioner. He admitted this was not legal betting. In explanation he testified, "I have been a gambler at heart." Although agreeing that raids could be initiated by his office on bookies in the city, Gilbert admitted it had not been done since 1939 despite the fact that practically every bookmaking establishment in the city of Chicago was listed in the recently published hearings before the McFarland subcommittee of the Senate Interstate and Foreign Commerce Committee.[14]

The Kefauver Committee conducted a spot check of the finances of Chicago policemen to determine the extent of interstate link-ups with national crime figures. Such a relationship did not exist, and the committee let it go at that. However, Commissioner O'Connor suspended Captains Joseph Goldberg of Sheffield Avenue and Harry J. O'Connell of Pekin Inn pending a broader-based investigation of their personal finances. Goldberg's personal assets exceeded $43,000. He had received gift shares of stock with a par value of $5,321. In 1948 Goldberg accepted "gifts" of $1,820, and approximately $42,285 a year later.

In the case of O'Connell the commissioner pointed out that his living expenses were not commensurate with his salary. His monthly rent was $225, an exorbitant figure for 1950.

It was clear that the only way to get rich in law enforcement was to become a Chicago police captain, especially in a politically "sensitive" district like East Chicago Avenue, as evidenced by the foibles of Tommy Harrison, who was roasted alive by the Kefauver Committee. U.S. Treasury Agent Arthur Madden estimated that at least 40 captains were worth at least half a million dollars in 1950, because, as he explained, "cash in safe deposit vaults doesn't leave any trail." The average grunt who patrolled his beat in 1950 would look upon these revelations with a mixture of amusement and bitter resignation. Their reality was a world apart from a Harrison or a Goldberg who had reaped a rich harvest.

To be sure, the cop on the beat would have welcomed any pay raise or improvement in working conditions. Between 1933 and 1950 patrolmen's pay increased 39.2 percent plus certain benefits added in the way of pensions and vacations. By comparison, the aldermen routinely voted pay increases of 100 percent to members of favored trade unions. In 1950 the plasterer's union benefited from two ordinances that raised their pay from $20 to $22 per day. Per diem appropriations for routine work in all departments doubled in the 1933–50 period, except for the lowly patrolman. The system, as it was constituted in 1950, required patrolmen to be on the job 44.5–48 hours per week, usually spread over six-day shifts (see Table 7).

The city was niggardly in providing the equipment necessary for the men to carry out their duties. Each officer was required to purchase his own uniform from department stores and licensed outlets, despite yearly protests from the Patrolmen's Association that they be provided with a stipend for the care and upkeep of their clothing. In some station houses, officers had to spend their own money or scurry about to locate equipment such as typewriters and office furniture. By 1953 there were still no target ranges provided for the men's use.

Certain Chicago policemen had not fired their guns in years, which made them dangerous not only to themselves but to the public at large. The police were often hampered in their ability to safeguard lives and property by law suits filed against them by private citizens. Because legal statutes designated the city as the secondary defendant in such cases, officers in many cases had to dig into their pockets to hire private attorneys to defend them against false arrest and

Table 7
Comparative Patrolmen Salaries, 1931–55

	First Year Salary	After Two Years on Force
1931	$2,140	$2,500
1941	$2,140	$2,500
1951	$3,782	$4,250
1955	$4,442	$4,925

Source: Report of the Superintendent to the City Council, 1931, 1941, and 1955. In 1919 first-year patrolmen earned a salary of $1,400 per year; $1,500 in year two; and $1,800 in the third year of service. Beyond the third year there were no provisions for a salary increase. In the next dozen years beginning salaries increased only 11 percent. During labor strikes, crime waves, overtime, and various hazardous duties, a police officer was required to be on duty without added compensation. Neither did the city provide credit in time or wages for the police when they were required to make their compulsory appearances in court.

brutality suits. Between 1945 and 1953 there were 142 of these cases, of which 53 were settled by privately retained counsel.

Shrewd politicians like Richard J. Daley, Democratic candidate for sheriff of Cook County in 1946, pandered to the ill-feeling in the ranks by promoting himself as the "friend of Chicago police."

[State] Senator Daley introduced, sponsored and passed legislation in the 1945 session of the Illinois General Assembly which permitted the salary increase for city of Chicago policemen.

As Minority Leader of the State Senate, Senator Daley handled all pension legislation, increasing pension rights for city policemen and their wives and children.

Since 1935 Daley has worked in every General Assembly session for improvement of working conditions and other benefits of the Chicago police department and its members.

Vote for Richard J. Daley for Sheriff November 5. Vote Democratic![15]

Daley cultivated the policemen's good will at election time. He lent a sympathetic ear to the police lobbyists in Springfield, which translated into Democratic votes.

The rank-and-file could not rely solely on the legislature or City Council to appropriate pay raises. Most of the men held outside jobs, contrary to police regulations. As we have seen, a number of officers invested in saloons, a natural extension of the police "culture." Still others worked as department store security guards, or crowd watchers at the city's two baseball parks.

Estes Kefauver uncovered widespread abuse of the police rule against moonlighting. Working as a security guard was one thing, but serving the interests of the syndicate was quite another matter. As one of his last official acts as commissioner, John Prendergast was forced to take disciplinary action against Detective Walter Carrigan of the East Chicago Avenue Station, who had been earning $25 a day as the unofficial "chief of police" at Sportsman's Park. The track had been mentioned in committee hearings in connection with a gangland murder and an $80,000 loan to Paul "the Waiter" Ricca.

Carrigan was one of many policemen who not only worked at Sportsman's Park, but the Hawthorne Track as well. The assignments were doled out to favored patrolmen by the district captain. In the case of Carrigan, Captain Thomas Harrison selected him for off-hours track duty. "He'll be working days tomorrow!" Prendergast fumed. The police who moonlighted at the race tracks often made handsome profits by betting on certain horses. The Chicago Crime Commission and the Kefauver investigators called for a thorough cleaning out of the Honky-Tonk district, watched over by Harrison.

Kefauver left town with the satisfaction of having torpedoed John Prendergast, Scott Lucas, Tommy Harrison, and Dan Gilbert. The Continental Press, which had claimed a score of lives in the 40 or so years of its existence, was soon driven out of business, and the alliance of West Side politicians with the members of the Mafia—a hitherto unknown word up to this time—was exposed for what it was. In the next two years the Chicago press was awakened to the scourge of the crime syndicate. The *Sun-Times* in particular rose to the vanguard of the anti-crime drive.

On a national level, Congress enacted a measure to prohibit the interstate shipment of slot machines, which put a major dent in Eddie Vogel's operation. Narcotics laws were tightened, and deportation proceedings were begun against undesirable aliens at Senator Kefauver's urging. But the Tennessee Democrat had only scratched the surface of labor racketeering. In 1957 Senator John McClellan, working in tandem with Robert Kennedy, conducted an exhaustive three-year probe into organized crime and its linkup with the labor unions.[16] Estes Kefauver had paved the way, despite formidable obstacles. In Chicago alone, his chief witness was assassinated and a file folder of documents was stolen from his chief investigator.

Regrettably, the fine work of the committee was overshadowed by Kefauver's hidden agenda: his desire to occupy the White House. And to these ends he failed. The exposures of political graft and protected crime in the big cities cost Senator Kefauver the support of the party machinery in Chicago, New York, Philadelphia, Kansas City, and Miami. The best he could accomplish was an unsuccessful vice-presidential bid in 1956.

Something Rotten in Chicago

The West Side bloc cast a long ugly shadow across nine city wards, all the way down to the state house in Springfield. No fewer than 17 state senators voted down Governor Adlai Stevenson's bill to allow local municipalities to revoke liquor licences of taverns that permitted backroom gambling. The power of the bloc in Springfield was absolute because neither Republicans nor Democrats enjoyed a clear majority in the house. Political parity permitted the bloc—

composed of six Republicans and three Democrats—to cast the deciding votes on key issues affecting the livelihood of the syndicate.

In Chicago the bloc was an ever-expanding entity squeezing out old-time machine aldermen like Democrat George Kells, who refused to accept the new mandates. The Kefauver Committee drew attention to this alarming development, but there was little that honest political leaders and civic organizations could do other than decry the gangster infiltration into local government.

The police, as the only agency standing between law and mob rule, were held accountable for each new eruption of gang warfare that flared anew in the early 1950s. On February 6, 1952, the battleground was the West Side 31st Ward, and the victim was the unobtrusive Charles Gross, acting committee man sworn to oppose the encroaching West Side bloc. Gross owned a soft-drink company, and had been carrying a gun for protection. It was later alleged that the 56-year-old committee man was not an innocent victim after all, and may have in fact been mixed up in the rackets. But in the wake of his shotgun murder, Gross was for the moment a fallen martyr. Alderman Thomas Keane vowed to "hold the line" against the gangsters. "They're not going to make another George Kells out of Tom Keane," he said. But as the *Sun-Times* observed wryly, "They didn't make a Kells out of Keane, but they made a corpse out of Gross."[17]

The charges against the police were flying thick and fast. Five aldermen demanded the removal of Commissioner O'Connor and another investigation of police graft. The mayor stated, "I'm not going to let anybody make a goat out of O'Connor. There will be no action taken without a complete investigation." In response to the outspoken criticism of his department, O'Connor turned the case over to his crack Scotland Yard detail under the direction of Frank Pape, 40, who sported six notches on his gun handle. "I've heard reports there are supposed to be some allegedly tough hoodlums involved in this deal," O'Connor said. "Pape's record will prove he knows what to do with tough guys." After a week the only arrest made in connection with the Gross slaying was that of William E. Block, who had beaten a well-worn path to headquarters during the Ragen murder investigation of 1946. Before another fortnight had passed, O'Connor reorganized Scotland Yard under the aegis of Lieutenant Joseph Morris.

Mayor Kennelly, who had won reelection in April because of his reputation for honesty and political independence from the machine, was asked to provide answers to difficult questions. Why had certain bloc aldermen like John D'Arco and Pat Petrone been provided with lavish office accommodations down the hall from the mayor? Kennelly and O'Connor sat tightlipped while 600 business and civic leaders raked them over the coals at an anti-crime rally held at the LaSalle Hotel on February 12, 1952. They were asked: "Will you demand no one in your department take orders from anyone except their superior officers?" The mayor and his new commissioner were stone-faced. Austin Wyman of the Crime Commission recalled the words spoken by the chief of police in Los Angeles: "I wouldn't last fifteen minutes in Chicago as police commissioner."

A two-pronged attack was launched, as noble as any ever conceived by reform politicians dating back to the era of John Wentworth. The business and reform groups organized a blue-ribbon committee of 19 to consider ways of separating the court system from politics, and the larger problem of curbing the power of the bloc through reapportionment. Phase two offered greater promise. On February 15, Mayor Kennelly appointed nine aldermen—the "Big Nine"—to investigate crime. The mayor opposed the demands of the young, liberal faction of the City Council that a civilian commissioner be appointed. He offered instead this compromise measure, which was passed by the aldermen. Alderman Robert Merriam of the 5th Ward, son of the noted Progressive-era politician who fought Carter Harrison and then Bill Thompson, called for the appointment of at least five members of the reform bloc. Instead, the powers-that-be derailed the committee before it had a chance to get started. The original nine was quickly subverted by a coalition of bloc-machine politicians.

THE BIG NINE

Minority Reform Bloc:

Ald. Robert E. Merriam (5th Ward)

Ald. Herbert Geisler (34th Ward)

Ald. John J. Hoellen (47th Ward)

Ald. Allen A. Freeman (48th Ward)

Machine/Bloc Faction:

Ald. Reginald Du Bois (9th Ward)

Ald. Clarence Wagner (14th Ward)

Ald. Robert Bremer (50th Ward)

Ald. P. J. Cullerton (38th Ward)

Ald. Wm. Lancaster (37th Ward)

Chairman:

Reginald DuBois

Present at the first meeting of the Big Nine were two politicians from the hoodlum-backed West Side bloc: Aldermen John D'Arco and Patrick Petrone. They were there to make sure that a "loose cannon" like Bob Merriam failed in his bid to become permanent chairman. The professor's son might have carried the day if not for the sell-out to the spoilsmen by Robert Bremer, a freshman alderman who had demonstrated surprising independence in his dealings up to this point. Bremer was the son-in-law of James J. Quinn, a cog in the old Kelly-Nash machine of years gone by. Casting a furtive glance at the two unsavory bosses charting his every move, Bremer threw the deciding vote in DuBois's favor. Merriam and his three allies believed that Bremer might vote with them on this one, but they were wrong. It was as fine a piece of political chicanery to come out of the smoke-filled rooms in many a year.

Still, there was hope that the Big Nine could overcome the obstacles and pick up where Estes Kefauver had left off. This was especially true after the committee hired a tough former FBI investigator from Philadelphia to step in and serve as special counsel. Aaron Kohn was his name, and after hearing about the formation of the Big Nine, he wrote a letter to Virgil Peterson saying that he would be happy to lend his talents to the task at hand. His appointment was enthusiastically endorsed by Attorney Charles Bane, responsible for preparing the Big Nine's report on police graft.

As it turned out there was no cause for optimism. By August the "Little Four" reform bloc was crying foul. Attorney Bane charged that at least 800 police were collecting money from syndicate figures. When Bane sought approval on an ordinance that would require policemen to complete income disclosure statements, the City Council voted the measure down 40 to 7. Before the committee report could be released, Bane and Kohn tendered their resignations, citing political "sabotage." The aldermen routinely ignored the standing order to refrain from peeking at classified documents collected by the investigators. The subpoena powers of the Big Nine were being challenged in court by parties interested in derailing the course of investigation.

Down, but certainly not out, Alderman Merriam pressed ahead with the investigation. Meanwhile, the Chicago Crime Commission renewed its call for the creation of a police intelligence unit that would have as one of its prime responsibilities the job of rooting out unfit men and exposing internal corruption. The proposal had been laid on the table in 1932, but Mayor Cermak, his successor, and three police chiefs refused to sanction any plan in which "cops would rat on cops." "Such an intelligence unit should be no more resented by the force than the staff of a bank should resent the presence of a bank examiner," the Commission's report stated. The notion was contrary to the prevailing attitudes. Such resentments against "outsiders," and those individuals who would dare to criticize a policeman without first-hand experience in the trenches, were rooted deep in the culture. But the day of reckoning was soon at hand, when the old-fashioned ways would simply not be acceptable any more.

The Little Red Book

The test of fire for the Big Nine began in March 1953, when the *Sun-Times* turned over to committee members a memorandum book that belonged to Captain Redmond Gibbons of the Hudson Avenue Station, situated in the lair of Alderman Mathias "Paddy" Bauler. "This book contained my name and address on the fly leaf, data on my camera, and data on my Ford automobile which I bought in September 1949," said Gibbons. Turning the pages of the little red book, the reporters also found dozens of listings of gambling dens, nightclubs, and other illicit establishments in the 43rd Ward, with numbers ranging from 10 to 100 after each entry. There were names of collectors and criminals, and notations about the still-unsolved murder of attorney Marvin Bas. Home addresses of key suspects identified by police investigators were also listed. One telephone number in particular caught the attention of the Big Nine—that of Fred Romano, an assistant state's attorney in the employ of "Honest" John Gutknecht. The new state's attorney hired Romano with the full knowledge that he was a close friend of Ross Prio, North Side boss of gambling and vice. The phone number was traced to the LaSalle Street offices of Prio and Romano, who had joint interests in a dairy company. Attorney William Mannion, who had screened Romano as a candidate when Gutknecht took office, said that as far as he was concerned, Prio was "a respectable businessman" with no prior criminal record. The truth was that Prio's record dated back to 1929, but a court order was handed down by a sympathetic judge who ruled that it be destroyed. Romano obligingly stepped down to avoid further embarrassment.

The same could not be said of Captain Gibbons, who gave his statement to Commissioner O'Connor. He then requested a leave of absence so that he could go to San Francisco, where he hoped to find evidence that would clear his name of the allegations. The Big Nine was incensed. In January, two months before the existence of the little red book was made known, the Big Nine had attempted to question Gibbons about his income and assets, but Gibbons refused on the grounds that they invaded his constitutional right to privacy. The superior court ruled in Gibbons's favor, but in light of the new evidence the Merriam faction renewed its efforts to compel the captain to testify before the committee. For his part, Commissioner Tim appointed his deputy Philip Breitzke and Captain William Balswick of Scotland Yard to study the book and make their report. Beyond that, O'Connor refused to reveal the whereabouts of Gibbons to committee members. That he was recovering his health, was all O'Connor would say. In "Notes from Town Hall," the *Police Digest* reported that "Captain Redmond Gibbons, the new skipper at Town Hall is quite a guy, well-liked by the men and a good policeman. The captain came up the hard way and knows all the angles. Square and on the level, he'll go a long way in the Police Department."[18]

Redmond Gibbons learned police work at his daddy's knee. Like so many other South Side Chicago families, police work was a multigenerational occupation. For years his father James was a detective. The younger Gibbons joined the force in 1922, after serving a hitch aboard a U.S. Navy gunboat. Gibbons disdained frivolity, and seems to have resisted the temptation to partake in the enormous bootleg profits the syndicates were using to pay off friendly patrolmen at the time. Instead, he attended night classes at DePaul University, and later the John Marshall Law School. In May 1938 Commissioner Allman sent him to the FBI Bureau for training, and Gibbons became the second Chicago policeman to be so honored. After the war there were more honors awaiting Gibbons. He was personally selected to go into Berlin to help in the reorganization of the post-Nazi police force. When he returned, there were several promotions ahead.

Between the time he assumed command of Hudson Avenue in 1949 and his 1952 promotion to commander of the uniformed patrol, Gibbons seems to have been corrupted. He moved into a deluxe apartment on Lake Shore Drive, but steadfastly refused to tell Big Nine committee members how much rent he paid, or other outside sources of income. Frustrated by his stone-walling tactics, the Big Nine voted to issue a subpoena for Gibbons to appear at a public hearing on April 27. Meanwhile, Mayor Kennelly dismissed the significance of the notebook. "This book dates from 1949," he said. "Gambling was running wide open before I became mayor in 1947. We closed hundreds, yes, thousands of places. It took a little time but gambling is down compared to what it once was."

Robert Butzler testified before the committee that during the time he worked undercover in the Hudson Avenue District there was an understanding that Ross Prio, Alderman Bauler, and Bauler's point man William Goldstein, alias "Bill Gold," were the boys to see about vice and gambling. Each of their names was entered in the ledger. A telephone listing for Gold turned out to be the number of a drugstore at North Avenue and LaSalle Street at which syndicate cash was doled out to members of the detective squad on "payday." Gold Coast residents recalled seeing as many as three or four squad cars parked outside while the envelopes were being distributed inside. Gibbons replied: "The owner of this store had made complaints about teenagers on the street around the store. I had called this drug store in checking on the police service rendered on these complaints. I have no knowledge, nor did I ever receive any complaints that this drug store was ever used for any illegal transactions."

Other notations listed after the names of taverns and gambling resorts referred to ticket sales made by the policeman for the mayor's annual prep championship football game. "There never was any pressure brought to bear by the administration in the sales of benefit tickets," Kennelly said, but it was common practice for the politicians to use the police for these purposes. The notebook contained a checkoff list of cash bonuses and "gifts" paid out to the police by grateful merchants at Christmas time. The owner of a Dearborn Avenue restaurant explained that he slipped $50 into a sealed envelope along with a business card. The "gift" was hand-delivered to Gibbons at the station. What had been originally intended as a goodwill gesture had turned into a highly organized collection system. Across the city, police would line up a few days before Christmas to receive their reward. Fearful business people paid out these bonuses in the form of cash or merchandise in order to assure themselves of continuous protection through the coming year. In the likelihood of a burglary or harassment by young toughs, the stores that cooperated could expect the full and undivided attention of the local police.[19]

Such practices were in violation of police ordinances, but as long as the captains were included on the gift list, rarely was the rule enforced. It was the normal way of doing business, and few people questioned it. It was not until O. W. Wilson arrived in 1960 to put an end to these extortions that the issue was ever discussed in the context of proper police ethics.

As the Big Nine futilely tried to force Gibbons into a dialogue, there were reports of other little red books, equally incriminating, popping up around the city. Detective Joseph P. Galvin of the vice-ridden Wabash Station, where the South Side policy kings held sway, said that his book had been "tampered" with by political enemies. Galvin was regarded as a "captain's man," the nefarious designation given to the officer selected to function as the liaison between the commander of the Fifth Police District and the illegal or borderline enterprises going on in defiance of local statutes. In olden days these individuals were simply known as "bag men." In the new order the shadowy captain's man was usually a plainclothes detective who worked the same shift every day, and was transferred at the commander's discretion when assignments changed. Commissioner O'Connor struck at this system by forcing many of them to work "around the horn," or "steady midnights," so that they would take three shifts at once, just like the ordinary patrolman. Still, it was impossible to strike at the root of this long-standing system.

"You can be sure I wasn't a captain's man," Galvin said. He dismissed the line item showing that someone in the Fifth District was pocketing $100 a day as pure fiction. There was nothing glamorous and daring about the Fifth. Unlike East Chicago Avenue, where vice was cloaked with an air of respectability, the Wabash District had the highest crime rate per capita in the city. The police station was a lonely outpost of white officers attempting to enforce unpopular laws in an all-black neighborhood. The knifings, prostitution, purse-snatchings, and street muggings were so commonplace that the police at the Wabash Avenue Station kept it off the blotter unless the complainant was a white person. The attitude of the black community was at odds with the aim of the police, who desired to clean up this district. Complaints of racial prejudice against white patrolmen discouraged the police from going after knife-wielding assailants or policy agents who enjoyed syndicate protection. As a result the district was often under-policed, when a complement of black officers assigned by the commissioner might have provided short-term solutions.

The captain with the clout was Kinzie Blueitt, whose district had become a syndicate battleground of late, as the last of the policy gamblers were picked off one by one. In 1955 Captain Blueitt was indicted by the grand jury for lying about his associations with gambler Claude Murphy. The two men had been seen together in off-hours, contrary to Blueitt's earlier testimony. During the two-year investigation into South Side policy operations that followed, U.S. Attorney Kinsey James employed two detectives to gather evidence against Blueitt and Congressman William Levi Dawson, the city's most formidable black politician. The two plainclothes men had been promised captaincies for their cooperation. On November 14, 1957, Judge William Campbell issued a directed verdict of not guilty in the perjury trial of Blueitt. Predictably, the undercover case against the influential Dawson, who was the vice chairman of the Democratic Committee, and his police stooge collapsed.[20]

In the wake of the continuing Gibbons turmoil, Commissioner O'Connor suspended Captain Joseph Vojtech, who had assumed command of Hudson Avenue in 1952. Vojtech professed ignorance about the existence of a handbook on Sedawick Avenue. He took the fall for Gibbons, who slipped back into Chicago to continue the fight to clear his name.

In 1954 the Illinois Supreme Court ruled that the Big Nine had the right to obtain information about Gibbons's sources of income, if that was its wish. In November Gibbons went before the committee and said that his income was derived solely from his salary as a police officer and the interest he earned from a passbook account. His August 25, 1953, suspension was lifted by O'Connor, and shortly afterward Gibbons was placed in command of the Maxwell Street Station, and later North Avenue. At the time of his death in 1957, Gibbons was attending an FBI "refresher" course in Washington. He was praised by Mayor Richard Daley as "an outstanding police officer and a dedicated public servant."

The City Council Emergency (Big Nine) Crime Committee continued to be plagued by the pernicious influence of politics. Despite much rhetoric it accomplished very little during its three and a half-year whirlwind existence. On March 3, 1955, nine months before the Big Nine submitted its final report to the City Council, Chief Investigator Downey Rice tendered his resignation and offered a candid assessment of the problems of this committee. "I'm disgusted," he said. "We're not getting anywhere. The politicians in Chicago are making monkeys out of us."[21] Armed with enough information to blow the lid off Chicago corruption, Rice said he had photostatic evidence of payoffs to policemen. He pushed for immediate open hearings, but Chairman Irwin N. Cohen—the fourth committee head since 1952—blocked him. Rice charged that Cohen was under the influence of the Democratic organization.

Rice flew back to Washington to resume his career in federal law enforcement. "I have a reputation to maintain!" he said. The Big Nine suspended operations in January 1956. In its final report it called for a new investigative unit in the city government, stopping well short of endorsing the Chicago Crime Commission's proposal for an internal affairs division within the Police Department. On June 6, 1956, the new mayor submitted the name of Irwin Cohen to the City Council for approval as the first commissioner of the Chicago Department of Investigation (CDI), aimed at tracking corrupt officials in all branches of municipal government. "Since the agency had been set up exclusively for the benefit of the mayor, I feel it can be of real help to him in his job," Cohen said, in praise of his new boss—Richard J. Daley.

The Resurgent Democratic Machine

Mayor Martin Kennelly, more than anyone, suffered the most at the hands of the Big Nine. The crime probe did little to change the prevailing system, but it succeeded in turning the searchlight on Kennelly's failure to reform the Police Department despite his persistent claim that he alone was responsible for closing down syndicate gambling in Chicago. Mayor Ed Kelly's tolerance of policy gambling earned him the support of a large black voting constituency—Dawson's people. Kennelly, however, antagonized South Side blacks, while leaving the

North Side cabaret districts alone. More than anything else, this influenced the decision of the Democratic slate-making committee to dump Kennelly as its standard-bearer in the 1955 mayoral election.

During this time, County Clerk Richard Daley had been quietly marshaling support among veteran aldermen like Paddy Bauler and Thomas Keane. With over 30 years of rough-and-tumble experience behind him, Clerk Daley had assembled a large patronage army, much the same way as Tony Cermak had 25 years earlier. Nervous ward bosses, who feared that Kennelly would dismantle the patronage system if given a third term, looked to Daley to deliver them to graft nirvana in 1955. Robert Merriam, the declared Republican candidate for mayor said as much in a blistering speech delivered March 8: "I've been hearing reports that Democratic precinct captains around town are spreading the word that after the election—if their man becomes mayor—everything is going to go. Every syndicate operation is going to open up in Chicago: open for high stake, high pressure gambling, crooked dice games and all the rest."[22]

Merriam charged that Daley would kill the Big Nine (which he did), and that a certain crooked police captain known to all would be appointed commissioner (which never happened). Kennelly was angry and bitter at the sell-out by the party regulars, but he would not support Alderman Merriam, whom he partly blamed for his downfall.

During the primary the scorned mayor ran as an independent, under the banner of the "Greater Chicago Committee to Reelect Martin H. Kennelly." Cook County Assessor Frank Keenan, who personally hated Dick Daley, directed the mayor's primary campaign. Keenan was not averse to using dirty tricks to achieve an advantage, and was said to have masterminded the bugging of Daley's private telephone line at the Morrison Hotel. Lieutenant Joe Morris of the Scotland Yard detail was given the assignment but botched it miserably. This cast Tim O'Connor, a Kennelly man, in an exceedingly unfavorable light. The two dirty tricksters identified themselves as policemen to the desk clerk, saying that they were tapping into the line of a New York hotel thief known to be staying in one of the rooms. Daley campaign workers caught them in the act.

Alderman Merriam boldly declared that he could defeat any Democrat sent his way. He was already making plans to appoint a civilian commissioner of police, which would have been the first since LeRoy Steward in 1909. But Merriam, for all of his quixotic, University of Chicago, goo-goo views, had underestimated the power of the West Side bloc/Dawson wards which delivered Daley a 125,179 plurality on April 5, 1955. Daley was in, and the Chicago press, which had endorsed Merriam, expressed their support with trepidations.

On election night, Charley Weber lifted his stein in salute to Dick Daley. "Chicago ain't ready for reform!" he cried, and all his cronies gathered round to toast. Fine airs and fine graces—well, this was no Sunday social after all. Chicago was in safe hands now. Paddy Bauler, who by now was a seasoned elder statesman of the machine, thought perhaps his friends may have underestimated this Daley: "Keane and them fellas—Jake Arvey, Joe Gill—they think they are gonna run things. Well, you listen now to what I'm sayin' they're gonna run nuthin'. They ain't found out yet, but Daley's the dog with the big nuts, now that we got him elected. You wait and see, that's how it is going to be."[23]

The Citywide Crime Picture: 1950s

Taking the very words out of Bauler's mouth, Mayor Daley ordered the police to arrest "without fear of reprisals" gambling wherever they found it. Traffic Chief Michael Ahearn and Detective Chief John O'Malley raised their eyebrows. No one could ever remember anyone, except the special detective units of Captain William Balswick's squad, being permitted to raid the gambling dens. There were to be no reservations about this, Daley said. All 7,000 men and women in the rank-and-file were given carte blanche to carry out their tasks. Daley had sent a signal to the Dawsons, D'Arcos, Libonatis, and all the other "dogs with the big nuts" that he alone would decide what went down and what didn't.

To further confound the "experts," Daley retained Commissioner Tim, not because of any personal high regard for the man but only because James B. Conlisk, administrative assistant to four previous superintendents, turned down the mayor's offer. Conlisk was arguably the most powerful man in the department but few outside City Hall knew who he was. He drew up every transfer and promotion order, and authorized all vouchers, requisitions, and budget revisions. Conlisk performed his tasks quietly for Alcock, Allman, Prendergast, and O'Connor, in that order. He was Chicago's J. Edgar Hoover and he deferred to only one boss—his wife Margaret, who reportedly told Daley to his face, "You leave him right where he is." Keeping Tim O'Connor on the job made good political sense. Chicago's crime rate had dropped in 1953 and 1954 as the national rate was soaring. There were fewer murders, rapes, and assaults. In the face of manpower shortages, the "single 24-hour command" instituted in 1950 seemed to be working. O'Connor judiciously avoided the common temptation to saturate high-crime areas with added men, as was the case in New York when the commissioner added 259 recruits to patrol Harlem. In Chicago's troubled Fillmore District, an area so tough that Captain Eugene McNally resigned in May 1954, O'Connor reported a decrease in crime. Refusing to deplete other neighborhoods for the benefit of Fillmore, O'Connor "sprinkled" the district with just ten rookies and 20 reassigned traffic police.

The numbers did not tell the whole story, however. Inefficiency and corruption still undermined the detectives' bureau and patrol squads, which imperiled the safety of Chicago residents. Any wise motorist who owned a car in the 1950s knew that the best way to beat a traffic ticket was to keep a $10 bill wrapped around the driver's license at all times. Typically, a patrol officer would pull an offender over to the curb and ask the driver to accompany him to the front seat of the squad car, where the money would be passed. More serious traffic violations might be handled in much the same way as a 1959 case involving a drunk driver named Jack W. Ferris, and his arresting officer, John McGuire. The policeman told Ferris that the matter could be settled for $200, whereupon he drove the intoxicated motorist to the private residence of one Robert Woods, a precinct captain who doubled as clerk of traffic court. Woods took the $200 and promised to find Ferris a lawyer who would represent him in traffic court, but the meaning was perfectly clear, even to a thoroughly intoxicated driver. The case would be "squared" before Ferris's name was even called. Ferris didn't even bother to show up in court that day; but his astonishment, he later found out that Judge Grover Niemeyer had suspended his license and slapped him with a $125 fine. Ferris was issued a $50 refund by Woods, but the matter didn't end there. McGuire and Woods were each sentenced to six months in the county jail.

The Woods-McGuire case sparked a broad investigation into traffic court ticket-fixing. Thirty-five indictments were returned against judges, clerks, and bailiffs in a scandal that predated the all-encompassing "Greylord" judicial investigation of the 1980s. "Politicians often call up judges and ask them to give earnest consideration to a certain case," explained 4th Ward Alderman Claude Holman.[24]

The 1950s were also characterized by a series of puzzling, unsolved murders involving politicians and adolescent youths, which revealed the sorry state of Chicago's police and court system. The police never found out who killed Charles Gross, the 31st Ward politician whose death raised such a public furor that the Big Nine was organized to provide answers. No solutions could be found. Clem Graver was another politician tied in with the West Side bloc. The 21st Ward Republican Committeeman drove into the garage of his home the night of June 11, 1953. He waved to his wife, who was sitting on the porch as a car pulled up in the alley. Three men got out. They spoke a few words with Graver inside the garage, and then all four drove off in the sedan—never to be seen again. There was no ransom note or clue. Graver went into the books as Police File no. MPV91903: missing person.

Most ghastly of all was the fate that befell Robert Peterson, the Schuessler brothers, Judith Mae Anderson, and Barbara and Patricia Grimes, who were abducted and murdered by unknown killers in a two-year period. The far Northwest Side of Chicago was a pleasant tree-lined community populated by thousands of middle-income immigrants and Chicago police and firemen who bought homes to comply with city residency requirements and still be as close to the suburbs as possible. It was also the scene of the Schuessler-Peterson tragedy of October 18, 1955.

John and Anton Schuessler, ages 13 and 11 respectively, and their friend Bobby Peterson, 14, left their homes on a Sunday afternoon to attend a downtown movie. The mangled bodies of three youngsters were found two days later in a forest preserve ditch on the outskirts of the city by a liquor salesman who had parked his car in a small lot nearby where he ate his lunch. The grief-stricken father of the Schuessler boys complained bitterly, "We couldn't get any action

Sunday night [when the boys turned up missing]; now we're getting all kinds of action.'' Coroner Walter McCarron disclosed that death was caused by asphyxiation. There was evidence of head wounds, sexual assault, and extreme violence. Dr. Harry Hoffman, former state psychiatrist, explained that the killer was a psycho-sexual deviate who probably acted alone. He added that the killer, if found, would prove to be someone with a long history of these kinds of crimes.[25]

The police and the county patrol worked feverishly around the clock on this case. Numerous suspects were arrested and a house-to-house search was conducted, resulting in little in the way of tangible evidence. The police were doomed to failure. Hindering the course of the investigation was the constant bickering between the detectives assigned to Lieutenant James Lynch, who headed up the Chicago side of the case, and 100 men under the jurisdiction of Sheriff Joseph Lohman, the University of Chicago intellectual who had been plucked from the lecture halls by the Democratic organization to run for office. Lohman was under constant fire during much of his four-year term for waste, inefficiency, and corruption. Lohman became addicted to the narcotic spell of politics, and had his eyes on the governor's office while his men had their hands in the cookie jar. Captain Richard Boone and Under-sheriff Thomas Brennan would later resign in disgust, telling a Cook County grand jury in 1958 that the sheriff's department was mired in graft. It was clear that little had changed since the regime of ''Blind'' Tom O'Brien out in the county.

The Chicago police interviewed 20,000 persons, tracked down 1,296 leads, and took 2,340 suspects into custody. They failed to locate the actual killer but they identified 80 other criminals who were wanted on other charges. Of this group, 17 were convicted and sent to jail. The Schuessler-Peterson slayings became a lesson in terror for a generation of school children in the 1950s: never talk with strangers, and be home before dark. The police were slow to enforce existing curfew laws, the Chicago Crime Commission pointed out.

The tragedy was still fresh in everyone's minds when, on December 28, 1956, the South Side experienced its own horrific murders that in many ways were an eerie carbon copy of the Schuessler murder. The Grimes girls exited the Brighton theater on December 28, 1956, after watching an Elvis Presley movie. At some point between the movie house and their home on Damen Avenue, they got into a car and were not seen alive again. In a tersely worded message issued by Captain McCarthy on January 23, 1957, it was reported that the missing person's search was at an end: ''Cancel message No. 54428. Barbara and Patricia Grimes, 5634 S. Damen. Bodies now at the County Morgue.'' The unclad bodies of the missing girls were found in a ditch off German Church Road in Palos Hills, a winding two-lane highway flanked by tall trees and spacious houses off the road. There was no clue as to the make of the vehicle or the drivers who left the girls in the desolate spot. Four hours of postmortem surgery failed to reveal the cause of death. Neither was there visible evidence of sexual molestation. ''The murderer in this case was diabolically clever,'' said Dr. Jerry Kearns of St. Elizabeth Hospital. ''He used a method which we are unable to detect. Perhaps he is a person trained in chemistry and with a knowledge of unusual poisons.''

Sheriff Lohman had primary jurisdiction in this case, promising to avoid the same mistakes that plagued the Schuessler investigation. ''We want to avoid duplication of effort and to use men and services as economically as possible,'' he said. This was not the case. Once again the Chicago police and the sheriff bumped heads after Mayor Daley ordered Tim O'Connor to take ''personal charge.'' The police had no clues. A 225-pound truckdriver told of dreaming about the location of the bodies in the same spot at which they were found two weeks later. This only sensationalized a tragedy that might have been resolved through a coordinated effort between the county and city. The investigation was hampered by a lack of highly specialized forensic pathologists who might have been able to provide some insights into the cause of death. Until November 1957, there was only one pathologist assigned to the coroner's office. The City Council eventually appropriated the funds to hire additional doctors, but at the expense of children's lives.[26]

The third agonizing child murder involved a 15-year-old West Side girl named Judith Mae Anderson who disappeared under mysterious circumstances on August 15, 1957, prompting the widest manhunt in Chicago Police history to date. Commissioner O'Connor called up 650 extra men to conduct a block-by-block search of the North and Northwest Sides. Incredibly, 515 of the men were rookie patrol officers fresh out of the Training Academy and supervised by 42 instructors.

The Anderson girl had telephoned her parents at 11:00 PM to say she was on her way home from a friend's house. When she did not return by midnight, the girl's father began a neighborhood search. He waited two days before notifying the Austin District police. It later came out that only 13 officers instead of the normal force of 42 were at the captain's disposal on the night of Judith's disappearance. That unlucky number of policemen were responsible for a five and a half-mile radius, populated by 150,000 residents. A sergeant and three detectives and a patrolman were on duty during the four-to-midnight shift when the girl vanished. The ranks had been depleted due to furloughs, days off, and reassignment of men to districts plagued in recent days by racial tensions.

On August 18 a ransom note arrived at the Anderson home. It read: ''If you want your daughter leave $10,000 at 3419 Jansson Avenue''—a rooming house. The note was taken to the crime lab and analyzed for fingerprints, but it proved to be only a hoax. ''Even if they asked me for a couple hundred dollars I would be lucky if I could raise it,'' said Ralph Anderson, the agonized father. ''There are a lot of cruel people in this world.''

The terrible suspense ended on August 22 when the torso and parts of a girl's body were found in an oil drum bobbing in Montrose Harbor, a dozen miles east of Judith's home. The remaining body parts were found in a second metal drum two days later. Dental charts were used to establish positive identification.

As the police combed in vain the lakefront and empty warehouses fronting the soon-to-be constructed Northwest Expressway for clues, the *Chicago Sun-Times* wondered just what it would take to put a stop to the "jungle terror that will keep children penned up in their homes, keep young people and women off the streets, and band together in restless vigilance against the jungle beasts." The paper stated, "If more policemen are the answer then they must be provided. If the answer is greater utilization of present manpower for more efficient patrol duty, then they must be put into effect."[27]

Sheriff Lohman's men could not get in the way this time. The Anderson murder occurred well within the city limits. But the Chicago Police Department had another wholly independent law enforcement agency to contend with: the 1,000-member Park District police force that enforced curfew and traffic laws, vagrancy statutes, and had primary jurisdiction over criminal investigations in the city parks and boulevards. The white-gloved park police did a competent job during their years of existence, but the agency was bossed by Jack Arvey, Democratic favor-giver who appreciated the political pull it entailed. By 1957 the park police were controlled by William McFetridge, a veteran labor union official from the AFL, who was one of Daley's closest allies. The Chicago Park District divided the scope of responsibility into four geographical regions: Lincoln Park (northern city limits to Oak Street); Central (Oak to 22nd Street South); Washington Park (22nd Street to southern city limits); and Garfield Park (West Side). It goes without saying that the Chicago police were jealous and mistrustful of the "sparrow cops," who were perceived to have an easier time of it—while taking home the same pay as the men who worked Wabash Avenue and other no-man's-lands. For their part, the Park District officers referred to their brethren across the boulevards as "alley cops." Chicago police officers were easily distinguishable by the markings on their uniforms. Park patrolmen also wore blue, but the striping on their trousers set them apart. The natural antagonisms and rivalry between Chicago's two policing agencies was understandable, but not desirable during a murder investigation of the scope of the Anderson case, in which the Lincoln Park detail could rightfully claim primacy. A state senate bill to merge the Park District force into the mainstream of the Chicago police force was up for consideration just three months before the fiendish murder of Judy Anderson. Senator William J. Lynch predicted that the bill would save the city from $3,000,000 to $5,000,000 annually. The tax levy that paid for the salaries of the park police and the maintenance of the street boulevards would have been transferred from the Park District to the city. The usual foot-dragging accompanied senate passage of the bill, and the merger wasn't accomplished until 1959.

Trained police dogs might have aided in the search for clues. Items of clothing were found in a West Side apartment building in which residents had reported hearing shots the night of August 15. The clothing had been burned before police could arrive on the scene. But a trained canine corps was rejected as "impractical" by O'Connor in a letter to the Chicago Crime Commission on December

17, 1957. The advantages of a bloodhound unit had been successfully demonstrated by the London police and the Baltimore Police Department.

Hideous crimes like the Anderson murder were once the province of Scotland Yard, the super-secret crime detection unit created on June 2, 1931, by Captain William Schoemaker and (then) Acting Commissioner John Alcock. The intention was to organize under one roof a group of crack detectives who were free of political interference, and given carte blanche to solve a backlog of unsolved murders. The old verbal "shoulder shrug" that the "deceased came to his death at the hands of person or persons unknown" given by dozens of coroners' juries over the years was to be removed from the police lexicon by virtue of Scotland Yard. The detail was patterned after the famous investigation bureau within the London Metropolitan Police Force that had solved many puzzling crimes through patient search and waiting.

"With the present organization of the force it proves difficult to pursue an investigation for long," Alcock said. "Captain Schoemaker will not be hampered by routine police duties such as clothesline fights, dog licences, and the like. The new branch will never drop a case."

The undercover detail, whose membership remained a mystery to the press, was headquartered at the Canalport Station on the West Side. Over the years the focus of the Scotland Yard detail changed. Originally assigned to provide answers to puzzling murder mysteries, the detail eventually concerned itself with organized crime activity. The veil of secrecy and the code of silence was observed by every police chief from Alcock to O'Connor. Scotland Yard became Chicago's most elusive and controversial police unit in the city's history. Nobody was talking because what went on inside was often in direct violation of a suspect's civil rights. On the second floor of the drab, two-story brick building was a torture chamber in which the rubber hose, the hot light, and the clenched fist often forced a confession from unwilling suspects. Police officers unfamiliar with what went on inside the station would complain that even the supposedly incorruptible Scotland Yard man was willing to release a high-profile gang figure if the price was right.

Scotland Yard continued an old tradition. During the 1890s and early 1900s, the "blue room" was headquartered in the Harrison Street lockup. The inquisitor was Herman Schluetter, and his methods were equally brutal. The casual disregard for human rights was a necessary weapon in a successful war on crime, its proponents would say. "I can only say this much—our men would adopt any disguise, they'd dress like working men to get what they were after, and what they were after was a chain reaction, little links leading to bigger ones," said William Balswick, who commanded the detail from 1940–52. In 1952, when the Gross killing led to a major skakeup in personnel, Lieutenant Joe Morris was placed in charge. He was a high-profile foe of the syndicate, and very acceptable to the Big Nine and the citizens' groups demanding changes.

Morris did commendable work over a four-year period. He dared top suburban crime figures to enter his turf, and when they didn't, Morris went out to theirs.

During one of Tony Accardo's famous Fourth-of-July garden parties at his River Forest compound, Joe Morris disguised himself as an ice cream vendor. As he pushed his cart past the house, Jake "Greasy Thumb" Guzik came out to buy an ice cream bar. Only then was his cover blown. In 1954 Alderman Patrick Petrone tried to order Morris and his men away from the funeral home in which Mrs. Sam Giancana was being waked. The syndicate answered such intrusions with a spray of bullets into the windows of the old Racine Avenue Station one day. Still others filed lawsuits, charging Morris with false arrest and intimidation. The fine work of Scotland Yard in this regard was overshadowed in its final years by allegations of wire tapping and illegal surveillance against political opponents of the mayor. The bugging of Daley's campaign headquarters had everything to do with the decision to disband Scotland Yard on June 15, 1956. Under the decentralization order issued by O'Connor, the remaining 73 members of the squad were reassigned to three outlying district stations—"little detective bureaus"—on the North, South, and West Sides. Lieutenant Morris was placed in charge of detail assigned to the Schuessler-Peterson murders.

Commissioner O'Connor remained noncommital about the demise of Scotland Yard, which he had infused with new talent in 1952. "All we're going to do is straight police work," he said. Virgil Peterson, director of the Chicago Crime Commission, was particularly vocal about the ill-advised plan to close Scotland Yard at a time that many Chicago parents were close to paranoia. Perhaps sensing that this was not a judicious move, O'Connor unveiled a new anti-crime tactical unit known as the "OP Task Force." Under the new plan, 132 patrolmen riding the three-wheel cycles set up command operations in selected districts each day. Similar to the flying squads of former days, the OP Task Force received different assignments each day, depending on the daily crime statistics and the greatest need.[28]

Judging by the report card submitted by Virgil Peterson for the three-year period ending on December 31, 1958, the OP Task Force and other anti-crime programs were a miserable failure. Robbery was up 13.3 percent in 1957, and 20.7 percent over 1956.[29] Major criminal offenses reached an all-time high in 1958 for the third straight year. However, the national increase was only 8 percent. The failure of the courts to dispense proper justice was not a new problem. The 1920s witnessed a tug-of-war between syndicate-controlled judges and the few earnest police officials that were serious about putting criminal offenders away. Although the corruption was not publicized, the decade of the 1950s was notorious for graft in the municipal court system. Justice had broken down because of lenient sentences doled out by judges who allowed criminal cases to drag on for months on end. In April 1959, a major bail-bonding scandal was uncovered in the courts when it was shown that $250,000 in bond forfeitures had been vacated. The central figure in this latest courtroom imbroglio was a shady bondsman named Joseph Perry, who was a friend of Chief Justice Raymond Drymalski. Drymalski was indicted for conspiracy in connection with his role in the ticket-fixing scandal. Half of the vacated bonds were in Perry's favor.

The city had ignored, as it usually did, the commission's annual calls for Perry's removal from the halls of justice.

Chicago was not a well-policed city in the 1950s; in fact, it was a dangerous place to live. The *Tribune* noted with concern that "there are too many political influences in the appointment and promotion of policemen, and these same influences inhibit the department in dealing effectively with the underworld, even if it sought to do so." The tragedy of the murdered children bore this out. In the words of Anton Schuessler Sr., a German immigrant who arrived on these shores to carve a new life for his family in one of Chicago's so-called "crime-free" neighborhoods: "When you get to the point that children can't go to the movies in the afternoon and get home safely, something is wrong with this country"—and city.

Prelude to Disaster: The DeGrazio Case

In the fall of 1959 the "Don" took a little vacation for himself. Anthony "Big Tuna" Accardo had recently turned over the reins of the Chicago syndicate to Sam Giancana, a ferret-faced mobster who was utterly ruthless when provoked. (The same could certainly be said of Accardo, who earned the name "Joe Batters" because of his skill with a baseball bat on the heads of his adversaries.) Tony Accardo's European tour began at Midway Airport on October 13, 1959. Desiring a little company during his junket to England, France, Italy, and Switzerland, Accardo invited a pal from the West Side. He chose someone who had also tagged along on his honeymoon in 1934—Lieutenant Anthony DeGrazio of the Damen Avenue Police Station.

A member of the department since 1922, DeGrazio had been fired by the Civil Service Commission on August 22, 1924, for accepting a bribe. He was reinstated in January of the following year and promoted to sergeant at the same time that Accardo married. The lieutenant was delighted and honored to accept the generous invitation after Hollywood producer Howard J. Beck had judiciously cancelled at the last moment. DeGrazio negotiated with his superiors in order to receive a furlough to accommodate "Big Tuna's" travel itinerary. In Europe, he proved most useful in fending off inquiring reporters and the cameramen who wanted to know how a U.S. police officer could be entrusted with the security and welfare of a well-known mafiosi. Tim O'Connor asked these same questions just as the Accardo party landed in Florence. DeGrazio was suspended for violating Police Rule 309, which read: "No member of the department shall associate or fraternize with persons known to have criminal records."

DeGrazio would answer his critics by saying that had he known about Accardo's bad record, he would have never embarked on the trip. "It is the worst black eye the Police Department ever had!" O'Connor snorted, unaware that he sat atop a volcano that was about to send his department up in smoke and shake the roots of the system. This was the second time within three months that a ranking police officer from North Damen Avenue was reprimanded for a personal association with Accardo, whose reputation as a ganglord was known worldwide. Captain Louis Possehl was relieved of his duties and assigned to Loop traffic after being photographed shaking hands with the "boss." On January 27, 1960, the Civil Service Commission fired DeGrazio from the force after hearing testimony from Virgil Peterson about Accardo's criminal background.[30]

The lieutenant persisted in his fairy tale that Accardo's record was a press invention. "Because I read it in the papers I shall believe it?" he asked. The fraternization of police with leading underworld figures was nothing new. It dated back to the Civil War era, when Cap Hyman and Jack Nelson visited each other's homes. The police and the crooks shared a kind of gallows humor when they encountered each other socially, or by chance. In the 1960s it was not unusual for Joseph "Pops" Panczko, the prolific master burglar, to drop by a North Side police station with a box of doughnuts for the same detectives who had arrested him dozens of times before. Some, but certainly not all policemen treated the profession as a game of cat and mouse. When the distinctions blurred and the police lost sight of their responsibility to the community the end result was a political-criminal tie-up and the inevitable scandal.

Summerdale

Shortly before 9:00 A.M. on October 1, 1958, Ralph Smiley, manager of LeBolt Jewelers at 119 Wabash Avenue, disengaged his burglar alarms. In a few minutes customers would be streaming through the front doors to begin a new business day on "Jeweler's Row" under the elevated tracks in the heart of the Chicago Loop. As the last alarm was turned off, two masked bandits stepped out of the rear storeroom, pointing a pistol at Smiley's head. "You do what we say and you won't get hurt!" one of the robbers said. Meanwhile, his accomplice herded the four salesmen into the washroom and locked the outer door. The men had slipped into the store from an alley fire escape and had hidden on the second floor until Smiley opened the store.

The gang ordered him to open the four safes behind the counter laden with diamonds and jeweled watches. Smiley stood helplessly aside as two men furiously stuffed the loot into a cement sack and two paper bags. The thieves exited the premises and climbed into an illegally parked car on Garland Court, a narrow alley way feeding out onto Randolph Street.

A traffic policeman who noticed the suspicious-looking car moved forward to take a closer look, but the two thieves sped away. The patrolman wrote down the licence plate number, and ran a check on the plates. They were traced to Patrick Groark, Jr., a policeman assigned to the North Side Summerdale Station. When asked to give an accounting of himself, young Groark explained that he had recently been in an accident, and that his car was undergoing repairs at a garage. Someone had removed the plates from the bumper, obviously. The police seemed satisfied with this explanation and did not pursue the matter further.

Earlier that same morning a second gang of burglars emptied out the Western Tire and Auto Supply at 5100 Broadway. Television sets, automobile tires, and auto repair tools were quickly loaded into the backseats of the blue and white getaway cars driven by eight patrolmen assigned to the graveyard shift of the 40th District—Summerdale. That night the police-robbers divided up their loot in the presence of their wives.

Summerdale. It was a scandal of unprecedented magnitude, even in wicked old Chicago. Summerdale jarred a complacent city into reality, illustrating that the rules of the game were no longer valid. Throughout the sonambulent 1950s, the newspapers of Chicago, the ever-vigilant Crime Commission, and various independent civic agencies stated repeatedly that influence peddling, lax discipline, low pay, long hours, and the absence of internal self-regulation was a cancer.

Chicago operated under much the same system as it had in 1895 when Civil Service came into being, and during the visits of Alexander Piper in 1904, and Bruce Smith 27 years later. When the reformers left town, the pendulum swung back when the heat was off.

Summerdale, however, was the one scandal that demanded far-reaching solutions. It would linger until Mayor Daley—triumphant with each new gleaming superhighway he opened up, a White Sox pennant, and a massive civic works project that bulldozed miles of slum housing—was forced to deal with it. But not even Daley could adequately foresee the changes wrought by a smirking 23-year-old "yegg" out of Senn High.

His name was Richard Morrison, and he committed his first theft at the age of 15. Dickie Morrison's first arrest was recorded on May 6, 1953, when he was sentenced to ten days in the County Jail for possessing burglar's tools. In the next two years his record showed a dozen "pick-ups" as a burglary suspect. In December 1955, he took his act on the road, serving nine months for a burglary in Los Angeles and 30 days for prowling the street of his favorite resort town west of the Mississippi—Las Vegas, Nevada.

Morrison slipped back into town in 1957 and was promptly arrested on a charge of petty larceny. When he was released, the glib cat burglar vowed to go straight. He took a job delivering pizzas for Wesley's at 1116 Bryn Mawr Avenue. Things were going well for Morrison. He looked forward to his impending wedding and was leaving his burglar tools at home. The Summerdale police, though, were hassling him and the other pizza drivers who attempted to park their cars outside the building during rush hour. The police were issuing so many parking tickets that Wesley decided to pay them off, if he could. He told them to come in and eat free—a common practice of many wise restaurant and coffeeshop owners in Chicago. At first the privilege was granted only to the sergeant of the district and the men assigned to patrol the Bryn Mawr Avenue vicinity. But soon the word got out in the station house, and Morrison found himself delivering hot pizzas directly to the 40th District.

It was a natural arrangement and it made good sense. Morrison was a neighborhood boy who could josh with the 40th District police. He grew up with many of them, shooting marbles and playing baseball on the cinder playlot of Swift School. Officer Sol Karras and his pretty blonde wife Gail continued their friendship with Morrison long past grammar school. Morrison was a frequent dinner guest at their home on Ardmore Avenue, and he often brought along expensive gifts, like fine damask draperies. Now, however, the stakes of the game suddenly changed. One day as Morrison was walking down Berwyn Avenue, Officer Frank Feraci, 42, bumped into him in front of a liquor store. ''Well, if it isn't the little burglar Richie,'' he said in a condescending manner. The smell of booze was unmistakable. Morrison nervously asked how things were going at home. ''Well, they would be a little better if you would cut us guys in on some of your jobs,'' he said. ''You know, Al Karras and some of the other fellows, and we'll go along with the show. After all, we like nice things too.''[31]

Patrolman Allan Brinn, a two-year veteran, desperately wanted to own a deluxe set of golf clubs, but it was a luxury he could not afford. Morrison went off one night on a fool's errand to find Brinn's clubs. By chance he found a similar set in a parked car in neighboring Evanston, a suburb just a few miles north of Summerdale. Before he could lift them out of the back seat, an Evanston cop appeared. Bullets whizzed by Morrison's head as he made it back to Chicago, but he was apprehended a few hours later. ''I figured as long as the clubs were for a cop . . . I would accept their offer and start doing burglaries with them, so I could get the money to beat the case,'' he claimed.

Freed on bond Morrison went back to Feraci and the two Karras brothers, agreeing to cut them in on his burglary operation. He was resigned to his lot in life. After all, once a thief. . . .

At 22, Morrison was one of Chicago's cleverest burglars. He had completed his apprenticeship by posing as a buyer of industrial safes and vaults in order to learn the locations of tumblers, the thickness of the steel, and the particular vulnerabilities of the strong boxes. Richie Morrison carried with him armor-piercing ammunition capable of blowing the locks off the most resilient safes. With a rope ladder he could easily gain after-hours entry through the ventilation or skylights. Armed with the finest tools available in the trade, Morrison was a craftsman not likely to be caught.

And so, each night at 1:00 AM while the North Side slept, seven of the eight Summerdale policemen—Feraci, Al and Sol Karras, Allan Brinn, Henry Mulea, Patrick Groark, Jr., and Alan Clements—met with Morrison outside Wesley's to plan the next day's job. *They*, not Morrison, picked out the places to burgle, based on a current need. At World Series time the police required portable TVs. With a hint of snow in the air, they told Morrison to find them some antifreeze for their radiators.

What Morrison did not fully comprehend was that his ''pals'' were making a monkey out of him. North Side detectives began picking him up for ''ques-

Figure 13

Long Arm of the Law

A view of the Summerdale scandal, by Cliff Birklund, *Chicago American*, January 21, 1960. (Đeckert/Birklund)

tioning'' on jobs that Faraci, Karras, and company has masterminded. How could they know? The Summerdale Eight were secretly tipping off their buddies in D–3 (Detective Bureau North Side). It was a way of cutting them in on a good thing, and an even better way of ensuring Morrison's continuing cooperation. The hush money extorted from Morrison by D–3 was then in turn split with the original eight, the denouement of a twisted sequence of events.

In determining the manner in which the burglaries were to be carried out, the police acquiesced to Morrison's superior judgments. There were three marked squad cars circling the area at all times (120, 207, 245), while Morrison and Robert Crilly, a former employee of Western Tire & Auto Supply, opened the store. During the Western Auto heist, he ordered the four police vehicles to remain two blocks away from the store, but to be ready to come to their assistance with ''flashing reds'' in the event of trouble. Morrison and Crilly entered the store at 3:00 AM. First, they located an expensive Browning Automatic shotgun and a set of tools for Sol Karras. Since Karras was assigned to the Rogers Park Station at the time, the implication seemed clear enough. Karras had tacitly agreed to arrange for the burglars to expand their base of operations a few blocks northward into his district, if Morrison could deliver the goods without a hitch.

Under the cover of darkness, and protected by the patrol cars cruising the neighborhood on the look-out for other squadrons, Morrison loaded up his car and prepared to make a second haul when Allan Brinn sped by on a three-wheeler, scaring them half to death. Richie gave him a severe dressing down for that one.

Western Tire & Auto was hit several times, according to the owners. ''Those guys broke into this store four times and cleaned it out—guns, TV sets, appliances, everything that wasn't nailed down,'' the manager said. ''Then, I'll be a son of a bitch if one of them didn't come around at Christmas time and ask for a handout.'' The loot from this first big score was divided up at the home of Sol Karras. Encouraged by the ease with which they gained entrance to the tire and supply store, additional jobs were planned. A furniture store was burgled on October 9. The location had been ''scouted'' by the Karras twins and Officer Faraci beforehand. Sometimes the personal greed of the eight officers overrided their loyalty to each other. On March 29, 1959, Morrison broke into a tavern on Sheridan Road, carrying out 15 cases of liquor and a set of carpentry tools for the personal use of Al Clements, former owner of the bar.

With the threat of snow hanging in the air, and the January skies a leaden gray, Al Karras dreamed of going sailing on Lake Michigan, but he needed an outboard motor for his boat. Morrison was told to evaluate the Anderson Marine Sports Supply Store on Broadway and report back to the gang. Morrison hesitated. He knew it was a risky venture. Too many all-night saloons in the area, he said. Karras grumbled about it but decided to hold off. With the coming of warm weather he, thought long and hard about that lake cruise. ''Listen, Dick,'' he said. ''You have been stalling on Marine Supplies and spring is here now, and tonight you're going to open that place up for us.''

Morrison agreed to smash the windows but that was all: "You'll have to get the motors and whatever else you guys want because I don't want to be in that place with the front window broken out." Morrison and Floyd Wilde threw the bricks, and lingered in the background while Karras and Pat Groark—whose father commanded the Cragin District until his death in 1954—carried the outboard through the shattered display window.

On another occasion Richie Morrison acted as the lookout while two officers looted a store singlehandedly. With each new robbery the police gained new courage, and soon they had thrown all caution to the winds. Morrison drove around the neighborhood in their squad car listening to the police radio for a possible alarm about the burglary then in progress. The police even volunteered to provide Morrison with a uniform and star, but he declined. Too much trouble maintaining the upkeep, he said.

The Summerdale police kept Morrison on a short leash. They attempted to restrict his movements and didn't like it very much when he went off on a short vacation to Las Vegas. When Morrison returned he was told that his colleagues had pulled a few jobs on their own. Things were starting to get crazy. The eight policemen no longer seemed to care about getting caught or the likely consequences of their actions. All that mattered was the next night's action.

Their greed almost got the best of them one night. After breaking into a Devon Avenue shoe store and taking out $14,000 in discounted footwear, they drove to a neighborhood tavern where they hoped the patrons would purchase them for $2 a pair. The driver—a policeman, according to Morrison—was stone drunk. He ran a light at Broadway and Bryn Mawr and drove the car down the sidewalk. "They all chewed him out for doing that stunt," Morrison said. "Everybody around the tavern was talking about him selling the shoes. He was a real nut. He was wild. He wanted to do anything for money."[32]

It ended abruptly on July 30, 1959, when Richie Morrison was arrested in a North Side flat by some honest burglary detectives apparently unaware of his operations. It was the second time in less than four months that the "master burglar," as he liked to think of himself, had been taken into custody. On March 3, U.S. Secret Service agents broke up a counterfeiting ring in which Morrison figured prominently. At the time his eight friends scolded him for carelessness. Why had he not printed $20 bills instead of hundreds? Even a sucker knew that $100 bills were tough to pass in Chicago.

After this latest arrest, the burglars hesitated. Inside the County Jail, Morrison had time to ponder his fate. Where were his friends now? Protecting their careers, of course. Morrison was not going to be anybody's martyr. If he was to go down the hole, there was no reason why he couldn't take a few of the Summerdale boys with him. As the prospects of a lengthy prison sentenced loomed larger, he sent word to State's Attorney Benjamin Adamowski that he had sensitive information to share. Chief Investigator Paul Newey, who held down Dan Gilbert's old job, went to the jail to see what this was all about. Morrison said he would cut a deal. In exchange for a reduced sentence he would tell the story of eight, maybe more, crooked cops forming their own burglary ring. At first Newey refused any deal. Adamowski wanted to put Morrison away for twenty years, and that was that.

Talks continued with the public defender and the state's attorney's man, until Morrison agreed to be placed in a secret witness program. At first the "babbling burglar" provided two or three names of crooked policemen, but not enough to launch a full-scale investigation. But as the full scope of the operation slowly came out, Adamowski realized he was dealing with much more than a common thief trying to beat a rap.

An election was coming up. It was inevitable that Adamowski, a political maverick who parted the waves with Daley and the Democrats years earlier, would make this a political issue. In Springfield Governor William Stratton delighted in each new revelation coming out of the state's attorney's office in Chicago. What a chance to discredit Daley, who had run the Republican governor through the gauntlet in 1956 after State Auditor Orville Hodge embezzled $1,576,344 through bogus warrants.[33] The sagging fortunes of the Republican Party could soar in 1960 if Adamowski played his hand right. The carrot they dangled in front of Morrison was the state's promise to drop 20 charges of burglary in return for his full cooperation in court. The diminutive thief readily agreed. His confession filled 77 pages.

Ben Adamowski established a command post at the swant Union League Club and at the Hilton Hotel. Here he mapped out a plan of attack. The danger was that the eight lowly patrolmen might be tipped off; even worse, other burglary rings yet to be detected might be driven underground. The prospect of the scandal being manipulated by Daley and his commissioner of investigation was of even greater concern to Adamowski. The state's attorney and his assistants Paul Newey and Frank Ferlic had been judicious in choosing with whom they shared their secret. But in his zeal to bring this scandal to the forefront of his anti-Daley crusade, Adamowski crossed the line of propriety. He hired two renegade burglary detectives to play a high-priced game of cat and mouse with city commissioner of investigations, Irwin N. Cohen. The detectives, Richard B. Cain, and Gerald Shallow, were paid $1,750 through two banks, one in Michigan and the other in Chicago, where Adamowski served on the board of directors. Cain rented an office next door to Cohen's at 64 East Lake Street. The office was used as a stakeout from which the two cops (on vacation furlough at the time) took secret photographs of persons leaving and entering the building. They hoped to gain after-hours admittance and plant a wireless tap in order to record Cohen's private discussions, but the building's janitor refused to cooperate. The janitor said he was "sick and tired" of seeing them around. The surveillance was conducted in January, and revealed in April when Detective Chief James McMahon and Deputy Commissioner Albert Anderson made their findings public.

Cain was suspended for his transgressions, but it was soon reported that these same two men acting in concert had shaken down a gray-haired 68-year-old prostitute named Grace Van Scoyk, whose $30,000 life savings were removed from a bank safety deposit box while she was in the lock-up on a soliciting charge. Acting on the advice of an attorney provided by the ever-obliging Cain, Mrs. Van Scoyk turned over the keys to the box. Because of a tax lien on the money she did not discover that the money was gone for a year. State's Attorney Adamowski refused to discuss this, or the covert surveillance that was conducted at his behest. Richard Cain went on to accept an appointment with Cook County Sheriff Richard Ogilvie in 1962 before linking up with the Chicago mob on a permanent retainer basis. Before he was gunned down in a cheap Northwest Side grill in 1973, Cain served as Sam Giancana's business advisor, golfing partner, and bag man.

On January 15, 1960, a hand-picked detachment of crack detectives were given sealed orders that were not to be opened until they were on the streets. The ultra-secret orders directed them to the homes of the eight Summerdale burglars where they were to search the premises thoroughly for stolen goods. The warrants were issued at 10:30 PM, when all the men were likely to be home with their families.

By 4:00 AM the next morning the raids were complete. Stolen merchandise was removed from the homes of the Karras twins, Brinn, Feraci, and Mulea. At the home of Peter Beeftink, fondly described as a "stupid policeman" by his own lawyer, the state's attorney's men removed a brocaded chair. It was the only item they could find in the house, but enough to brand him a cop-thief. Beeftink placed a frantic call to a retired policeman living in Florida, with whom he had worked in years past. "Bill, I am in trouble," he whispered. "Please do me a favor. They raided my house and they found a chair. I was so nervous and excited that I said I bought it from you." It was too late. Supervising Police Captain Jerome Looney had already talked to retired officer Bill Mandell and had learned that he knew nothing about any chair. Morrison later testified that the Beeftink was deliberately left out of any planning sessions and had merely helped himself to a free chair by virtue of showing up on the night the gang burglarized the E. J. Self Furniture Store. Nothing was found at the home of Pat Groark.

Four truckloads of stolen items were impounded by the state's attorney. The Summerdale burglars were driven to the Union League Club for questioning. Brinn, Faraci, Clements and the Karras Brothers admitted to receiving stolen property but denied taking part in the burglaries. The other three denied any knowledge or involvement. At detective headquarters the men pushed their way past a swarm of newspaper photographers. Their faces and heads were concealed by trench coats—certainly a riveting moment in Chicago police history.

"Instead of police protection, people in that North Side area were getting police participation in crime. If I were police commissioner, I think I would be concerned that similar situations might exist in other police districts," Adamowski said hopefully.

The politicians were not the only ones who were stunned by the Summerdale

Table 8
The Summerdale Police

Name	Age	Residence	District Assigned	Year of Appointment	Date of Suspension
Peter Beeftink	50	Chicago	Summerdale	1942	3/30/60
Allan Brinn	30	Skokie	Summerdale	1956	4/01/60
Alan Clements	29	Chicago	Summerdale	1951	1/20/60
Frank Faraci	43	Skokie	Albany Park	1951	4/01/60*
Patrick Groark, Jr.	28	Chicago	Summerdale	1956	5/09/60*
Alex Karras	26	Chicago	Summerdale	1955	4/01/60
Sol Karras	26	Chicago	Town Hall	1955	4/01/60
Henry T. Mulea	45	Chicago	Summerdale	1947	4/01/60

* This was not the first suspension for these two men. On April 23, 1959, Faraci and Groark were reprimanded and suspended for surrendering their weapons to a 16-year-old robber.

arrests. The omnipotent outfit recoiled in horror at the thought of their hand-picked police captains being shifted out of politically sensitive districts. Corrupt alliances between the mobsters and the police that were years in the making were shattered overnight as the Mafia "old-guard" pressured their contacts in the 1st Ward—Pat Marcy and John D'Arco—to try to influence Mayor Daley to maintain the status quo. The Chicago FBI office learned through their various wire taps that Richie Morrison's aunt, Billie Jean, dated Murray "the Camel" Humphreys. Once when Morrison was arrested for car theft on the North Side, Humphreys brought in syndicate mouthpiece Mike Brodkin to get the kid off the hook. In desperation Humphreys tried to locate Billie Jean in order to give her $5,000 in hush money to silence her talkative nephew. The scheme failed only because Agent William Roemer and his men alerted Adamowski to the present danger. Morrison went right on talking. Aunt Billie Jean conveniently disappeared.

Toward a New Professionalism

On the heels of Morrison's confession were new disclosures of police impropriety across the city. The scandal was spreading like a prairie fire out of control. Mayor Daley cut short a trip to Florida to assess the damage of his administration and to placate a jittery city. "Naturally, we are disappointed to see anything like this happen," he said. "We have 10,000 men and the majority are doing a good job. We are asking these men to help in finding those who are guilty of irregularities." Privately, the mayor was stunned beyond comprehension. Journalist Len O'Connor reported that Daley was "hitting the sauce" in the basement of his South Side home.[34]

Meanwhile, three more policemen connected to the Summerdale burglars were arrested on January 18 and charged with extorting $1,200 from Richard Morrison. Officers George Raymond, Robert Ambrose, and Jackson Whelen had switched crucial evidence in a pending case against Morrison in order to influence an acquittal. The indictments against these three men were quashed on October 6, 1960, because a clerk-typist had inserted a comma instead of a semicolon in the documents.

On the South Side, Patrolman Charles Jamieson, 28, was suspended after he was arrested on charges of robbery and abduction. Officer Jamieson of the Wabash Avenue Station, was identified as one of three policemen who knocked on the door of Alphonso Nichols's home. Jamieson demanded $513 from Nichols after failing to locate a cache of drugs he believed to be hidden on the premises. The patrolman was discharged from the force on March 22, 1961, but was found not guilty by Judge Daniel Covelli on July 17, 1960. The decisions of the courts in these matters were construed as classic Chicago cronyism between a highly suspect judicial system, the mob, and a corrupt police force.

Summerdale was not only a blow to the fragile integrity of the city, but to local businesses, the cornerstone of neighborhood economy, as well. Insurance companies like West Bend Mutual, which had served the needs of small businessmen in the Rogers Park-Edgewater neighborhoods for nearly 45 years, suffered a 288 percent loss in ratio to the premiums received. Company spokesmen said they would stop writing open stock burglary insurance to retailers along the Clark, Sheridan Broadway, and Ashland business corridors. The district had shown a 48 percent increase in burglary during the first ten months of 1959, as compared with a comparable period in 1958.

Someone had to assume responsibility for this fiasco. Tim O'Connor, by virtue of his position, became the scandal scapegoat. Mayor Daley had stood behind his "inherited" commissioner for the better part of five years but this time he issued a terse "no comment" to questions about O'Connor's status. "Somebody has to be the sucker and it could be me," O'Connor said. Daley stalled on the fate of Commissioner Tim for nine days while he conferred with top city officials to outline a plan of action.

O'Connor caved in to Ben Adamowski's demand that polygraph experts be brought in from out of state to administer lie detector tests to 130 police officers at the Summerdale Station. Captain Herman Dorf considered this a personal affront to his integrity. He submitted his resignation 17 months short of reaching the compulsory retirement age of 63. The Summerdale commander said he was moving to California and would take no part in the investigation.

Pleading ill health, Tim O'Connor ended his 31-year career with the police department on January 23. "This task will call for a tremendous additional effort on the part of the commissioner. My physician informs me that this additional effort combined with the burden of administering the Police Department is beyond my physical condition," he stated in his resignation letter to the mayor. O'Connor had only four interests in life: his family, athletics, good police work, and reading history. Daley lauded O'Connor's fine record, but in the same breath let it be known where he believed the ultimate fault rested: "Tim was always telling me how he went home at night and watched TV instead of running around getting into trouble. I should have asked him why he wasn't running around checking on his policemen at night instead of sitting home watching TV."

There were few who doubted O'Connor's personal honesty—or Mayor Daley's intention to bring in an outsider to silence the diatribes reverberating around the State House in Springfield, where Governor Stratton had turned up the heat. Stratton had threatened to step in and take personal charge of the situation, whatever that meant. "Cheap politics!" Daley snorted, as he dredged up the carcass of the four-year-old Hodge scandal.[35]

Kyran Vincent Phelan was appointed acting commissioner, with the clear understanding that the assignment was a temporary one. Phelan had risen steadily through the ranks and had been a fixture in the detectives' bureau since 1922, and had the blessing of the mob. Daley was perceptive enough to realize there had been far too many "fixtures" and chair warmers in this department over the years. For one of those rare occasions in his mayoral career, Richard Daley looked past the inner circle of ward committee men and Democratic payrollers

Figure 14

ALI BABA AND THE FORTY THIEVES—ACT I

In league with the criminal classes, 1960s. A persistent theme of newspaper cartoonists throughout the twentieth century. (Deckert/Orr)

to name a bipartisan committee that would select the next commissioner, someone who would be given broad administrative powers to enact reform.

Committee appointments were announced the same day Mayor Daley accepted O'Connor's resignation. There were few people in the professional community who quarreled with Daley's committee selections. Virgil Peterson of the Chicago Crime Commission would finally be given his say in policymaking at the highest level. Peterson was a veteran crimefighter, a recognized expert on the inner workings of the national crime syndicate. He was an FBI agent for the 12 years prior to his appointment as director of the Crime Commission in 1942.

Serving with Peterson on the committee were Paul W. Goodrich, president of the Chicago Association of Commerce; Franklin W. Kreml, head of the Northwestern University Transportation Center, and author of the 1947 traffic plan enthusiastically adopted by John Prendergast; William L. McFetridge, vice president of the Chicago Federation of Labor, and Daley's point man on all civic projects of note; and Orlando W. Wilson, dean of criminology and professor of police administration at the University of California. Wilson was the unanimous choice to chair the selection process. He was assured by Daley that there would be "no restrictions on the activity or scope of the committee."

The selection of O. W. Wilson was a real coup for the city. Daley knew very little about this tall, angular Norwegian from Veblen, South Dakota. He had probably never heard of Wilson's book *Police Administration*, a standard text in university curricula for aspiring criminologists since 1950. Wilson came highly recommended by Fred Hoehler, superintendent of the Chicago House of Correction. Hoehler was well familiar with his track record, and remained an enthusiastic supporter when the two men were thrown together during police board deliberations.

Wilson believed that organization and tight discipline were the hallmarks of a successful police force. The corruptive arrangements that had existed between the police and the underworld could be circumvented by instilling a new professionalism through the ranks. Dean Wilson was a proponent of advanced technology. He advocated the adoption of up-to-date equipment, improved mobile communications, and the implementation of community out-reach programs to encourage a dialogue between the police and their constituents.

O. W. Wilson blended scholarship with a hard-nosed approach to law enforcement. To these ends he was a disciplinarian who believed that the police executive should be more than a figurehead, a situation that had existed far too long in Chicago.

Described by a Wichita mayor as "too damned efficient," Orlando Wilson was a dynamic force in U.S. law enforcement. He was both reformer and martinet, an advocate of military discipline but sympathetic to the needs of his men and the community at large. He believed that those men who demonstrated efficiency and honesty should be advanced according to merit, not political pull. This was the bane of the Chicago Police Department, and Wilson gave it immediate attention. Police work was a lifetime avocation for Wilson, dating back to 1921 when he applied for the position of patrolman in the Berkeley, California Police Department. The department was administered by August Vollmer, who took the young college student under his wing.

Because of the paternal interest shown by Vollmer, Wilson abandoned his plans to become a civil engineer in order to dedicate himself to law enforcement. Largely through the efforts of his benefactor, young Orlando secured a position as chief of police in Fullerton, California. The experience he gained in the next three years was valuable, but the intransigent political administration was not ready to allow an upstart with high ideas to damage the infrastructure. In 1928,

Wilson moved on to his next assignment: Wichita, Kansas. At a time that most U.S. police departments suffered through unchecked Prohibition lawlessness, O. W. Wilson ran his city in a capable, forthright manner. He served as Wichita police chief until 1939, when he returned to the University of California to provide direction to the fledgling School of Criminology, serving as its dean until he got the call from Mayor Daley in 1960.[36]

What made Wilson attractive to Daley, Hoehler, and the members of the Chicago Crime Commission were the innovative reforms he had introduced to police work. Wilson authored a complete law enforcement code of ethics, sorely needed as big-city police departments evolved from their nineteenth-century machine roots.

Wilson appointed the first woman police captain. He initiated psychological profile testing during the recruitment and hiring stage. The first college cadet program was pioneered under his auspices, a recognition that if a modern police department was to maintain professional standards, it was of primary importance that university men with fresh perspectives be provided with career opportunities. Police work since the mid-nineteenth century was a blue-collar occupation. The salary structure was low, and the rewards so meager that talented young professionals naturally gravitated toward the private sector.

Wilson came to Chicago knowing that he would be given the opportunity to implement his ideas and reform the most poorly run, bankrupt police department in the nation. It is unlikely that the dean would abandon his tenure merely to chair a three-month committee to "find the best man in the nation," to head up the Chicago Police Department. O. W. Wilson was that man, but he had to go along with the facade, and screen worthwhile applicants before the coronation could take place.

The screening committee met for 28 days behind the closed doors of the staid University Club. At its first meeting, the members established three criteria to guide the selection process:[37]

Integrity: The police head must not only be incorruptible, but he must also be a man of intellectual honesty and moral courage.

Professional Skill: The effective organization, management, direction, and control of a large police force requires a high degree of professional knowledge and skill most likely to be found in a career policeman but which might also be found in persons from other fields. Included in this category are qualities of leadership and command, the ability to win both police and public confidence, skill in organizing community efforts, and ability to gain the support and organize the cooperation of public officials and agencies.

The Test of Experience: The present situation in Chicago is such that the committee felt impelled to apply the criterion of demonstration of on-the-job performance, and top administrative capacity to insure ability to deal effectively with the problems of a Police Department. This capacity is most convincingly demonstrated when the person has held a top police command position.[38]

The committee interviewed 53 applicants, of which 24 were from within the department. Too often the stature of the candidate did not match up to the accomplishments listed on the resume. According to Wilson's biographer, William J. Bopp, the committee selected five finalists whose names were to be submitted to the mayor for consideration. "Can we go to the mayor with this guy and really say he has all we need?" asked one member. William McFetridge broke the silence by suggesting that the rightful commissioner sat in the room, in the person of O. W. Wilson or Franklin Kreml.

Kreml immediately withdrew his name from consideration, leaving Wilson as the only viable candidate. Modesty prevented the taciturn criminologist from accepting their nomination right away. He had to be persuaded by Kreml and McFetridge, who had scripted this likely scenario after conferences with Daley. Wilson continued to play hard ball. He demanded a three-year contract at $30,000 per annum, and political independence from the mayor. He proposed the creation of a police board composed of these same committee members to insulate his office from the pressures of aldermen, office seekers, and special-interest groups. Two days later, February 22, Mayor Daley announced to the city that O. W. Wilson had accepted the committee's nomination to head up the Police Department. The full City Council approved his selection on March 2, amidst deafening silence from the press and the police. Certainly the veteran officers were bitter and resentful. Here was another "expert," an "outsider." Wilson would deal with this problem in good time. Recalling these hectic days four years later, Wilson recalled his decision to accept.

The challenge of Chicago, however, was too much for me. This was an opportunity to demonstrate to the world the simple truth of the police theories that I had spent a lifetime teaching and talking about. In my younger years I had been Chief of Police in Wichita, Kansas and had instituted many new and progressive ideas. But this was Chicago, our second largest city—and by reports one of the wickedest. Would the ideas that had worked in Wichita work in Chicago? I felt I owed it to the whole police profession to demonstrate that they would.[39]

Wilsonian Ideals

The Chicago Police Department at long last was ready to reform. It began and ended with the silver-haired Wilson, who summoned 5,000 policemen to the International Amphitheater during his first week in office to set forth his plans of reorganization. Wilson encouraged an ongoing dialogue with the men, either through face-to-face meetings or by way of personal memoranda, which he called "PAX 501."

The police in attendance that day greeted him with a mixture of polite applause and catcalls from the rear of the auditorium. The selection of Wilson was not a popular one. He was taking the place of an Irish Catholic considered "one of the boys." O'Connor had been cashiered out of the ranks because the old way of doing things was no longer tolerable to the city or the state government. The men neither understood this logic nor appreciated it. It was an inauspicious start, but Wilson was not out to win a popularity contest—just their respect. It would come, in time.

The Chicago Police Department was in a precarious state of disarray. The station houses were run-down, grimy, and short of supplies. Tim O'Connor's yearly austerity program ensured that the department came in under budget, which pleased the mayor, but required desk sergeants to purchase small items like carbon paper out of their own pockets. There were just two radio frequencies serving the city's three million inhabitants. It was not uncommon for a citizen to wait three hours for a policeman to arrive in response to a distress call. At times it was necessary for operators at the central complaint room to call the district station with outside telephone lines. Under the direction of Ray Ashworth, who had been brought to Chicago from Wichita to oversee the reorganization, the communications center was upgraded and expanded.

The city was split into eight radio communications zones, with calls and complaints routed to the appropriate dispatcher representing the district. The new communications center was housed in the second floor at 1121 South State, the old headquarters building that had not undergone any significant renovations since it was built in 1928. Under Wilson's direction the "Old Central" was modernized and expanded by some 87,900 square feet. Computer systems and data processing operations were installed in the new building to allow for easy storage and quick recall of sensitive data.[40] The new comprehensive record-keeping system, which eliminated reams of paper files, was the brainchild of Everett Leonard, an FBI man hired by Wilson. The remodeled police head-quarters was dedicated on March 5, 1963, at a cost of $39,801.12. Thirty-seven percent of the construction costs were defrayed by savings in 1961 operating funds. Eleventh and State, as it came to be known to Chicagoans, represented state-of-the-art technology.

The chain of command was arranged in pyramidal form, with Wilson at the top. The chief reduced the number of police districts from 38 to 21, which broke up the borders of ward districts and curtailed and dictatorial powers of the bosses. Wilson created three important bureaus: (1) the Bureau of Staff Services, which reflected his commitment to tightening up organizational lines. The Crime Laboratory, Records and Communications, Training, Automotive Maintenance, Radio Maintenance, and a new division of Central Services grouped together various custodial and operational functions. Pierce J. Fleming was appointed deputy superintendent of staff services; (2) the Bureau of Field Services, comprised of the Patrol, Traffic, Detective, Criminal Intelligence, and the Youth Divisions was given over to Captain James Conlisk, one of the youngest members of the "ancien regime." The appointment of Conlisk to head up the largest and most important bureau was no doubt a concession to Daley, who was an intimate friend of James B. Conlisk, Sr., who had served for years as the administrative assistant to five previous police commissioners. The elder Conlisk was fired by Wilson while the son was promoted to deputy commissioner at the same time. It was an interesting piece of political maneuvering by Wilson, who was gaining a baptism by fire to Chicago-style politics; (3) the Bureau of Inspectional Services. At the heart of the reform effort was the formation of the Bureau of Inspectional Services. It was composed of four divisions—Internal Investigations, Inspection, Intelligence, and Organized Crime—all vital to the proper functioning of the department. Captain Joseph Morris, who had drifted in limbo after the dissolution of Scotland Yard, was appointed by Wilson because of his reputation for integrity. Morris was one of the applicants who had been interviewed by the search committee, but had been found wanting. This did not preclude him from further advancement, and Wilson rewarded his fine record without the slightest reservations. The four specialized units were placed under his command, and given their own separate facility in Washington Park on the South Side. Named to head up the Internal Investigations Division (IID) was Captain William Szarat, who, like Morris, held a rank that was exempt from Civil Service protection. This meant that Wilson exercised firm control over their day-to-day activities.[41]

The IID was charged with ferreting out corruption on all levels. For years the politicians and the governing body of police had fended off any attempts to "Piperize" the department with "spys" in any way, shape, or form. Yet without such an agency, systematized graft and the disgraceful Summerdale burglary ring were allowed to flourish. The absence of internal self-regulation resulted in a breakdown of discipline. In the late nineteenth century, the "drillmaster" was responsible for imbuing the military ideal through constant inspection, cadence marching, and target shooting. By 1960 this position had long since been abolished. The IID and the Inspection Division, which reported to Wilson on the physical conditions of police property, took the place of the drillmaster and the inspector positions of past years. Wilson's mandate to these agencies was simple: end corruption by whatever means necessary. IID men posed as traffic violaters in order to catch officers soliciting bribes. They dressed in the garb of Madison Street bums and congregated with the winos and panhandlers in front of the 25-cent hotels awaiting the inevitable shakedown from the policeman on the beat—rousting "piss bums"—a favorite Skid Row sport for many years. Joe Morris deployed his men to the city jails to make sure booking procedures were handled correctly. Where incidents of corruption or job malfeasance were detected, the offender was brought before the board for a hearing. If there was a measure of doubt, the accused would be asked to submit to a polygraph test. Those who refused were summarily dismissed. Detecting police misconduct was one phase of the job. It was also the responsibility of this agency to clear innocent officers wrongfully accused of corruption. The progress made by the IID in the span of a few short months was heartening. By the end of 1960, the unit had gone a long way toward repairing the image of the police in the public's eyes.

The Organized Crime Unit was assigned to Captain James Riordan, formerly of the Monroe Station. Riordan reported to Morris and Wilson about vice arrests and syndicate operations in the cabaret districts. Applications for liquor licences were cleared through Riordan's office, which closed off an important source of graft for the politicians and the syndicate. "In all but small departments," Wilson wrote, "the chief finds it difficult to ascertain vice and organized crime conditions in his community and the integrity of his force except by using an intelligence unit working directly under him."

It was found that between 1948 and 1960, no officer had been permitted to take the Civil Service promotional exams. There was a good reason for this, because after every major exam that was administered there was an inevitable wave of lawsuits filed by disappointed office seekers. Sensitive and fearful about this, the commission simply avoided the bother. Wilson badgered the commission relentlessly in the first few months of his regime.[42] Finally the Civil Service Commission caved in, and held the first major exam in over a decade. On September 29, 1960, 137 patrolmen were promoted to sergeant. Henceforth, exams would be held every two years, thus providing an opportunity for younger, talented men to advance without the interference of politics.

Among the 137 new sergeants were 50 black men. Wilson discovered to his dismay that for years the Civil Service Commission had rejected the applications of black males to the force, because of a standing rule against flat feet. O. W. Wilson urged that the Commission relax this rule. By 1962 there 1,200 black patrolmen on the force, an increase of 500 in just two years. Race relations was not a concern to big-city police departments until the mid–1950s. The landmark Supreme Court decision *Brown v. the Board of Education* (1954) desegregated public schools in the United States. This sweeping decision, coupled with an exodus of U.S. blacks into the cities of the industrial north, forced many police departments to reexamine their standards of community relations. The old maxim that the police were there to protect whites and isolate blacks changed in the wake of the Brown decision. The St. Louis Police Department pioneered a new thinking in race relations through the formation of a special unit organized to consider the matter.[43] Such a unit was never adopted in Chicago, but Wilson was the first commissioner to champion the cause of civil rights within the department. In the mid–1960s, he authorized the human relations section to work with black leaders in the hope of improving racial tensions in Chicago. In March 1965, Wilson appointed Sergeant Samuel Nolan to serve as liaison. Nolan was one of group of young black men coming of age during the Wilson years—men like Renault Robinson, who founded the Afro-American Patrolman's League in the 1970s to further the aims of the black community, and Fred Rice, who would eventually become the city's first Afro-American superintendent.

Wilson was a dynamic force of social change, impervious to the criticisms of the old guard, and the coterie of newspaper reporters who often found him surly and uncommunicative. It was a small price to pay for the tasks that had to be performed. He instituted a policy of shifting district commanders whenever he thought their job performance was lacking. He advocated tighter gun control laws, and sought permission to wiretap leading mob figures. A stop-and-frisk measure that Wilson had advocated was pushed through the Illinois General Assembly, only to be vetoed by Governor Otto Kerner. His controversial views on these matters put him at loggerheads with many civil libertarians, but hard-nosed Wilson did not care.

Wilson the academician would greet delegations of criminologists from all over the world who came to Chicago to survey the progress of reform. They would elicit his theories of reform, and he would proudly show them the fruits of his labor: the $1,000,000 communications center, computerized record-keeping, a K–9 Corps inaugurated in 1961, freshly painted squad cars equipped for the first time with blue roof flashers and an oscillating whistle that skeptics likened to a peanut vendor's wagon.

The public paid a high price for reform. The 1960 police budget was $72,000,000. A year later it had swelled to an astronomical $186,000,000. Daley and the politicians grumbled but raised property taxes all the same. Someone had to pay for this, so the costs were passed on to the public. In return, Wilson permitted the citizens of Chicago to view their Police Department at first hand. Throngs of curious spectators observed the impressive communications center and the data processing area through glassed-in partitions. Wilson believed in good public relations, and the 1963 expansion made all this possible.

O. W. Wilson accepted the challenge of Chicago, as he called it, with full assurance from the mayor that he would be immune from political interference. He demonstrated his independence by moving the superintendent's office (the title of commissioner was dropped—again) to Eleventh and State. Indeed, Orlando Wilson had been given extraordinary latitude by Daley, who understood the inherent value of allowing the dean to call the shots. Daley's most vocal critics, who hoped to ride the law and order issue to election victory, were effectively silenced. Governor Stratton and State's Attorney Adamowski were voted out of office in 1960, and in their place loyal machine men Otto Kerner and Daniel Ward stood tall, ready to serve the mayor without reservation.[44]

Richard J. Daley also gained a police board that, after Wilson was gone, would prove to be a very useful political tool. The board was empowered to review and approve police budgets, establish internal rules and regulations, serve as the appellate authority in disciplinary actions, and guide the selection process of future superintendents. The original board was composed of three holdovers from the search committee: McFetridge, Goodrich, and Kreml. Two new mayoral appointees, Morgan Murphy, vice-president of Commonwealth Edison, and Theophilus Mann, a prominent black attorney and member of the Chicago Housing Authority, were approved by the City Council without reservation. With Fred Hoehler acting as secretary pro tem, the mayor had a majority interest. Kreml, the duly elected president of the board, was an independent. Goodrich and Mann straddled the fence, but McFetridge, Murphy, and Hoehler were Daley's men. Interestingly, neither Kreml nor Goodrich were Chicago residents. Ben Adamowski cried foul, and renewed his demands for the state to take control of the Police Department, a proposal that did not get very far in the 1960 legislative session, thanks to the pervasiveness of the Chicago machine in Springfield.

The lone dissenter in the City Council was Alderman Leon Despres of the 5th Ward, who correctly pointed to the inherent flaws in this legislation. First, the mayor, and not the board, would make the final appointment of a superintendent. The police board would make only the nominations. Second, no restriction was placed on the mayor's power to fire a superintendent at will. And third, the police chief was stripped of his powers to supervise and control the force, make and enforce rules, maintain the efficiency rating system, and have custody of stations, buildings, equipment, books, and records.

Only Wilson would be unaffected by these impediments. Only Wilson would be able to hold it all together. He was a "push-button Sherlock Holmes" who transformed one of the worst policing agencies in the nation to one of the best. His achievements were reflected in a declining crime rate and the President's Crime Commission Report, which listed Chicago and New York as the only two U.S. cities to "mobilize" against the threat of mob rule. Wilson instilled pride through the ranks. He all but eliminated petty graft and bribe-taking while removing the "clout" that saw ward committee men dictating to the superintendent who was in and who was out.

In 1960, when he took over the reins of this graft-plagued, ill-begotten police force, 3,000 members of the Chicago Patrolmen's League threatened to picket City Hall demanding his ouster. By the time he retired seven years later there were few who doubted the wisdom of Wilson's many reforms. The *Kansas City Star* credited him with taking a "rinky-dink police department—sloppy, corrupt, and clownish and fashioned it into a respected major leaguer."[45] If there was any fault to Wilson's logic, it was perhaps an underestimation of his own abilities. When he walked away from the job in 1967, he left the department in the hands of lesser men. Control reverted to the mayor, whom Wilson once described as the "finest administrator [I] ever knew." Did he truly believe that the organization he had built would endure the challenges of the tumultuous 1960s when blacks, women, youth, and the disenfranchised demanded equal justice under the law?

Under O. W. Wilson, the Chicago Police Department was forced to break from its historic nineteenth-century roots. The period of modernity had at last begun.

Epilogue

The trial of the Summerdale burglars began in the Chicago criminal court on June 26, 1961. The prosecution team, headed by Barnabas Sears, Louis Garippo, Charles Rush, and Daniel McCarthy, based its case around nine separate burglaries committed between October 1, 1958, and April 10, 1959. No doubt there were many more burglaries that the all-woman jury never heard during the course of the deliberations.

Throughout the two-month trial, defense attorney Julius Lucius Echeles accused high police officials of deceit, duplicity, intimidation, and kidnapping.

The defense objected to the pre-dawn seizure and interrogation of the eight burglars on January 15, 1960. They were not told they were under arrest and had been "threatened" with the loss of their jobs by First Assistant State's Attorney Frank Ferlic unless they answered all of the questions put to them by a battery of police captains and investigators from Adamowski's office. Sol Karras had been without sleep for 19 hours at the time he was questioned. "Those defendants were held incommunicado and given no opportunity to obtain counsel," complained Attorney Stephen Levy.

Echeles attempted to confuse the issue with screaming harangues about the integrity of the state's star witness Morrison, and the war record of Attorney Rush. The carnival sideshow aspects of the trial dominated the last few days of the proceedings as Defense Attorney Charles Bellows bestowed upon Echeles the Congressional Medal of Honor after Rush replied to the insinuation that his service record was unworthy of respect. "I have wrung more salt water out of my socks that Mr. Echeles ever sailed on!" Rush shot back. Bellows burst out of his chair and cried in a rasping voice, "Well, you didn't get the Congressional Medal of Honor like Mr. Echeles did!"

Judge James B. Parsons, the first black man to receive a lifetime appointment as a U.S. district judge, lectured them about proper courtroom ethics: "I know that for years in this building both defense and prosecution have used tricks. They don't use tricks in this courtroom, nor do they use tricks to retrick each other!"

Attorney Echeles, who defended a score of mob luminaries over the years, including Jimmy "Monk" Allegretti, Sam DeStefano, and Frank "Hot Dogs" Lisciandrello, stared at Bellows wide-eyed. He had never won the Medal of Honor but had spent some time in the federal penitentiary in Terre Haute, Indiana, after being convicted of selling jobs and promotions in the Chicago Post Office. During his jail sentence Echeles had voluntarily withdrawn from his practice but was readmitted to the law profession by the Illinois supreme court upon his release.

Unquestionably, the star of this trial was Richard Morrison, the pint-sized burglar who appeared shy and uneasy on the witness stand. He answered the lawyers' questions in a hesitating, self-conscious manner. Echeles portrayed him as a diabolical criminal genius. "Richard Morrison lied his way into the house of poor dumb, stupid Frank Faraci—Faraci the schnook!" he said in a near-hysterical tone. Charles Bellows assailed the state for deals made with Morrison, and the privileged status he enjoyed in the county jail. "He was promised he would not have to spend one day in the regular jail," Bellows charged. "When they put him in a cell briefly he kicked up a big fuss. He wanted to be back in his private bath and his beddie and they sent him back."

The case against the eight accused police officers seemed airtight. There was little else the defense lawyers could do but appeal to the sympathy of the female jurors. And it nearly worked. "It wasn't so much over the fact that they were guilty," one of the women explained. "With the exception of Beeftink we all thought they were guilty on the first ballot. But when it came to fixing penalties, oh my Lord!''

The case nearly blew up in the face of the prosecution when, after five hours of deliberation, the jury refused to attach recommendations for the length of jail sentences. To ease their troubled consciences they left that task to Judge Parsons. On August 24, 1961, he sentenced Clements, Faraci, and Alex Karras from two to five years. Sol Karras, who elicited the most sympathy from the jury because of his "sad hang-dog" look, received two to three years. Next came Allan Brinn, whom several of the jurors described as the "most honorable" of the bunch for having the good sense to warn Morrison that several of his pals were contemplating killing him. Brinn was ordered to serve one to three years. Peter Beeftink and Henry Mulea, a big, square-shouldered man who had dropped out of grammar school to work, was let off with a $500 fine. Patrick Groark, whose matinee idol looks left a lasting impression on the female jurors, asked for a bench trial. He steadfastly maintained his innocence throughout the trial, reminding the court at opportune moments that no stolen merchandise was found in his house. It was true of course, but a curious aside to the Summerdale case was the unexplained presence of a Chicago Police squad car in front of the Groark residence hours before the State's Attorney's raid. This suggests that Adamowski's secret plan was not so secret after all. During the trial, Pat Groark seemed unwilling to seek mercy from Judge Parsons. Had he done so, it is probable that he might have escaped the six-month jail sentence handed down by the court.

And what about Chicago's babbling burglar? Dickie Morrison disappeared from Chicago shortly after the trial. He lived in Florida for a few years, but was called back to testify in another Summerdale-related case that came before the docket. Prosecution attorneys were interested in hearing about his encounter with Dr. Leonard Macaluso, a physician reputed to have mob ties. This same doctor reportedly treated Morrison for a bullet wound he sustained during one of the burglaries. The reformed burglar was preparing to testify about this and other matters when a speeding car barreled around the corner at 26th and California Avenues. The attendant in the back of the vehicle pointed a shotgun at Morrison who was about to cross the street. A vicious blast from the gun nearly tore his arm off. The car sped away, leaving Morrison in the street outside the Criminal Court screaming in helpless agony. Frank Sullivan, then a beat reporter for the *Chicago Sun-Times* helped administer emergency first aid. An ambulance was summoned, but Morrison was understandably fearful of riding to the hospital in the company of the cops. He pleaded for his attorney to sit with him in the back, lest he end up lying on a slab in the county morgue. The lawyer agreed. Morrison was treated for his wounds and was eventually released. Later, on the witness stand the babbling burglar suffered a sudden memory loss. Morrison said he could not remember who it was that treated him the first time, nor could he say whether the doctor's office was north or south of North Avenue. The syndicate boys had sent him a message he understood. The case collapsed and Morrison took leave of Chicago, this time for good. At last report he still resided in Florida.

And so ended the Summerdale Scandal, a bleak chapter in Chicago history ended satisfactorily in the minds of police officials who looked ahead to a brighter day. There would be no more scandals of this magnitude, Superintendent Wilson prophesied: "I feel members of the Chicago Police Department today have a sense of public service and integrity which will tend to dessuade any new members from engaging in activities that would discredit the department." The bitter fruit of scandal had yielded many positive results. Chicago had served notice that the police star was not a badge of immunity or a license to commit crime. It was up to the governing agencies to make sure this lesson was never forgotten.

Notes

1. Herman Kogan, "Honky Tonk U.S.A.," *Chicago Sun-Times*, October 19–21, 1950. After the Levee was forced to close during World War I, the vice-keepers moved further south to the black belt in the 2nd Ward, and the wild "frontier" towns like Stickney, Burnham, and Chicago Heights where police control was minimal, and suburban chiefs were easily bribed. The Rialto district of North Clark Street, once the political fiefdom of James "Hot Stove" Quinn, became the city's new Levee beginning in the 1920s. During Prohibition, Albert J. Prignano, Democratic committee man, alderman, and state representative, protected the lucrative gambling and liquor interests in the ward. Prignano faced a difficult task. Endless gang warfare thinned the ranks of the O'Bannion-Weiss-Moran mob, forcing Prignano to accommodate Al Capone. He skated on thin ice until December 1935, when Frank Nitti ordered Prignano's removal. The assassin was thought to be Angelo Lazzia, wanted in Italy by the Mussolini government for three other murders. Political control reverted to Botchie Connors and later Ross Prio. The North Side nightclub remained a syndicate battleground well into the 1980s.

2. Ibid., October 19, 1950. After a police shakeup commenced, the word went up and down Clark Street that "Tommy's in trouble." Harrison was a member of the Police Department for 37 years. In World War I he served in the 129th Infantry in France, and won the welterweight championship of the 33rd Division. He was appointed to the city police on January 7, 1922. Harrison's rise in rank and reputation were rapid. He became a sergeant in 1928, a lieutenant in 1935, and a captain two years later. At the time of his death in 1960 Tommy Harrison was serving as acting undersheriff of Cook County, a political plum given to him by Frank Sain.

3. Lindberg, *Chicago Ragtime*, (South Bend: Icarus Press, 1985), pp. 210–11. Alvin Karpis and Freddie Barker formed the nucleus of the most dangerous robbery-kidnap gang of the 1930s. For four years (1931–35) the Barkers and Karpis masterminded dozens of major crimes, including the Lynch abduction. See Jay Robert Nash, *Bloodletters and Badmen*, vol. 3 (New York: Warner Books, 1975), pp. 180–82.

4. *Chicago Tribune*, October 17, 1950. In addition to his business dealings with Lynch, Harrison borrowed $10,000 from syndicate gambling boss William Skidmore in 1935. The captain was introduced to Skidmore through Attorney William Goldstein, the

same Bill Gold who figured so prominently in the 1953 "little red book" payoff scandal. The loan was disclosed during Skidmore's trial on income tax evasion charges.

5. Kreml began his work on August 15, 1947. A new traffic division was established and the personnel strength was increased twofold from 569 to 1,100 officers. The city appropriated funds to pay for 150 solo motorcycles, 116 enforcement and accident investigation squad cars, and 65 three-wheeled cycles. The number of ambulances was increased and additional snow removal equipment was purchased.

6. Dominic A. Pacyga and Ellen Skerrett, *Chicago: A City of Neighborhoods* (Chicago: Loyola University Press, 1987), pp. 37–52. The Gold Coast and the slum are stark reminders of a troubled past and an uncertain future in this North Side enclave populated by some of the wealthiest citizens and its poorest ghetto inhabitants.

7. John T. Flynn, "Smart Money," *Collier's*, September 13–27, 1940. See also Smith, *Syndicate City*, (Chicago: Henry Regnery, 1954), pp. 167–70. The backbone of illegal bookmaking operations in the United States was the Continental Press Service and its competitors, which dispersed the latest up-to-the minute racetrack information to poolrooms across the country. From the days of Mont Tennes right up to the Kefauver investigation, Continental flourished in the same downtown offices on Dearborn Street. See also *The Third Interim Report of the Special Committee to Investigate Organized Crime in Interstate Commerce Pursuant to Senate Activities, 1950–51*, (New York: Arco Press, 1952), pp. 53–54.

8. Demaris, *Captive City*, (New York: Lyle Stewart, 1969), pp. 53–54.

9. Mortimer and Lait collaborated on three other confidential books on New York, Washington, and the U.S.A. at large.

10. Reprinted in the *Chicago Tribune*, September 26, 1950.

11. The Chicago police and the state's attorney agreed there was no connection between the Drury and Bas slayings. Drury maintained to his dying day that he and captain Connelley were dismissed from the force in 1947 because of syndicate pressure on State's Attorney William Touhy and his First Assistant Wilbert Crowley, whom they accused of instigating the Civil Service charges.

12. *Chicago Sun-Times*, June 21, 1951. Marshall Caifano and his brother "Fat" Lenny were two rising stars of the Chicago underworld in the early 1950s. Gambling and policy boss Theodore Roe, a black man, were gunned down in August 1952, allegedly by Marshall Caifano who was avenging the death of his brother a year earlier. Captain Kinzie Blueitt ordered the wholesale arrests of 14 Mafia chieftains, including Tony Accardo, Sam Giancana, and Sam "Golf Bag" Hunt, who were squeezing out the South Side policy kings. Caifano later ran the Chicago interests in Las Vegas.

13. *Chicago Tribune*, October 18, 1950. Dan Gilbert was not legally obligated to appear before the Kefauver Committee, but did so in order to silence his critics in the press on the eve of the election. Describing himself as a gambler at "heart," Tubbo Gilbert testified that he began buying stocks at the suggestion of the late George Brennan, Democratic Party boss in the 1920s. Gilbert "pyramided" his holdings during the bull market but lost all his paper profits in the 1929 crash. Afterward he speculated in grain, and diversified his holdings by purchasing shares of Pepsi Cola, the Union Pacific Railroad, and AT&T. By the mid–1950s, when Gilbert was in comfortable retirement, his personal fortune was estimated to be $350,000. Dan was appointed a Chicago patrolman on April 6, 1917, the day the United States entered World War I. At the same time he pursued a separate career in labor union politics, eventually becoming secretary-treasurer of the Baggage & Parcel Driver's Union, Local 725. During one labor war Gilbert was

indicted on a charge of assault. The indictment was later suspended with leave to reinstate. However, the records mysteriously disappeared from the criminal court files. His rise in police circles in those years was unprecedented. Gilbert became a captain in 1926 and was viewed as a "real comer." In the City Council at the same time, an even younger man, Thomas J. Courtney, was sergeant-at-arms. Gilbert's slavish loyalty was rewarded in 1932 with appointment to the post of chief investigator and personal command of 100 detectives assigned to the state's attorney's office. In April 1935 Gilbert initiated a very shady internal move within the department. He temporarily left his job with Courtney to accept command of the uniformed patrol, placing him in the number-two slot behind Allman. Captain Martin Mullen, who headed up the morals and gambling squad, reported directly to Gilbert. In July he quietly stepped down from this post to return to his former position as Courtney's chief investigator after disbanding the gambling unit. At the same time a bill sponsored by the Kelly-Nash forces that would have permitted the Chicago City Council to licence off-track betting crossed Governor Horner's desk. Horner vetoed the measure, which led to a permanent schism in Democratic ranks. But was it just a coincidence that Gilbert was in the middle of this gambling controversy at the time that this bill hung precariously in the balance? See Robert H. Williams, *Vice Squad* (New York: Thomas Crowell Co., 1973), p. 29. Gilbert was accused of protecting Frank Nitti's interests by former Circuit Court Judge Oscar F. Nelson, who ran for state's attorney in 1940. He charged that on May 6, 7, and 8, 1939, Gilbert was vacationing with Nitti at the Arlington Hotel in Hot Springs, Arkansas. He was using a set of gold-plated clubs, believed to be a personal gift from the gang boss. The Nitti gambling dens enjoyed virtual immunity during the Kelly years, which became a campaign issue in more than one city election. In 1947 John Boyle promised the civic reformers that he would fire Gilbert if elected. Once in office he changed his tune and said he would fire Gilbert only with the mayor's approval—which never came. In 1949 Boss Arvey slated him for sheriff but his elective ambitions crumbled when John Babb claimed the office by a whopping 390,000-vote margin. Forced into retirement, "Two Ball" Dan spent his next few years reminiscing about the good old days as he played high stakes gin rummy in the basement of Fritzel's Restaurant on Randolph Street. He maintained quarters in a deluxe Lake Shore Drive high-rise, but spent the winter months vacationing in Hot Springs and Miami Beach. When asked if he had any sympathy for the ever-extended and fretful Babb, Gilbert said, characteristically, "I'm glad it happened to him and not me."

14. *Third Interim Report*, p. 61.

15. Richard J. Daley campaign literature, *Police Digest*, October 1946. Daley was slated to run for sheriff by Boss Arvey, who discussed the issue with Federal Judge Abraham Lincoln Marovitz when the political figures were stationed in the Philippines during World War II. Marovitz and Daley were inseparable friends in the Illinois State Senate—part of a troika that once included Benjamin Adamowski. Fortunately for Daley, he lost this particular race to Elmer Walsh. The Cook County sheriff's office historically has been the boneyard for washed-up Chicago politicians.

16. Robert F. Kennedy, *The Enemy Within* (New York: Harper Brothers, 1960), p. 151. One of the problems that hampered the various senate committees investigating organized crime in the 1950s was the absence of a national crime commission to disseminate information to local law agencies.

17. *Chicago Sun-Times*, February 8, 1952. Alderman George Kells of the 28th Ward retired from public office after receiving death threats. He was replaced by Patrick Petrone, cousin of Robert "Happy" Petrone, 26th Ward boss and an intimate of Tony Accardo.

18. *Police Digest*, July 1946.

19. In December 1960, O. W. Wilson appealed to the business community to support the policy of the department forbidding police officers from accepting gratuities, financial or otherwise, at Christmas time. This subtle form of bribery was greatly curtailed after 1960; *Chicago Sun-Times*, March 23, 1953.

20. Ibid., November 15, 1957. Captain Blueitt ordered arrest warrants for the 14 mobsters believed responsible for the murder of Theodore Roe. For years he defended the interests of South Side policy gamblers against the incursions of the mafiosi in the Wabash District.

21. Ibid., March 4, 1955. When Washington attorney Downey Rice quit the committee he left an unfinished file on "Mr. Big," a powerhouse in Chicago politics and local gambling. The identity of this Mr. Big remained a mystery of the 1950s, known only to certain members of the City Council. The file folder turned up missing from the committee records and could not be located when U.S. Attorney Robert Ticken subpoenaed the aldermen in 1956 for access. After Ticken had his look, the Big Nine files were "bottled up." In 1960 Robert Merriam, then an aide to President Dwight Eisenhower, accused Police Commissioner Tim O'Connor and State's Attorney John Gutknecht of suppressing the report. The Big Nine died in January 1956, six months after Merriam accepted a federal appointment.

22. Ibid., March 7, 1955. Alderman Merriam was the better known of the two candidates and stood a reasonably good chance of winning the election. However, when Daley swept the ghetto wards he described William Dawson not as a boss, but a leader of men. Len O'Connor, *Clout: Mayor Daley and His City* (Chicago: Henry Regnery, 1975), p. 111.

23. Ibid., p. 125. Daley vowed to reorganize the department but very few steps were taken before 1960 to address the key recommendations of the 1953 and 1956 reports of the Big Nine. These had accused the police of being "incapable of conducting or unwilling to conduct a vigorous, aggressive investigation of possible misconduct on the part of its personnel." The first report, drawn up by Charles A. Bane, the committee's first chief counsel, was pigeonholed, ignored, and allowed to gather dust. The same was true of the blistering report submitted by Aaron Kohn. Volume six dealt with the Chicago Police Department Detectives' Bureau. It described the system of "rooting," whereby bureau cars looked for payoffs from bookmakers, policy operators, and after-hour taverns. A radio call of a major crime in progress on one end of the city would often result in a cross-city ride at high speeds to reach the scene. Although the gamblers were aware that bureau men would probably not make an arrest, they nevertheless paid a tribute. Not to do so might result in an anonymous phone call to the uniformed squad reporting a serious crime in the gambler's domain. This could force a "protection" arrest or closure of the establishment until the shakedown money was paid. A detective could earn for himself $300 a month through rooting, according to Kohn's section, entitled "An Experienced Policeman Speaks His Mind." Was it any wonder that the captains, sergeants, and patrolmen's associations were antagonistic to the Big Nine?

24. Virgil W. Peterson, *Report on Chicago Cime for 1959* (Chicago: The Chicago Crime Commission, 1959), pp. 43–44. Chief Justice Raymond P. Drymalski was indicted for malfeasance in his handling of two cases. Joseph Gill, clerk of the municipal court and a wheelhorse in Chicago politics, was also indicted for malfeasance and omission of duty in ten different cases. The other 33 defendants were indicted for conspiracy to obstruct justice. Drymalski was acquitted by Judge Casimir Griglik on March 2, 1960.

The ten indictments against Gill were quashed by Judge David Canel on March 25, 1960. Judges Henry Ferguson and John T. Sullivan entered pleas in bar and were dismissed on March 3, 1960, by Judge John Gutknecht, who elevated himself to the bench after completing his term as state's attorney. The municipal court system of Cook County continued to be a trough of graft and cronyism until 1977, when U.S. Attorney Thomas Sullivan laid the groundwork for a massive probe of judicial corruption. The ambitious work of two undercover FBI agents, Terrence Hake and David Ries, unearthed evidence of bribery and case fixing, resulting in the conviction of 14 judges and 69 municipal employees and police officers between 1977 and 1989. In the early months of Operation Greylord—named after a racehorse and not the bewigged jurists of Britain, as was commonly believed—Hake posed as a corrupt lawyer seeking breaks for his clients. Later, as the investigation expanded in scope the agents bugged the private chambers of Judge Wayne Olson, who presided over narcotics court. Olson, a judge since 1962, told attorney Bruce Roth that he "loved people that take dough because you know exactly where they stand." In order to systematize the payoffs, Judge Richard Lefevour, who headed up the Chicago branch courts from 1980 until his conviction in July 1985, organized a "Hustler's Club" of lawyers who would pay $2,000 a month directly to him and $500 to his cousin James Lefevour, a former Chicago policeman. On several occasions Police Sergeant Cy Martin agreed to pose as Judge Raymond Sodini during the early morning call of vagrants and winos at Chicago's notorious Branch 26 Court. Donning the traditional black robe, Martin filled in for Sodini when the judge was hungover or otherwise incapacitated.

25. *Chicago Tribune*, October 19, 1955. Hoffman believed the Schuessler-Peterson murders committed by a solitary murderer who would be classified as a sexual sadist. The psychological profile and an artist's sketch of a "puffy faced," sly-looking teen-age boy seen in the company of Robert Peterson convinced writer Richard Vachula and police wife Rosemary Sarnowski that the killer may have been John Wayne Gacy. Detective Sergeant John Sarnowski was one of 52 officers assigned to special duty on this case. When mass-murderer Gacy was arrested in 1978 at his Northwest Side home, Mrs. Sarnowski recalled the 1955 police sketch of the "Mr. Potato Head" suspect. At the time, 13-year-old John Gacy lived on Marmora Avenue, not far from the Peterson residence. Whether Gacy was involved in homosexual hustling at this stage in his life, no one knows. His psychological problems are documented only back to 1958. Vachula speculates that Bobby Peterson and his friends kept an appointment with the youthful Gacy at the Garland Building, a favorite meeting place for gay males in the later 1950s. From there they may have returned to 4505 Marmora, where Gacy accosted them. Detective Robert Ekenburg said he questioned a boy matching Gacy's description at a Milwaukee Avenue tavern, but let him go. The Police Department kept detectives on the case until 1965. However, the trail was cold much earlier than that. The Gacy theory is compelling, but unproven. The only one who can prove or disprove the thesis currently languishes on death row in Illinois—John Wayne Gacy. See Richard Vachula, "The Gacy Connection," *Chicago Magazine*, July 1989, pp. 113–14.

26. Peterson, *Report on Chicago Crime for 1957*.

27. *Chicago Sun-Times*, August 29, 1957. The Anderson investigation was not hampered by the presence of Cook County sheriff's police or other suburban law enforcement personnel. Various suspects were questioned, including an entire Italian family on the West Side who were subjected to polygraph tests and photographed for the front page of the morning papers. The tests failed to establish a degree of guilt.

28. *Report of the General Superintendent to the City Council* (1956), pp. 6–7.

29. Peterson, *Chicago Crime*, 1957. (See also *Superintendent's Report.*)

30. Ibid., 1960, p. 9. DeGrazio asserted that his friend Accardo never committed a felony. Overlooked apparently was the rash of publicity accompanying his income tax records made public during the Kefauver hearings, or the McClellan investigation at which he evoked the Fifth Amendment 172 times. *Chicago Tribune*, January 12 and January 28, 1960.

31. Robert Wiedrich, "A Burglar's Confession," *The Chicago Crime Book*, (New York: Pyramid Books, 1969), p. 384. See also *Chicago Tribune*, January 20, 1960. There have been other police-burglars over the years but none quite so spectacular as the Summerdale Eight. In 1936, for instance, an Evanston patrolman named Philip Reiman looted a sporting goods emporium on Sherman Avenue, one of 21 stores he broke into while pounding the beat. Reiman accidentally left behind a notebook containing data on his "jobs." He was caught and sentenced from one year to life. In 1946 a 17-year-veteran of the Chicago police named Anthony Crane was dismissed from the force after his role in the heist of $100,000 worth of pens from the Reynolds International Pen Company was uncovered. Crane received two to seven years. When he was released from prison Crane took up burglary on a full-time basis. Facing a two-count indictment and a likely prison sentence, former officer Crane committed suicide on January 3, 1955.

32. *Chicago Tribune*, January 20, 1960. Morrison believed that someone inside the gang was trying to kill him. When he was told to break into a meat market he thought twice about choosing a lookout for the job. During an earlier burglary on Lawrence Avenue, someone—a police officer, perhaps—took a pot shot at him. During the meat market operation his partner sat outside on a three-wheeled cycle while Morrison looted the safe. After $1,300 in cash had been removed Morrison gave the all-clear sign and retreated to the safety of a nearby garage roof while the squad cars and a paddy wagon converged on the store like a vulture to carrion. "Anyways," he recalled, "they cleaned out the whole meat market. I was eating some of the steaks taken out of there at their houses quite a few times.

33. The *Chicago Daily News* broke the Hodge scandal on June 4, 1956, in a front-page exclusive. The reporters won a Pulitzer Prize for their efforts. Governor Stratton demanded Hodge's immediate resignation and doubled his $50,000 bond before declaring the auditor's office vacant. Orville Hodge was sentenced to 15 years in prison. Chicago Policeman William D. Lydon was fired by the Civil Service Commission as a direct outgrowth of the scandal. His decorating firm did work for Hodge on the side, and he was the payee on $478,091 in state warrants cashed by Hodge.

34. O'Connor, *Clout*, p. 172. Daley was "scared" into reforming the department. The high-strung mayor had a history of overreacting to political crises, real or perceived. Viewing the Summerdale scandal from Washington, Robert Merriam said that he believed that it never would have happened if the mayor had followed the recommendations of the Big Nine three years earlier.

35. *Chicago Tribune*, January 24, 1960. The governor demanded that Daley resign his chairmanship of the Cook County Democratic Committee to devote more time to putting his house in order. Stratton precipitated the dispute over the direction of reform by calling for the creation of a state-run police board, a variation on a 100-year-old theme. The ulterior motive of the Republican governor was to embarrass Daley and usurp control from the Democrats. It was a typical election-year power play. The state senate was Republican-controlled, and the lower house a tool of the Chicago Democrats. Stratton counted on the support of Paul Powell, the Democratic speaker of the house from down-

state who was known to buck the machine on occasion. However, the Democrats closed ranks behind Daley. Stratton, an otherwise capable executive, was defeated in his bid for a third term.

36. William J. Bopp, *O. W.: O. W. Wilson and the Search For a Police Profession* (Port Washington, NY: Kennikat Press, 1977), pp. 81–82. Wilson's 21-year career at the University of California was interrupted only by his work in occupied Germany at the end of World War II when he served as a member of the de-Nazification team sent in to reorganize a new police force in the western sector. Prior to his acceptance of the "Chicago challenge," Wilson successfully thwarted an attempt by university administrators to abolish the Department of Criminology on the grounds that it was "too technical." Wilson was supported by the governor, the state attorney general, and every major law enforcement agency in California.

37. Peterson, *Chicago Crime*, 1960, pp. 10–11.

38. O. W. Wilson, "How the Chief Sees It," *Harper's*, April 1964, p. 140. Wilson was only a few years away from his well-deserved retirement when he accepted the committee offer. He had toyed with the idea of retiring to Hawaii, where he hoped to write another book.

39. *The Chicago Police: A Report of Progress, 1960–64*, Public Information Division of the Chicago Police Department, p. 1.

40. Tim O'Connor took pride in the fact that Chicago's Police Department had more graduates of the FBI Academy in Washington than any other big-city force in the United States. It was all well and good, but it did little for the rank-and-file seeking advancement. The antiquated Civil Service Commission protected inefficient and corrupt officers while inadvertently holding back qualified men for advancement. In practice, a policeman had one chance every five or ten years to be promoted. The officer's entire career often depended on that one examination. The lawsuits filed by disgruntled applicants destroyed the purpose of the Civil Service system by preventing regular promotion based on merit, outstanding work, and frequent exams. *Chicago American*, January 12, 1960.

41. Between 1960 and 1964, 873 men were promoted to sergeant, 226 to lieutenant, and 94 to captain. The old-line party hacks were weeded out and the great intangible— the inititive to succeed—suddenly became an attainable dream for a younger generation of policemen. The promotion ceremony was a great morale-boosting event as relatives and friends could share the pride in achievement. Appointment to the detectives' bureau rested with the superintendent and not the Civil Service Commission under the new arrangement. Selections were based on competitive exams rather than political reward.

42. Renault Robinson, *The Chicago Police Department: An Agenda for Change* (Chicago: University of Illinois Symposium, September 13, 1974), pp. 2–3. Police and minority relations before the flowering of the Civil Rights movement of the 1960s meant two separate things to whites and blacks. The black community disliked and distrusted the local police, who reinforced stereotypical behavior, uttered racial epitaphs, and were generally the authority figures to be most feared. The absence of black police officers in ghetto communities further aggravated the situation. Until 1960 black officers were rarely assigned to patrol cars in what must be construed as a policy of de facto segregation. In some police districts, if no white police officer was present for duty the radio cars were not dispatched. However, the appearance of a black person in an affluent white neighborhood encouraged the police to detain and question the individual about his purpose for being there. At the same time, black leaders complained bitterly about the levels of protection afforded them during Civil Rights gatherings. For a discussion of the plight

of blacks in U.S. police agencies, see Stephen H. Leinen, *Black Police, White Society* (New York: New York University Press, 1984).

43. In 1963 Adamowski challenged Daley for the mayoralty. The Summerdale scandal, still fresh in the former state's attorney's mind, was a non-issue by 1963. Despite running the strongest campaign of any of Daley's five mayoral opponents over the years, Adamowski was defeated by a strong voter turnout, and the usual rubber-stamp approval from the black South Side and machine-infested West Side "river" wards.

44. There were no guarantees that the Wilson reforms could stand up after this dynamic administrator was gone. The success of those 1960 moves had everything to do with the willingness of Mayor Daley and the City Council to assume a vigilant posture against corruption. The formation of an IID unit was a positive step, certainly long overdue. But the IID alone could not be counted on to maintain standards of professional ethics if future mayors and their sychophants assumed an attitude of official tolerance, or were reluctant to expose corruption in all forms because of fears of political repercussions. The city of New York provides an abject lesson about the perils of short-term drives. The history of the New York police, best told by James Richardson, is studded with numerous civic drives against corruption, beginning in 1853 when the City Reform Party sponsored a law that created a board of commissioners consisting of the mayor, the recorder, and the city judge. The board guaranteed that no one solitary individual would reign supreme over the department. It was a noble sentiment, to be sure, until Mayor Fernando Wood made short work of it by appointing his cronies to positions on the force and then requiring them to canvass the precincts at election time. In 1857 a bill was introduced to transfer control from the municipal authorities to the state board. Wood defied the Metropolitan Police Board and a riot ensued in Manhattan. By 1869 William Marcy Tweed succeeded in marshaling control of the legislature and the state house. The Tweed Charter of 1870 (price tag: $600,000) returned control of the police to municipal authorities—the mayor and his lackeys serving on the Board of Aldermen. New York had the dubious distinction of becoming the first city in the United States to institute a state board and the first to take it away. In 1873 the police board was reshuffled and a new reform administration vowed to clean house. Mayor William Havemeyer quarreled with the board and died in office. Ultimately, the Tammany spoils men prevailed. The battle for a meaningful reform in the 1890s pitted Reverend Charles Parkhurst and Chief of Police Theodore Roosevelt against boss Tom Platt in Albany and a resurgent Tammany in New York City. In 1895 an investigating committee of the New York state senate headed by Clarence Lexow uncovered a web of graft in all shapes and forms. The corresponding Lexow Bill was a halfway measure that did not go far enough to permit Roosevelt to see through the transformation of the department. The cycle of reform and scandal and more reform characterized Chicago and New York for much of the nineteenth and twentieth centuries. The pace was unending. Mayor Seth Low wore the white hat in 1901 but was unable to reform the department in just one term of office. In 1912 District Attorney Charles Whitman's sensational exposure of a criminal-police tie-up during the prosecution of Police Lieutenant Charles Becker for the murder of gangster Herman Rosenthal put him in the governor's chair. Becker, seemingly above the law after attaching his star to Big Tim Sullivan, Tammany boss of the entire East Side, was executed in July 1915. Two decades later, Judge Samuel Seabury who presided over Becker's second trial, exposed the magistrate's courts and the Police Department for what they truly were, and Mayor Jimmy Walker was forced to step aside. In 1947 the head of the Department of Investigation (formerly the Commissioner of Accounts) issued a terse statement saying

that his agency had driven out all of the major bookmakers in New York. When the Kefauver Committee confronted the sheepish investigator he admitted the statement ''was made in the heat of a political campaign'' to elect Mayor William O'Dwyer. District Attorney Miles McDonald launched another investigation of the links between the New York Police Department and the racketeers. O'Dwyer called it a witchhunt, but McDonald succeeded in driving 400 crooked police officers from the force.

45. *Chicago Sun-Times*, April 24, 1961. In a statement issued through Public Defender Gerald Getty, Morrison expressed satisfaction with the outcome: ''I'm very happy with the verdict. The defendants made me the issue and the jury must have believed me. I am happy that my testimony was useful to the community. Chicago may now be a better city.''

Appendix I: Statistical Data, 1866–1960

	Number of Police	Number of Arrests	Departmental Expenses
1866	218	n/a	$239,180
1867	n/a	n/a	n/a
1868	297	n/a	$373,480
1869	374	n/a	$473,052
1870	377	n/a	$614,877
1871	451	26,448	$465,361
1872	455	21,931	$498,297
1873	458	31,585	$505,328
1874	552	27,995	$653,259
1875	575	24,899	$722,877
1876	517	27,291	$639,887
1877	516	28,035	$534,843
1878	442	27,208	$432,759
1879	453	27,338	$445,195
1880	473	28,480	$493,672
1881	506	31,713	$577,038
1882	557	32,800	$659,260
1883	637	37,187	$703,580
1884	924	39,434	$779,721
1885	926	40,998	$1,079,345
1886	1,036	44,261	$1,192,770
1887	1,145	46,505	$1,305,563
1888	1,255	50,432	$1,400,437
1889	1,624	48,119	$1,602,595
1890	1,900	62,230	$2,200,127
1891	2,306	70,550	$2,622,046
1892	2,726	89,833	$3,035,044
1893	3,189	96,976	$3,550,558
1894	3,188	88,323	$3,643,936
1895	3,255	83,464	$3,421,876
1896	3,425	96,847	$3,375,740
1897	3,594	83,680	$3,457,666
1898	3,594	77,441	$3,441,870
1899	3,267	71,349	$3,438,574
1900	3,314	70,438	$3,385,160
1901	2,782	69,442	$3,409,007
1902	2,732	70,314	$3,338,783
1903	2,773	77,763	$3,569,478
1904	2,676	79,026	$3,545,942
1905	2,590	82,572	$3,961,274
1906	3,578	91,554	$4,071,202
1907	4,110	63,132	$5,388,110
1908	4,293	68,220	$5,703,917
1909	4,288	70,575	$5,810,619
1910	4,260	81,269	$5,825,455

	Number of Police	Number of Arrests	Departmental Expenses
1911	4,437	84,838	$6,141,632
1912	4,436	86,950	$6,637,452
1913	4,443	109,764	$6,662,655
1914	4,420	116,895	$6,985,905
1915	5,331	121,714	$7,276,440
1916	5,277	111,527	$7,274,164
1917	5,199	137,910	$7,290,942
1918	4,706	110,819	$7,815,142
1919	5,120	96,676	$9,454,332
1920	5,152	94,453	$10,498,622
1921	5,140	117,719	$10,896,707
1922	6,184	132,290	$11,735,866
1923	5,965	181,980	$12,788,318
1924	6,010	242,602	$13,044,219
1925	5,862	264,494	$14,025,560
1926	6,080	211,317	$14,201,536
1927	6,078	161,239	$15,715,923
1928	6,098	150,885	$16,258,413
1929	6,712	194,999	$17,151,408
1930	6,719	183,434	$17,400,511
1931	6,581	150,197	$17,143,871
1932	6,330	106,767	$13,581,408
1933	6,561	93,455	$14,058,843
1934	6,313	85,320	$14,425,087
1935	6,642	78,270	$15,320,455
1936	6,625	77,562	$15,904,437
1937	6,606	75,605	$16,103,587
1938	6,763	69,639	$17,350,622
1939	6,641	82,137	$17,014,720
1940	6,629	77,947	$17,363,772
1941	6,778	76,285	$17,354,773
1942	6,378	62,657	$17,175,057
1943	6,418	57,002	$18,809,754
1944	6,360	61,901	$19,794,410
1945	6,749	61,160	$19,983,088
1946	7,827	70,415	$25,272,724
1947	7,657	n/a	$25,174,902
1948	7,771	84,558	$27,552,917
1949	7,584	139,036	$27,745,854
1950	7,694	133,013	$27,411,399
1951	7,895	162,495	$30,273,052
1952	7,525	189,803	$33,900,102
1953	7,324	196,511	$35,240,253
1954	7,425	218,368	$38,598,535
1955	8,238	209,201	$42,310,871

	Number of Police	Number of Arrests	Departmental Expenses
1956	8,905	209,977	$47,348,629
1957	9,600	217,992	$54,053,745
1958	9,739	209,558	$58,417,495
1959	9,215	n/a	*$68,577,381
1960	10,091	*129,742	**$72,792,963

Source: *Reports of the General Superintendent to the City Council* (1872–1920). Data for period prior to 1872 extracted from the *Chicago Tribune*, January 9, 1867, and April 11, 1870.

Note: The figures herein are cited from official reports submitted each year to the mayor and City Council. In 1929, the Chicago Crime Commission noted with alarm that thousands of criminal offenses never appear on official records. Virgil Peterson accused the police of deliberately underreporting statistics to reflect favorably upon the administration.

*Due to the Summerdale scandal, statistical data for the year 1959 were not published. The number of arrests are listed in *Crime in the U.S.*, an FBI document published by the U.S. Justice Department for the years 1958–62.

**Extracted from the city budget for 1960.

Appendix II: Law Enforcement in Cook County, 1855–1960

Year	Mayor	Head of Police Department	State's Attorney	Cook County Sheriff
1855	Levi D. Boone (KN)	Cyrus Bradley	Daniel McIlroy	James Andrews
1856	Boone/Thomas Dyer (D)	James Donnelley	Carlos Haven	Andrews/John Wilson
1857	Dyer/John Wentworth (R)	James Donnelley	Carlos Haven	John L. Wilson
1858	Wentworth/John C. Haines (R)	Jacob Rehm	Carlos Haven	Wilson/John Gray
1859	John C. Haines (R)	Jacob Rehm	Carlos Haven	John Gray
1860	Haines/Wentworth (R)	Iver Lawson (City Marshal)	Carlos Haven	Gray/Anton Hesing
1861	Wentworth/Julian Rumsey (D)	Cyrus Bradley	Carlos Haven	Anton C. Hesing
1862	Rumsey/Francis Sherman (D)	Cyrus Bradley	Haven/Joseph Knox	Hesing/David L. Hammond
1863	Francis Sherman (D)	Cyrus Bradley	Joseph Knox	David L. Hammond
1864	Francis Sherman (D)	Bradley/William Turtle	Knox/Charles Reed	Hammond/John A. Nelson
1865	Sherman/John Rice (R)	William Turtle	Charles Reed	John A. Nelson
1866	John B. Rice (R)	Turtle/Jacob Rehm	Charles Reed	Nelson/John Beveridge
1867	John B. Rice (R)	Jacob Rehm	Charles Reed	John L. Beveridge
1868	John B. Rice (R)	Jacob Rehm	Charles Reed	Beveridge/Gustav Fischer
1869	Rice/Roswell Mason (Union)	Jacob Rehm	Charles Reed	Gustav Fischer
1870	Roswell Mason (Union)	Rehm/William Kennedy	Charles Reed	Fischer/Henry Cleaves
1871	Mason/Joseph Medill (Union)	William W. Kennedy	Charles Reed	Henry L. Cleaves
1872	Joseph Medill (Union)	Kennedy/Elmer Washburn	Charles Reed	Cleaves/Timothy M. Bradley
1873	Medill/Bond/Colvin	Washburn/Ward/Rehm*	Charles Reed	Timothy M. Bradley
1874	Harvey D. Colvin (Peoples)	Jacob Rehm	Charles Reed	Bradley/Francis Agnew
1875	Harvey D. Colvin (Peoples)	Rehm/Michael Hickey	Charles Reed	Francis Agnew
1876	Colvin/Monroe Heath (R)	Michael C. Hickey	Reed/Luther L. Mills	Agnew/Charles Kern
1877	Monroe Heath (R)	Michael C. Hickey	Luther L. Mills	Charles Kern
1878	Monroe Heath (R)	Hickey/Valorius Seavey	Luther L. Mills	Kern/John Hoffman
1879	Heath/Carter Harrison (D)	Seavey/Dixon/O'Donnell*	Luther L. Mills	John Hoffman
1880	Carter Harrison (D)	O'Donnell/William McGarigle	Luther L. Mills	Hoffman/Orrin L. Mann
1881	Carter Harrison (D)	William McGarigle	Luther L. Mills	Orrin L. Mann
1882	Carter Harrison (D)	McGarigle/Austin J. Doyle	Luther L. Mills	Mann/Seth Hanchett
1883	Carter Harrison (D)	Austin J. Doyle	Luther L. Mills	Seth F. Hanchett
1884	Carter Harrison (D)	Austin J. Doyle	Mills/Julius Grinnell	Seth F. Hanchett
1885	Carter Harrison (D)	Doyle/Frederick Ebersold	Julius Grinnell	Seth F. Hanchett
1886	Carter Harrison (D)	Frederick Ebersold	Julius Grinnell	Hanchett/Canute R. Matson
1887	Harrison/John Roche (R)	Frederick Ebersold	Julius Grinnell	Canute R. Matson
1888	John A. Roche (R)	Ebersold/George Hubbard	Grinnell/J. Longnecker	Canute R. Matson

Year				
1889	Roche/Dewitt Cregier (D)	George Hubbard	Joel M. Longnecker	Canute R. Matson
1890	Dewitt Cregier (D)	Frederick Marsh	Joel M. Longnecker	Matson/James H. Gilbert
1891	Cregier/Washburne (R)	Marsh/Robert McLaughery	Joel M. Longnecker	James H. Gilbert
1892	Hempstead Washburne (R)	Robert McLaughery	Longnecker/Jacob Kern	James H. Gilbert
1893	Harrison/John Hopkins (D)	McLaughery/Michael Brennan	Jacob Kern	James H. Gilbert
1894	John P. Hopkins (D)	Michael Brennan	Jacob Kern	Gilbert/James Pease
1895	Hopkins/George Swift (R)	Brennan/Kipley/Badenoch*	Jacob Kern	James Pease
1896	George B. Swift (R)	John J. Badenoch	Kern/Charles Deneen	James Pease
1897	Swift/Carter Harrison Jr. (D)	Badenoch/Joseph Kipley	Charles Deneen	James Pease
1898	Carter H. Harrison Jr. (D)	Joseph Kipley	Charles Deneen	Pease/Ernest Magerstadt
1899	Carter H. Harrison Jr. (D)	Joseph Kipley	Charles Deneen	Ernest J. Magerstadt
1900	Carter H. Harrison Jr. (D)	Joseph Kipley	Charles Deneen	Ernest J. Magerstadt
1901	Carter H. Harrison Jr. (D)	Kipley/Francis O'Neill	Charles Deneen	Ernest J. Magerstadt
1902	Carter H. Harrison Jr. (D)	Francis O'Neil	Charles Deneen	Magerstadt/Thomas Barrett
1903	Carter H. Harrison Jr. (D)	Francis O'Neill	Deneen/John J. Healy	Thomas E. Barrett
1904	Carter H. Harrison Jr. (D)	Francis O'Neill	John J. Healy	Thomas E. Barrett
1905	Harrison/Edward Dunne (D)	O'Neill/John Collins	John J. Healy	Thomas E. Barrett
1906	Edward F. Dunne (D)	John M. Collins	John J. Healy	Barrett/Pease/Strassheim
1907	Dunne/Fred Busse (R)	Collins/George Shippy	Healy/John Wayman	Christopher Strassheim
1908	Fred Busse (R)	George Shippy	John E. W. Wayman	Christopher Strassheim
1909	Fred Busse (R)	Shippy/Leroy T. Steward	John E. W. Wayman	Christopher Strassheim
1910	Fred Busse (R)	LeRoy T. Steward	John E. W. Wayman	Strassheim/Michael Zimmer
1911	Buse/Carter Harrison Jr. (D)	Steward/John McWeeney	Wayman/Maclay Hoyne	Michael Zimmer
1912	Carter H. Harrison Jr. (D)	John McWeeney	Maclay Hoyne	Michael Zimmer
1913	Carter H. Harrison Jr. (D)	McWeeney/James Gleason	Maclay Hoyne	Zimmer/John Traeger
1914	Carter H. Harrison Jr. (D)	James Gleason	Maclay Hoyne	John E. Traeger
1915	Harrison/Wm. H. Thompson (R)	Gleason/Charles C. Healey	Maclay Hoyne	John E. Traeger
1916	William Hale Thompson (R)	Charles C. Healey	Maclay Hoyne	John E. Traeger
1917	William Hale Thompson (R)	Healey/Herman Schluetter	Maclay Hoyne	Traeger/Charles W. Peters
1918	William Hale Thompson (R)	John Alcock/John Garrity*	Maclay Hoyne	Charles W. Peters
1919	William Hale Thompson (R)	John J. Garrity	Hoyne/Robert Crowe	Charles W. Peters
1920	William Hale Thompson (R)	Garrity/Charles Fitzmorris	Robert E. Crowe	Charles W. Peters
1921	William Hale Thompson (R)	Charles C. Fitzmorris	Robert E. Crowe	Peters/Peter M. Hoffman
1922	William Hale Thompson (R)	Charles C. Fitzmorris		

Year	Mayor	Head of Police Department	State's Attorney	Cook County Sheriff
1923	Thompson/Wm. E. Dever (D)	Fitzmorris/Morgan A. Collins	Robert E. Crowe	Peter M. Hoffman
1924	William E. Dever (D)	Morgan A. Collins	Robert E. Crowe	Peter M. Hoffman
1925	William E. Dever (D)	Morgan A. Collins	Robert E. Crowe	Peter M. Hoffman
1926	William E. Dever (D)	Morgan A. Collins	Robert E. Crowe	Hoffman/Carr/Graydon
1927	Dever/Wm. H. Thompson (R)	Collins/Michael Hughes	Robert E. Crowe	Charles Graydon
1928	William Hale Thompson (R)	Hughes/William F. Russell	Crowe/John A. Swanson	Graydon/John E. Traeger
1929	William Hale Thompson (R)	William F. Russell	John A. Swanson	John E. Traeger
1930	William Hale Thompson (R)	William F. Russell	John A. Swanson	Traeger/Wm. Meyering
1931	Thompson/Anton J. Cermak (D)	Russell/John A. Alcock*	John A. Swanson	William D. Meyering
1932	Anton J. Cermak (D)	Alcock/James P. Allman*	Swanson/Courtney	William D. Meyering
1933	Cermak/Edward J. Kelly (D)	James P. Allman	Thomas J. Courtney	Meyering/John Toman
1934	Edward J. Kelly (D)	James P. Allman	Thomas J. Courtney	John Toman
1935	Edward J. Kelly (D)	James P. Allman	Thomas J. Courtney	John Toman
1936	Edward J. Kelly (D)	James P. Allman	Thomas J. Courtney	John Toman
1937	Edward J. Kelly (D)	James P. Allman	Thomas J. Courtney	John Toman
1938	Edward J. Kelly (D)	James P. Allman	Thomas J. Courtney	Toman/Thomas O'Brien
1939	Edward J. Kelly (D)	James P. Allman	Thomas J. Courtney	Thomas O'Brien
1940	Edward J. Kelly (D)	James P. Allman	Thomas J. Courtney	Thomas O'Brien
1941	Edward J. Kelly (D)	James P. Allman	Thomas J. Courtney	Thomas O'Brien
1942	Edward J. Kelly (D)	James P. Allman	Thomas J. Courtney	O'Brien/Peter Carey
1943	Edward J. Kelly (D)	James P. Allman	Thomas J. Courtney	Michael F. Mulcahy
1944	Edward J. Kelly (D)	James P. Allman	Courtney/Wm. Touhy	Michael F. Mulcahy
1945	Edward J. Kelly (D)	Allman/John C. Prendergast	William J. Touhy	Michael F. Mulcahy
1946	Edward J. Kelly (D)	John C. Prendergast	William J. Touhy	Mulcahy/Elmer M. Walsh
1947	Kelly/Martin H. Kennelly (D)	John C. Prendergast	William J. Touhy	Elmer M. Walsh
1948	Martin H. Kennelly (D)	John C. Prendergast	Touhy/John S. Boyle	Elmer M. Walsh
1949	Martin H. Kennelly (D)	John C. Prendergast	John S. Boyle	Elmer M. Walsh
1950	Martin H. Kennelly (D)	Prendergast/Timothy O'Connor	John S. Boyle	Walsh/John E. Babb
1951	Martin H. Kennelly (D)	Timothy J. O'Connor	John S. Boyle	John E. Babb
1952	Martin H. Kennelly (D)	Timothy J. O'Connor	Boyle/John Gutknecht	John E. Babb
1953	Martin H. Kennelly (D)	Timothy J. O'Connor	John Gutknecht	John E. Babb
1954	Martin H. Kennelly (D)	Timothy J. O'Connor	John Gutknecht	Babb/Joseph D. Lohman
1955	Kennelly/Richard J. Daley (D)	Timothy J. O'Connor	John Gutknecht	Joseph D. Lohman
1956	Richard J. Daley (D)	Timothy J. O'Connor	Gutknecht/Adamowski	Joseph D. Lohman

334

1957	Richard J. Daley (D)	Timothy J. O'Connor	Benjamin S. Adamowski	Joseph D. Lohman
1958	Richard J. Daley (D)	Timothy J. O'Connor	Benjamin S. Adamowski	Lohman/Frank G. Sain
1959	Richard J. Daley (D)	Timothy J. O'Connor	Benjamin S. Adamowski	Frank G. Sain
1960	Richard J. Daley (D)	O'Connor/Phelan/O. W. Wilson	Adamowski/Daniel Ward	Frank G. Sain

*Ward, Dixon, Kipley, Alcock, and Phelan served on an "acting" basis.

provides an accurate rendering of the city as it appeared to the ever-vigilant Chicago Crime Commission during the 1930s and 1940s. Demaris picks the story up in the mid–1950s with *Captive City*. It is hoped that a post–1969 sequel to this fine volume may one day appear in print.

From time to time various line officers have published their memoirs of years spent policing Chicago. Michael Schaak's *Anarchy and Anarchists*, and Clifton Rodman Wooldridge's *Hands Up in the World of Crime* were noteworthy examples from the early years of this study. Woodridge's accounts of the urban underworld of the 1890s is both entertaining and far-fetched. This self-serving autobiography apes similar late nineteenth-century police fare, particularly David Cook's *Hand's Up! Or Twenty Years of Detective Work in the Mountains and on the Plains* (1882). Apparently, Wooldridge had difficulty finding a publisher. In desperation he solicited financial help from the gambler Jim O'Leary and several downtown business contacts. Schaak had no such problems getting his rambling discourse about the dangers posed by socialism into print. Not even his contemporaries could take this silly tome seriously.

Another 70 years would pass before police memoir again made its way into the book stores. In 1971 Jack Muller, the famous ticket-writing traffic cop who got into trouble when he decided the politicians were not above the law, came out with an angry polemic against the system. It was called *I Pig, or How the World's Most Famous Cop, Me, Is Fighting City Hall*. Less blunt, but even more to the point was *Joe D: On the Street With A Chicago Homicide Cop*. This memoir of Joe DiLeonardi, the stylish homicide detective who rose in the ranks at a rapid clip until he ran afoul with Mayor Jane Byrne and her press-agent husband in 1980, was actually penned by Richard Whittingham.

The newspapers of the day provide the only continuing link to Chicago policing during the period under consideration. But there are problems interpreting the checkered and often biased accounts submitted by nineteenth-century police reporters. The city editor frequently assigned the lowest-paid, most inexperienced writer to a station house. The hours were sporadic and the work was often drab. Since the metropolitan dailies paid their reporters based on the number of column inches, descriptions of routine arrests were elaborated in the most florid prose.

Police reporters had to use cunning and charm to pry newsworthy items from officers. Close acquaintances with the bluecoats and plainclothes men was the first essential of good police journalism. In return for choice bits of gossip, reporters favored their contacts by publishing their names in the papers when it could do some good and holding back during times of censure. Conversely, some editors made it a point to "get" certain offending officers who, through personal insult or by virtue of their political affiliation, incurred the wrath of the papers. This seems to be the case with James West and Joseph Dunlop of the *Chicago Times*, who "stalked" Michael Schaak and John Bonfield for four weeks during the winter of 1889.

Competition between the daily newspapers in those days was fierce. To scoop a rival in the days of the "yellow" press was an industry reward. To this end stories were occasionally manufactured. The fly-by-night newspapers came and went. For these reasons it is wise to avoid the scandal sheets, except when some local color is desirable. In 1891 gambler Mike McDonald bought the *Chicago Globe* to rail against Carter Harrison. A few years later Charles Tyson Yerkes turned the good gray *Inter Ocean* into a mouthpiece to further his goal of franchising the street railway system in the city. And while the *Tribune* barely wavered from its rigid philosophy, their reporters were less inclined to "work up" a story than someone who worked for McDonald's paper, for example.

Notes on Sources

Until now, there has never been an all-encompassing study of the Chicago Police Department. Various civic commissions have been appointed to examine departmental structure, community relations, and overall discipline within the rank-and-file. A summary of findings with appropriate recommendations most often appeared in pamphlet or booklet form. Rarely, however, were the issues placed in a proper historical content.

The first and only published history of the Chicago Police Department was written by John J. Flinn and John E. Wilkie, under the auspices of the Benevolent Association—hardly an unbiased source. Flinn's book, published in 1887, is worthy of consideration for it contains the only surviving biographical record of men who were active in the pre-fire period. The *History of the Chicago Police* was a "civic booster" project, never intended to provide historical substance for future generations of scholars. It was published during the Haymarket era, when the actions of the police were increasingly coming under attack. They portrays the department in an exceedingly favorable light, when the facts suggest otherwise. Because publication costs were absorbed by the policing agency itself, any critical judgments he may have cared to offer were tempered. To the researcher, their work is rather slipshod. Subjects that demand further investigation were given only cursory treatment, or in some cases were so obscure that the events could not be traced based on time-frames he provided. John Flinn's *History* was published concurrently with projects of a similar nature in New York, Philadelphia, Pittsburgh, and Cincinnati.

Good secondary sources about the Chicago Police Department are scarce. John Landesco's investigation of the urban underworld in the first quarter of the twentieth century ties together the relationship between gambling, commercialized vice, and the police, but fails to offer supporting evidence to back up some critical assertions. To say that gambling was eclipsed in popularity by wartime constraints does not hold up under careful scrutiny. Virgil Peterson and Ovid Demaris capture better than anyone crime conditions in Chicago in the post-Depression period. Peterson's book *Barbarians in Our Midst*

In the 1920s the *Chicago Daily News*—the writer's newspaper—and the *Herald-Examiner* were particularly good sources. However, the *Tribune* had on its staff two exceptional police reporters: John Kelley and James L. Doherty, whose father was a lieutenant. Doherty was credited with smashing a parole racket in 1948 in which top Capone gangsters were granted their freedom after a short incarceration. Without exception, the top crime writers of the 1950s were Ray Brennan and Sandy Smith of the *Chicago Sun-Times* and *Tribune* respectively. Brennan's career dated back to 1929. He bore witness to the tragedy of the murdered children, the futile struggle to reform the department during the O'Connor years, and the Summerdale scandal, which signaled the end of an era.

The dearth of archive materials at the Chicago Historical Society is not surprising. The Chicago Police Department shreds its papers on seven-year cycles, a tradition that prevents historians and researchers from cataloging material of enduring impact. The Society does have in its manuscript division—the *Register of Police*. These three tract books list interdepartmental transfers, disciplinary measures, and some choice items from the pen of the secretary who maintained the ledger during the 1890s.

At the present time the Chicago Police Department continues to deny the serious researcher access to a subbasement reputed to house the collective flotsam and jetsam of a hundred years. The News Affairs Division, cooperative in other matters, will reaffirm the department policy in this regard. Perhaps at some future time it will take a more enlightened view, and the historian's job will be an easier one.

Bibliography

Books

Allsop, Kenneth. *The Bootleggers: The Story of Prohibition*. New Rochelle: Arlington House, 1961.

Anderson, Jack, and Blumenthal, Fred. *The Kefauver Story*. New York: Dial Press, 1956.

Asbury, Herbert. *Gem of the Prairie: An Informal History of the Chicago Underworld*. New York: Alfred Knopf, 1940.

Bayley, David, ed. *Police and Society*. Beverly Hills: Sage Publications, 1977.

Biles, Roger. *Big City Boss in War and Depression: Mayor Edward J. Kelly of Chicago*. DeKalb: Northern Illinois University Press, 1984.

Boettiger, John. *Jake Lingle*. New York: E. P. Dutton, 1931.

Bopp, William J. *"O. W." O. W. Wilson and the Search for a Police Profession*. Port Washington: Kennikat Press, 1977.

Carwardine, William H. *The Pullman Strike*. Chicago: Charles H. Kerr & Co., 1973.

Cook, Frederick Francis. *Bygone Days in Chicago*. Chicago: A. C. McClurg & Co., 1910.

Darrow, Clarence. *The Story of My Life*. New York: Charles Scribner's & Sons, 1932.

David, Henry. *The History of the Haymarket Affair*. New York: Russell & Russell, 1936.

Dedmon, Emmett. *Fabulous Chicago: A Great City's History and Its People*. New York: Atheneum, 1981.

Demaris, Ovid. *Captive City*. New York: Lyle Stuart, 1969.

Dobyns, Fletcher. *The Underworld of American Politics*. New York: Fletcher Dobyns, 1932.

Duis, Perry. *The Saloon: Public Drinking in Boston and Chicago: 1880–1920*. Champaign: University of Illinois Press, 1983.

Fehrenbacher, Donald. *Chicago Giant*. Madison: American History Research Center, 1957.

Flinn, John J. and Wilkie, John E. *The History of the Chicago Police*. Chicago: The Policemen's Benevolent Association, 1887.

Fogelson, Robert M. *Big Ciy Police*. Cambridge: Harvard University Press, 1977.

Fraley, Oscar, and Ness, Eliot. *The Untouchables*. New York: Julian Messner, 1957.

Funchion, Michael. *Chicago's Irish Nationalists: 1881–1890* New York: Arno Press, 1976.

Gottfried, Alex. *Boss Cermak of Chicago: A Study of Political Leadership*. Seattle: University of Washington Press, 1962.

Green, Paul M., and Holli, Melvin G. *The Mayors: The Chicago Political Tradition*. Carbondale and Edwardsville: Southern Illinois University Press, 1987.

Griffin, William D. *The Irish in America*. New York: Charles Scribner's & Sons, 1981.

Halper, Albert, ed. *The Chicago Crime Book*. New York: Pyramid Books, 1969.

Harrison, Carter. *The Stormy Years*. New York: Bobbs-Merrill, 1935.

Higdon, Hal. *The Crime of the Century: The Leopold-Loeb Case*. New York: G. P. Putnam's Sons, 1975.

Hofmeister, Rudolf A. *The Germans of Chicago*. Chicago: University of Illinois Press, 1976.

Howard, Robert P. *Mostly Good and Competent Men: Illinois Governers 1818–1988*. Illinois Issues, Sangamon State College and The Illinois State Historical Society, 1988.

Hunt, Henry M. *The Crime of the Century: The Assassination of Dr. Patrick Cronin*. Chicago: H. L. Kochersperger Publishers, 1889.

Johnson, Claudius O. *Carter Harrison I: Political Leader*. Chicago: University of Chicago Press, 1928.

Johnson, David. *Policing the Urban Underworld: The Impact of Crime on the Development of the American Police: 1800–87*. Philadelphia: Temple University Press, 1979.

Kennedy, Robert F. *The Enemy Within*. New York: Harper Brothers, 1960.

Kirkland, Joseph, and Moses, John. *History of Chicago*, vol. 1. Chicago and New York: Munsel & Co., 1895.

Kobler, John. *Capone: The Life and World of Al Capone*. New York: G. P. Putnam's Sons, 1971.

Kogan, Herman, and Wendt, Lloyd. *Lords of the Levee: The Story of Bathhouse John and Hinky Dink*. New York: Garden City, 1944.

———. *Big Bill of Chicago*. New York: Bobbs-Merrill, 1953.

Lait, Jack, and Mortimer, Lee. *Chicago Confidential*. New York: Crown Publishers, 1950.

Landesco, John. *Organized Crime: Part Three of the Illinois Crime Survey*. Champaign: University of Illinois Press, 1929.

Lane, Roger. *Policing the City: Boston 1822–1920*. Cambridge: Harvard University Press, 1967.

Leinen, Stephen H. *Black Police, White Society*. New York: New York University Press, 1984.

Lindberg, Richard C. *Chicago Ragtime: Another Look at Chicago 1880–1920*. South Bend: Icarus Press, 1985.

Lyle, John H. *The Dry and Lawless Years*. Englewood Cliffs: Prentice Hall, 1960.

McCaffrey, Lawrence J., Fanning, Charles, Funchion, Michael, and Skerrett, Ellen. *The Irish in Chicago*. Urbana and Chicago: University of Illinois Press, 1987.

McPhaul, Jack. *Johnny Torrio: First of the Ganglords*. New Rochelle: Arlington House, 1970.

Mollenhoff, Clark R. *Strike Force: Organized Crime in the Government*. Englewood Cliffs: Prentice Hall, Inc., 1972.

Monkkonen, Eric H. *Police in Urban America: 1860–1920*. London and New York: Cambridge University Press, 1981.

Morn, Frank. *The Eye That Never Sleeps: A History of the Pinkerton National Detective Agency*. Bloomington: Indiana University Press, 1982.

Nash, Jay Robert. *Bloodletters and Bad Men*, vol. 3. New York: Warner Books, 1975.

———. *People to See: An Anecdotal History of Chicago's Makers and Breakers*. Chicago: New Century Publishers, 1981.

Nelli, Humbert. *Italians in Chicago, 1880–1930: A Study in Ethnic Mobility*. New York: Oxford University Press, 1970.

O'Connor, Len. *Clout: Mayor Daley and His City*. Chicago: Henry Regnery, 1975.

Peterson, Virgil W. *Barbarians in Our Midst*. Boston: Little, Brown & Co., 1952.

Reppetto, Thomas. *The Blue Parade*. New York: The Free Press, 1978.

Richardson, James A. *The New York Police: Colonial Times to 1901*. New York: Oxford University Press, 1970.

Roemer, Bill. *Man Against the Mob: The Inside Story of How the FBI Cracked the Chicago Mob by the Agent Who Led the Attack*. New York: Donald F. Fine, Inc., 1989.

Schaak, Michael. *Anarchy and Anarchists*. Chicago: F. J. Schulte & Co., 1889.

Sherman, Lawrence. *Scandal and Reform*. Berkeley: University of California Press, 1978.

Smith, Anson J. *Syndicate City: The Chicago Crime Cartel and What To Do About It*. Chicago: Henry Regnery, 1954.

Spiering, Frank. *The Man Who Got Capone*. New York: Bobbs-Merrill, 1976.

Stead, William. *If Christ Came to Chicago*. Chicago: Laird & Lee, 1894.

Thrasher, Frederick. *The Gang: A Study of 1,313 Gangs in Chicago*. Chicago: University of Chicago Press, 1927.

Touhy, Roger, and Brennan, Ray. *The Stolen Years*. Cleveland: Pennington Press, 1959.

Tuttle, William H. *Race Riot: Chicago in the Red Summer of 1919*. New York: Atheneum, 1978.

Walker, Samuel. *A Critical History of Police Reform: The Emergence of Professionalism*. Toronto: Lexington Books, 1977.

Washburn, Charles. *Come Into My Parlor*. New York: National Library Press, 1936.

Weinberg, Arthur, and Weinberg, Lila. *Clarence Darrow: Sentimental Rebel*. New York: G. P. Putnam's Sons, 1980.

Wendt, Lloyd. *The Chicago Tribune: The Rise of a Great American Newspaper*. Chicago: Rand McNally, 1979.

Williams, Robert H. *Vice Squad*. New York: Thomas Crowell, 1973.

Wooldridge, Clifton R. *Hands Up In the World of Crime! Or Twelve Years a Detective*. Chicago: Stanton & Van Vliet, 1901.

Periodicals

Baumann, Edward, and O'Brien, John. "The Sausage Factory Mystery." *Chicago Tribune Magazine*, August 3, 1986.

Bonfield, John and McLaughery, Robert. "Police Protection at the World's Fair." *North American Review*, June 1893.

Bukowski, Douglas. "William Dever and Prohibition." *Chicago History*, Summer 1978.
———. "Judge Edmund K. Jarecki: A Rather Regular Independent." *Chicago History*, Winter 1979–80.
Bulletin of the Chicago Crime Commission, 1919–20.
Chicago Police Digest, 1939–60.
Chicago Police Star Magazine, 1960–78.
"Chicago's Police Investigation." *The Outlook*, January 24, 1917.
"Chicago's Police Scandal." *Literary Digest*, January 27, 1917.
Cooper, S. W. "Abuse of Police Powers." *North American Review*, May 1890.
Doherty, James. "History of the Chicago Crime Commission." *Police Digest*, December 1960.
Duis, Perry. "The World's Greatest Fireman." *Chicago Magazine*, May 1978.
———. "Playing the Ponies on Lake Michigan." *Chicago Magazine*, August 1981.
Fenner, Richard W. "In A Perfect Ferment." *Chicago History*, Fall 1976.
Flynn, John T. "Smart Money." *Collier's*, September 13–27, 1940.
Flynt, Josiah. "The Man Behind the Poolrooms." *Cosmopolitan Magazine*, March 1907.
———. "Allies of the Criminal Poolrooms." *Cosmopolitan Magazine*, March 1907.
———. "The Poolroom Vampire." *Cosmopolitan Magazine*, February 1907.
Griffin, Richard T. "Big Jim O'Leary: Gambler Boss 'iv th' Yards." *Chicago History*, Winter 1976–77.
Haller, Mark. "Historical Roots of Police Misbehavior in Chicago: 1890–1925." *Law and Society Review* 10 (Winter 1976).
———. "Bootleggers and American Gambling: 1920–1950." U.S. Government document.
Hallgren, Mauritz A. "Chicago Goes Tammany." *The Nation*, April 22, 1931.
Hopkins, Albert A. "Science Trails the Criminal." *Scientific American*, February 1932.
"Look Here, Mr. Mayor!" *Police Digest*, May 1947.
Marohn, Richard C. "The Arming of the Chicago Police in the 19th Century." *Chicago History*, Spring 1982.
Martin, John Bartlow. "Al Capone's Successors." *American Mercury*, June 1949.
McCarthy, Kathleen. "Nickel Vice and Virtue: Movie Censorship in Chicago: 1907–1915." *Journal of Popular Film* 1, 1976.
McLaughery, Matthew Wilson. "History of the Bertillon System." *Fingerprint Magazine*, April 1922.
Morgan, Gene. "Detective Chief for Ten Years." *Police Digest*, December 1947.
Nelson, Bruce C. "Anarchism: The Movement Behind the Martyrs." *Chicago History*, Summer 1986.
O'Leary, Nealis. "A Criminologist to the Rescue." *Literary Digest*, October 6, 1934.
Peattie, Donald Culross. "The Most Unforgettable Character I've Met." *Reader's Digest*, January 1944.
Peterson, Virgil W. "The Chicago Police Scandals." *Atlantic Monthly*, June 1960.
"Policewomen in Chicago." *Literary Digest*, August 23, 1913.
Russell, Charles Edward. "Chaos and Bomb Throwing in Chicago." *Hampton's Magazine*, March 1910.
"Sandy Hanley and John W. Norton." *Police Digest*, April 1960.
Smith, Carl. "Cataclysm and Cultural Consciousness: Chicago and the Haymarket Trial." *Chicago History*, Summer 1986.
Taylor, Graham. "The Police and Vice in Chicago." *The Survey*, November 6, 1909.

"Ten Years a Chief Investigator: The Story of Captain Daniel Gilbert." *Police Digest*, December 1942.

"Timothy O'Connor: Commissioner of Police." *Police Digest*, December 1950.

Vachula, Richard. "The Gacy Connection." *Chicago Magazine*, July 1989.

Wheeler, Keith. "John Prendergast: Career Policeman." *Police Digest*, December 1950.

Wilson, O. W. "How the Police Chief Sees It." *Harper's*, April 1964.

Unpublished Materials

Forkosh, Bonnie J. "History of the Chicago Police Department: 1820–1886," Chicago Police Department, Public Information Division, 1968.

Forthal, Sonya. *Six Hundred Precinct Captains in the Chicago Party System: 1926–1928*. Ph.D. dissertation, American University, Washington, DC, 1938.

Goddard, Calvin H. "A History of Firearm Identification." An address delivered to the student body of the Southern Police Institute, University of Louisville, on May 11, 1953.

Johnson, David R. *The Search for an Urban Discipline: Police Reform as a Response to Crime in American Cities*. Ph.D. dissertation, University of Chicago, 1972.

Ketcham, George A. *Municipal Police Reform: A Comparative Study of Law Enforcement in Cincinnati, Chicago, New Orleans, New York, St. Louis: 1844–1877*. Ph.D. dissertation, University of Missouri, 1967.

Myers, Howard Barton. *Policing of Labor Disputes in Chicago: A Case Study*. Ph.D. dissertation, University of Chicago, 1929.

Pruter, Robert. *The Prairie Avenue Section of Chicago: The History and Examination of its Decline*. Graduate thesis, Roosevelt University, 1976.

Reckless, Walter Cade. *The Natural History of the Vice Areas in Chicago*. Ph.D. dissertation, University of Chicago, 1925.

Winslow, Charles. *Biographical Sketches of Famous Chicagoans*, vols. 3–4. Chicago Public Library Collection.

Federal, State and Municipal Documents and Reports

Chicago City Council Proceedings (Chicago IL: 1868, 1874–75, 1895).

Chicago Police Department: A Report of Progress 1960–64, Public Information Division.

Chicago Police Department: An Agenda for Change, Renault Robinson, chairman (Chicago). An Agenda For Change. University of Illinois Chicago Circle Campus Symposium, September 13, 1974.

Chicago Police Problems: By the Citizen's Police Committee (Champaign: University of Illinois Press, 1931).

Discipline and Administration of the Police Department of the City of Chicago, Alexander Piper, chairman (Chicago: The City Club of Chicago, March 17, 1904).

Final Report of the Police Investigation, An Inquiry conducted by authority of His Honor the Mayor: Carter Harrison II (Chicago: Western Newspaper Union Press, 1912).

Report of the General Superintendent to the City Council (1872–1958).

Reports on Chicago Crime, 1950–1960 (Chicago: Chicago Crime Commission).

Senate Report On the Chicago Police System, Committee of Investigations appointed by the Fortieth General Assembly Special System, 1897–98 (Springfield: Philips Brothers, State Printers, 1898).

*Testimony of the Chicago Crime Commission before the U.S. Senate Permanent Sub-
committee on Investigations Hearing on Organized Crime* (Chicago: Chicago
Crime Commission, March 4, 1983).

*Third Interim Report of the Special Committee to Investigate Organized Crime in Interstate
Commerce Pursuant to Senate Resolution 202 of the 81st Congress: A Resolution
to Investigate Gambling and Racketeering Activities* (New York: Arno Publishing
Co., 1952).

Manuscript Collections

Charter Constitution and Bylaws of the Paid Fire Department of the City of Chicago.
Chicago Historical Society Collection (Hazlitt & Reed Printers, 1877).

Cyrus Parker Bradley Memorial: 1865. Chicago Historical Society Collection.

Detective Bureau General Order Book: November 1915 through July 1931. Chicago
Historical Society Collection.

First Precinct Arrest Book: January 2, 1875 through June 30, 1885. Chicago Historical
Society Collection.

Matthew Wilson McLaughery Scrapbooks. Includes newspaper clippings, articles, and
correspondence to his father, Robert McLaughery, chief of police. Chicago Historical Society Collection.

Policemen's Benevolent Association of Chicago: Bylaws and handbook. Chicago Historical Society Collection (Collins & Hoffman, printers, 1877).

Register of the Chicago Police Department, vol. 1, 1890–1897. Includes roster of department, transfers, appointments, suspensions, and resignations. Chicago Historical Society Collection.

Herman Schluetter Scrapbooks, vols. 1–2. Includes newspaper clippings. Chicago Historical Society Collection.

John D. Shea scrapbooks, newspaper clippings, testimonials. Chicago Historical Society
Collection.

Edward Steele papers. Includes a letter written from John Bonfield to the mayor, 1886.
Chicago Historical Society Collection.

Newspapers

Chicago American (1839; 1900–10; 1960)
Chicago Daily Journal (1900–10)
Chicago Daily News (1875–1960)
Chicago Democrat (1835)
Chicago Herald-Examiner (1922–40)
Chicago Inter Ocean (1890–1900)
Chicago Sun-Times (1948–60)
Chicago Times (1854–90)
Chicago Times-Herald (1891–1900)
Chicago Tribune (1854–1960)
New York Times (1881–1935)

Index

About the Author

RICHARD C. LINDBERG is a Chicago historian and author. He holds a master's degree in history from Northeastern Illinois University, and is the author of *Who's on Third? The Chicago White Sox Story*, the *Macmillan White Sox Encyclopedia*, and *Chicago Ragtime: Another Look at Chicago, 1880-1920*. He has also contributed articles to *U.S.A. Today Magazine*, the *Chicago Tribune Magazine*, *Chicago History*, and *Inside Chicago*.